D1379169

# Contents

Introduction, *by Bruce A. Elleman, Andrew Forbes, and David Rosenberg*                                                    1

CHAPTER ONE            A Modern History of the International
                       Legal Definition of Piracy                    19
                       *by Penny Campbell*


PART ONE: PIRACY IN EAST ASIA AND THE SOUTH CHINA SEA

CHAPTER TWO            Piracy on the South China Coast through
                       Modern Times                                  35
                       *by Robert J. Antony*


CHAPTER THREE          The Taiping Rebellion, Piracy, and the
                       Arrow War                                     51
                       *by Bruce A. Elleman*


CHAPTER FOUR           *Selamat Datang, Kapitan:*
                       Post–World War II Piracy in the South
                       China Sea                                     65
                       *by Charles W. Koburger, Jr.*


CHAPTER FIVE           The Political Economy of Piracy in the
                       South China Sea                               79
                       *by David Rosenberg*


PART TWO: PIRACY IN SOUTH AND SOUTHEAST ASIA

CHAPTER SIX            The Looting and Rape of Vietnamese
                       Boat People                                   97
                       *by Bruce A. Elleman*


CHAPTER SEVEN          Piracy and Armed Robbery in the
                       Malacca Strait: A Problem Solved?            109
                       *by Catherine Zara Raymond*

**CHAPTER EIGHT**   Piracy in Bangladesh: What Lies Beneath?  121
*by Samuel Pyeatt Menefee*

**CHAPTER NINE**   Confronting Maritime Crime in
Southeast Asian Waters: Reexamining
"Piracy" in the Twenty-first Century    137
*by Sam Bateman*

PART THREE: PIRACY IN AFRICA

**CHAPTER TEN**   President Thomas Jefferson and the
Barbary Pirates    157
*by Robert F. Turner*

**CHAPTER ELEVEN**   The Limits of Naval Power:
The Merchant Brig *Three Sisters,*
Riff Pirates, and British Battleships    173
*by Andrew Lambert*

**CHAPTER TWELVE**   Guns, Oil, and "Cake": Maritime
Security in the Gulf of Guinea    191
*by Arild Nodland*

**CHAPTER THIRTEEN**   Fish, Family, and Profit:
Piracy and the Horn of Africa    207
*by Gary E. Weir*

Conclusions, *by Bruce A. Elleman, Andrew Forbes, and
David Rosenberg*    223
Bibliography    243
About the Contributors    249
Index    253

# Introduction

BRUCE A. ELLEMAN, ANDREW FORBES, AND DAVID ROSENBERG

Piracy, or "robbery on the high seas," has existed for as long as people and commodities have traversed the oceans. The ancient Greeks, Romans, and Chinese all complained of it, and all created naval forces to fight pirates. The word "piracy" comes from the Latin *pirata,* "sea robber," and before that from the Greek *peirates*—"brigand," or "one who attacks." Piracy, however, has evolved over time, and this volume examines how piracy and ocean governance have changed from 1608, when the Dutch jurist Hugo Grotius published his *Mare Liberum* [*The Freedom of the Seas, or the Right Which Belongs to the Dutch to Take Part in the East Indian Trade*]. As modern nation-states emerged from feudalism, privateering for both profit and war supplemented piracy at the margins of national sovereignty. More recently, an ocean enclosure movement under the aegis of the United Nations Convention on the Law of the Sea 1982 has granted states access to maritime resources far beyond their territorial limits. This in turn has given states more responsibility for providing safe passage through their waters. This monograph provides case studies on how these developments have changed the ways in which nations deal with piracy.

Who owns the sea? Who has rights of navigation through its waters? Who is responsible for protecting ships at sea? For most of human history, the high seas were seen as vast, dangerous, uncharted regions filled with demons and dragons. In premodern times, the sea was a space apart from society. 'Amr ibn al-'As, a seventh-century Arab military leader who was responsible for the conquest of Egypt in 640, observed, "The sea is a boundless expanse, whereon great ships look tiny specks; nought but the heavens above and waters beneath; when calm, the sailor's heart is broken; when tempestuous, his senses reel. Trust it little, fear it much. Man at sea is an insect on a splinter, now engulfed, now scared to death."[1]

Throughout much of human history, therefore, it was assumed that the seas could not be owned, occupied, or governed. Fighting pirates at sea, although desirable, was beyond the jurisdiction and ability of most "states," whether feudal or national. As

Grotius asserted in *Mare Liberum,* "The sea is common to all, because it is so limitless that it cannot become a possession of any one, and because it is adapted for the use of all, whether we consider it from the point of view of navigation or of fisheries."[2]

Grotius's view was developed to counter the activities of, in particular, Spain and Portugal, who were using their navies to assert their global maritime spheres of influence. The Dutch and other Europeans also wanted to pursue maritime interests. In this fashion, Grotius's "freedom of the seas" doctrine became a widely accepted foundation of modern international law.

Historically, a state's sovereignty stopped at the shoreline. The world's oceans remained open-access, "common pool" resources. "How can a country control the seas?" asked the ruler of Macassar in the early seventeenth century, when the Dutch were attempting to monopolize the spice trade: "God has made the earth and the sea, has divided the earth among mankind and given the sea in common. It is a thing unheard of that anyone should be forbidden to sail the seas."[3]

As commercial trade expanded, coastal communities over time evolved maritime practices to earn money from passing merchantmen. These practices ranged from the piloting and provisioning of ships, to extortion, to outright pirating. In these early years, piracy was not just an enterprise of criminals but a widespread practice of some seafaring communities, including the Bugis and Riau in the Malay world, Iban raiding and pirating communities on the west coast of Borneo, the Iranun around Jolo and the Sulu Sea, and others in Vietnamese and Chinese coastal areas.[4]

Lured by the spice trade, and later by the tea trade with China, Western European powers competed with each other to expand their trade networks and overseas colonies in these regions. Grotius provided an ideological justification for the Dutch to use their own growing naval power to break up other European countries' trade monopolies.

### Maritime Piracy in Historical Perspective

As maritime trade increased, so did piracy. Many navies were created in the fourteenth and fifteenth centuries to protect their shipping and trade from piracy, which was then widespread. However, absent a navy, a state had only limited means of redress or protection. Three distinct but complementary legal concepts evolved by which states without strong navies could attempt to control attacks on their commerce: letters of marque, commissions for privateering, and prize law. The first two provided for the issuance of "letters of marque" or commissions as privateers, conferring limited authority upon individuals to capture ships and cargoes, for which service they would receive recompense. Prize law asserted state control over the process, by determining the value and distribution of captured ships and goods.

How did the letters of marque work? Generally, if a merchant lost ships or goods through the hostile actions of another state or countrymen of that state, he would first seek direct restitution. This attempt would usually be made through the legal system of the offending state. If no compensation was forthcoming, the merchant could petition his own sovereign for assistance. If no solution was reached through diplomatic channels between monarchs, the merchant's sovereign could, as a last resort, issue a letter of marque giving the merchant the right to attack the commerce of the offending state to obtain full restitution for his original losses. The letter of marque was directed not at the individuals who had committed the original theft but against any goods originating from the offending country.

The earliest known letter of marque issued in England dates to 1295, when Bernard Dongresilli was given a letter against Portugal, the people of Lisbon in particular.[5] This letter was valid for five years. It allowed the recipient to regain his losses plus the costs of gaining restitution. If he died before this was achieved, the right of restitution was passed on within his family. If the recipient of a letter took more than had been lost, plus expenses, he would have to answer to his king. If restitution was received, reprisals were to cease.

Thousands of such letters were issued in England. For example, in 1414, King Henry V of England granted letters of marque against the property of the town of Leydon (now Leiden, in the Netherlands) to the value of the debt owing to John de Waghen; previous English kings had sought legal restitution for de Waghen's losses without response. In 1569, Queen Elizabeth I granted letters of marque to the Winter brothers against the Portuguese in recompense for losses, but unlike under previous letters, the brothers were specifically required to surrender the letters when the losses were satisfied.[6] The letter of marque allowed what today might be considered minor acts of war while guaranteeing the maintenance of a general state of peace between states.[7] To ensure that seafarers acted appropriately and did not precipitate open conflict, letters of marque became more regulatory in nature. The Crown could take legal action against letter holders who acted outside the prescribed terms.

Thus, in 1484, the king made a proclamation against piracy, specifying that all ships leaving English ports must leave behind sureties for their behavior. Similarly, in 1578 all English ships were required to carry letters signed by the Admiralty before they could leave English ports.[8] Initially the issuance of letters of marque in England was the prerogative of the Lord Chancellor, but from 1357 they were issued by the Lord High

Admiral in the High Court of the Admiralty.[9] This began a process of defining which actions were acceptable and which were not. A "captor"—that is, the holder of a letter of marque who captured a foreign ship or goods—now had legal sanction within his own country for attacking the shipping of another state. Without this protection, his actions would have been considered piracy.

In 1652, the Admiralty judges published an opinion stating that before a letter of marque could be issued, a demand for reparation had to be made and proof of the level of loss provided. This would establish that the applicant had been wronged and had sought legal redress without success and would prove the extent of his losses. A letter could then be issued in good faith for a just cause. However, not all captors operated within the bounds of their letters. In 1595, a letter was revoked because a captor recovered more than he had lost.[10]

Privateering, as distinct from attacking shipping under letters of marque, was evident as early as the eleventh century; by the seventeenth century it was widespread in the evolving global economic system. By the end of the seventeenth century, the issuing of letters of marque was widely considered a belligerent act, and so they were used less often, replaced by commissions for privateering. Personal seeking of restitution for private losses through authorized theft at sea disappeared, in favor of privateering in time of war—in effect, *guerre de course* under contract. There were a number of reasons why a sovereign might commission privateers. Most important, it offered a way to destroy a rival's shipping and create economic turmoil at virtually no cost to the issuing state.[11] Large professional navies were expensive and often nonproductive; privateering represented a cheap form of naval warfare.

There are numerous examples of English sovereigns commissioning privateers. In 1543, the king licensed as many ships as possible against the Scots and the French; the privateers could keep all spoils and acted under the protection of their sovereign.[12] But the British government did not want to lose all control—in 1563 instructions were issued condemning piracy and privateering without commissions. Suspected perpetrators were to be arrested, and all armed ships had to pay securities before sailing to ensure their good behavior.

For a state that had no navy or only a small one, privateers often constituted the only way to conduct naval warfare. Early examples are the three Anglo-Dutch Wars (1652–54, 1665–67, and 1672–74), which were among the first great oceanic wars fought over trade. England actively sought war, on the assumption that by taking another state's trade it would be able to increase its own wealth. In the first war, English privateers wreaked havoc on Dutch shipping, although toward the end the Dutch responded in a similar manner. Estimated shipping losses were between three and four hundred vessels for the English and about 1,250 for the Dutch. In the second war, shipping losses appear to have been about the same, but since England's merchant fleet was smaller, its losses were proportionally greater. In the third war, the Dutch kept their own vessels in harbor and used privateers to attack English shipping. The resulting losses undermined business confidence in England, leading eventually to withdrawal from the war.[13]

In England, numerous sets of "instructions to privateers" were issued between 1649 and 1780. In general, prospective privateers had to fulfill the requirements in the instructions before appearing in the High Court of the Admiralty to request commissions. The claimant would have to provide a list of ships and crews to be used, a budget for reimbursable costs, and a sufficient bond. Prizes had to be kept whole and be brought into English ports, and there be assessed by the High Court of the Admiralty.

A key issue for captors, whether holders of letters of marque or commissions as privateers, was their rights over the ships and goods they took as prizes. It was through the regulation of prizes—how they were valued, who received shares—that the state placed controls on privateering.

However, the use of private ships to harass one's enemies has a long history, predating letters of marque and commissions for privateering. Many early documents show that the English king could lay claim to all or part of the value of prizes under the concept of the "droits," or rights, of the Crown. This tradition maintained that all prizes belonged to the sovereign, who might give them in full or in part to the captor. For example, in 1205, the king granted a captor half of the captures taken from the king's enemies. The sovereign could be fickle. In 1337 the king directed the bailiffs at Great Yarmouth to give all the ships and goods taken to the captors but in 1341 reclaimed these prizes. In 1544, King Henry VIII issued a blanket authorization against France for privateers, allowing privateers to keep all of their prizes.[14]

In 1563, the Lord High Admiral required inventories and bail for prizes so that the courts would know precisely what had been captured and its exact value. Privateers had to promise not to break up their prizes and sell them, to turn in their prizes to the government, and to pay the Admiralty a tenth of the value. In 1603 a ship captured without proper letters was condemned and confiscated by the Lord High Admiral.[15] This became a precedent, whereby prizes taken illegally would go to the Lord High Admiral, while the captor could be considered a pirate and treated as such.

A number of other regulations were issued to control the distribution of prizes. In 1589, an order of council was issued requiring all captures to be brought for adjudication before the High Court of the Admiralty; the first formal sentence of condemnation of a lawful prize appears in the records for that year. In 1590, the Lord High Admiral instructed the High Court of the Admiralty that all prizes should be fully inventoried. In 1649, a distinct Prize Division was created in the High Court of the Admiralty to handle prize cases. Thereafter the High Court of the Admiralty dealt with peacetime captures, the Prize Court with wartime captures.[16]

In 1665 and 1677 the king issued a number of rules to be observed by the High Court of the Admiralty in adjudicating prizes. In 1692 the first Prize Act was passed, containing provisions for the sharing of proceeds. Before this act was passed, shares had been apportioned by agreement, custom, or the Crown. The sale of prizes in neutral countries was common in early times but discouraged later, probably due to the difficulty of the king and the Lord High Admiral in getting their shares—a tenth and fifteenth, respectively. The Prize Act gave captors a statutory right to their prizes, which had previously been at the pleasure of the Crown.

Over time, national prize courts were authorized to act for the Crown, without its direct control. For example, in 1702, the High Court of the Admiralty was empowered to judge prize cases. In 1708 under the Cruiser's Act, Queen Anne waived her rights to droits of the Crown; captors would receive all the value of their prizes. In 1709, a regulation provided that all prizes of holders of commissions or letters must be brought before the High Court of the Admiralty. Finally, in 1739, the lords of the Admiralty required that the judge of the High Court of the Admiralty hear all prize cases.[17]

One major cause for the sudden rise in piracy during the seventeenth and eighteenth centuries was the passage of the British Navigation Acts in 1651. These directed that goods could be brought into England or English possessions only by English ships or by ships of the countries where the goods originated.[18] As a result, foreign tobacco and other agricultural products imported on English ships could be sold in England and its colonies at low prices. The same goods imported on non-English ships were charged with additional duties.

Rejecting this monopoly, many merchants in the American colonies traded with privateers, often with the knowledge and tacit support of local officials. Undoubtedly, many privateers could really be considered pirates, since they did not take their spoils back to England to be divided, as they were required to do. In cities and towns all along the Atlantic coast, privateer loot was "imported" in defiance of the Navigation Acts: "Very often the same merchants and officials who furnished the illegal market for privateer plunder also outfitted expeditions in exchange for guaranteed shares in a ship's loot."[19]

This trade reached its climax in 1700, when there were so many pirates along New England's coastline that one official described the region as being in a "state of war."[20]

A second reason behind the upsurge in piracy was the War of the Spanish Succession (1702–13), between England and Spain. During that conflict privateering was legal so long as the privateer had a valid commission. If it was lost, privateers could expect to be treated as pirates. This was the cause of William Dampier's sojourn in a Dutch prison as an accused pirate.[21] In May 1720, Captain Shelvocke risked drowning to reboard his sinking ship *Speedwell* to retrieve his "commission scroll and the chest containing eleven hundred dollars of the owners' money."[22]

Spain and England signed a peace treaty in 1713, but thousands of privateers refused to quit and instead became pirates. There was especially stiff competition to control the lucrative resources of the Caribbean. By 1715 an estimated two thousand pirates operated out of Nassau, preying on Spanish galleons carrying gold and silver back to Europe. The profits that could be made from even one successful attack were enormous. Piracy reached a peak during the ten years between 1716 and 1725, a period called "the Golden Age of Piracy." It was "during those decades [that] the world experienced the most intense outbreak of seaborne banditry ever recorded."[23]

Many pirates began to focus on the lucrative trade between England and its North American colonies. James Logan, colonial secretary of Pennsylvania, estimated in 1717 that "there were at least fifteen hundred pirates cruising at any one time off the coast of North America and that no one could travel safely by ship."[24] During this period, piracy reached new heights, including the infamous exploits of Edward Thatch (or Teach), alias Blackbeard the Pirate, who was finally killed in 1718, and Captain Bartholomew Roberts, who reportedly pirated some four hundred ships during just "three years of looting and burning" before he was finally captured and executed.[25]

The Royal Navy responded to the piracy threat by setting up convoys to protect merchant ships, or even offering—for a hefty fee—to transport cargo on its warships. Nevertheless, it proved extraordinarily difficult to track down and eliminate the pirates. There was simply too much money in piracy, and "the profit to be made from such convoy duty made many Royal Navy captains less than zealous to destroy the pirates who were the indirect source of their profits."[26] It took a concerted effort by naval authorities to suppress piracy; only by 1725 had the most infamous pirates been captured and hanged.

Competing colonial powers continued to use privateers to supplement their naval forces against enemies. Weak governments often turned to privateers. For example, during the American Revolutionary War, the Continental Congress commissioned over 2,500 privateers, and "the Americans captured 2,300 prizes from the British, losing fewer than half that number to the enemy." Later still, during the War of 1812, American privateers played a major role; the "U.S. brig *Yankee,* for example, was credited with destroying or capturing some five million dollars' worth of English shipping and cargo during that time."[27] Sometimes privateering and blockade could work hand in hand: from 1793 to 1796, some 2,100 British ships were seized by French privateers even while the British fleet blockaded France.

Once a state could build up and maintain its own navy, it was very dangerous for the government to allow "independent" armed naval forces to persist. In such circumstances, as Lord Nelson put it, "all privateers are no better than pirates."[28] Governments began to justify the use of naval force against pirates. By this time Western European countries had largely established their global spheres of influence, and suppressing piracy was now in their economic interest. By the nineteenth century, with superior firepower, better charts, and steam-powered ships, governments would be better able to police the seas and curb piracy.

Privateering, for its part, continued during the 1700s but slowly petered out after the final defeat of Napoleon in 1815, as neutral countries took greater exception to the prospect of their own trade being attacked in war. By the mid-1800s, privateering was no longer practiced by the major naval powers. With the growth of the Industrial Revolution, colonial empires, and global trade, most states agreed that attacks on commerce should be a last resort of states and should not be undertaken at all by private individuals for personal profit. In the 1856 Declaration of Paris, major naval powers—with the United States a notable exception—agreed that privateering should be outlawed.

### Piracy in International Law and Practice

Another factor influencing the ability of states to respond to piracy comprised efforts to limit the freedom of the seas. This trend began in the late 1700s, when the newly founded United States of America became the first nation-state to extend its claim as sovereign territory to three miles offshore. Thomas Jefferson, as secretary of state, argued in 1793: "The greatest distance [of the outer boundary of territorial waters] to which any respectable assent among nations has at any time been given is the extent of human sight, estimated upward of twenty miles, and the smallest distance, I believe, claimed by any nation whatever, is the utmost range of a cannon ball, usually stated at one sea league."[29] The "cannon-shot rule" declared that the ability to exert naval power over a coastal area was sufficient to establish a property interest in its marine resources, such as fish stocks or pearls.[30] The area within the three-mile limit, however, was not private property but would be administered by each state as a common natural resource under public stewardship. In these waters, acts of robbery would be considered maritime crime, not piracy.

Many countries followed the American lead. The three-mile limit largely remained in effect worldwide until 1945, when President Harry Truman issued a unilateral proclamation that natural resources in the waters, the subsoil, and the seabed of the continental shelf adjacent to the United States were subject to its jurisdiction and control. Truman's decision was motivated by the discovery of offshore oil deposits and the anticipated surge in postwar resource demands. It was unlikely that private companies would invest if mineral rights were disputed or rich fishing grounds could not be secured.

The United States having established a new standard for enclosing the seas, several countries rapidly followed suit. In 1946, Argentina claimed control of its continental shelf, which extends beyond two hundred miles, and of the seas above it. In 1947, Chile and Peru extended their jurisdictions to two hundred miles, as did Ecuador in 1950. In 1948, Iceland declared conservation zones beyond its three-mile limit out to the extent of its continental shelf and then in 1949 unilaterally invoked a "headland to headland" rule, which in 1958 became a self-declared twelve-mile territorial sea. In 1976, Iceland adopted a two-hundred-mile limit on maritime resources.

The process of increasing state jurisdiction continued around the oceans of the world. In an attempt to negotiate a single international standard for the continental shelf, in 1958 the United Nations convened in Geneva the First Conference on the Law of the Seas. Amid growing concerns over the possible privatization or militarization of the seabed, the UN General Assembly in 1968 established the Committee on the Peaceful Uses of the Seabed and the Ocean Floor beyond the Limits of National Jurisdiction. In 1970, the General Assembly unanimously adopted the committee's Declaration of Principles, which states that "the seabed and ocean floor, and the subsoil thereof, beyond the limits of national jurisdiction . . . as well as the resources of the area are the common heritage of mankind," and should be reserved for peaceful purposes, not to be subjected to national appropriation, explored, or exploited except in accordance with an international regime to be established.[31]

The UN, recognizing that the many problems of ocean space were interrelated and needed to be considered as a whole, also decided to convene a new conference to prepare a single, comprehensive treaty. This new treaty was to encompass all aspects of the establishment of a regime and machinery for the high seas and seabed, the continental shelf, and territorial sea. Adding pressure to the diplomatic efforts, a series of "Cod Wars" between Britain and Iceland ensued after Iceland adopted a fifty-mile territorial sea limit in 1972. British warships rammed Icelandic coast guard vessels and shot over their bows, while the Icelanders cut the nets of British fishing trawlers and eventually broke off diplomatic relations with the United Kingdom.

In 1974, the UN convened the Third Conference on the Law of the Sea. By 1982, it had produced a treaty for international ratification. Among its many provisions, the treaty grants coastal states the right to declare sovereign rights and resource control over an exclusive economic zone (EEZ) up to two hundred nautical miles off their coastlines. In the case of countries bordering semienclosed seas, like the South China Sea, in such a way that their EEZ claims overlap, the United Nations Convention on the Law of the Sea 1982 calls for establishing joint resource-management areas and provides guidelines for doing so, even where conflicting territorial claims are unresolved. The treaty entered into force in November 1994.[32] To date, 155 countries have signed this agreement. Also to date, the U.S. Senate has declined to ratify it, although the U.S. Navy largely adheres to its provisions.

In accordance with the principles of the 1982 convention, many coastal countries have asserted greater management control over their newly acquired EEZs.[33] Most recently, in April 2008, the UN agreed to the proposed outer limits of Australia's continental shelf, increasing the size of that shelf from 8,200,000 square kilometers to over 10,700,000. By the early twenty-first century, the early tradition of the freedom of the seas had been thoroughly circumscribed by an ocean enclosure movement sanctioned by the United Nations. This in turn has substantially affected how states deal with piracy.

Data on piracy are often limited to statistics on attacks on commercial shipping, as recorded by the international shipping industry. Sea robbery and violence toward fishing boats, yachts, and recreational ships are usually excluded. Given these reporting limitations, one must view the figures on frequency and trends in piracy with considerable caution.

The two major methodologies used in reporting piracy reflect the various priorities of international organizations and commercial enterprises. The International Maritime Organization (IMO) is an agency of the United Nations, while the International Maritime Bureau (IMB) is a division of the International Chamber of Commerce and represents the shipping industry. Their divergent definitions of piracy are summarized in table 1.[34] The existence of two approaches to defining and reporting piracy often causes confusion about the scale and types of attacks. Further, it inhibits the development of effective policy responses.

**TABLE 1**
*Contrast between the IMO and IMB Definitions of Piracy*

| IMO | IMB |
|---|---|
| Piracy must be committed on the high seas or in a place outside the jurisdiction of any state. A criminal attack with weapons on ships within territorial waters is an act of armed robbery and not piracy. | Distinctions do not exist between attacks on the high seas and in territorial waters. |
| Piracy necessitates a "two ship" requirement. Pirates need to use a ship to attack another ship. This excludes mutiny and privateering from acts of piracy. | A "two ship" requirement is abolished. Attacks from a raft or even from the quay are acts of piracy. |
| Piracy is committed for private ends. This excludes acts of terrorism and environmental activism. | Piracy may not only be committed for private ends. Attacks on a ship for political or environmental reasons qualify as piracy. |
| Because pirate attacks have to be committed by the crew or passengers of privately owned vessels, attacks by naval craft fall outside the bounds of piracy. | The acts of government naval craft can be deemed as piracy in certain circumstances. |

*Source:* Graham Gerard Ong-Webb, "Introduction: Southeast Asian Piracy: Research and Developments," in *Piracy, Maritime Terrorism and Securing the Malacca Straits,* ed. Graham Ong-Webb (Singapore: Institute of Southeast Asian Studies, 2006), p. xiii.

Of the two, the IMO methodology conforms more closely to the international legal view about piracy; nonetheless, the most widely used source of data on piracy is the IMB. For statistical purposes, the IMB defines piracy and armed robbery as "an act of boarding or attempting to board any ship with the apparent intent to commit theft or any other crime and with the apparent intent or capability to use force in the furtherance of that act. This definition thus covers actual or attempted attacks whether the ship is berthed, at anchor or at sea. Petty thefts are excluded unless the thieves are armed."[35]

A compilation of Asian piracy attacks is detailed in table 2. Notably, the 2007 IMB annual report finds that "over the last five years, there has been a significant drop in the incidents reported in Indonesia, where in 2003, there were 121 reported incidents and in 2007, there have been only forty-three incidents."[36]

However, when the summary data are disaggregated, there is significant volatility in piracy from year to year and from place to place. Many factors might explain these anomalies. IMB director Eric Ellen once estimated that half or more of all incidents of piracy go unreported: "The problem is that the industry does not want incidents reported," he said. "They don't want their reputations scarred. Shippers fear that official investigations will delay shipments, increase insurance premiums, prompt demands for higher pay by nervous crews, and raise questions about their credibility among clients who can switch carriers at a moment's notice."[37]

The IMB also estimates that these statistics do not include more than half of all pirate attacks on commercial vessels generally. For instance, attacks on fishing boats and other

TABLE 2
*Piracy Reports, South China Sea Region, 1992–2008*

|  | 1992 | 1993 | 1994 | 1995 | 1996 | 1997 | 1998 | 1999 | 2000 |
|---|---|---|---|---|---|---|---|---|---|
| China* | 28 | 18 | 38 | 13 | 13 | 6 | 2 | – | 2 |
| Indonesia | 49 | 10 | 22 | 33 | 57 | 47 | 60 | 115 | 119 |
| Malacca Strait | 7 | 5 | 3 | 2 | 3 | 0 | 1 | 2 | 75 |
| Malaysia† | 2 | 0 | 4 | 5 | 5 | 4 | 10 | 18 | 21 |
| Myanmar | 0 | 0 | 0 | 0 | 1 | 2 | 0 | 1 | 5 |
| Philippines | 5 | 0 | 5 | 24 | 39 | 16 | 15 | 6 | 9 |
| Singapore | 0 | 0 | 3 | 2 | 2 | 5 | 1 | 14 | 5 |
| Thailand | 0 | 0 | 0 | 4 | 16 | 17 | 2 | 5 | 8 |
| South China Sea | 6 | 31 | 6 | 3 | 2 | 6 | 5 | 3 | 9 |
| Vietnam | 0 | 0 | 2 | 4 | 0 | 4 | 0 | 2 | 6 |
| TOTAL | 97 | 64 | 83 | 90 | 138 | 107 | 96 | 166 | 259 |

|  | 2001 | 2002 | 2003 | 2004 | 2005 | 2006 | 2007 | 2008 |
|---|---|---|---|---|---|---|---|---|
| China* | – | – | 1 | 3 | 4 | 1 | 0 | 0 |
| Indonesia | 91 | 103 | 121 | 94 | 79 | 50 | 43 | 28 |
| Malacca Strait | 17 | 16 | 28 | 38 | 12 | 11 | 7 | 2 |
| Malaysia† | 19 | 14 | 5 | 9 | 3 | 10 | 9 | 10 |
| Myanmar | 3 | 0 | 0 | 1 | 0 | 0 | 0 | 1 |
| Philippines | 8 | 10 | 12 | 4 | 0 | 6 | 6 | 7 |
| Singapore | 7 | 5 | 2 | 8 | 7 | 5 | 3 | 6 |
| Thailand | 8 | 5 | 2 | 4 | 1 | 1 | 2 | 0 |
| South China Sea | 4 | 0 | 2 | 8 | 6 | 1 | 3 | 0 |
| Vietnam | 8 | 12 | 15 | 4 | 10 | 3 | 5 | 11 |
| TOTAL | 165 | 165 | 188 | 173 | 122 | 88 | 78 | 65 |

*Source:* ICC-International Maritime Bureau, *Piracy Reporting Centre, Piracy and Armed Robbery against Ships, Annual Reports, Actual and Attempted Attacks.*

* Includes Hong Kong, Macau, Hainan; excludes East China Sea.

† 1995–2002 Malaysia data from J. N. Mak, *Incidents at Sea: Shipjacking, Maritime Muggings, Thefts and Illegal Migration in Southeast Asia* (Maritime Institute of Malaysia), available at http://www .southchinasea.org/docs/JMMak-piracy.pdf.

small craft are "rarely reported."[38] Additionally, many kidnappings of crew members of commercial vessels also are kept secret.[39] Shipmasters may be reluctant to report piracy attempts because they might reflect poorly on them. An investigation would take time and disrupt the ship's schedule, thus incurring substantial costs of delay. The data are further confounded by the IMB practice of reporting both attempted and actual attacks and of failing to distinguish between attacks at sea and theft from ships at anchor.

For all of these reasons, it has been extremely difficult to detect and measure piracy, calculate its true costs, and determine how best to prevent it. The existing piracy data are indicative, at best; they have so many limitations that no specific policy can be based upon them. This makes evaluation of piracy and maritime crime through the use of historical case studies particularly useful.

### Comparative Historical Analysis

As we have seen, sovereign nations have sought to extend their maritime territorial claims as population growth, market demand, and technology extended their economic and political interests at sea. Today, however, major naval powers and commercial shipping stakeholders are at the same time attempting to preserve the freedom of the seas and free access to archipelagic waterways, to benefit commercial vessels, free trade, and warship transit. Between these two policy domains, piracy has continued to flourish. The historical case studies presented in this work investigate nineteenth- and twentieth-century piracy in East Asia and the South China Sea, South and Southeast Asia, and Africa to gain a greater understanding of how best to counter the piracy threat.

The first chapter, "A Modern History of the International Legal Definition of Piracy," a preliminary to the three sets of essays that follow, is devoted to a legal analysis of the various definitions of piracy. Commander Penny Campbell, Royal Australian Navy, argues that whereas the accepted international definition of piracy has changed very little over time, various international organizations' working definitions of piracy have been altered, the better to combat the threat. As a result, the maritime community seems destined to have to balance several conflicting definitions of piracy, making choices that can often mean the difference among "marine insurance coverage, successful prosecution in a domestic court, or international cooperation in such things as piracy patrols through the Malacca Strait."

Part 1 examines piracy in East Asia and the South China Sea. Robert J. Antony opens this investigation in "Piracy on the South China Coast through Modern Times." In Chinese history, the execution of pirates was commonplace; during the late eighteenth century officials along the coast could summarily execute pirates immediately after trial. Today in China, most of the large-scale professional piracy syndicates have moved southward to the waters around Indonesia and the Malacca Strait, although "many syndicate bosses still hail from Hong Kong and Macau."

Bruce A. Elleman evaluates in "The Taiping Rebellion, Piracy, and the Arrow War" how Chinese piracy threatened to undermine British trade, especially during the early 1850s when the Taiping Rebellion broke out in China. The origins of the Arrow War (1856–60) revolved around piracy suppression; new treaties signed after the war obtained Chinese cooperation in suppressing piracy and granted the British expanded rights "to operate in Chinese waters against pirates."

Charles W. Koburger, Jr., discusses post–World War II piracy in the South China Sea. In the wake of World War II, when the traditional European security providers had been sapped by six years of constant warfare, piracy rapidly increased throughout the region. In particular, during the period of decolonization new countries were not overly concerned with suppressing piracy, which they all too often saw as a "patriotic reaction against global commerce. So the international machinery for suppressing piracy became largely impotent, and cases of piracy soared."

In chapter 5, David Rosenberg examines the political economy of piracy in the South China Sea. Piracy in the South China Sea has increased substantially in the past two decades, accounting for approximately half of the world's incidents since the 1990s. Due to continuing territorial disputes, however, no durable burden-sharing system exists. To date, "regional states and shippers have yet to put aside their individual stakeholder interests and then negotiate and implement an effective regional maritime antipiracy security system. Unfortunately, it may take an event equivalent to the 11 September 2001 attacks on the United States, a spectacular collision, or a devastating oil spill to overcome contending stakeholder interests and institutional inertia and to galvanize the political will needed for effective antipiracy security measures."

Part 2 presents four case studies examining piracy in South and Southeast Asia. In the sixth chapter, Bruce Elleman examines the looting and rape of Vietnamese "boat people." Beginning soon after the end of the Vietnam War, approximately three million people—many of Chinese heritage—fled Vietnam, Laos, and Cambodia. Those who fled by sea became known as "boat people." Many Southeast Asians felt threatened by this influx and looked the other way when local pirates began to prey on "boat people." However, piracy was allowed to get out of control, at which point it "was no longer the realm of occasional pirates but of professionals, many of whom now preyed as well on unsuspecting international shipping, thereby dramatically increasing overall cases of piracy within the region."

Catherine Zara Raymond analyzes piracy and armed robbery in the Malacca Strait in chapter 7. Once the most pirate-infested area in the world, with seventy-five reported attacks in 2000, in 2007 the Malacca Strait saw only three successful and four attempted attacks by pirates out of the ninety thousand vessels transiting the strait that year. While antipiracy measures already in place should keep pace with the changing nature of piracy in the waterway, at the same time: "Lessons learned in the fight against piracy in the Malacca Strait should be applied to other regions to make these waters more secure. . . . [I]t is time for it to be held up as an example to the rest of the world of how piracy can successfully be reduced."

Samuel Pyeatt Menefee discusses piracy in Bangladesh. Due to growing piracy problems in Bangladesh, Chittagong was recently labelled by the IMB as the "most dangerous port in the world," a characterization that produced little international reaction, because Chittagong does not sit astride major sea-lanes. In fact, Bangladesh is afflicted by varying types of piracy; in some areas pilfering ship supplies—including rope and zinc anodes—predominates, while in others stealing fishing boats or kidnapping fishermen is more common. Over time, however, both the number of attacks and the level of violence have generally increased. Piracy in Bangladesh might one day impact international trade throughout the region: "Attacks on simple fishing boats in Bangladesh might in time grow to piracies against supertankers."

In the final case study in part 2, Sam Bateman discusses maritime crime in Southeast Asian waters. Changes in the nature of maritime crime have occurred over the years, due in part to declines in fish stocks and loss of access to traditional fishing grounds, which have led to unemployment and loss of income in coastal villages throughout Southeast Asia. Piracy and sea robbery should be viewed not in isolation, therefore, but as part of a continuum of maritime crime that also includes smuggling, illegal fishing, and unlawful pollution of the marine environment. In that light, "there remains a fundamental need for international cooperation to redress the underlying causes of piracy and maritime criminality in the region, such as depressed social conditions, poverty, and unemployment."

Part 3 offers four cases connected to African piracy, starting with Robert F. Turner's study "President Thomas Jefferson and the Barbary Pirates." While Jefferson was by nature a peaceful man, when faced with the threat of uncontrolled piracy against American ships his response was to use the nation's new naval forces to face down and destroy the pirates. Two-thirds of the American navy was sent to attack from the sea. In addition, General William Eaton's bold invasion against Tripoli over land forced Yusuf Karamanli to abandon his attempts to extract tribute from the United States. Following the American victory, European governments quickly announced their own refusals to continue paying tribute, and "centuries of terror on the high seas soon came to an end."

Andrew Lambert's chapter, "The Limits of Naval Power: The Merchant Brig *Three Sisters,* Riff Pirates, and British Battleships," shows how fifty years after the U.S. war against the Barbary pirates, Britain faced a similar threat from Riff pirates preying on a major Mediterranean trade route. The Riff pirates could have been stopped only by a substantial deployment of naval forces and troops ashore, which, however, would have risked complex and dangerous frictions connecting Britain, France, and Spain with Morocco, Algeria, and Gibraltar. Instead of attacking the pirates, therefore, the British helped the Moroccan state to assert greater control. An effective Moroccan customs system, with low tariffs and adequate policing, proved to be the best solution to Riff piracy. One enduring lesson of this case study is that "because pirates—like all other people—must live on the land, it is on the land that they must often be stopped; naval power alone is not sufficient to fight piracy."

Arild Nodland, in "Guns, Oil, and 'Cake': Maritime Security in the Gulf of Guinea," addresses contemporary piracy in Nigeria. Since 1990, oil firms have invested more than US$20 billion in exploration and production activity in Africa, with another $50 billion on the way. Nigeria, the most populous country in Africa, has a serious and growing piracy problem over the control of "cake," government-owned resources. Local initiatives to fight piracy include a proposed "Gulf of Guinea Guard Force," while the recent establishment of AFRICOM, the U.S. Africa Command, is a clear sign of American interest in fighting piracy. However, Nigeria's systemic problems can only be solved by "balanc[ing] its security needs and U.S. courtship with the interests of other significant players—notably China, the country's large Muslim population, and other states that might resent American meddling in the region's internal and regional affairs."

In chapter 13, Gary Weir evaluates piracy in the Horn of Africa. The recent increase in piracy off the coast of Somalia is directly linked with the inability of local fishermen to preserve their traditional fisheries, which are threatened by foreign fishing fleets, and by the constant civil wars that serve to undermine domestic authority. On 22 April 2008, France, the United Kingdom, and the United States called for a United Nations resolution to support nations determined to fight piracy off Somalia, and on 2 June 2008 the UN Security Council adopted Resolution 1816 allowing international patrols in Somali waters. But naval patrols merely address the symptoms of piracy, not the cause. For Somalia, the real "solution to piracy is as local as the lost livelihood of a pirate recruit in one of the Harardhere camps along the Somali coast, and as global as Admiral Mullen's international city at sea. If we can see the connection and act on it, the region can once again find both the rule of law and a way to sustain itself."

In a concluding chapter, the editors review all the historical cases studies in terms of factors encouraging piracy, international shipping, and multilateral naval responses to piracy. They evaluate the uses and limitations of naval antipiracy operations with new maritime technologies and within a wider range of modern national policy goals. A comparative analysis of historical cases of piracy and maritime crime can stimulate new and original thinking about an overlooked naval duty—the suppression of piracy.

## Notes

1. George F. Hourani, *Arab Seafaring in the Indian Ocean in Ancient and Early Medieval Times* (Beirut: Khayats, 1963), pp. 54–55, quoting W. Muir, *The Caliphate: Its Rise, Decline and Fall,* rev. T. H. Weir (Edinburgh: n.p., 1924), p. 205.

2. Hugo Grotius, *Mare Liberum: The Freedom of the Seas, or the Right Which Belongs to the Dutch to Take Part in the East Indian Trade,* trans. Ralph Van Deman Magoffin (New York: Oxford Univ. Press, 1916), p. 28, published in the original Latin in 1608.

3. Ram P. Anand, *Origin and Development of the Law of the Sea* (The Hague: Nijhoff, 1983), p. 83.

4. For the Iranun, Eduardo Ma. R. Santos, "Piracy and Armed Robbery against Ships in the Philippines," in *Piracy, Maritime Terrorism and Securing the Malacca Straits,* ed. Graham Gerard Ong-Webb (Singapore: Institute of Southeast Asian Studies, 2006), p. 38. For the Vietnamese and Chinese, Adam J. Young, *Contemporary Maritime Piracy in Southeast Asia: History, Causes and Remedies* (Singapore: Institute of Southeast Asian Studies, 2007), chap. 2.

5. Reginald G. Marsden, *Documents Relating to Law and Custom of the Sea,* vol. 1, *1205–1648* (London: Navy Records Society, 1915), pp. 38–41.

6. Ibid., pp. 126–27; 184–89.

7. David J. Starkey, *British Privateering Enterprise in the Eighteenth Century* (Exeter, U.K.: Univ. of Exeter Press, 1990), p. 20.

8. Marsden, *Documents Relating to Law and Custom of the Sea,* vol. 1, pp. 136–38, 221–22.

9. P. Kemp, *The Oxford Companion to Ships and the Sea* (New York: Oxford Univ. Press, 1988), pp. 86, 615.

10. Reginald G. Marsden, *Documents Relating to Law and Custom of the Sea,* vol. 2, *1649–1767* (London: Navy Records Society, 1916), pp. 13–14, 289.

11. Starkey, *British Privateering Enterprise in the Eighteenth Century,* pp. 13, 20.

12. Marsden, *Documents Relating to Law and Custom of the Sea,* vol. 1, p. 19.

13. J. R. Jones, *The Anglo-Dutch Wars of the Seventeenth Century* (New York: Longman, 1996), p. 29.

14. Marsden, *Documents Relating to Law and Custom of the Sea,* vol. 1, p. 19; Janice E. Thomson, *Mercenaries, Pirates and Sovereigns* (Princeton, N.J.: Princeton Univ. Press, 1994), p. 23.

15. Marsden, *Documents Relating to Law and Custom of the Sea,* vol. 1, p. 20.

16. Ibid.; Starkey, *British Privateering Enterprise in the Eighteenth Century,* pp. 22–23; P. K. Kemp, *Prize Money: A Survey of the History and Distribution of the Naval Prize Fund* (Aldershot, U.K.: Gale and Polden, 1946), p. 9.

17. Marsden, *Documents Relating to Law and Custom of the Sea,* vol. 2, pp. 191–92, 213–14, 287–88; Nicholas Tracy, *Attack on Maritime Trade* (Toronto: Univ. of Toronto Press, 1991), p. 11.

18. E. B. Potter, ed., *Sea Power: A Naval History,* 2nd ed. (Annapolis, Md.: Naval Institute Press, 1981), p. 17.

19. Frank Sherry, *Raiders and Rebels: The Golden Age of Piracy* (New York: Hearst Marine Books, 1986), pp. 24–25.

20. Cyrus H. Karraker, *Piracy Was a Business* (Rindge, N.H.: Richard R. Smith, 1953), p. 67.

21. Christopher Lloyd, *William Dampier* (London: Faber and Faber, 1966), p. 21.

22. Kenneth Poolman, *The* Speedwell *Voyage: A Tale of Piracy and Mutiny in the Eighteenth Century* (Annapolis, Md.: Naval Institute Press, 1999), p. 82.

23. Sherry, *Raiders and Rebels,* p. 7.

24. Ibid., p. 212.

25. Karraker, *Piracy Was a Business,* p. 217.

26. Sherry, *Raiders and Rebels,* p. 216.

27. Ibid., p. 360.

28. A. G. Course, *Pirates of the Western Seas* (London: Frederick Muller, 1969), p. 2.

29. Anand, *Origin and Development of the Law of the Sea,* p. 139.

30. John Joy, "The Cannon-Shot Rule and Exclusive Economic Zones," *Navigator* (2001), available at www.wob.nf.ca/ (accessed 7 November 2005).

31. "Declaration of Principles Governing the Seabed and the Ocean Floor, and the Subsoil Thereof, beyond the Limits of

National Jurisdiction," *Center for Oceans Law and Policy,* www.virginia.edu/colp/pdf/LOS -Resolution-2749.pdf.

32. "United Nations Convention on the Law of the Sea 1982," available at www.un.org/Depts/ los/index.htm.

33. J. N. Mak, "Unilateralism and Regionalism," in *Piracy, Maritime Terrorism and Securing the Malacca Straits,* ed. Ong-Webb, p. 140.

34. Young, *Contemporary Maritime Piracy in Southeast Asia.*

35. International Chamber of Commerce, *Piracy and Armed Robbery against Ships: Annual*

*Report, 1 January–31 December 2006* (London: International Maritime Bureau, 2007), p. 3.

36. Ibid., p. 24.

37. Phillippe Moulier, "Pirates? What Pirates?" *US News & World Report,* 23 June 1997.

38. Carolin Liss, "Private Military and Security Companies in the Fight against Piracy," in *Piracy, Maritime Terrorism and Securing the Malacca Straits,* ed. Ong-Webb.

39. Stefan Eklöf, "Political Piracy and Maritime Terrorism: A Comparison between the Straits of Malacca and the Southern Philippines," in ibid., p. 55.

# CHAPTER ONE

# A Modern History of the International Legal Definition of Piracy

PENNY CAMPBELL

> *The definition of piracy is discussed at length. . . . It suffices here to give*
> *advance warning of the great variety of opinions as to the scope of the*
> *term and to emphasize the important difference between piracy in the*
> *sense of the law of nations and piracy under municipal law.*
>
> AMERICAN JOURNAL OF INTERNATIONAL LAW

This cautious introduction to the Harvard Draft Convention on Piracy, written in 1932 by some of America's most eminent jurists, shows just how important they thought varying definitions of piracy could be.[1] This warning holds as true today as it did then. For example, the International Maritime Bureau's (IMB) Piracy Reporting Center reported a total of 263 acts or attempted acts against shipping in 2007, an overall increase of approximately 10 percent over the previous year.[2] Over the same reporting period, the International Maritime Organization (IMO) received 282 reports of attacks or attempted attacks, which was a 17 percent increase over the previous year.[3] Meanwhile, the more Asia-focused group Regional Cooperation Agreement on Combating Piracy and Armed Robbery against Ships in Asia (ReCAAP) reported "that the piracy and armed robbery situation in Asia had improved significantly in the last year with a reduction in the total number of reported incidents from 135 in 2006 to 100 in 2007."[4]

Which report is correct? Could they all be correct? Given piracy's obvious importance, it is surprising that there remains little or no agreement on how many attacks occur every year. Different definitions also produce different estimates of losses due to piracy. While many contemporary sources would appear to agree that piracy costs the international shipping community many billions of dollars per year, it has been extremely difficult to identify or capture all costs associated with this illegal activity; for example, the International Chamber of Commerce loosely estimates the cost of piracy to world trade at US$16 billion annually, of which four billion is attributable solely to attacks in the Malacca Strait.[5]

There are many reasons for these wide discrepancies in numbers of attacks and total losses, not the least of them that many piratical acts are simply never reported to authorities. However, another key reason, and the focus of this chapter, is that arriving at a common definition of piracy under international law can sometimes present just as much a challenge as combating it in the first place. As a result, acts of piracy and armed robbery at sea can be reported very differently, depending on the legal definitions applied.

## Piracy as a Universal Crime Sui Generis

Pirates "are peculiarly obnoxious because they maraud upon the open seas, the great highway of all maritime nations. So heinous is the offence considered, so difficult are such offenders to apprehend, and so universal is the interest in their prompt arrest and punishment, they have long been regarded as outlaws and the enemies of all mankind."[6] Because of this link between a violent act committed on the "great highway of all maritime nations" and the view that the seas are beyond the jurisdiction of any one state, piracy has long been regarded as a universal crime—that is, as sui generis.

In the *Lotus* decision in 1927, the Permanent Court of International Justice recognized that piracy was a crime against the law of nations. The Permanent Court had been asked to adjudicate on whether Turkey could exercise criminal jurisdiction over the *Lotus*'s French officer of the watch for a collision with a Turkish steamer on the high seas. In seeking to deny Turkey jurisdiction over the matter, France argued that the flag state of the vessel had exclusive jurisdiction over the incident.[7] The Permanent Court rejected this argument but reaffirmed the "elemental" principle that all nations—and hence their flagged vessels—have equal rights to the "uninterrupted use of the unappropriated parts of the ocean for their navigation," a view harking back to the seventeenth-century Grotian dictum of the freedom of the high seas. The only exception to this freedom in peacetime was in the case of piracy or extraordinary cases of self-defense: "Piracy by law of nations," noted the court, "in its jurisdictional aspects, is sui generis."[8]

While some aspects of the court's decision were controversial at the time, no eminent jurist challenged its characterization of piracy as sui generis—an offense against the law of all nations. The reasoning behind this characterization dates back to 1608, when the Dutch lawyer Hugo Grotius published *Mare Liberum* [*Freedom of the Seas*]. In it he argued that as the seas are vast and fluid, they cannot be controlled or defended by any state against another in the same way that land territory can be. As a state generally has the means to defend its immediate coastal waters, it thus has the ability to exercise jurisdiction over a narrow coastal belt of sea. But beyond that limited range, Grotius argued, all states should enjoy free access to the high seas and be denied exclusive juris-diction over them.[9]

Accordingly, any illegal acts such as piracy committed on the high seas must likewise be beyond the jurisdiction of one state. Instead, jurisdiction over a piratical act is vested in *all* states. This notion of universal jurisdiction is a unique concept in international law. International law usually allows states to exercise jurisdiction over their own territories or over crimes committed by their own nationals wherever committed. In all other cases, a state's ability to exercise jurisdiction over another state's territory or nationals is extremely limited.

Piracy, however, is an exception by which the jurisdiction of a state's municipal law is permitted to extend over the high seas and over any national, because by engaging in an act of piracy the pirate has placed himself beyond the protection of any state. As the perpetrator of an act contrary to international law, a pirate will find himself treated as an outlaw, an enemy of all mankind, *hostis humani generis*. Thus, for both practical and theoretical reasons, any state may, "in the interest of all," take appropriate action against that perpetrator. However, defining exactly what constitutes a "piratical act" has never been easy, and it was centuries before a single definition was accepted.

### Moving Toward a Single Definition of Piracy

In the early years of the twentieth century, when the international community was moving toward codifying aspects of international law, piracy was just one of a number of subjects that seemed worthy of international regulation. In 1927, the same year as the *Lotus* case, a subcommittee report of the League of Nations found that the unset-tled state of the concept of piracy was due to failure to distinguish between piracy in its international legal sense and piracy as proscribed under the municipal laws and statutes of individual states.

Agreeing to an international definition of piracy meant limiting each and every state's jurisdiction over piracy, as a universal crime, to that conduct reflecting all—and only—those elements. The problem with maritime crimes on the high seas as defined by international law is that international law has no means of trying or punishing them. That body of law merely provides a generally accepted definition under which one state may act to suppress or punish piracy without condemnation from another state for acting out of turn. Of course, there is nothing to prevent states from incorporating the international-law definition into their municipal criminal codes, including any varia-tions they might desire from that internationally agreed definition, provided they do not then exercise that municipal jurisdiction within an international setting.

In 1927, the League of Nations' subcommittee reported that "piracy consists in sailing the seas for private ends without authorization from the Government of any State with the object of committing depredations upon property or acts of violence against persons." Nevertheless, despite this fairly concise view, the report concluded that "it would be preferable for the Committee to adopt a clear definition of piracy applicable to all States in virtue of international law in general."[10]

Though it had now been established in an international tribunal that piracy constitutes a crime against the law of all nations, it was usually under municipal law that a piratical act would be prosecuted. Sometimes a domestic court was asked to consider the international, rather than the domestic, legal position on piracy. This was the case when in 1934, following a superior—and ultimate—Hong Kong Supreme Court decision, the United Kingdom's Judicial Committee of the Privy Council was asked whether "actual robbery" formed an essential element of the offense of piracy in international law.[11] The Hong Kong Court had concluded it did.

In arriving at the opposite conclusion, the Privy Council conceded that in embarking upon international law it had been "to a great extent in the realm of opinion" and permitted itself "to select what appear to be the better views upon the question."[12] Their lordships canvassed earlier judgments, including the "sheet anchor" decision of *Dawson,* for those that considered sea robbery as piracy. Equating sea robbery with piracy, however, results in a definition both too wide and too narrow. Too wide, because it would be ludicrous to contemplate a situation where, the court suggested, one cruise-line passenger committing a petty theft against another could be guilty of a crime carrying the death penalty; such an act would not be considered piracy under the modern definition in any event, as the act was committed within the one ship, and not by one vessel against another. Too narrow, because many a heinous crime could be committed on the high seas, and it would be an anathema to the law of nations if such an act were considered piracy only if the perpetrator "stole, say, an article worth sixpence." The Privy Council ultimately concluded that the definition of piracy had gradually widened over the centuries, in part because international law is a "living and expanding code."[13]

At about the same time that the Judicial Committee of the Privy Council determined that actual robbery is not an essential element of piracy, the Supreme Court of the Philippines arrived at a contrary view. In *People v. Lol-Lo and Saraw,* the Court found that piracy was robbery and that because piracy had no jurisdictional limits, it could be committed within the jurisdictional three-mile limit of a coastal state. Such a conclusion was based more on an interpretation of the Spanish penal code than on a proper examination of international law.[14] In any event, the Court referred to the opinion of

Grotius that "piracy by the law of nations is the same thing as piracy by the civil law, and he [Grotius] has never been disputed."[15]

Obviously, a state's domestic law would seek to extend the principle of territorial jurisdiction over its nationals, and this has often had the effect of broadening the international law definition of piracy. For example, in English common law until the mid-fourteenth century, piracy was punishable as a *petit treason* if committed by a subject and as a felony if committed by a foreigner. Likewise, the Slave Trade Act of 1825 provided that British subjects who carried or conveyed a person on board a ship for the purpose of bringing him or her as a slave to any place would be guilty of piracy.[16]

It is entirely appropriate for the municipal interpretation of piracy in its international sense to incorporate these other elements, but those laws would only be valid as against the state's own nationals or against foreigners committing the wider category of piratical acts within that state's territory. It would not enable a state to seek to exercise the universal jurisdiction of piracy sui generis on the high seas against a foreigner.

From the early twentieth century onward, there was no common understanding among nations on the basic definition of piracy at the domestic level. The only thing that virtually all nations agreed on was that piracy was an international crime granting them universal jurisdiction. In 1932, a committee put together by Harvard University tried to resolve these fundamental differences in definition.

### The Harvard Draft

In 1932, the Harvard Research Group, a group of American academics headed by Professor Joseph Bingham of Stanford University, met to address these weighty piracy questions. In a voluntary undertaking, they produced a draft convention, widely referred to as simply "the Harvard Draft," that contained nineteen articles on piracy, with associated commentary.[17] The Harvard Draft is noteworthy for two main reasons. First, it was an impressive undertaking, analyzing the contemporary views of piracy as espoused by numerous municipal courts and eminent jurists. It thus provides an excellent snapshot of the concept of piracy at that time. Second, and perhaps more important, the Harvard Draft became a foundational text for the piracy provisions ultimately agreed to in the 1982 United Nations Convention on the Law of the Sea. For these reasons, it is illuminating to consider it carefully.

The first article of the Harvard Draft deals with jurisdiction. Article 1 sets the framework for the draft convention, affirming that in this context "jurisdiction" is that granted to states by international law, not by states to themselves in a domestic sphere. Article 1 also defines the "high seas" as any part of the sea not included in the territorial waters of any state.

Article 3 of the draft is as follows:

> Piracy is any of the following acts, committed in a place not within the territorial jurisdiction of any state:
>
> 1.  Any act of violence or of depredation committed with intent to rob, rape, wound, enslave, imprison, or kill a person or with intent to steal or destroy property, for private ends without *bona fide* purposes of asserting a claim of right, provided that the act is connected with an attack on or from the sea or in or from the air. If the act is connected with an attack which starts from on board ship, either that ship or another ship which is involved must be a pirate ship or a ship without national character.
>
> 2.  Any act or voluntary participation in the operation of a ship with knowledge of facts which make it a pirate ship.
>
> 3.  Any act of instigation or of intentional facilitation of an act described in paragraph 1 or paragraph 2 of this article.[18]

There are some important elements in this definition of piracy. First, it should be noted that the Harvard Group agreed with the Privy Council that an intention to rob *(animus furandi)* is not an essential element of the offense. However, if an act at sea is to constitute piracy, it must involve some element of violence or depredation.

Second, an act of violence at sea can only be considered to be piracy if it is committed for "private ends." This requirement has caused much debate and continues to have repercussions for states seeking to exercise universal jurisdiction over particular acts at sea. The term "private ends" is not defined, but it seems in this context that the Harvard Research Group intended to draw a distinction between acts committed by "unrecognized insurgents against a foreign government who have pretended to exercise belligerent rights on the sea against neutral commerce or privateers whose commissions violated the announced policy of the captor" and those by offenders acting for private ends only.[19] In the modern context, the phrase "for private ends" is usually interpreted to distinguish piracy from state-sponsored violence or from terrorism, which is considered to have ideological, not private, ends.

Third, piracy occurs only when the act is committed on or from the sea or in or from the air against a ship. Thus, an uprising by a crew against its own ship and master cannot be considered piracy, as it is not directed from one ship against another. This would be classified as the crime of mutiny, which would not qualify as a crime against mankind, punishable by all states. The label of piracy, however, would attach if "the successful mutineers then set out to devote the ship to accomplishment of further acts of violence or depredation."[20] The requirement that more than one ship be involved is due to "the insistence on some international factual element in the definition of piracy" in order to exclude from the definition those offenses that "involve only ships and territory under the ordinary jurisdiction" of a single state.[21]

The inclusion of an implied reference to aircraft in the Harvard Draft is curious, especially noting the long association of piracy as a maritime crime. Often, international law is criticized for not keeping up with the changing needs of states or reflecting developments in technology. Conscious of the requirement to look to the future, the Harvard Research Group noted that "with rapid advance in the arts of flying and airsailing, it may not be long before bands of malefactors, who now confine their efforts to land, will find it profitable to engage in depredations in or from the air beyond territorial jurisdiction." Thus, attacks from the air were included for reasons of foresight; the Harvard Draft was not necessarily to reflect "only cases raised by present conditions of business, the arts, and criminal operations."[22]

However, perhaps because blimps and zeppelins never caught on, the article has been condemned as a "virtually useless provision"; when applied to fixed-wing aviation, the practicalities involved in committing an act of violence from one aircraft against another make it "something which defies the imagination unless one of the aircraft is totally destroyed."[23] In the modern context, violent acts by one aircraft against another aircraft would probably be dealt with under relevant aviation conventions and not treated under the rubric of piracy.

Finally, and perhaps most important in the current geopolitical environment, under this legal definition piracy can only occur on the high seas. The importance of the reference to "high seas" has particular relevance in article 101 of the 1982 UN convention, because areas that were deemed high seas in 1932 had ceased to be characterized as such some fifty years later. A casual read of any IMO piracy or armed-robbery report will reveal that many more violent acts against shipping are committed in internal or territorial waters than on the high seas. The legal definition of piracy, therefore, can determine which nation has the relevant jurisdiction or obligation to act to prevent and punish those acts.

## Modern Definition under Law of the Sea Conventions

During the early 1950s, the International Law Commission was tasked by the UN General Assembly to review the customary international law of the sea with a view to proposing conventions to the international community. In preparing the articles on piracy, the commission was greatly assisted by the work of the Harvard Research Group and was generally able to endorse the findings of that research.[24]

The International Law Commission drafted four conventions on various aspects of the law of the sea. These and the piracy articles ultimately agreed to in the 1958 Geneva Convention on the High Seas introduced some new elements into the definition of the term.[25]

For example, article 15 of the 1958 convention stated:

Piracy consists of any of the following acts:

(1) Any illegal acts of violence, detention or any act of depredation, committed for private ends by the crew or the passengers of a private ship or a private aircraft, and directed:

(a) On the high seas, against another ship or aircraft, or against persons or property on board such ship or aircraft;

(b) Against a ship, aircraft, persons or property in a place outside the jurisdiction of any State;

(2) Any act of voluntary participation in the operation of a ship or of an aircraft with knowledge of facts making it a pirate ship or aircraft;

(3) Any act of inciting or of intentionally facilitating an act described in subparagraph (1) or subparagraph (2) of this article.

The first part of the definition of piracy was slightly more simple than the Harvard Draft, requiring only that the act constitute any "acts of violence, detention or any act of depredation." These acts were not further defined.

Subparagraph (1) introduced two new concepts. The first was that piracy could only be committed by the crew or passengers of a "private ship or private aircraft"—excluding, therefore, acts committed by a government ship or warship or government aircraft or warplanes. The International Law Commission was firmly of the view that piracy could be committed only by private vessels and that to "assimilate unlawful acts committed by warships to acts of piracy would be prejudicial to the interests of the international community."[26] Indeed, article 16 of the 1958 convention stresses the point that acts of piracy as previously defined, if "committed by a warship, government ship or government aircraft whose crew has mutinied and taken control of the ship or aircraft[,] are assimilated to acts committed by a private ship."[27]

By removing piratical mutineers from the main definition of piracy and placing the definition in article 16, the convention strengthened the two-ship—or two-aircraft—requirement. Piracy will only occur when the relevant violent act originates in one vessel and is directed at another. An act of mutiny in itself would not qualify as piracy, unless those mutineers go on to take action, for private ends, against another ship.

The second new concept in subparagraph (1) was the introduction of the "illegal." The word, which necessarily could be taken to imply that there existed acts of legalized violence on the high seas, was highly controversial. It is difficult to envisage "legal" forms of violence committed by private ships. Of course, the laws of armed conflict permit warships to exercise belligerent rights in times of conflict, but stricter limits on the methods and means of warfare could render some belligerent acts "illegal."

The commentary in the report of the International Law Commission noted the existence of the 1937 Nyon Arrangement, which condemned the sinking of a merchant vessel by submarines as a piratical act, but the commission denied that this indicated a change to the legal position that piracy could be committed only by private ships. The commission noted the complexity of dealing with violent acts committed by warships or "rival governments" in a civil war, suggesting that there was no need to go beyond granting all states a general right to repress piracy perpetrated by private ships.[28]

Nevertheless, it seems clear that the introduction of the word "illegal" was intended to preserve the illegality of some naval acts of violence characterized as such under different treaties, such as the Nyon Arrangement. Attempts to have the word "illegal" removed in the negotiating conferences for the 1982 Convention on the Law of the Sea were defeated.[29] The term "illegal" remains to this day.

There are few duties imposed in the 1958 convention. Notably, article 14 of the convention calls on all states to "co-operate to the fullest possible extent in the repression of piracy on the high seas or in any other place outside the jurisdiction of any State." Note, however, that the duty on states is to *co-operate,* not to *act,* in the prosecution or prevention of piratical acts. Such a duty would be too onerous and would run the risk that another state might seek to initiate proceedings if the first failed to act in a positive manner.

### The United Nations Convention on the Law of the Sea 1982

Although the International Law Commission contended that it had to consider certain controversial points, the definition of piracy it ultimately drafted was adopted, virtually word for word, in the United Nations Convention on the Law of the Sea 1982 (UNCLOS). UNCLOS was opened for signature in 1982 and came into force on 16 November 1994.

While the contemporary legal definition of piracy as expounded in article 101 of UNCLOS is arguably representative of the position in international law, it is not without its difficulties. It has been argued that some of the limiting features of UNCLOS have been derived from bias or errors contained in the Harvard Draft.[30] For example, the definition in article 101 mirrors article 15 in the 1958 Geneva Convention on the High Seas, which relied in turn mainly on the Harvard Draft. While that definition was the result of much compromise and debate in the negotiating conferences of the 1958 convention, it seems to have received little attention during the Third Conference on the Law of the Sea, which produced the draft text of UNCLOS.

Indeed, of the sixty declarations or reservations made by states parties to UNCLOS, none dealt with piracy. However, other important law of the sea concepts debated during the three conferences did influence the effect of the piracy definition. As noted above, piracy can be considered as such only if it occurs on the high seas. Confusingly,

UNCLOS has two definitions of "high seas." One refers to those waters beyond the seaward limits of a coastal state's territorial sea—that is, typically beyond twelve nautical miles from a coastal state's baselines. The other, supported by article 86 of the convention, is that "high seas" refers to "all parts of the sea that are not included in the exclusive economic zone, in the territorial sea or in the internal waters of a State, or in the archipelagic waters of an archipelagic State."[31]

This ambiguity arises because certain so-called high-seas freedoms are enjoyed by all states in other states' exclusive economic zones (EEZs)—such as to exercise freedom of navigation and to lay submarine cables. This potential legal vacuum covering piratical acts on certain parts of the high seas is resolved by article 58(2), which states that articles 88 to 115, which cover piracy, and other pertinent rules of international law apply to the exclusive economic zone insofar as they are not incompatible with Part V of UNCLOS, which deals with the exploration and exploitation of resources. Thus, piracy is a relevant act committed on the high seas as measured from the seaward limit of a state's territorial sea, now generally recognized as twelve nautical miles from shore.

The importance of the definition of high seas lies in the historical and legal lessening of the high-seas area. The increasing demands of coastal states over their adjacent waters led UNCLOS to recognize exclusive economic zones extending up to two hundred nautical miles from a coastline. The area of high seas available for the freedom of all was vastly shrinking. Arguably, the stage on which pirates could act was likewise diminishing. The jurisdiction of coastal states over violent acts committed against shipping near their coastlines was extending to a degree directly proportional to the decreasing sphere of international jurisdiction over those sui generis acts.

The import of this definition is that certain acts against shipping that had previously been in the jurisdiction of all states now became mere criminal or civil offenses under the coastal state's municipal laws. The obligation on other states to cooperate in the repression of piracy would not lead automatically to an obligation to assist in maritime law enforcement tasks within territorial waters.[32]

As of 1 January 2008, 155 countries were parties to the 1982 convention, giving it near universal ratification. Notably, the United States is not a party;[33] recent government announcements (in the previous and current administrations) suggest that this may soon change.[34] Nevertheless, the sheer weight of numbers now provides strong support to the view that the convention's provisions are representative of the customary international law of the sea and definition of piracy. However, it is not the only definition in common use in the international shipping community.

### Other International Legal Definitions

There is no organization under UNCLOS that is dedicated to monitoring or preventing piracy. In some UNCLOS provisions, though not in those relating to piracy, there is mention of a "competent international organization."[35] It is widely accepted that this is a reference to the IMO, a UN specialized agency that predates UNCLOS. In its regulatory role of shipping, maritime security, and safety, the IMO has also taken an interest in piracy.

The IMO refers to both piracy and sea robbery in its reports. It uses the UNCLOS definition of piracy, but it defines "armed robbery against ships" as "any unlawful act of violence or detention or any act of depredation, or threat thereof, other than an act of 'piracy,' directed against a ship or against persons or property on board such ship, within a State's jurisdiction over such offences."[36] The IMO has urged governments to cooperate with each other and the IMB with a view to combating maritime fraud in a coordinated manner.[37]

The International Maritime Bureau, in turn, is a specialized division of the International Chamber of Commerce. It thus has a very commercial focus, and as maritime crime can have a huge financial impact on the world's shipping community, in 1992 it created a dedicated Piracy Reporting Center. For statistical purposes the IMB chooses not to use the relatively narrow UNCLOS definition of piracy. Instead, it speaks collectively of "Piracy and Armed Robbery," which it defines as "an act of boarding or attempting to board any ship with the apparent intent to commit theft or any other crime and with the apparent intent or capability to use force in the furtherance of that act."[38] It is clear that this definition will cover any act of violence against a ship, whether that vessel is berthed in internal waters or under way on the high seas. The definition thus crosses the jurisdictional boundary of international and domestic law.

Commercial interests affect the definition of piracy in yet another way. Various court decisions seem to indicate that the international and relevant municipal legal definitions of piracy are not applicable to cases involving the interpretation of marine insurance provisions. In a United Kingdom decision in 1909, for example, the court held that an attack on a government vessel transiting up the Amazon River was not piracy. From a strictly international-law position, one would have to agree. But in finding that the particular marine insurance policy did not cover this attack, the court held that the word "pirates . . . must be construed in the popular sense and in a way businessmen would generally understand it."[39]

The cumulative effect of the various "legal" definitions of piracy—both in international treaties and domestic legislation—and of the "working" definitions adopted by international agencies and marine insurers has been the broadening of both the geographical and jurisdictional standing of certain violent acts against shipping. There are a large number of commercial and political reasons for this broadening, including to pressure certain nations to improve their law enforcement efforts, especially in harbors and ports. However, the plethora of competing definitions of piracy has also obfuscated the true extent of the problem, often making piracy look worse than it really is.

## Conclusions

The accepted international legal definition of piracy has changed little from the Harvard Draft of 1932. Even recent Security Council Resolutions dealing with piracy and armed robbery off the coast of Somalia have not changed the accepted legal definition of piracy as it is understood in UNCLOS. But as the maritime commercial environment and the modus operandi of sea bandits, however defined, have changed, the international community has responded by adopting various working definitions of these threats against shipping, the better to combat them. Changing a definition in an international document like UNCLOS is an onerous and protracted business.

From a legal perspective, an international convention "codifying the international law of piracy is not to unify throughout the various municipal laws of piracy, nor to provide uniform measures for punishing pirates, but to define this extraordinary basis of state jurisdiction over offences committed by foreigners against foreign interests outside the territorial and other ordinary jurisdiction of the prosecuting state."[40] Nevertheless, the maritime community seems destined to have to balance several definitions of piracy. Choice of a definition can mean the difference between the ability to obtain marine insurance coverage, successful prosecution in a domestic court, or international cooperation in such things as piracy patrols through the Malacca Strait. As the following case studies show, context will determine whether the courts (either domestic or international), the boardroom, the Security Council, or the popular media will ultimately prevail in this ongoing process.

---

### Notes

1. "Part IV: Piracy," *American Journal of International Law* 26, Supplement: Research in International Law (1932) [hereafter Harvard Draft], p. 749.

2. International Chamber of Commerce, *Piracy and Armed Robbery against Ships: Annual Report, 1 January–31 December 2007* (London: International Maritime Bureau, 2008).

3. International Maritime Organization [hereafter IMO], *First Quarterly Report*, MSC.4/Circ.105, 20 August 2007; *Second Quarterly Report*, MSC.4/Circ.106, 18 September 2007; *Third Quarterly Report*, MSC.4/Circ.110, 7 December 2007; *Fourth Quarterly Report*, MSC.4/Circ.114, 28 January 2008; all available at www.imo.org/.

4. *ReCAAP Information Sharing Centre,* www.recaap.org/.

5. "The Shipping News: Combating Pirates and the Threat of Terrorism," *APEC Currents* (September 2006).

6. Edwin Dickinson, "Is the Crime of Piracy Obsolete?" *Harvard Law Review* 28 (1925), p. 358.

7. Lotus *Case,* Publications of the Permanent Court of International Justice (1927), Series A, no. 10.

8. Ibid., p. 62.

9. While the United Nations Convention on the Law of the Sea 1982 (UNCLOS) recognized the growing jurisdiction of coastal states over their contiguous maritime zones, the underlying Grotian philosophy is still preserved in articles dealing with high-seas freedoms.

10. *Report of the Sub-committee of the League of Nations Committee of Experts for the Progressive Codification of International Law,* quoted in Harvard Draft, p. 749.

11. Judicial Committee of the Privy Council, *In re Piracy Jure Gentium 1934,* reprinted in *American Journal of International Law* 29 (1935), p. 141.

12. Ibid.

13. Ibid.

14. The Penal Code of Spain, 1870, applied to the Philippines (with minor amendments—but none to the provisions dealing with piracy) and remained in force after the transfer of the Philippines to the United States in 1898. It was thus the applicable municipal law at the time.

15. *The People of the Philippine Islands v. Lol-Lo and Saraw,* GR no. L-17958, 27 February 1922, as per Malcolm, J.

16. Stanley Morrison, "Part V: A Collection of Piracy Laws of Various Countries," *American Journal of International Law* 26, Supplement: Research in International Law (1932), p. 911.

17. Harvard Draft.

18. Ibid., art. 3.

19. Ibid., p. 798.

20. Ibid., p. 810.

21. Ibid., p. 807.

22. Ibid., p. 809.

23. Bary Hart Dubner, *The Law of International Sea Piracy* (Leiden, Neth.: E. J. Brill, 1980), p. 52.

24. "Report of the International Law Commission to the General Assembly," document A/2934, reprinted in United Nations, *Yearbook of the International Law Commission* (New York: International Law Commission, 1955), vol. 2, p. 25.

25. Entered into force 30 September 1962.

26. "Report of the International Law Commission to the General Assembly."

27. "Convention on the High Seas," 1958, United Nations *Treaty Series* 450, art. 16.

28. "Report of the International Law Commission to the General Assembly."

29. Alfred Rubin, "Notes and Comments: Is Piracy Illegal?" *American Journal of International Law* 70 (1976), p. 93.

30. See, for example, Goldie's argument that Bingham's policy choice to remove rebels from universal jurisdiction saw the definition of piracy limited to acts for "private ends." L. F. E. Goldie, "Terrorism, Piracy and the Nyon Agreements," in *International Law at a Time of Perplexity: Essays in Honour of Shabtai Rosenne,* ed. Yoram Dinstein and Mala Tabory (Boston: Nijhoff, 1989).

31. "United Nations Convention on the Law of the Sea 1982," art. 86.

32. The 2007 IMB *Piracy and Armed Robbery against Ships* annual report records a steady decrease in the incidents reported in the Malacca and Singapore straits, commenting: "This welcome reduction has been the cumulative result of increased vigilance and patrolling by the littoral states." However, because of the restrictions of the definition of piracy under UNCLOS, this form of international cooperation cannot be strictly ascribed to the legal obligation to cooperate under article 100.

33. President Reagan refused to sign the treaty because Part XI of UNCLOS, which created the deep-seabed-mining regime and the International Seabed Authority, was considered to be contrary to U.S. national interests (see President Ronald Reagan, "Statement on United States Ocean Policy," 10 March 1983, available at Oceanlaw.org). The 1994 Agreement Relating to the Implementation of Part XI of the United Nations Law of the Sea repealed the convention's mandatory

technology transfer provisions, addressing U.S. concerns.

34. See "President's Statement on Advancing U.S. Interests in the World's Oceans," 15 May 2007, available at www.whitehouse.gov/. "That starts with the Law of the Sea Convention, which President Obama and I are committed to ratifying . . . ." Hilary Clinton, "Remarks at the Joint Session of the Antarctic Treaty Consultative Meeting and the Arctic Council, 50th Anniversary of the Antarctic Treaty" (Washington, D.C., 6 April 2009).

35. See, for example, convention article 22, dealing with traffic separation schemes through the territorial sea; article 60, dealing with safety zones around artificial islands; article 119, dealing with exchange of scientific information relating to the conservation of high-seas fish stocks; article 208, dealing with marine pollution; and so forth.

36. IMO, "Code of Practice for the Investigation of the Crimes of Piracy and Armed Robbery against Ships," Resolution A.922(22), annex, para. 2.2.

37. IMO Resolution A.504 (XII), adopted 20 November 1981.

38. *Piracy and Armed Robbery against Ships.*

39. *Republic of Bolivia v. Indemnity Mutual Marine Assurance Company Limited* [1909] 1 KB 785, in Donna Sinopoli, "Piracy: A Modern Perspective," *Queensland University of Technology Law Journal* 14 (1998), p. 25.

40. Harvard Draft, p. 760.

# PART ONE

Piracy in East Asia and the South China Sea

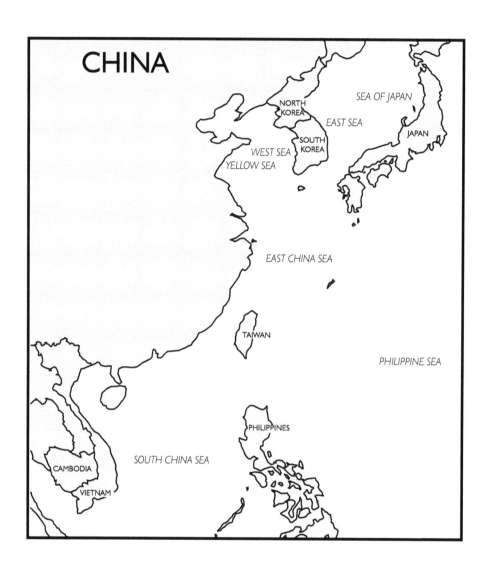

# CHINA

*SEA OF JAPAN*

NORTH
KOREA

*EAST SEA*

JAPAN

SOUTH
KOREA

*WEST SEA*
*YELLOW SEA*

*EAST CHINA SEA*

TAIWAN

*PHILIPPINE SEA*

PHILIPPINES

*SOUTH CHINA SEA*

CAMBODIA

VIETNAM

# CHAPTER TWO

# Piracy on the South China Coast through Modern Times

ROBERT J. ANTONY

Piracy in China has deep historical roots, and it has continued through modern times. For example, on 28 January 2000, in Shanwei, a grisly sight, but one not uncommon in China, unfolded as thirteen men, hands bound, feet shackled, drunk, and singing wildly, were led off by armed policemen to the execution ground—in this instance, a vacant field packed with gawking villagers, fishermen, soldiers, women, and children. At the designated spot the prisoners were lined up in single file and forced to kneel down. Then the executioners shot each man, one by one, once in the back of the head and then again in the chest. Spectators gasped; some cried. Later, relatives came to claim the blood-soaked bodies. As was the custom, officials charged them for the bullets that had killed their family members.

The thirteen executed men were pirates. In November 1998, in the Taiwan Strait, they had hijacked *Cheung Son,* a ten-thousand-ton bulk carrier loaded with furnace slag bound for Malaysia. The pirates had brutally murdered the twenty-three crew members after holding them hostage for ten days. Afterward, the corpses, weighted with engine parts, had been thrown overboard. After extensive police investigations in China, over fifty persons were arrested. It is unclear why they had hijacked the ship; the cargo of furnace slag was almost worthless, and the twenty-one-year-old ship was itself of little value. It has been speculated that *Cheung Son* may have been used for smuggling Chinese weapons or perhaps illegal emigrants. After the hijacking, the ship was given a new identity and sold, first in China for US$36,000 and later to an unknown buyer in Singapore for $300,000.

The court in Shanwei found thirty-eight men guilty of the piracy and sentenced thirteen of them to death. After sentencing, the local authorities duly noted, "Doomsday arrives for 'evil monsters' of the sea," and police immediately led the condemned men off for execution. Among the condemned was one Weng Siliang, a Chinese businessman who was said to have ordered the hijacking and killings. Also, an Indonesian named Wei Suoni implicated at the trial Liem Sioe Liong, a wealthy Chinese-born Indonesian tycoon with close connections to the former Indonesian president Suharto. No further arrests followed, however, and the case was closed.[1]

In Chinese history, the execution of pirates has been commonplace. In imperial China, beheading was the chief form of capital punishment for piracy; in the most serious cases—those involving the murder of officials or foreigners—the sentence was death by slicing, the "lingering death." So relentless had piracy become by the late eighteenth century that the Qianlong emperor (r. 1736–95) took the extraordinary step of allowing officials along the coast to execute pirates summarily, immediately after trial. As an explicit warning to others, the severed heads were afterward displayed in public, usually in port towns and fishing villages in the vicinity where the pirates had committed their crimes. Hundreds, usually thousands, of convicted pirates were disposed of each year in this manner. Today in China several thousand people annually receive the death penalty, but few have been convicted for involvement in piracy; in fact, piracy is no longer a specific crime in China. In recent years piracy has not been as pervasive in Chinese waters as it was a hundred or even just fifty years ago.

In China's comparatively recent history—starting from the seventeenth century—we can discern three major forms of piracy along the South China coast: opportunistic, professional, and sanctioned. Opportunistic, or petty, piracy always has been by far the most common. This form of piracy has been perpetrated mostly by small gangs, generally working independently in a restricted, relatively small, local area. Attacks have normally been sporadic and spontaneous, and the motive has usually been immediate, personal economic gain. Professional piracy, as the name suggests, has historically been well organized, the heists well planned and carried out on a much larger scale than opportunistic piracy. Pirates have been associated with large pirate leagues or criminal syndicates, such as in the *Cheung Son* case mentioned above. For the individuals involved, piracy has been a business and a livelihood. Sanctioned piracy—usually referred to in the West as privateering—historically involved maritime raiding that was approved and supported by a state or political regime. These three forms of piracy, however, have not been necessarily exclusive. Sanctioned piracy, such as occurred during the Taiping Rebellion, has often merged with professional piracy, and opportunistic piracy has continued even when the other forms of piracy were flourishing.

Examples of all of these types of piracy can be found in a number of major cycles of piracy along the South China coast. First, in the middle of the seventeenth century, during the tumultuous Ming–Qing transition, huge syndicates, particularly one led by the Zheng family of Fujian, took advantage of the anarchy to carve out a piratical empire in the South China Sea. The second cycle occurred during the late eighteenth and early nineteenth centuries, when charismatic pirate chiefs like Zheng Yi, Zheng Yi Sao, Zhang Bao, and Cai Qian organized formidable leagues that vied with the Qing state for control over the southern littoral. This cycle was soon followed by resurgences in piracy between 1840 and 1890, in the wake of the Opium War, the Taiping Rebellion, and China's other foreign wars. Then, after a respite of about twenty years, a new wave of piracy flared up during the chaotic years between the revolution of 1911 and the Nanking Decade, ending in 1937. Finally, in recent years there has been a resurgence of all forms of piracy in the South China Sea.

### Early Modern Chinese Piracy

Piracy is as ancient as China itself. The earliest official mention of pirates dates from the Han dynasty (106 BCE–220 CE), but surely it existed before that time. Thereafter, piracy tended to rise and fall with changes in regimes and fluctuations in the economy. Whenever opportunities arose—during wars, natural disasters, and economic depressions, and the like—piracy occurred. It increased when governments were weak and either unable or unwilling to cope with the problem; it also increased when commerce was vibrant.

In the mid-seventeenth century, piracy arose out of the anarchy produced by the Ming–Qing dynastic wars. Without a strong government to control the coastal population, large numbers of seafarers took to their boats to engage in piracy and smuggling. At first competition was fierce between the various pirate leaders, but gradually, through force and intrigue, one man, Zheng Zhilong, defeated his rivals to become the master of the southern coast. The ailing Ming dynasty was powerless to stop him and so "pacified" him by incorporating him and his pirates into the imperial navy. He received an admiral's rank and thereafter levied "water fees" *(baoshui)* on all junks sailing along the southern coast. According to Shao Tingcai (1648–1711), "All of the merchant junks passing through the South China Sea had to have Zhilong's safe conduct pass." Many local and court officials were also on his payroll. From bases in and around Amoy, the Zheng syndicate openly levied duties on all fishing and merchant vessels, as well as on fishing villages and ports in Fujian and Zhejiang. Those unfortunate few who refused to pay his tolls were ruthlessly attacked and murdered.[2]

By the mid-1640s, with Ming defeat imminent, Zheng Zhilong switched sides and joined the rising Manchus. But he was quickly arrested and brought to Beijing, where he lived out the rest of his life in confinement.[3] The arrest of Zhilong, however, did not mean the end of the Zheng piratical empire. In fact, it grew even stronger over the next several decades under his son Zheng Chenggong (better known in the West as Koxinga). Raising the banner of Ming loyalism, he gained the support of tens of thousands of people all along the southern coast. Through a combination of trade and extortion, his piratical empire came to embrace the waters from South China to Japan, to Southeast Asia. With a retreat to Taiwan in 1661 and his untimely death later that year, the Zheng syndicate began to unravel, finally collapsing in 1683, when the Manchus conquered Taiwan.[4]

During the forty years between 1644 and 1684, the new Manchu rulers paid close attention to the unruly southerners. Exterminating Zheng Chenggong and other lawless bands of pirates was a priority. The new government not only continued to enforce the earlier Ming bans on overseas trade but also initiated a drastic scorched-earth policy whereby the entire coastal population was forced to relocate ten to twenty miles inland. Soldiers torched the empty villages and towns, and anyone caught trying to return home was beheaded.

The results were mixed. In the short run, these draconian measures alienated large numbers of people and did not eliminate but actually ignited further piracy and dissent. In 1650 in the Chaozhou area, Wang Huizhi; in 1653 in the Zhengzhou area, Huang Ting; in 1656 in the Funing area, Zhang Mingzhen; and in 1663 in the Canton area, Zhou Yu—all became pirates and rebels.[5]

In the long run, however, these domestic policies, in combination with government-sponsored naval campaigns, eventually succeeded in wearing down the pirates and pacifying the coastal population. Once Taiwan was conquered in 1683, the Kangxi emperor (r. 1662–1722), now convinced that national security depended on the prosperity of the southern littoral, quickly reversed earlier policies and opened ports to trade. With the government stabilized and the economy prosperous, piracy for a time diminished.

### Chinese Piracy in the Mid-Qing Dynasty

After a lull of nearly a century, by the last decades of the eighteenth century piracy was once again on the rise in South China. In fact, between 1780 and 1810 piracy reached heights unprecedented in China and unmatched anywhere else in the world. This period, often depicted by scholars as the start of the decline of the Qing dynasty, was a time of rising crime and disorder throughout the southern provinces—banditry, feuds, secret-society disturbances, and urban riots, as well as piracy. Distracted by several major rebellions—the Lin Shuangwen Rebellion on Taiwan (1787–88); the Miao uprisings in Sichuan, Hubei, and Guizhou (1795); the White Lotus Rebellion in central China (1795–1804); and the Triad Uprising in Guangdong (1802–1803)—the Qing dynasty at first paid little attention to the resurgence of piracy on the periphery. By the time officials turned their attention to the pirates, several powerful leagues had developed that took many years to subdue.

This era too was "an age of prosperity," but one in which wealth was unevenly distributed. Despite the burgeoning economy, population pressure intensified competition and kept wages low for most seafarers. What is more, the 1780s and 1790s witnessed an unusually large number of natural disasters that threw many sailors out of work.[6] It is hardly surprising, given these circumstances, that tens of thousands of fishermen and sailors readily engaged in occasional piracy to survive in a harsh and competitive world. Opportunity and desperation were at work here in the upsurge in piracy.

Between 1780 and 1810 South China was plagued by several competing pirate leagues, each with its self-contained fleet. Petty gangs of pirates operated in the shadows of the larger, better organized pirate leagues. Large-scale piracy reappeared in the South China Sea in the 1780s, when Tâyson rebels in Vietnam sanctioned raids into Chinese waters to bolster their revenues and increase their manpower with Chinese pirates. Pirate fleets set out each spring and summer from bases on the Sino-Vietnamese border to plunder vessels and villages between Guangdong and Zhejiang. With the defeat in 1802 of the Vietnamese Tâyson, however, the Chinese pirates fled back into China. After a brief bloodbath between gangs, several chieftains consolidated their power and organized themselves into three major associations: Cai Qian in Fujian, Zhu Fen on the Fujian–Guangdong border, and Zheng Yi and others, who led the Guangdong Confederation.

At the height of power in 1806, Cai Qian, who commanded over five thousand pirates in several hundred ships, called himself the "Majestic Warrior King Who Subdues the Sea" *(Zhenhai weiwu wang)*. His capable and courageous wife, known to us only as Cai Qian Ma ("Wife of Cai Qian"), was said to have commanded her own junks with crews of women warriors *(niangzijun)* and to have died fighting off the coast of Taiwan in 1804.[7] After several attempts to take Taiwan, Cai Qian himself was killed in a naval battle on the Zhejiang coast in 1809. Zhu Fen, for his part, had a smaller but still formidable fleet, with several thousand followers who were active on the waters around Fujian, Guangdong, and Taiwan until his death, also in 1809.

By far the most impressive group of pirates in Chinese history was that of the Guangdong Confederation between 1802 and 1810. At its height in 1809 the confederation was composed of hundreds of vessels and anywhere from forty to sixty thousand followers. Until his death in 1807, Zheng Yi—who hailed from a family of professional pirates—led the confederation, which was divided into seven, later six, well armed and highly organized fleets.

In China, as elsewhere, people became pirates for many reasons—survival, adventure, wealth, greed, or power. They came from all walks of life and races; pirate gangs included men, women, and children. Most pirates, however, were just ordinary people, simple sailors and fishermen. For some, like Zheng Yi, piracy was a family tradition; as they grew up they were expected to become pirates. After Zheng Yi's death, leadership passed into the hands of his widow, Zheng Yi Sao, and of the capable, young Zhang Bao. They jointly commanded the largest of the Guangdong pirate fleets, the so-called Red Banner fleet, numbering nearly twenty thousand followers.

If some inherited the pirate trade and some volunteered, a large number of others were coerced into joining pirate gangs. Sometimes chiefs would induce men to join with offers of money, boats, weapons, positions of authority, and even sexual favors from among the captive women.[8] A number of people joined gangs of their own free will after having first been abducted by them; that was the case with Zhang Bao. Sometimes bandits, murderers, and rebels fleeing from the law on land ended up at sea and among the pirates.

But there were also many reluctant pirates, who had been forced to join gangs against their will. Sometimes hostages who could not pay their ransoms were obliged to turn pirate. In the early nineteenth century, Richard Glasspoole described witnessing the capture of nine rice boats. Since the captives put up no resistance, they were allowed the choice of becoming pirates. When four of them refused, they were tortured until they either "died or complied with the [pirates'] oath."[9] Occasionally seamen were tricked into becoming outlaws. One popular method was to hire sailors on false pretenses, disclosing the true situation only after the ship left port and the sailors had little choice but to submit.

Pirate gangs were not only transient but also often ethnically diverse. Oceans by their very nature were transnational spaces, and ships were melting pots.[10] Like crews on merchant ships, pirate gangs were often racially and linguistically mixed. In the mid-seventeenth century it was not uncommon to find Chinese pirate ships crewed by Japanese, Southeast Asian, European, and Chinese sailors; in the late eighteenth and early nineteenth centuries, Vietnamese pirates often worked alongside Chinese counterparts.

From lairs along the Guangdong coast and offshore islands the pirates extended their domination over most of the fishing and coastal trade, as well as over many towns and markets, through a formal protection racket. By 1805 the confederation had virtual control over the state-monopolized salt trade, and even Western merchants had to pay "tribute" to the pirates to protect their ships. Zhang Bao and other chieftains defiantly established "tax bureaus" in cities, towns, and villages along the coast where their agents collected protection money and ransom fees.

The confederation, in fact, operated a sophisticated and efficient protection racket. Its tentacles stretched outward from headquarters in Macau and Canton throughout coastal Guangdong to Fujian in the north and Vietnam in the south. The entire system was highly institutionalized, with trained clerks and bookkeepers at each node who compiled registration certificates, issued safe-conduct passes, kept account books, and collected ransom and protection payments. Agents collected duties semiannually or annually; the pirates even had installment plans. The Chinese pirates not only attacked Chinese junks who had not paid them off but also Western merchant ships en route to Canton. John Turner in 1806 and Richard Glasspoole in 1809 were kidnapped for ransom when their vessels were attacked near Macau.

In particular, Wushi Er, one of the confederation's leaders, oversaw a huge operation, centered on Hainan and the Leizhou Peninsula but extending to southern Fujian. Because each year his fleet collected several thousand taels of silver from extortion, ransoms, and robberies, he had to employ a small bureaucracy to write blackmail letters and keep accounts of the loot, weapons, and provisions.[11] At the height of the confederation's power in 1809, Bai Ling, the viceroy in Canton, observed that the pirates were "like ants attaching themselves to honeycombs."[12]

By 1805 to 1809 the confederation had extended its activities from water to the shore. Protection rackets were not only the confederation's chief means of income but also the basis of regional domination. Through them the pirates were able to penetrate the structure of local society. Through systematic extortion, bribery, and terror, the pirates gained a firm hold over coastal villages, towns, and markets, as well as over fishing and shipping enterprises. The Guangdong Confederation became a state within a state, exercising over maritime society a control independent of, and even overshadowing, that of the government and local elites. Piracy therefore became a significant and pervasive force in South China's coastal society in the early nineteenth century.

At the height of its power in 1809, within a year the confederation collapsed. The Qing navy, even with the aid of Portuguese warships from Macau, had been unable to quell the pirates. The Jiaqing emperor (r. 1796–1820) now offered the pirates pardons and rewards for their surrender, and the confederation began to fall apart as rogue gangs returned their allegiance to the state. Finally, in April 1810, Zheng Yi Sao and Zhang Bao surrendered. The government quickly rewarded Zhang Bao with money and a naval commission and then sent him and his fleet to fight the remaining pirates in western Guangdong. The confederation quickly and completely collapsed.[13]

### Late Nineteenth-Century Chinese Piracy

Never again would Chinese waters see such huge pirate leagues. But piracy persisted, with a marked upsurge between 1840 and 1890, prompting one foreign shipmaster to describe the period as a piratical "reign of terror."[14] Once again political distress—brought on by the Opium War (1839–42), the Taiping Rebellion (1850–65), and other domestic and foreign disturbances—provided new opportunities for an upsurge in sanctioned piracy. The piracy threat even prompted foreign intervention, notably the Arrow War during the 1850s (see the next chapter, which examines the Arrow War in greater detail).

During the first Opium War numerous Chinese junks acted as privateers, and once the war ended many of them became outright pirates. Actually, the first several years of the new British colony at Hong Kong (formally ceded in 1842) witnessed a marked increase in pirate activity, resulting in part from the corruption and inefficiency of the Hong Kong government and from the increase in Chinese and foreign trade. It was said that pirates easily purchased all the firearms they needed in Hong Kong and Singapore. Many opportunistic and well armed gangs of Chinese pirates regularly plied the waters between Hong Kong and Southeast Asia, attacking both native craft and foreign merchantmen.[15] One such instance was the capture in October 1854 off Macau of the Chilean ship *Caldera* bound for California. Among the passengers taken prisoner and held for ransom was a French woman, Fanny Loviot, who later wrote about her harrowing experience in a popular adventure book, *A Lady's Captivity among Chinese Pirates* (1859).

The two most notorious Chinese pirates at that time were Shap-ng-tsai and Chu-apoo. The former commanded a gang of three thousand men and over sixty junks, and the latter 1,800 men and about twenty junks. In the years following the Opium War, they repeatedly pillaged ships and villages between Hong Kong and Hainan Island. Fishing and trading vessels paid them regular protection fees. They gained notoriety when in February 1849 Chu-apoo's gang killed two British officers serving in Hong Kong and, that summer, Shap-ng-tsai's robbed a junk registered to a British subject. Later that same year, in two separate campaigns, the Royal Navy nearly destroyed the two armadas; Shap-ng-tsai escaped, but Chu-apoo was captured and committed suicide in jail. Despite these naval successes, opportunistic piracy continued to flourish in the South China Sea, and new pirate fleets quickly replaced those that had been destroyed.[16]

Adding to the turmoil of Chinese piracy was the reappearance of foreign pirates along the China coast. American and European renegades, "Manila-men," and escaped African slaves served on the same ships with Chinese pirates throughout the nineteenth century.[17] After 1840 an increasing number of British, American, French, and other foreigners worked with Chinese merchants in Hong Kong, Macau, and other treaty ports to organize piratical syndicates. In the 1850s, an American sailor, Eli Boggs, was the most notorious of these men, so much so that the Hong Kong government offered a $1,000 bounty for his capture. In 1857, Boggs was finally apprehended near Shanghai by his equally colorful compatriot Captain Bully Hayes, himself deeply involved in smuggling opium and illegal emigrants.

There were also gangs of Portuguese sailors, working in conjunction with several Macau merchants; under the pretence of providing convoy services for coastwise shippers, these gangs extorted protection fees that brought them between fifty thousand and two hundred thousand U.S. dollars annually. They openly robbed and murdered anyone who did not comply with their demands. According to George Cooke, the *Times* correspondent in China, the crews of these "convoys" committed the "most frightful atrocities," burning down villages, kidnapping the women and murdering the men. "They became infinitely greater scourges than the pirates they were paid to repel."[18]

To rid themselves of this foreign menace, Chinese officials in Ningbo hired their own pirates. Their leader was a Cantonese man known as A'Pak. This pirate was now sanctioned—much like Captain William Kidd—to hunt down and destroy other pirates and, in particular, those Portuguese gangsters. A'Pak was "made a mandarin of the third class" by Ningbo officials in 1856, and he responded by building up his own protection racket under official sanction.[19] Many of the fishing and merchant vessels that had previously paid tribute to the Portuguese convoys shifted their allegiance to him. Several American, French, and British deserters joined A'Pak's gang, which numbered about five hundred men by 1857. After a bitter fight the Portuguese pirates were soundly defeated, and A'Pak became the undisputed master of the South China coast for the time being.[20] However, the British and French took action later that year, in the Arrow War, to put an end to A'Pak's piratical activities.

In most cases, piracy was not a lifelong vocation or relied upon as a sole or even major source of income. Rather, piracy was a sideline, turned to when opportunity arose and in time of need. While the men involved made piracy an important part of their overall survival strategies, they also engaged at least part of the time in lawful activities, as sailors, fishermen, laborers, and so forth. They either joined gangs to supplement honest wages or went on sprees of criminality between periods of legitimate work. One Western observer remarked in 1899 that most of the gangs that he had seen were composed of individuals "who do perhaps a little fishing or occasional agriculture for their living, but combine illegal courses with their more legitimate occupations, and plunder a passing junk or wealthy pawnshops in the neighboring towns."[21] For the occasional pirate, piracy was typically a seasonal job.

"Occasional pirates" were not only the major source of recruits for opportunistic piracy but an important source of recruits for professional piracy. Membership in gangs was never fixed; around a core of career criminals there were always part-timers. Many gangs, as noted previously, were transient in nature; they formed, splintered, and re-formed with relative ease. Individuals rarely spent many years with the same group of men. For many people piracy was just another job, and jumping ship and switching gangs were common.

Gradually, with the increasing presence of the Royal Navy in the region, and especially after Hong Kong became the headquarters of the China station, old-style piracy began to recede. In 1847, the Hong Kong government also enacted its first antipiracy legislation, and the Royal Navy began to take a more active role in suppression. By the Treaty of Tianjin in 1860, British warships were for the first time allowed to pursue pirates into Chinese harbors. But it was the steam warship, which first appeared on the China station in the mid-nineteenth century, that was to become the most effective weapon in the fight against pirates. Fleets of sailing junks were no match for the heavily armed and more maneuverable steamers. By the 1860s, most of the foreign coasters were steamers as well, and a new age of piracy was dawning. "The steamship, more than the Royal Navy," A. D. Blue explains, "was responsible for the decline in the old-fashioned style of piracy, in which a fleet of junks had an overwhelming advantage over a sailing ship becalmed in coastal waters."[22]

But pirates quickly adapted to the new circumstances, switching their tactics from direct attacks to hijacking. Gangs boarded steamers as passengers and once under way took control of the vessel. The pirates would rob the passengers and crew and sometimes take hostages for ransom.

One of the first recorded incidents of the new-style piracy was the attempted hijacking of the steamer *Iron Prince* in 1862. A more successful heist occurred twelve years later, when pirates hijacked the river steamer *Spark* as it sailed from Canton to Macau. But the first major incident to gain public attention was the hijacking of the British coastal steamer *Namoa* in December 1890. The vessel had left Hong Kong bound for Shantou with five European passengers in first-class cabins and roughly 250 deck passengers. Only a few hours into the voyage, shots rang out: forty or fifty pirates, who had come aboard as deck passengers, quickly seized the bridge and engine room and rounded up the Europeans, who were having lunch with Captain Pocock in the saloon. In the scuffle that ensued, the pirates mortally wounded Pocock and a Danish man. They then forced the Chinese pilot to sail the ship to Bias Bay, where six small junks came alongside to off-load the booty (later valued at US$55,000). Once the pirates departed, the *Namoa*'s officers and passengers regained their ship and returned to Hong Kong.

Chinese local authorities sent a punitive force to Bias Bay. Soldiers rounded up ten suspects, quickly tried them, found them guilty, and summarily executed them. Later another twenty-three men were arrested, of whom thirteen were found guilty of piracy. On 17 April 1891, these thirteen pirates were beheaded, together with six other men, on the beach in Kowloon before a group of Western spectators.[23] As a result, at least in part, of these draconian measures to quell piracy, many Chinese pirates withdrew up China's inland rivers and into the waters of Southeast Asia. Of course, coastal piracy did not end, but it did decrease for about twenty years.

### Chinese Piracy in the Early Twentieth Century

In the early twentieth century, once again, turmoil—the revolution of 1911, warlordism, and the civil war between the Nationalists and the Communists—provided opportunities for a resurgence in piracy along the southern coast. Despite the disorder, there was still a flourishing sea trade out of Hong Kong, Shanghai, and other Chinese ports. Both opportunistic and professional piracy flourished under these new circumstances. Isolated harbors, bays, and offshore islands became pirate retreats, from which gangs sallied forth to raid villages and plunder coastal shipping, and to which they fled back. These no-man's-lands formed states within a state. Successive Chinese governments were too weak or corrupt to curb piracy, and foreign governments were often reluctant to get involved, because of the sensitive issue of Chinese sovereignty.

Between the two world wars there were fifty-one reported cases of piracy against modern coastal steamers, most of which were British ships. The worst years were 1922, 1927, and 1928, when there were five, six, and eight piracies, respectively.[24] These were the "Bias Bay piracies," named after the haven out of which the pirates operated.[25] During the 1920s, "buccaneering was quite a natural means of livelihood among a certain class of the seafaring gentry" in the Pearl River Delta. "The pirate chiefs of to-day have inherited their junks and property from their fathers and forefathers."[26] As might be expected, most pirate chieftains were professional criminals who made piracy a way of life. It provided their main incomes.

What was particularly important about these piracies was that they all involved professional gangs and what was still a relatively new modus operandi, hijacking. Pirates had already adapted to the modern world of steamships, and now they adapted to modern shipping practices. In the Pearl River Delta, pirates worked in syndicates and spent weeks in preparation for heists. During that time pirates traveled back and forth as passengers on the steamers they planned to rob, reconnoitering and smuggling firearms on board. Ultimately the pirates would embark as ticketed passengers, and once everything was set the leader gave the signal to attack. One group stormed the bridge and took control of the ship, another stormed the engine room, and a third kept the passengers at bay. Rich passengers, both Westerners and Chinese, would be taken ashore in Bias Bay and held for ransom. While relatively few foreign ships were affected by piracy, the number of plundered Chinese vessels remains unknown.

These were well organized, professional heists, often run by business tycoons in Macau and Hong Kong.[27] Professional crime syndicates controlled most piracy, which was but one of several illegal activities in which they were involved; syndicates also engaged in prostitution, gambling, money laundering, loan-sharking, and drug trafficking. These syndicates, which were organized by tycoons in Hong Kong and Macau, were established "along sound business lines, replete with boards of directors." The foreign press, perhaps in an attempt to sensationalize an otherwise dull story, claimed that attractive Chinese women headed several of the syndicates.[28]

During those same years there was also a more traditional form of piracy, involving robbery, kidnapping, and extortion. The American journalist Aleko Lilius vividly described several encounters with this variety of pirate from firsthand experience. One of the most unforgettable was a woman named Lai Choi San (Lai Caishan), whom he dubbed the "Queen of Macau pirates." She apparently had inherited the business and ships from her father, a pirate who had been granted refuge in Macau in return for protecting the colony's enormous fishing fleets. He had owned seven heavily armed junks when he died. Lai Choi San had taken over the business, added five more junks to her fleet, and soon had complete control over the fishing trade. According to Lilius, she was cunning, ruthless, and cruel; she had "barrels of money, and her will is law." She owned a house in Macau and had close connections with important men in that city. This pirate queen maintained her power over rival gangs through murder, kidnapping, and blackmail.[29] Lai Choi San also received official recognition, when an official in Macau gave her the title of "inspector," which gave her operations the appearance of legality.[30] This meant Lai could lead her fleet in the waters around Macau collecting tribute from local fishermen.

Those who paid were protected from rival gangs in the area, but as in previous eras, those who refused were either murdered or kidnapped for ransom. This sort of extortion, which was common throughout this period, was in fact a major source of pirate income. To avoid being attacked, merchant junks and fishing craft paid large sums of money to the pirates, who then issued passports guaranteeing safe passage.[31]

With the outbreak of the Sino-Japanese War in 1937, piracy in Chinese waters began to decline; at least, there were fewer reported cases. It picked up for a time during the Chinese Civil War (1945–49) and during the first few years of communist rule, but by late 1950s piracy seemed almost a thing of the past along the south coast of China. One of the last major acts of piracy against a foreign vessel occurred in 1952, when pirates hijacked *Hupeh*, brought their hostages to Bias Bay, and held them for ransom.[32] During the 1990s, piracy once again revived in Chinese waters.

## Conclusions

Historically, Chinese pirates were outlaws who committed a multiplicity of crimes on both sea and shore. They robbed, killed, raped, committed kidnapping and extortion, burned down villages, and scuttled ships. They bribed and colluded with soldiers, officials, and merchants. On water they attacked any vessel, large or small, that appeared easy prey. On shore they raided villages and markets, plundering them of valuables and food, even carrying off women and children as hostages. They also became deeply involved in such organized crimes as prostitution, gambling, and opium smuggling. By the late nineteenth century, pirates had added hijacking to their repertoire, and this type of piracy increased rapidly after the collapse in 1911 of the Qing dynasty.

Today, although most of the large-scale professional piracies have moved southward to the South China Sea, and also around Indonesia and the Malacca Strait, many syndicate bosses still hail from Hong Kong and Macau.[33] Pirates depend upon friendly ports and secure bases, since they need confederates ashore for food and supplies, as well as for handling booty, providing information, and finding new recruits. Also, inns and taverns were traditionally important oases of merriment and rest where pirates could spend their earnings freely and wildly.

It is important to reiterate, therefore, that Chinese pirates built strongholds not only on remote islands but also in and around such key commercial and political hubs as Canton, Macau, Chaozhou, Shantou, Amoy, Ningbo, and Shanghai. In those cities and in smaller port towns they set up "tax bureaus" to collect tribute and ransom payments and to conspire with soldiers, *yamen* underlings, and officials who were on their payrolls. Lantau and Cheung Chau islands, near Hong Kong, and Taipa and Coloane islands, near Macau, were for centuries home to thriving populations of pirates, smugglers, and fishermen. In the twentieth century, Bias Bay (Daya Wan) and Mirs Bay (Dapeng Wan), which are only about fifty kilometers northeast of Hong Kong, were important pirate retreats, and they had served the same purpose since at least the seventeenth century.

It made good sense for pirates to locate their lairs near major trade routes and convenient sources of supply. The close proximity of pirate lairs to economic and political centers throughout South China has historically been a clear indication of how deeply entrenched piracy is in China's maritime society. Not surprisingly, therefore, the most recent upswing in piracy is also focused in these same areas. In 1993, for example, the Hong Kong *Morning Post* reported the murder of local fishermen by mainland pirates.[34] The *Cheung Son* case of 1998, of course, was another famous example of piracy involving hijacking, but in this case the crew was murdered, not held for ransom.

If the number of cases of piracy in Chinese waters is waning, pirates nevertheless live on in legends, folklore, movies, and popular imagination. Often ignoring the facts, writers, journalists, and tour guides have used and misused pirates in many interesting ways. In China, as in the West, pirates have been depicted variously as treacherous villains, swashbuckling heroes, champions of the poor, and avengers against injustice. For example, even before Zheng Chenggong's death in 1661 and Zhang Bao's surrender in 1810, both men had become folk heroes in South China. In fact, in Taiwan, Zheng Chenggong was deified; today there are several temples dedicated to the pirate-hero, the largest one in Tainan.[35] Throughout the Pearl River Delta, every schoolchild knows stories about Zhang Bao. For some, he is a Chinese Horatio Alger figure—a downtrodden boy who achieves fame, wealth, and success against all odds in a cruel and oppressive society. For others—especially in more recent Chinese historiography—he is a primitive rebel in the vanguard of the revolution that overturned the alien Manchu dynasty in 1911.[36]

The female pirates of South China are perhaps not as famous as their male counterparts, but several have not been forgotten. Lai Choi San, the pirate queen, was the only daughter in a family with four male siblings, who had all died before she reached adulthood. She grew up on ships: "Her father used to take her with him on his trips along the coast. . . . And now she loved the sea." What is more, she had no ambition to settle down to a peaceful life on shore.[37] Lai Choi San is still remembered as a feminine Robin Hood who robbed the rich and gave to the poor. In 1935, she was immortalized as the archetypical "Dragon Lady" in the American comic strip *Terry and the Pirates*.[38]

Zheng Yi Sao and Cai Qian Ma were other female pirates able to survive in a man's world by proving themselves more capable than their male counterparts. After her surrender in 1810, Zheng Yi Sao continued to receive some notoriety in the Canton region, where she is said to have opened a successful brothel and gambling den. She died of old age in her home. Another female pirate, the sister of a Ming dynasty chieftain named Wu Ping, was killed on Nan'ao Island, where today she is worshipped as the "Treasure Protecting Goddess." People come from all around the vicinity to pray to her for good luck and good fortune.

One of the most persistent pirate legends concerns buried treasures. In fact, dozens of caves in the Pearl River Delta are said to be genuine sites where Zhang Bao hid his booty. On Longxue (Dragon Cave) Island, in Dongguan County, there is a "Gold Cave" that today displays a small painted statue of Zhang Bao. Another cave, on Cheung Chau Island, has been a popular tourist attraction for Hong Kong visitors for decades. Even Hong Kong schoolchildren go on "treasure hunting" field trips to the cave on Cheung Chau Island.[39] Along the Nan'ao coast there is a speck of land called "Gold-Silver

Island" where pirates were said to have hidden their treasures; perched on this rock is a statue of the Treasure Protecting Goddess overlooking the sea. These monuments to pirates have become staple tourist sites.

While few people today remember much about the thirteen pirates who were executed in Shanwei in 2000, the front page of the 29 January 2000 *South China Post* published an unforgettable photo of Yang Jingtao, dressed in a suit and tie as he was led off to the firing squad. Drunk, defiant, and cursing the Chinese government and the Communist Party, Yang went to his death singing a popular Ricky Martin song.[40] The irony of this event, of course, is that a society that has worked so diligently to eliminate piracy has in the end immortalized the condemned pirates as folk heroes. Even in death, pirates defy Beijing's attempt to assert unchallenged authority over all forms of maritime activity.

## Notes

The author wishes to thank Bill Guthrie and Kit Kelen for helpful comments and suggestions, and the Faculty Research Committee at the University of Macau for a generous grant that has enabled the author to do this research.

1. Bertil Lintner, *Blood Brothers: The Criminal Underworld of Asia* (New York: Palgrave Macmillan, 2003), pp. 1–2; Stefan Eklöf, *Pirates in Paradise: A Modern History of Southeast Asia's Maritime Marauders* (Copenhagen: Nordic Institute of Asian Studies Press, 2006), pp. 78–79.

2. *Xiamen zhi* ([1832] 1961), pp. 665–67; the quote is cited in Robert J. Antony, *Pirates in the Age of Sail* (New York: W. W. Norton, 2007), p. 113.

3. Leonard Blussé, "Minnan-jen or Cosmopolitan? The Rise of Cheng Chih-lung alias Nicolus Iquan," in *Development and Decline of Fukien Province in the Seventeenth and Eighteenth Centuries* [hereafter *Fukien Province*], ed. E. B. Vermeer (Leiden, Neth.: E. J. Brill, 1990), pp. 245–64.

4. Patrizia Carioti, "The Zhengs' Maritime Power in the International Context of the 17th Century Far Eastern Seas: The Rise of a 'Centralized Piratical Organization' and Its Gradual Development into an Informal 'State,'" *Ming Qing Yanjiu* (1996), pp. 29–67; Cheng K'o-ch'eng, "Cheng Ch'eng-kung's Maritime Expansion and Early Ch'ing Coastal Prohibition," in *Fukien Province*, ed. Vermeer, pp. 228–44.

5. *Quanzhou fuzhi* (1870), pp. 73/32a–34a; *Xiapu xianzhi* (1929), pp. *dashi*/16b–17b; and *Shantou dashiji* (1988), pp. 2/38–60.

6. See Robert J. Antony, *Like Froth Floating on the Sea: The World of Pirates and Seafarers in Late Imperial South China,* Institute of East Asian Studies China Research Monograph (Berkeley: Univ. of California, 2003), p. 38.

7. *Maxiang tingzhi* (1893), addendum 1/56b–57a.

8. *Gongzhongdang* [Palace Memorials] (3749) JQ 3.2.29 and (3728) JQ 3.2.19; *Xingke tiben* [Routine Memorials] (136) QL 46.3.25 and (147) JQ 14.4.23.

9. Richard Glasspoole, "A Brief Narrative of My Captivity and Treatment amongst the Ladrones," in *History of the Pirates*, ed. Charles Neumann (London: Oriental Translation Fund, 1831), pp. 114–15.

10. Some writers have described today's pirate syndicates as huge multinational corporations. For example, see Jack Hitt, "Bandits in the Global Shipping Lanes," *New York Times Magazine*, 20 August 2000; and Eklöf, *Pirates in Paradise*, p. 83.

11. *Gongzhongdang* (3728) JQ 3.2.19 and (10138) JQ 13.3.2.

12. *Gongzhongdang* (14804) JQ 14.7.15.

13. On the demise of the Guangdong Confederation see Robert Antony, "State, Community, and Pirate Suppression in Guangdong

Province, 1809–1810," *Late Imperial China* 27, no. 1 (June 2006), pp. 1–30.

14. Ralph Reid, "Piracy in the China Sea: Some Aspects of Its Influence upon the History of the Far East" (MA thesis, University of Hawaii, 1938), p. 244.

15. C. R. Boxer, "Piracy in the South China Sea," *History Today* 30 (December 1980).

16. Grace Fox, *British Admirals and Chinese Pirates, 1832–1869* (Westport: Hyperion, 1973), pp. 107–109.

17. See the Zhang Rensheng case in Liu Fang, ed., *Qingdai Aomen zhongwen dang'an huibian* [Collection of Chinese Archives from the Qing Dynasty in Macau] (Aomen: Aomen jijinhui chuban, 1999), vol. 1, p. 344. The so-called Manila-men was a catchall category that included Malays, Chinese, Oceanians, and mixed races of Asian sailors.

18. Donald Pittis and Susan Henders, comps., *Macao: Mysterious Decay and Romance* (Hong Kong: Oxford Univ. Press, [1940] 1997), pp. 139–40.

19. Ibid., p. 140.

20. Ibid., pp. 140–42; Fox, *British Admirals and Chinese Pirates*, p. 128.

21. Ernest Alabaster, *Notes and Commentaries on Chinese Criminal Law and Cognate Topics* (London: n.p., 1899), p. 469.

22. A. D. Blue, "Piracy on the China Coast," *Journal of the Hong Kong Branch of the Royal Asiatic Society* 5 (1965), p. 75.

23. John Kleinen, "De Kaping van de *Namoa*," *Amsterdams Sociologisch Tijdschrift* 25 (1998), pp. 99–103; Harry Miller, *Pirates of the Far East* (London: Robert Hale, 1970), pp. 151–55. Because Bias Bay was under the jurisdiction of the Kowloon submagistrate, the execution was carried out there.

24. Blue, "Piracy on the China Coast," p. 79.

25. Bias Bay lies just outside Hong Kong territorial waters. J. M. Sheridan's fictionalized account *The "Shanghai Lily": A Story of Chinese Pirates in the Notorious Regions of Bias Bay* and the 1935 American film *China Seas*

popularized and glamorized the Chinese pirates for Western audiences. Today on the shore of Bias Bay is a French-built nuclear power plant, the largest in China and perhaps a symbol of the government's destruction of the pirate threat.

26. Aleko E. Lilius, *I Sailed with Chinese Pirates* (Hong Kong: Oxford Univ. Press, [1930] 1991), p. 27.

27. Ibid., pp. 15–22.

28. Blue, "Piracy on the China Coast," p. 77.

29. Lilius, *I Sailed with Chinese Pirates*, pp. 37–57.

30. Ibid., pp. 39–40.

31. On the protection rackets in the early nineteenth century see Antony, *Like Froth Floating on the Sea*, pp. 118–21.

32. Blue, "Piracy on the China Coast," p. 85.

33. Hitt, "Bandits in the Global Shipping Lanes"; Eklöf, *Pirates in Paradise*, p. 73.

34. B. J. Lofland, "Piracy: A Selective Historical Account," *Boletim de Estudos de Macau* 3 (November 1995), p. 36.

35. Ralf Croizier, *Koxinga and Chinese Nationalism: History, Myth and the Hero* (Cambridge, Mass.: Harvard Univ. Press, 1997); Gao Zhihua, *Zheng Chenggong xinyang* (Hefai: Huangshan shushe, 2006).

36. Xiu Guojian, *Yuedong mingdao Zhang Baozai* (Hong Kong: Xiandai jiaoyu yanjiu she chuban, 1992). For an earlier popularization about Zhang Bao see Ye Linfeng, *Zhang Baozai de chuanshuo he zhenxiang* (Hong Kong: Shanghai shuju, 1970).

37. Lilius, *I Sailed with Chinese Pirates*, pp. 53–54.

38. See Wikipedia.org, s.v. "Dragon Lady (character)."

39. Personal communication from Prof. Joseph Lee, 16 October 2007.

40. Christopher Kelen, "In China, the Last Picture of Yang Jingtao," *Peace Review* 13, no. 4 (2001), pp. 553–59.

# CHAPTER THREE

# The Taiping Rebellion, Piracy, and the Arrow War

BRUCE A. ELLEMAN

Piracy can sometimes lead to war. The Taiping "Rebellion" (1851–64) was in fact a Chinese civil war that sparked the Second Opium War (1856–60), also known as the "Arrow War." This conflict was named after the Chinese-owned ship *Arrow*, which was given permission by Hong Kong authorities to fly the British flag as part of an anti-piracy convoy. When Chinese authorities violated the flag, the British government used this provocation to force China to agree to a number of trade revisions, including closer cooperation in eliminating piracy. Thus, an increase in piracy in Chinese waters resulting from the Taiping Rebellion eventually led to a major foreign war and equally dramatic changes in Sino-British relations.

The early nineteenth century witnessed an enormous expansion in the British Empire. In addition to establishing the Sydney (Australia) naval base in 1788, the British set up key trading bases in Penang in 1786, in Singapore in 1819, and finally in Hong Kong in 1842, all with the goal of increasing trade. To support its maritime trade routes, Britain established naval bases at crucial geographic locations, including the Cape of Good Hope in 1806, in Mauritius in 1810, in the Falkland Islands in 1833, in Aden in 1839, and in Karachi in 1842. During this process of empire building, the Royal Navy actively fought piracy throughout the world; in 1856 the Declaration of Paris even outlawed privateering, which by this point was often seen as little better than state-sanctioned piracy.

Not too surprisingly, the origins of the Arrow War with China were closely linked with Britain's "suppression of piracy" policies, since the Taiping Rebellion aggravated piracy in Chinese waters. Protecting trade from the Chinese pirates required treaty revision, and Great Britain and France—with the tacit support of Russia and the United States—launched a successful war to obtain that revision. While the new treaty achieved greater trade privileges and rights from China generally, this chapter will show that one of the Arrow War's prime strategic goals was to ensure the safety of foreign trade from pirates.

### Chinese Piracy and the Origins of the Arrow War

A leading cause of the First Opium War (1839–42) was not the opium trade per se but the injurious effects of the illegal trade on China's overall foreign trade. The Opium War was not a war about drugs, therefore, so much as a war about trade. In 1852, a former governor and commander in chief of the colony of Hong Kong, Sir John Francis Davis, even wrote that "at no time was the [opium] traffic deserving of the full load of infamy with which many were disposed to heap it," since the "worst effect" of the opium trade was the "piracy it engendered." Further, "Of the war it [the illegal trade] certainly was mainly the cause."[1]

As the previous chapter discussed, piracy was common throughout all of East Asia and in the South China Sea specifically. Asian waters saw a dramatic increase in piracy that "dated from the early 1840s when, no doubt, it was stimulated by the disorders of the Opium War in China." Although this type of piracy, referred to as "junk piracy," because the pirates used traditional Chinese junks, was much reduced when the British instituted antipiracy measures during the late 1840s, it revived in the 1850s.[2] In those years there were reports of a pirate raid near Hong Kong almost every day, and many others went unreported. Opium was the major commodity sought by the pirates, who then smuggled it into China. The Royal Navy was tasked with suppressing pirates, but "there were too few ships and too many responsibilities for the Royal navy in the China seas for continuous protection to be given to any one place."[3]

The spark that eventually resulted in the Arrow War was struck by the Taiping Rebellion. The founder of the Taiping movement, Hong Xiuquan, was a Chinese of the Hakka ethnicity, born and raised in Guangdong Province.[4] Growing up just thirty miles north of Canton, Hong saw firsthand how easily British forces defeated the Manchus during the First Opium War. Failing to pass the imperial civil service examinations in 1828, 1836, and 1837, Hong appears to have blamed himself, but after a fourth failure in 1843 he blamed China's Manchu leaders of the Qing dynasty and vowed to overthrow them.[5] The British victory in the First Opium War gave Hong hope that the Qing empire had finally lost its "Mandate of Heaven" by proving the Manchus' "military and political decadence."[6]

In preparation for his fight with the dynasty, Hong converted to Christianity in June 1843, perhaps equating Britain's recent military victory with its philosophical and religious foundation. In 1846, he formed a group known as the Society of God-Worshipers (Pai-Shang-ti Hui). Based at Mount Thistle, in Guangxi Province, this group gradually grew during the late 1840s. By 1851 Hong was ready, and on 11 January he declared himself "Heavenly King" and announced an anti-Manchu revolution.[7] The "Great Peace," or Taiping, he declared, had begun.

The Taiping army, numbering about seventy thousand troops, took the city of Hankou, on the upper Yangzi River, in December 1852.[8] From there it crossed the Yangzi River and laid siege to Wuchang, capturing it on 12 January 1853. The Taipings now controlled the upper Yangzi River and its trade, thus cutting off China's interior from the coastal regions. Beginning in February 1853, the Taiping army floated downstream (that is, generally northeasterly) in approximately twenty thousand boats. After a series of brilliant military victories it reached Nanjing, which the Taipings captured and made their capital in late March.

Soon afterward, the Taiping forces also took the terminus of the Grand Canal, which connected the seaport of Hangzhou, 110 miles south of Shanghai, with Beijing, thereby controlling "the great medium of communication between the southern provinces and the capital, and the route by which all of the grain supplies were conveyed to the north."[9] These victories convinced the Manchus that the Taiping drive to the north would eventually take Beijing, and they ordered all future provincial tax revenues to be delivered directly to the Manchu palace at Jehol.[10] However, in a last-ditch effort, they brought in additional troops and cavalry from Manchuria and Mongolia; on 5 February 1854 the Taipings' northern expedition failed and began a retreat to the south.

Although unable to take Beijing, the Taipings held out against imperial troops for the next ten years. From their capital in Nanjing, the Taipings quickly opened trade with Shanghai on the coast. In return for tea and silk, foreign merchants provided basic necessities, luxury goods, and also such black-market items as weapons and ammunition. The Taipings coined their own money and set up customhouses along the Yangzi to collect duties from boats transporting goods. By 1856 the Taipings held the heart of the Yangzi Valley, which gave them ultimate control over China's inland trade.

The volume of international trade grew gradually every year during the Taiping reign. The Taipings and Western merchants quickly clashed, however, over the sale of opium. Although the Taipings were pro-trade, their laws forbade the drinking of alcohol, gambling, and the smoking of opium. British authorities protested the Taipings' high duties, arguing that according to their agreements with Beijing such duties were illegal. In addition, there was a rapid increase of pirates, who regularly attacked foreign shipping, many claiming to be associated with the Taipings. "By 1854 the civil disturbances in China added rebels who were alternately pirates to the usual supply of marauders in the waterway between Hong Kong and Canton. The Canton River became impassable for Chinese vessels, foreign ships were attacked, and 'trade was at a standstill.'"[11]

In fact, the pirates, although not necessarily Taiping members, were clearly sanctioned by the government in Nanjing. By January 1856 the British had formed a squadron of ten ships to protect Hong Kong, and they instituted a system of scheduled north–south convoys under warship escort. Further, in tacit support of Britain's antipiracy policies in China, on 16 April 1856 the Declaration of Paris affirmed that "privateering is and remains abolished."[12] Although not specifically binding on China, which was not a signatory, the Paris declaration validated Britain's goal of eliminating Taiping-related piracy, in that many of the pirates were thought to be privateers, acting on behalf of the Taipings.

Chinese-owned ships registered in Hong Kong were allowed to join the convoys and given permission to fly the British flag for the purpose. This decision, however, quickly led to increased tension with Manchu authorities, who considered all Chinese-owned ships to be under their administrative authority. On 8 October 1856 Canton police boarded a Chinese-owned, but Hong Kong–registered, ship, *Arrow*. This ship had a British captain but a Chinese crew. After lowering the British flag, the police arrested twelve crew members. Immediately, Harry Parkes, the British consul, demanded that Ye Mingchen, the imperial commissioner in Canton, apologize for this "insult" to the British flag. Ye offered to release nine of the arrested sailors but insisted that the other three were "wanted on charges of piracy," and he refused to apologize.[13] He also disputed the British practice of registering Chinese ships and allowing them to fly British flags.

This incident gave the governor of Hong Kong, John Bowring, a long-sought-for opportunity to demand treaty revisions from China. Under the threat of naval shelling Commissioner Ye returned all twelve sailors, but he still refused to apologize for violating the British flag.[14] Tensions peaked during late May 1857, and on 1 June 1857 the Royal Navy defeated seventy to eighty Chinese war junks protecting Canton. Although it was a clear victory, Great Britain's position, according to Admiral Michael Seymour, remained precarious.[15] Thus, a relatively minor Sino-British disagreement over whether a Chinese vessel could legally fly the British flag while part of an antipiracy convoy had precipitated a major international war.

### Resolution of the *Arrow* Dispute

During the spring of 1857, the government of Prime Minister Lord Palmerston appointed James Bruce, the eighth Earl of Elgin, to be Her Majesty's High Commissioner and Plenipotentiary to China. His task was to lead a naval and military expedition first to Canton but ultimately to the mouth of the Bai River, near Beijing, to demand reparations for past injuries, diplomatic representation in Beijing, and treaty revisions that would grant Britain greater access to China's river trade and help quell the piracy threat for good.

The arrival of *Sans Pareil,* the Royal Navy's newest screw-propelled battleship, allowed Admiral Seymour's naval force to blockade Canton on 3 August. A British-French advance on Canton under Elgin began in early December, by which time thirty ships and over five thousand troops had been assembled. Elgin issued a final ultimatum on 12 December to Ye, who refused to accept it; on 15 December British troops took Honam Point, and the British warships *Nimrod, Hornet, Bittern, Actaeon,* and *Acorn* moved within range of Canton. Shelling commenced on 28 December, and on the following day the combined British and French forces scaled Canton's southeastern walls. The troops took control of the city; British casualties numbered ninety-six and the French thirty-four.

The next task was to find and capture Commissioner Ye. The wise thing for Ye would have been to move into the "hinterland to carry on the campaign," but Qing law stated that "any official who lost his city should lose his head."[16] Unable therefore to flee, Ye was captured on 5 January 1858 and was removed on board the warship *Inflexible* to life imprisonment in a villa outside Calcutta, India. The remaining Qing troops in Canton were soon disarmed.

With Canton safely in allied hands, the next goal was Beijing. The expedition was delayed while, in mid-April 1858, Elgin sailed northward aboard *Furious* for negotiations. Eleven weeks later the talks with Beijing failed, but due to this delay the size of the British forces had gradually increased. By 20 May everything was ready. A siege of the Dagu forts on the Bai River, protecting Tianjin, eighty miles southeast of the capital, met with light opposition, and after an hour and a half the fighting was over. British casualties were five killed and seventeen wounded; the unexpected explosion of a Chinese magazine had killed six and wounded sixty-one Frenchmen. With the taking of the Dagu forts, the road to Beijing was open; foreign ships docked for the first time at Tianjin, on 26 May.

Rather than fighting this foreign force, the Manchu emperor quickly sent imperial commissioners to Tianjin. On 26 June 1858 the fifty-six-article Treaty of Tianjin was signed with Great Britain; at almost the same time, separate treaties were signed with France, Russia, and the United States.[17] By means of this treaty, England received an indemnity of more than a million pounds for its losses in Canton, tariff revisions, the opening of five new treaty ports, and freedom of the Yangzi River as far inland as Hankou (which was at that point under sporadic Taiping control). Most important, Beijing was now open to a British representative, who would be treated by the Chinese officials as an envoy of an equal nation—not a tributary, as in the past. (Elgin later agreed to modify this clause by locating the British residence outside of Beijing so as to help prop up the Qing dynasty against the Taipings.)

Fighting piracy had been the underlying factor that had triggered warfare, and four articles of the Treaty of Tianjin (18, 19, 52, and 53) pertained to it. These articles read:[18]

18. The Chinese authorities shall at all times afford the fullest protection to the persons and property of British subjects, whenever these shall have been subjected to insult or violence. In all case of incendiarism or robbery the local authorities shall at once take the necessary steps for the recovery of the stolen property, the suppression of disorder and the arrest of the guilty parties, whom they will punish according to the law.

19. If any British merchant vessel, while within Chinese waters, be plundered by robbers or pirates, it shall be the duty of the Chinese authorities to use every endeavour to capture and punish the said robbers or pirates, and to recover the stolen property, that it may be handed over to the consul for restoration to the owner. . . .

52. British ships of war coming for no hostile purpose, or being engaged in the pursuit of pirates, shall be at liberty to visit all ports within the dominion of the Emperor of China, and shall receive every facility for the purchase of provisions, procuring water, and, if occasion require, for the making of repairs. The commanders of such ships shall hold intercourse with the Chinese authorities on terms of equality and courtesy.

53. In consideration of the injury sustained by native and foreign commerce from the prevalence of piracy in the seas of China, the high contracting parties agree to concert [discuss] measures for its suppression.

These antipiracy articles were a major boon to British efforts to eliminate the threat of piracy in Chinese waters. Many of these pirates were linked to the Taipings and so opposed China's central government in Beijing. The Treaty of Tianjin accordingly made the pirates a common enemy of the foreigners and the Manchus. Elgin had already formed a negative opinion of the Taipings, having encountered their forces along the Yangzi River and learned from locals that "the rebels were even more unpopular in the Yangzi than the Imperial forces because of the destruction which they inflicted."[19]

But it was not a forgone conclusion that the foreigners and the Manchu court in Beijing would join together against the Taipings. In fact, it would take the final ratification of the antipiracy articles agreed at Tianjin—the treaty had stipulated that ratification should occur within a year of signing—to form a solid basis of cooperation. Obtaining China's ratification of these treaty provisions was to prove more difficult than the British and French had thought.

## Sino-British Conflict and the "Dagu Repulse"

Following what appeared to be an almost complete diplomatic victory with the signing of the treaty, the British and French fleets withdrew to the south, and Lord Elgin returned home. However, with the immediate threat to Beijing over, the Manchus did their best to ignore the provisions of the treaty. In June 1859, the final month by when ratifications of the Treaty of Tianjin could be exchanged, the Manchus once again attempted to treat the British and French envoys as representing tributaries of China. This attempt to return to the status quo ante quickly led to a resumption of conflict.

To ensure that the Treaty of Tianjin would go into effect, the British and French now sent a sizable naval expedition. The fleet tried to enter the Bai River beginning on the morning of 25 June, but it was unexpectedly rebuffed by a strong Chinese force. By nightfall, five allied ships had been either sunk or disabled, and Admiral James Hope had been wounded twice. A final attempt, meant to take one of the Dagu forts by land, also failed, resulting in British casualties of sixty-four killed and 252 wounded or missing, while four Frenchmen were killed and ten wounded. During the entire battle, known as the "Dagu Repulse," a total of 519 British were killed and 456 were wounded.[20]

After this unexpected defeat, Elgin was once again made Britain's plenipotentiary to China. His new goal was to lead an expedition to Beijing to force the Manchus to ratify the Treaty of Tianjin, apologize for the recent attack, and provide an additional indemnity. But Elgin had no intention of overthrowing the Manchu dynasty; he warned that there was no satisfactory alternative to that dynasty and that accordingly it would be best for British trade to avoid creating even greater anarchy in China.

Palmerston agreed and authorized action to occupy Beijing in these terms: "The occupation by a barbarian army of a capital into which even a barbarian diplomatist is not to be admitted, would go further to proclaim our power, and therefore to accomplish our ends, than any other military success, and I must own I have no belief whatever in the supposition that such an occupation would overthrow the Chinese Empire. Depend upon it, that occupation would bring the Emperor to reason."[21] A British ultimatum was sent to Beijing in March 1860. The Manchu response was to insist that all negotiations take place away from Beijing; this reply made conflict inevitable. Elgin left London on 26 April 1860 for China.

Thirteen thousand British troops, commanded by General Hope Grant, were joined by seven thousand French troops under General Cousin de Montauban. It took time and numerous transport vessels to move these troops to China. On 12 August 1860, a flanking maneuver aimed at the Dagu forts began, with six thousand troops. On 20 August the British offered terms of surrender, but the Qing official in charge reportedly became abusive and replied "that if the Allies wanted the forts they had better come and take them."[22] On 21 August, storming parties were organized, with the French on the right flank and the British on the left. By nightfall the forts had fallen, with total British casualties numbering 201; the French had 158. Although the figure was difficult to determine, it was estimated that the Chinese had sustained approximately two thousand casualties.[23]

Beginning on 22 August the British ships began to make their way upriver to Tianjin, and on the 25th Elgin himself arrived in the city. He was met by three imperial commissioners, but he refused to negotiate with them; instead, he demanded that China accede unconditionally to the March ultimatum. The commissioners agreed to all of Britain's demands, but they questioned and delayed decision on the indemnity payment. This prompted Elgin on 8 September to order a march to within twelve miles of Beijing.

An unexpected Chinese ambush and the capture of thirty-nine members of the advance party (thirteen French, twenty-six British) led to battles on 18 and 21 September, which the better-equipped allied forces easily won. Splitting into two columns, the British in the north and the French in the west, the allied forces reached Beijing on 5 October. The hostages were returned on 8 October, but thirteen British soldiers and seven Frenchmen had either been murdered or died during their imprisonment. Beijing's Anding Gate fell to the British on 13 October. On the 18th the Summer Palace, just north of the capital, was burned at Lord Elgin's orders; several British prisoners had been tortured at that site, and he wanted to leave a permanent reminder, aimed specifically at the Manchus, of Western strength.

The final stage of the Arrow War was reached on 24 October 1860 for the British, and the next day for the French, when the Beijing Convention and ratifications of the Treaty of Tianjin were exchanged between China and its two opponents. By 9 November 1860 all the British and French troops had evacuated Beijing, although five thousand troops were stationed in Tianjin, and smaller garrisons were left to guard the Dagu forts. According to the now ratified Treaty of Tianjin, a British diplomatic mission could be located in Beijing. More to the point, the British had now secured greater trading rights throughout China, especially along the Yangzi River.

In the aftermath of this conflict, the treaty signed at Tianjin ensured Chinese cooperation in suppressing piracy. In particular, it granted the British expanded navigation rights, as "ships of the Royal Navy had complete liberty to operate in Chinese waters against pirates."[24] Similar agreements signed with France, Russia, and the United States furthered international cooperation against Chinese pirates.

### Taiping Piracy and the Abortive Lay-Osborn Fleet

As stated in the Treaty of Tianjin, the British and Chinese agreed to discuss measures for the suppression of piracy. The pirate and Taiping threats, between them, led to a British plan to sell China modern naval ships. This proposed force would have been China's first modern navy. Unfortunately for China, it was to be canceled, due to disagreement over how the ships would be used and which Chinese government agency would be in charge of them.

In 1861, soon after its various foreign treaties had been ratified, the Chinese govern-ment began to negotiate with Western countries to purchase foreign technology—including military technology—to support its effort to put down the Taipings. As part of this reform, the position of "Inspector General of the Imperial Maritime Customs" was given to a British civil servant, Horatio Nelson Lay. One of his main goals was to create China's first modern naval force to be used to quell pirates, many of whom were linked to the Taiping rebels. On 2 September 1862, during a visit by Lay to Britain, Queen Victoria gave permission for China to buy British vessels and hire crews.

During 1863, Lay and a British naval officer working for China, Sherard Osborn, helped to negotiate the purchase of seven modern steamships and one supply vessel from Britain. According to Lay's original plan, control over the ships would remain with the Imperial Maritime Customs, not the central Chinese government. To this end, on 16 January 1863 Lay appointed Captain Osborn as commander of the Chinese fleet—referred to as the "Lay-Osborn fleet"—for a term of four years.

These ships were intended to be used mainly for protecting foreign trade from Taiping-supported piracy. Queen Victoria had instructed that these "vessels should fly a recog-nized ensign in order to avoid any risk of capture and imprisonment" by Chinese or foreign ships; Lay proposed an ensign with a green field charged with a yellow saltire, colors that were not in widespread use in China at the time.[25] China's first modern fleet was canceled, however, when a dispute arose between the Chinese Customs Service, mainly staffed by British civil servants (like Lay), and the Chinese government, over which agency would actually control the navy. When the fleet was ready for delivery, the Chinese insisted that they should be able to appoint a Chinese commander in chief; Osborn would be his assistant, with authority only over the foreign naval officers.

On 18 October 1863, Osborn refused to work under the direct supervision of a Chinese officer, claiming that his agreement with Lay specified that he would take orders only from the Chinese emperor, as transmitted to him directly by Lay. This point was con-sidered crucial, since the ships, intended for antipiracy patrols, could also be used to bolster the Chinese military. The British government undoubtedly feared that a truly modern and Westernized Chinese fleet might one day be directed against British hold-ings in China. When it appeared that the ships might fall completely under China's authority, the plan was halted. The ships turned back en route and returned to England.

The British had every reason to fear that the Lay-Osborn fleet might one day be turned against them. Since the money to pay for the ships was from customs revenue, paid by the foreign countries, they had a clear self-interest in how that money was spent. The incident was quickly condemned by China, however, as yet one more example of its poor treatment by the West. As one Chinese naval historian was later to comment,

China had been forced to "spend money to buy humiliation," since it was not allowed the right to command its own fleet.[26]

The ships of the Lay-Osborn fleet were sold to a variety of foreign buyers. As a result, the creation (by purchase) of China's first modern navy was delayed by more than ten years. Lay was held responsible for this debacle by Beijing and was dismissed. Soon afterward, Beijing hired Robert Hart as inspector general of its customs. Hart would soon begin a long and distinguished career as one of the most famous foreigners in Chinese service.

### End of the Taiping Rebellion and the Final Suppression of Piracy

Although the British and French had handily defeated the Manchus, they did not attempt to overthrow the dynasty, for fear that (as Elgin had warned) an even worse government might take its place. The military success of the Taipings continued, and the threat to Shanghai was particularly great. The ratification of the Treaty of Tianjin and the Beijing Convention gave foreigners a compelling reason to back the Manchus, in particular since the Taipings refused to acknowledge the legitimacy of any treaty signed by the Manchu government concerning trade.

A Taiping eastern expedition in 1861 was initially very successful. With the bloodless capture of Ningbo on 9 December 1861, and a bloodier siege of Hangzhou that ended with victory on 31 December 1861, the Taipings finally had direct access to the sea. While this success promised increased trade with Western merchants, mainly in modern weapons and ammunition, it also opened the possibility of Taiping fleets attacking and destroying cities along China's seaboard.

This seaborne threat prompted foreigners to side more closely with the Manchu dynasty. When Taiping troops surrounded Shanghai (for the second time) during early January 1862, British and French forces under the command of Admiral Hope undertook to defend the city. On 1 March 1862, Hope's five hundred foreign troops and 750 Chinese and Western troops under the American mercenary Frederick Townsend Ward routed the Taiping force of about five thousand, inflicting about a thousand casualties and capturing three hundred prisoners.

From early April to May 1862, the foreign troops cleared out the most important Taiping strongholds within a thirty-mile radius of Shanghai. British steamships transported from Anqing to Shanghai a new imperial army, called the Huai Army, commanded by a Han Chinese official, Li Hongzhang. In mid-May, however, about ten thousand Taiping troops engaged these combined forces and forced them to retreat to Shanghai. By mid-June the Taipings had gathered a force fifty to sixty thousand strong; they approached Shanghai in twelve columns but were beaten back.

In what would prove to be their final attempt to take Shanghai, the Taipings attacked in late August. Opposed by the Huai Army, Ward's "Ever Victorious Army," and British and French troops, the Taipings were pushed back. In a series of battles during 22–24 October 1862, about 2,200 British and French soldiers, 1,500 of Ward's mercenaries, and a division from the Huai Army defeated the Taipings.[27] This battle ended the Taiping threat to Shanghai, and it was the last engagement of the campaign in which British and French troops participated.

Although the Taipings launched a final, and ultimately futile, expedition to the north to take Beijing, their hold over the Yangzi Valley became ever more tenuous. With the loss of Suzhou in 1864 and the death of Hong on 1 June of that year, the Taiping movement was doomed. Nanjing's walls were finally breached on 19 July 1864, and the city soon fell to the imperial forces. Isolated groups of Taipings continued to resist for the next year and a half, but on 9 February 1866 the last Taiping detachment was finally defeated.

Simultaneous with the Taiping defeat, the final step in Britain's fight against East Asian piracy was taken, when in 1866 the British government adopted new laws that all junks entering Hong Kong harbor had to buy licenses and all ships leaving the port had to obtain clearance permits. Strict penalties were adopted for anyone helping, arming, or protecting pirates or dealing in stolen goods. Finally, fishing and trading vessels were prohibited from carrying arms.[28]

If the Qing victory guaranteed the survival of the Manchu government in Beijing, the price China paid included giving foreign merchants unimpeded access to the Yangzi River basin. Granting foreigners direct naval access to China's interior violated one of the nation's oldest and most important coastal-defense traditions. The Lay-Osborn fleet project, though abortive, showed that China was at last willing to consider modernizing its naval forces. Its primary reason had been to gain foreign assistance in putting down the Taipings, but the government soon realized the necessity of building an indigenous, modern navy to patrol China's coastline against pirates.

## Conclusions

The Qing dynasty narrowly survived the Taiping Rebellion. In return for trade concessions along the Yangzi River, foreign powers sided with the Manchus and used their superior military might to oppose the Taipings. By playing the two sides against each other, the Manchus were able to defeat the Taipings while granting to the Western nations only nominally greater trade advantages than they had held before, mainly in areas that were under Taiping control at the time. However, the trading system put in force following the Arrow War would continue unchallenged for the next half a century. China's victory over the Taipings also gave new life to an imperial dynasty that had seemed on the verge of collapse.

As a direct result of the Arrow War, new treaties were signed at Tianjin and Beijing obtaining Chinese cooperation in suppressing piracy. These agreements allowed British ships to fight pirates not only within China's territorial seas along its lengthy coastline but also far inland on the Yangzi. In 1866 the British government invited other nations to assist in halting piracy in China; "Prussia, Russia, Austria, Holland, the United States, Portugal, France, Spain and Italy pledged support." For the first time, China also succeeded in purchasing modern steamships and organizing them against the pirates "under one distinguishing flag—a yellow flag with a red dragon on it."[29]

On its own initiative, China began to sign bilateral treaties with foreign nations to control piracy: "Between 1861 and 1869 China negotiated agreements with six [sic] other Western nations, Prussia, 1861, Denmark, 1863, the Netherlands, 1863, Spain, 1864, Belgium, 1865, Italy, 1866, and Austria-Hungary, 1869, each of which dealt in some measure with the problem of Chinese pirates." By exposing merchants who bought pirate spoils, the 1866 "ordinance, amended in 1867 and restated in 1868, was the greatest blow ever struck at piracy as it brought within legal restriction the haunts and stores of the robbers and the native dealers in marine supplies." Meanwhile, the registration of Chinese ships, which began in 1869, meant that vessels caught assisting pirates could be impounded and that piracy losses were spread to the other "members of the same tything and shipping division in proportion to the degree of their responsibility."[30] This mutual responsibility system exerted real social pressure within China to halt piracy, and it proved an extremely effective deterrent until the very last years of the Qing empire in the early twentieth century.

---

### Notes

1. Sir John Francis Davis, *China, During the War and Since the Peace* (Wilmington, Del.: Scholarly Resources, 1972), pp. 18–19.

2. Nicholas Tarling, *Piracy and Politics in the Malay World: A Study of British Imperialism in Nineteenth-Century South-East Asia* (Melbourne, Australia: F. W. Cheshire, 1963), p. 214.

3. Grace Fox, *British Admirals and Chinese Pirates, 1832–1869* (Westport, Conn.: Hyperion, 1973), pp. 118–22.

4. For a discussion of the Hakka's military prowess, see Mary S. Erbaugh, "The Hakka Paradox in the People's Republic of China: Exile, Eminence, and Public Silence," in *Guest People: Hakka Identity in China and Abroad*, ed. Nichole Constable (Seattle: Univ. of Washington Press, 1996), pp. 211–14.

5. C. A. Curwen, *Taiping Rebel: The Deposition of Li Hsiu-ch'eng* (London: Cambridge Univ. Press, 1977), p. 79.

6. *The Taiping Revolution* (Peking: Foreign Languages, 1976), p. 16.

7. C. A. Curwen, "Taiping Relations with Secret Societies and with Other Rebels," in *Popular Movements and Secret Societies in China,*

*1840–1950,* ed. Jean Chesneaux (Stanford, Calif.: Stanford Univ. Press, 1972), pp. 65–84.

8. Jen Yu-wen, *The Taiping Revolutionary Movement* (New Haven, Conn.: Yale Univ. Press, 1973), pp. 45–48.

9. Augustus Lindley, *Ti-Ping Tien-kwoh: The History of the Ti-Ping Revolution* (New York: Praeger, 1970), vol. 1, pp. 137–38.

10. Ssu-yü Teng, *New Light on the History of the Taiping Rebellion* (New York: Russell and Russell, 1966), p. 61.

11. Fox, *British Admirals and Chinese Pirates,* p. 123.

12. Available at *Yale Law School: Lillian Goldman Law Library—The Avalon Project, Documents in Law, History, and Diplomacy,* www.yale .edu/lawweb/avalon/lawofwar/decparis.htm.

13. Douglas Hurd, *The Arrow War: An Anglo-Chinese Confusion, 1856–1860* (London: Collins, 1967), p. 21.

14. Gerald S. Graham, *The China Station: War and Diplomacy 1830–1860* (Oxford, U.K.: Clarendon, 1978), p. 303.

15. Ibid., p. 317.

16. J. Y. Wong, *Yeh Ming-ch'en, Viceroy of Liang Kuang, 1852–8* (London: Cambridge Univ. Press, 1976), p. 187.

17. For a detailed description of these negotiations, see Immanuel C. Y. Hsu, *China's Entrance into the Family of Nations: The Diplomatic Phase, 1858–1880* (Cambridge, Mass.: Harvard Univ. Press, 1960), pp. 46–70.

18. Sr. M. Pampson, "Piracy in China," confidential memorandum to Sir Austen Chamberlain, 29 November 1927, Australian National Archives, Canberra, series A981 (A981/4), Control: CHIN 28, China-Piracy.

19. Hurd, *Arrow War,* p. 169.

20. Graham, *China Station,* pp. 375–77.

21. Ibid., p. 383.

22. Michael Mann, *China, 1860* (London: Michael Russell, 1989), p. 80.

23. Graham, *China Station,* p. 400.

24. Harry Miller, *Pirates of the Far East* (London: Robert Hale, 1970), p. 151.

25. For an example of the Lay-Osborn flag, see *Flags of the World,* www.fotw.net/flags/ cn~lo.html. Although the origins are unclear, apparently green and yellow were the colors of Charles George "Chinese" Gordon's family tartan; perhaps he helped choose them. Since China did not have a national flag, Prince Gong ordered that a triangular flag bearing a dragon design should be flown by all Chinese warships. For early examples of Chinese naval flags, see flagspot .net/flags/cn-dragn.html#1844 (which leads to the *Flags of the World* site noted above).

26. Yu Zufan, *Zhongguo Jiandui Shi Lu* [The Real Record of the Chinese Fleet] (Shenyang: Chunfeng wenyi chubanshe, 1997), pp. 9–12, cited in Bruce A. Elleman, "The Neglect and Nadir of Chinese Maritime Policy under the Qing," in *China Goes to Sea: Maritime Transformation in Comparative Historical Perspective,* ed. Andrew S. Erickson, Lyle J. Goldstein, and Carnes Lord (Annapolis, MD: Naval Institute Press, 2009), pp. 288–317; p. 303.

27. Jen, *Taiping Revolutionary Movement,* p. 460.

28. Miller, *Pirates of the Far East,* p. 152.

29. Ibid., pp. 151–52.

30. Fox, *British Admirals and Chinese Pirates,* pp. 145–82.

# CHAPTER FOUR

# Selamat Datang, Kapitan
## Post–World War II Piracy in the South China Sea
CHARLES W. KOBURGER, JR.

For well over a century,* from at least the mid-nineteenth century, East Asian waters were policed by European nations, including at various times Spain, Portugal, the Netherlands, France, and Great Britain. Britain had arguably done the lion's share, and during the *Pax Britannica* maritime piracy almost became a thing of the past. All of this changed after the end of World War II, with the traditional European security providers sapped by six years of constant warfare. As a result, piracy rapidly increased throughout the region.

During the *Pax Britannica,* British sloops and gunboats fought pirates whenever they were found, often pursuing, attacking, and capturing pirate ships, and when this was not possible, sending landing parties to destroy the coastal villages that supported the pirates, driving the men into the jungle, burning the houses, breaking up boats, and destroying nets. The theory of "hot pursuit" allowed the British ships to follow suspected pirates into territorial waters, even up a country's internal rivers. Nowhere seemed out of reach of the Royal Navy.

After World War II, however, this all changed, as newly created nations throughout the Far East began to assert their rights, including their right to deny foreign access into their sovereign waters. Certain areas remained under direct foreign control, including that of the United States in the Philippines; of the British in Malaya, Singapore, and Borneo; of the Dutch in the East Indies; and of the French in Indochina. But over time even these countries gained greater autonomy, many of them full independence. These new countries were not usually much concerned with suppressing piracy, which was all too often seen as a patriotic reaction against global commerce. So the international machinery for suppressing piracy became largely impotent, and cases of piracy soared. The South China Sea and adjoining waters, in particular, saw an enormous growth in

---

* *Selamat datang,* Malay for "good morning," is often heard on the waterfront in Singapore.

piracy during the postwar years. Piracy assumed many guises, including misguided patriotism, traditional family or clan practices, or simply the urge to make a quick buck.

### South China Sea Piracy

On first examination, the South China Sea looks like a large, unbroken expanse of
water. However, it is actually full of small islands, shoals, reefs, and rocks, many of
them marked on charts as "dangerous waters." Although the islands are small in size,
there are many island groupings, including the Tambelans, the Karimatas, the Rious,
the Linggas, the Natunas, the Anambas, the Tawis, the Paracels, the Poulo Condores,
and the Spratlys, to name just a few.

In terms of geography, Hong Kong and Manila lie at the top of the South China Sea,
cities like Saigon and Bangkok inhabit the middle, and the island nation of Singapore is
at the farthest western extreme. From Hong Kong it is 1,460 miles to Singapore, from
Manila 1,330 miles. The waters between are claimed, either entirely or in part, by many
countries, including China, Taiwan, Indonesia, Thailand, Vietnam, Cambodia, Malaysia, Brunei, and the Philippines. China, in particular, has claimed the entire South
China Sea, as has Taiwan; China has occupied the Paracel Islands and several atolls in
the Spratlys, but Taiwan controls the Pratas Islands and Itu Aba (Taiping Island), the
largest island in the entire South China Sea. In addition to land disputes, there are constant arguments over fishing and mineral rights.

During the interwar years, the British kept piracy to a minimum, but during World
War II the entire region was once again full of petty pirates; the Japanese and the Allies
were too busy fighting each other to patrol the sea-lanes. Most ships transiting the
South China Sea from the north came by way of Hong Kong or Manila, while those
from the south came by way of Singapore. Unlike the Malacca Strait and waters near
Singapore, which are relatively crowded, the nearly empty South China Sea lacked
enforcement by strong regional governments, so there was virtually no established law
and order in those waters. During the immediate post–World War II period much of
the South China Sea was a violent, scarcely regulated no-man's-land, in which pirates
could operate with relative impunity.

Soon after the war ended, the United States and the Philippines jointly turned against
the Moro pirates, and the British tried to reassert their control over Singapore and the
Malacca Strait, as did the French over Indochina and the Dutch over the East Indies.
However, the trend toward decolonization undermined many of these countries'
antipiracy efforts. With the formal independence of Malaysia, Singapore, Indonesia,
and the Philippines, piracy flourished; it took a decade or more for these newly created
states to return the region to some degree of equilibrium. In particular, local authority

declined, and conversely, the availability of weapons increased; for example, the number of small but fast boats rapidly grew—"Already after World War II, the availability of American surplus outboard engines in the Sulu region gave pirates there the means and equipment with which to overtake their victims at sea."[1]

Spurred by these innovations, by 1950 the Moros in the Philippines became active again. Isabelo "Beloy" Montemayor even became a local hero of sorts. From his base in Cebu he carried on a successful smuggling and raiding organization for almost two decades before his capture in 1975: "During night-time raids, Montemayor and his accomplices attacked and raided fish carrier boats and other inter-island vessels, including passenger vessels."[2] There were many more attacks in the 1980s, including one in August 1981 on the 135-ton *Nuria 767.*[3]

### Australian Involvement against Piracy

North Borneo also saw a particularly rapid increase in piracy. Between 1959 and 1962, British officials recorded 232 pirate attacks, and many more probably went unreported. In addition to attacking ships, these pirates would raid coastal towns: "In 1962 alone there were 20 armed raids on the coast of British North Borneo which left at least eight people dead and many more injured." The ethnic background of the pirates, known as "Tawi-tawi," was unclear, but they may have been descended from "the Samal pirates who settled there after the Spanish in 1848 sacked their strongholds on the island of Balangingi east of Jolo in the heart of the Sulu Archipelago."[4]

Beginning in 1957, the Australian government became concerned about piracy in its immediate neighborhood, in particular to the near north, "on account of the growing chaos in Indonesia." The Royal Australian Navy (RAN) agreed to conduct antipiracy operations off North Borneo, as requested by the Commander in Chief, Far East Station, in December of that year. But to "avoid the probability of becoming involved in incidents with Indonesia, we should not carry out antipiracy patrol duties in the internal and Territorial waters claimed by Indonesia. Antipiracy protection, should however, be given to registered British Ships about whose identity there can be doubt, which on the High Seas as recognized by us; that is, up to the 3 mile limit of Territorial waters."[5]

An "appendix" to the RAN directive, furthermore, made it clear that the intention was to protect "British merchant ships only."[6] However, a supplementary directive was debated that would have authorized RAN ships to oppose pirates off of Borneo. On 1 December 1959, D. W. Nichols, Esq., of the Australian Commission, Singapore, reported on a recent compilation of fifty-odd piracy cases: "The general picture as I see it is one of piracy purely for profit with no political motive or significance, and it is relevant to the Royal Navy's duty of policing the high seas that they should deal with this kind of menace."[7]

Piracy rates were high in this area. Between 1 November 1958 and October 1959, fifty-four piracies were reported (see table 1). Only three led to arrests and conviction. Eighty-three percent were from May to August, since this is "the period of fair weather in the Sulu and Celebes Seas which gives way to the boisterous northeast monsoon in the last quarter of the year." Almost all of the victims were Indonesian vessels on voyages to Tawau, and most piracies took place east of the island of Si-Amil (04°18' north, 118°53' west). Lost cargo was mainly copra (dried coconut) but also some nutmeg and spices. Total losses exceeded US$200,000. Most of the pirates—a total of thirty-two—were described as using Filipino or Suluk motor *kumpit*s, or speedboats. All cases in this list appeared to be carried out by Suluk natives of the southern Philippines.[8]

TABLE 1
*Piracy Reports between 1 November 1958 and October 1959*

| 1958 | November | 1 |
|------|----------|---|
| 1959 | January | 2 |
| | April | 1 |
| | May | 12 |
| | June | 12 |
| | July | 2 |
| | August | 19 |
| | September | 4 |
| | October | 1 |
| | Total | 54 |

"Proposed Use of RAN Ships on Anti-piracy Operations off North Borneo," supplementary directive of February 1958 on conduct of HMA ships in Indonesian waters, rescinded on 2 August 1960, Australian National Archives, Canberra, series A1838 (A1838/369).

The pirates were well armed. In twenty-eight cases they showed weapons or ammunition, in fourteen they used firearms or bombs, and in only nine were no arms visible (although that does not necessarily mean the pirates did not have them). Weapons included "shotguns, Garrand rifles, carbines, Sten guns, Bren guns, pistols, and fish bombs (i.e., homemade bombs for stunning fish, illegal in North Borneo but traditional in the area)."[9]

Territorial disputes between Malaysia and Indonesia made piracy suppression difficult. To counter the piracy threat, during spring 1960 HMAS *Tobruk* was assigned to carry out patrols of the Sulu Archipelago, followed by HMAS *Anzac* in June, HMS *Crane* in

July, and HMS *St. Bridges Bay* in September. These patrols were in support of local trade, what "in the Indonesian eyes would be deemed to be the protection of illegal traffic conducted by dissidents in armed revolt against their Government." Also, the Australian government was concerned that its ships not become involved in an incident with Indonesia over the latter's sovereign waters. For this reason, all such patrols would be on the high seas or in British waters, not in sea territory claimed by Indonesia.[10]

After *Crane* finished its final patrol, Australian antipiracy patrols were discontinued. It was envisioned that if future patrols were ever carried out, "it might be desirable to enlist the cooperation both of the Philipinos [*sic*] and the Indonesians." But, this would not "in any way [have] implied recognition of Indonesia's claim in relation to her territorial waters." Piracy had occurred on high seas and "also outside the arc of Indonesia's claim."[11]

Another group of modern pirates in the area were the Tausug, from Jolo. These young men considered piracy a traditional practice that allowed them to demonstrate "highly regarded virtues such as bravado, honour, masculinity and magnanimity." Instead of taking slaves, as their forefathers had, the modern Tausug pirates focused on "cattle, money, jewellery, weapons, brass work and gongs," plus "shoes, watches, transistor radios and sewing machines." One name given to local pirates was "jump buddies," because they often forced victims to jump overboard, presumably to drown. The Philippine Archipelago, in particular, was considered a dangerous region.[12]

In terms of the levels of violence and human suffering, however, the Sulu region stood out in the 1960s as probably the most dangerous in the world. Not only are piracy and maritime raiding culturally sanctioned among some maritime communities, but violence is triggered by a proliferation of firearms, including modern automatic weapons, since World War II. Moreover, many of the Muslim groups who traditionally inhabit the Sulu Archipelago are only weakly integrated into, and are even marginalized by, the Philippine nation. Piratical activity, in this context, may even be seen as a historically and religiously justified means of resistance against the attempts by Christians—whether Spanish, American, or Filipino—to control and dominate.

In fact, piracy has been a growing problem throughout the South China Sea since the 1950s, and it has often appeared to be linked to government actions. During decolonization, for example, it seemed as if government-sponsored privateering in Indonesia had returned: "Echoes of privateering continued well into the twentieth century. Sea raiding, thought to be condoned by Indonesia, was a factor that the Commonwealth naval forces had to take into account during the Malayan Emergency (1948–1960) and Sukarno's subsequent policy of Confrontation *(Konfrontasi)* against the newly created Malaysian Federation between 1963 and 1966."[13] Accordingly, the "piratical activity which did occur during the 1950s and 1960s seems to have been perpetrated by Indonesian regular and irregular forces and linked to international maritime and political disputes."[14]

### South China Sea Piracy during the 1970s and 1980s

Small-time pirates in the South China Sea and adjoining waters operated during the 1970s and 1980s in junks, *prahus* (outrigger sailboats), and dhows, many of them large enough for the high seas, but the vast majority suitable only for coastal attacks. Often pirates would board a ship, loot its safe and crew, and disappear before they could be captured by local authorities. Rape and murder were not uncommon, and there were many cases of kidnapping and holding of victims for ransom.

Larger pirate organizations, also present in these waters, would hijack ships and sell their cargoes, usually on the black market. Once a cargo was disposed of, the ship might be sold or be used to smuggle drugs or illegal emigrants. Referred to as "phantom ships," they were given new names, different paint schemes, and bogus registrations. Such ships might then be used to conduct legitimate trade or to smuggle, until the new owners sold them for scrap or scuttled them.

As noted above, pirates were able to obtain a wide range of weapons, mainly army surplus, manufactured in Japan, Britain, or the United States. These included automatic weapons of all types, and even modern field guns. During one incident, a British submarine surfaced next to a suspicious boat, which then fired on it with a British-made twenty-five-pounder howitzer. Fortunately the untrained crew missed, and the submarine used its own four-inch deck gun to retaliate, but the danger was real. During May 1975, the U.S.-flagged containership *Mayaguez,* out of Hong Kong en route to Sattahip, Thailand, was fired on and boarded by a Cambodian gunboat. It was escorted into the port of Wai and then the next day to Koh Tang. Four days later, the U.S. Air Force, Navy, and Marines conducted a "cutting out" operation that freed the ship.[15]

There are many other well known cases of piracy. In August 1981, the ferry *Nuria 767* mentioned above was about five hundred miles south of Manila en route to Sabah when it was hijacked by two stowaway pirates and two crew members. A total of eleven people were shot, and another twenty-five were drowned. The pirates escaped with US$380,000 in cash and about $126,000 in cargo. The same year, a Thai pirate group was reportedly robbing Malay fishermen, holding them and their boats for ransom. Since the boundary between the two countries was unclear, it was difficult for the Malay fishermen to avoid capture by pirates. Fortunately, Malay and Thai police were able to break up the ring.[16]

In 1981 a Liberian-flagged tanker, *Koei,* was boarded southwest of Singapore. In August of that year the 29,960-ton tanker *Corsicana* was boarded at the same place; pirates armed with machetes and knives forced the captain to open his cabin safe. During September, the captain of the forty-thousand-ton *Mammoth Monarch* left the bridge to visit his cabin, only to find "his cabin ransacked, the safe gone, and a length of rope (cut from a convenient reel) hung over the stern."[17]

A total of twenty-one pirate attacks were recorded in this area during 1981 alone. These incidents tended to be armed robberies, and the pirates did not attempt to hijack the ships or sell their contents. In a typical instance, a small number of pirates, perhaps half a dozen at the most, would sneak up behind a ship, grapple it, and then board and rob it. These attacks took place at night; often the pirates could board, steal what they could find, and then depart again without ever being detected. In extreme cases, the pirates forced the captain to open the ship's safe or stole the safe outright if they could not open it. Such attacks were rapid: "The whole attack will normally not last for more than 15–20 minutes, after which the pirates leave even if they fail to come across any booty. They may then move on to other targets, attacking up to three ships or even more in a single night's raiding."[18]

Piracy syndicates displayed the most organization when it came to hijacking ships. Reportedly, for as little as US$300,000 a client could point to any ship in the Manila harbor from the rooftop bar at the Pan Pacific Hotel, and a local syndicate would then arrange for it to be stolen. The ship would be given a new name and registration and delivered to a predetermined location.[19]

### Shipping Coming from Singapore

In the waters of Southeast Asia, where the Malacca Strait and the South China Sea meet, Singapore is the pivot around which all maritime communication revolves. Most of the shipping through the South China Sea stops at Singapore, which is the major East–West hub and has been for almost two hundred years. Aside from considerable legitimate trade, it has been comparatively easy to choose any rusting, old hulk anchored along the Phillip Channel, buy papers for it on the Singapore waterfront, crew it from Indonesia, and go into business.

While approximately a third of the world's trade passes through the Malacca Strait, for certain commodities the percentages are much higher; for example, Japan and China obtain most of their crude oil from the Persian Gulf, and virtually all of it must transit that strait. Ships could travel on the southwest side of Sumatra and then pass through the Sunda Strait, but that would involve a much more circuitous route, through many small islands; the other alternative route, through the Lombok Strait and then up through the Makassar Strait, would add over a thousand miles to the one-way trip from the Persian Gulf to Japan.

Historically, piracy has been worst for the South China Sea traffic coming from Singapore, since the Malacca Strait acts like a funnel, pushing commercial ships into a small area. For example, during the nineteenth century pirates preyed on opium being shipped from India via Singapore. South China Sea piracy syndicates, with representatives in Jakarta, Hong Kong, Nha Be, Bangkok, or Dubai, as well as Singapore, have access to data on ship routes, cargoes, and departure times. Using this information for planning purposes, the syndicates can often place their own men on board ships they want to take over or pay crew members to assist them.

The Phillip Channel, in particular, provides a convenient location to stage an attack. Although the far end is six hours' sailing from Singapore, the channel there is full of merchant ships. Usually twenty-five or more merchantmen pass through every hour; some are forced to anchor there to conduct repairs or wait their turn at Singapore's busy docks. The coastline is mainly mangrove swamps, which provide the perfect cover and hiding places for fast boats.

The Royal Malaysian Marine Police regularly patrols this area, but it is very difficult to distinguish the pirates from groups carrying out legitimate business; often pirates are also fishermen or have some other cover, which makes it even harder to identify them. In fact, for many centuries piracy was a time-honored way to supplement a fisherman's normal income, which is often adversely affected by weather, such as frequent monsoons. Pirates coming from the Indonesian side of the strait make law enforcement even more difficult, since they can quickly leave Malaysian waters and return to their own, where the Malaysian authorities cannot follow them.

When the goal is to take control of a ship, the pirates can often seize it before the crew is even aware that it is being attacked. Once on board, pirates split up; different groups take control of the bridge, engine room, and radio room. One of the obvious ways to combat piracy, therefore, is to keep all essential areas locked up, but this is generally not easy while the ship is under way. Once pirates take control of a ship, their goal is usually to steal money from the ship's safe, in the captain's cabin. Depending on the circumstances, the bridge of the ship—which is often sailing at between twelve and sixteen knots down one of the world's busiest waterways—is left unattended while they do so, for many minutes, an hour, or even longer. The danger of a collision, grounding, or some other disaster is high.

While most of the pirates are simply after a quick profit, others are connected to religious or nationalist organizations. These include the Abu Sayyaf Group in the Philippines, the Free Aceh Movement (Gerakan Aceh Merdeka, or GAM) fundamentalists in northern Sumatra, the Jamaah Islamiah in Malaysia and Indonesia, and the Moro Liberation Front in the Muslim-dominated southern islands in the Philippines. These are terrorist groups and might welcome an international incident as a way of advertising their causes. One good example of a near disaster involved the French-flagged tanker *Chaumont*, en route through the Malacca Strait to the Philippines. Passing through the Phillip Channel, it was boarded by pirates from small boats. While they were conducting their raid, *Chaumont* was left to steam out of control for an estimated thirty-five minutes. It was pure chance that the ship did not run aground or collide with another ship.[20]

During an incident in September 1992, the ships involved were not so lucky: as a result of a pirate attack, the twenty-seven-thousand-ton containership *Ocean Blessing* rammed the oil tanker *Nagasaki Spirit*. Although details are hard to discern, it would appear that *Nagasaki Spirit* was under the control of pirates at the time; four months later, ten charred corpses, later identified as probably from *Nagasaki Spirit,* were located in a cargo vessel, *Hai Sin,* that was being broken up at the Guangdong Shunde yard in southern China. *Hai Sin* proved to be the ex–*Erria Inge,* a missing Australian-flagged bulk carrier that had been pirated the year before.[21] These cases were arguably bad enough, but the number of piracy attacks increased even further during the early 1990s, especially after the collapse of the Soviet Union.

### Piracy after the End of the Cold War

In the years after the Cold War, Southeast Asia experienced some of its most dramatic increases in piracy. There are many possible reasons, but one of the most easily identifiable was the sudden decrease in the number of warships operating in the region: "The end of the Cold War and the demise of the USSR as the second superpower brought about a general withdrawal of warships, especially so in the Asia-Pacific and the Indian Ocean. A lower interest in maritime affairs and a lower number of warships on patrol means lower security for licit forms of trade and higher security for illicit activities."[22]

A particularly horrible instance of piracy involved the Panamanian-flagged bulk carrier *Cheung Son,* discussed in chapter 2. In November 1998, it was hijacked in the South China Sea on its way from Shanghai to Malaysia. The twenty-three members of its crew were eventually lined up, hooded, clubbed, shot, and stabbed, before being thrown into the sea. The ship's manifest stated that it was carrying furnace slag, which is of little commercial value; perhaps the pirates wanted the ship to smuggle other goods. Another example was *Inabukwa*, a 980-ton cargo ship registered in Indonesia. Although almost worthless—the ship was valued at less than US$100,000—it was carrying a cargo of tin ingots, zinc, and white pepper valued in excess of two million dollars. After being seized and its crew marooned, the ship steamed for the Philippines.

About the same time, a Philippine coast guard unit in Sabinagi, in Ilocos Sur, located a ship that did not have proper registration. The ship had a newly given name, which no ship registry carried. Apparently, the pirates had been preparing to off-load the goods at sea when they had had to put into port for repairs. The coast guard seized the ship. The pirate syndicate tried and failed to regain it. Eventually, the owner of the cargo paid fifty thousand U.S. dollars for its return.

The *Fu Tai* incident occurred in August 1998. The ship was at anchor off Batam Island, across from Singapore, when pirates boarded it and took control. They gathered the crew and ordered all overboard but the chief engineer, whom they needed to tend the engines; many drowned. *Fu Tai* was reportedly given a new identity and set to running drugs, from Bangkok across the South China Sea to the Philippines and back again. According to reports, it rarely went into port, stopping only long enough to off-load drugs and to take on new supplies.[23]

Tankers that are attacked are usually carrying refined petroleum, not crude oil, since the market for crude is highly controlled. A seized tanker is reflagged, given false papers, and repainted, and then the product is sold. Sometimes the ship is ransomed back to the owner. If not, after the cargo is sold off the vessel might become a phantom ship, carrying other petroleum supplies of suspect origin. Eventually, it would be sold for scrap. *Petro Concord*—a small, handy, twelve-thousand-ton tanker that usually carried jet fuel, diesel, fuel oil, or gasoline—was one such ship. This ship was hijacked a remarkable four times in three years.

Efforts to fight pirates can be simple or elaborate. For example, simply waiting for daylight before transiting some of the most dangerous areas has dramatically decreased the number of attacks. Other solutions have involved installing electrified fences to make it more difficult for pirates to board. Pirates who do board but find the bridge, engine room, and radio room locked often leave without taking anything of real value.

Shipowners advise crew members not to try to fight pirates. This is one reason why most ships do not carry weapons, including firearms. On petroleum tankers, in particular, any spark can start a fire; even such common household items as mobile telephones, cigarette lighters, radios, and unauthorized flashlights are usually prohibited. However, it is "common knowledge that Israeli and Russian ships do carry firearms and they are seldom declared to port officials. . . . Word gets around. In 2001 not one Russian or Israeli ship was attacked, compared to twenty-seven ships from the U.S. and the UK."[24]

The number of attacks fluctuates from year to year, but in recent years the numbers of ships attacked in port and at sea have increased. In 2001, for example, the Indonesian-flagged tanker *Tirta Niaga IV* was boarded and robbed while anchored off Aceh's western coast; the captain and second officer were abducted and ransomed, in the captain's case for thirty thousand U.S. dollars. Following this incident there was a rapid increase of similar crimes in the area.[25]

Fear of terrorist attacks has also increased, especially after reports suggested that in 2003 terrorists had hijacked *Dewi Madrim,* a small tanker, to practice navigation in the Malacca Strait; the ship's owner claimed, however, that it had been simply a pirate attack and that the captors had maneuvered the ship to "stop it colliding with other ships or running aground while they stole what they could from it."[26] Elsewhere the pirates have been more brutal, as in the 5 January 2004 hijacking of the Indonesian oil tanker *Cherry 201,* in which four of the sixteen crew members were eventually killed. However, despite the potential for a maritime terrorist attack, all "evidence that Islamist terrorists are plotting a maritime terrorist attack in Southeast Asia is mostly circumstantial."[27]

While it is difficult to know for sure, pirates at the northern entrance to the Malacca Strait may be connected to the Free Aceh Movement. Whereas pirates in the southern region of the Malacca Strait seem to take care not to attack Indonesian ships, in the north a large proportion of the victims are Indonesian-flagged, which may reflect the separatist goals of the pirates. Following the 26 December 2004 earthquake and tsunamis, however, piracy cases plummeted for several months. This was due not only to the destruction of the pirates' equipment but also to the large number of foreign military vessels in the region providing humanitarian aid. The U.S. Navy, for example, sent over fifteen thousand sailors and some twenty-five warships into the region, which could not help but have an impact on security in the region.[28]

Unfortunately, as the foreign ships left the piracy once again began to increase: "From the end of February 2005, piratical activity resumed off the Acehnese coast, still characterized by shootings, kidnappings and generally high levels of violence." On 15 August 2005, however, GAM and Indonesia signed a peace treaty and piracy attacks continued, which has led some scholars to suspect that local pirates could be posing as GAM or might be its supporters acting independently of higher authority.[29]

### Conclusions

In recent years, piracy in the South China Sea has been on the increase. Singaporean authorities have taken steps to halt piracy in their region, with some success. However, the surrounding waters remain unsafe, in particular in areas adjacent to Indonesia, to which pirates can retreat and where they can easily hide. To add to the problems inherent in controlling piracy, only an estimated 30–40 percent of pirate attacks on commercial ships are reported. There are many reasons for this reluctance, including the risk of higher insurance premiums and the delays and costs of being kept on the scene by police while they are investigating the crime, but the end result is that the true extent of the piracy is difficult to gauge accurately.

Although international shippers are the most important single group of users of the South China Sea, they are by no means alone. Numerous junks, *prahu*s, sampans, dhows, coastal freighters, and barges also use these waters. Some are local craft, many of them fishing boats, while others carry commercial goods strictly within the region. Because of the large number of vessels, as well as their almost infinite variety, it is impossible to tell a pirate ship from a legitimate fisherman or small commercial vessel. As a result, the number of piracies carried out against small craft, including fishermen, regional shipping, and local boats involved in "barter trade," is almost surely greater than that of pirates carried out against commercial ships.

The biggest single problem with patrolling these waters effectively arises from the continued disputes over sovereignty, discussed at greater length in the next chapter; most of the South China Sea is claimed by more than one country. The lack of defined borders makes locating and capturing pirates extremely difficult, especially if the pirates flee into an unfriendly country's waters. Until international efforts can be organized to halt piracy attacks, there is no reason to believe that they will end. In particular, the international maritime rules of engagement must be changed to allow police to enter a neighboring country's sea territory in "hot pursuit." Until then pirates will always enjoy a clear advantage.

---

### Notes

1. Stefan Eklöf, *Pirates in Paradise: A Modern History of Southeast Asia's Maritime Marauders* (Copenhagen: Nordic Institute of Asian Studies, 2006), p. 59.

2. Ibid., p. 37.

3. Roger Villar, *Piracy Today: Robbery and Violence at Sea since 1980* (London: Conway Maritime, 1985), p. 32.

4. Eklöf, *Pirates in Paradise,* pp. 38–39.

5. "Proposed Use of RAN Ships on Anti Piracy Operations off North Borneo," 1 October 1959, National Archives of Australia, Canberra, Australia, Series number A1838, Control Symbol 682/23/1/2, Secret (declassified 9 December 2004).

6. 17 July 1959, Australian National Archives, Canberra, Secret 682/23/1/2.

7. "Proposed Use of RAN Ships on Anti-piracy Operations off North Borneo," supplementary directive of February 1958 on conduct of HMA ships in Indonesian waters, rescinded on 2 August 1960, Australian National Archives, Canberra, series A1838 (A1838/369).

8. Ibid.

9. Ibid.

10. "Anti-piracy Patrols off North East Borneo, Memorandum by C-in-C Far East Station, 24 August 1959," 27 August 1959, Australian National Archives, Canberra, Secret DCC(FE)(59)207.

11. Ibid.

12. Eklöf, *Pirates in Paradise,* pp. 40–44.

13. Peter Chalk, "Contemporary Maritime Piracy in Southeast Asia," in *A Cooperative Monitoring Regime for the South China Sea: Satellite Imagery, Confidence-building Measures, and the Spratly Islands Disputes,* ed. John C. Baker and David G. Wiencek (Westport, CT: Praeger, 2002), p. 165, citing Michael Pugh, "Piracy and Armed Robbery at Sea: Problems and Remedies," *Low Intensity Conflict and Law Enforcement* 2, no. 1 (1993), p. 2.

14. Eklöf, *Pirates in Paradise,* p. 61 note 26.

15. Roy Rowan, *The Four Days of Mayaguez* (New York: W. W. Norton, 1975).

16. Villar, *Piracy Today,* p. 140.

17. Ibid., p. 140, 25.

18. Eklöf, *Pirates in Paradise,* pp. 46–47.

19. John S. Burnett, *Dangerous Waters: Modern Piracy and Terror on the High Seas* (New York: Dutton, 2002), pp. 225–26.

20. Ibid., pp. 146–48.

21. Ibid., pp. 135–37, 140–45.

22. Peter Lehr, ed., *Violence at Sea: Piracy in the Age of Global Terrorism* (London: Routledge, 2007), p. viii.

23. Burnett, *Dangerous Waters,* pp. 216–25.

24. Ibid., p. 88.

25. Eklöf, *Pirates in Paradise,* pp. 51–53.

26. Martin N. Murphy, *Contemporary Piracy and Maritime Terrorism: The Threat of International Security,* IISS Adelphi Paper 388 (London: Routledge, 2007), p. 8, citing Charles H. Cragonette, "Maritime Legends," *Bulletin of the Atomic Scientists* 62, no. 5 (September–October 2006), p. 18.

27. Eklöf, *Pirates in Paradise,* pp. 117–24.

28. See Bruce A. Elleman, *Waves of Hope: The U.S. Navy's Response to the Tsunami in Northern Indonesia,* Newport Paper 28 (Newport, R.I.: Naval War College Press, February 2007).

29. Eklöf, *Pirates in Paradise,* pp. 53–57.

# CHAPTER FIVE

# The Political Economy of Piracy in the South China Sea

DAVID ROSENBERG

Piracy is an ancient, persistent, and elusive phenomenon in the South China Sea. In the past two decades it has increased substantially, leading to a renewed interest in piracy and its possible nexus with maritime terrorism, especially after the 11 September 2001 attacks on the United States. Although it has been widely reported and investigated, piracy remains difficult to understand and to control. The oceans are "a domain increasingly beyond governmental control," says William Langewiesche. They are "vast and wild, where laws of nations mean little and where the resilient pathogens of piracy and terrorism flourish."[1] In the Asia-Pacific region, "maritime disorder prevails," observes Sam Bateman. "This includes unregulated pollution of the marine environment, over-fishing, marine environmental degradation and widespread illegal activities at sea."[2]

This chapter attempts to analyze piracy through the perspective of political economy, with an emphasis on state and market stakeholders and on the economic, technological, and institutional factors affecting ocean governance of piracy. The major area of concern here is the South China Sea, where approximately half of the world's reported incidents of piracy have taken place since the 1990s. Following the usage of the International Maritime Bureau (IMB), this estimate includes instances of both piracy as defined under international law—theft on the high seas—and armed robbery or theft in the territorial waters or ports of coastal states.[3]

This chapter will examine the scope and trends in piracy in the South China Sea as well as the factors that motivate this form of maritime crime. It continues with an analysis of the factors that impede antipiracy efforts, including uncertainties over definitions and legal jurisdiction, the underlying dynamics of piracy, and uncoordinated efforts at detection, pursuit, arrest, and conviction of pirates as well as recovery of crew, cargo, or ships. It concludes with an analysis of the limited progress made by state and market stakeholders to improve antipiracy security in the vital shipping lanes of the South China Sea.

### Maritime Trade and Shipping Traffic

The most important factor affecting piracy and government efforts to interdict pirates is the dramatic increase in shipping traffic. Maritime trade through the South China Sea has expanded rapidly in recent years, due to three major, long-term trends: the high growth rates of regional economies and increasing trade flows among them, rising energy demand and energy imports, and the automation of cargo handling in hub ports.

Seaborne trade has doubled every decade since 1945, and shipbuilding tonnage worldwide has doubled since 1990. It is estimated that 80 percent of all world trade, or about 5.7 billion tons of cargo, is transported by sea. This maritime superhighway in the world economy is supported by a massive infrastructure, including ninety-three thousand merchant vessels with 1.25 million seamen bound for eight thousand ports.[4]

Intra-Asian trade is growing more quickly than transpacific trade. For example, in 2003 South Korea's trade with China surpassed its trade with the United States for the first time. In 2004, Japan's trade with China surpassed its trade with the United States for the first time. More and more Asian states are reorienting their trade flows toward China. The several explanations for this trend include the recovery of Asian economies from the 1997 economic crisis, the dynamic China market, and trade-opening agreements between China and Southeast Asia.[5]

Asian countries had the largest share of the total tonnage of seaborne world exports in 2006, at 38.8 percent. Exports of crude oil from western Asia and manufactured goods from China and other countries of East and Southeast Asia contributed to this result. European countries accounted for 21.8 percent of world export tonnage, with the major share coming from countries belonging to the European Union. Industrialized countries in North America and developing countries in the Americas made up 21.1 percent of world export tonnage; the latter accounted for about two-thirds of the total tonnage for the hemisphere, owing to their considerable exports of crude oil, iron ore, coal, and grains. Africa's and Oceania's shares of overall world tonnage exported were 8.5 percent and 8.8 percent, respectively.[6]

Of the world's twenty busiest container-handling ports in the past five years, Asian ports accounted for the top six: Hong Kong, Singapore, Shanghai, Shenzhen, Busan, and Kaohsiung. The top twenty busiest global ports generally also include Port Klang and Tanjung Pelepas in Malaysia, Tanjungpriok in Indonesia, Laem Chabang in Thailand, and Manila in the Philippines.[7] The rapid growth of maritime trade has created enormous pressures for hub ports and shipping companies to speed up shipping traffic.

Port managers and shipping companies have tried to accelerate shipping traffic flows, including containerization, automation of cargo handling, and increased ship sizes.

Oil tanker traffic—already high—will increase substantially with the projected increase in Chinese oil imports. Almost all of this additional Asian oil demand, as well as Japan's oil needs, will be imported from the Middle East and Africa. Most tankers pass through the strategic Malacca Strait into the South China Sea. About sixty-five thousand vessels of all types passed through the Malacca Strait in 2005.

This rise in shipping has also created a corresponding increase in the risks of congestion and delay, collision, and crime, including in particular all forms of piracy, especially in the narrow and shallow choke points of the South China Sea. Clearly, there is a growing concern among coastal states and user states to ensure speedy and safe passage through the shipping lanes of the South China Sea. Efforts to halt piracy have been stymied, however, by differing views of what constitutes piracy and as to which countries should have jurisdiction over stopping it in highly disputed waters.

### The Detection, Cost, and Prevention of Piracy

Despite the problem of defining piracy and determining which stakeholder should be responsible for stopping it, several widespread generalizations about piracy set it apart from other maritime activities. These include the link between growing shipping volume and piracy, economic drivers (such as poverty), the role of organized crime, and the role that law enforcement agencies on land can play in stopping piracy.

First, the more the shipping, all things being equal, the more the opportunities for piracy. As shipping volume and velocity increase, targets of opportunity increase for pirates to seize valuable and accessible cargo from ships in port or at sea. Globalization has not only accelerated world trade. It has also seen a move to the use of flag-of-convenience shipping and a privatization of port cargo-handling services. It is increasingly difficult for port officials to distinguish legal from illegal trade, especially among the contents of millions of containers passing through their ports. All these factors enhance the opportunities for illegal trade in pirated goods.

Second, "piracy is largely driven by poor economic conditions."[8] "The vast majority of lower-end piracy . . . is largely motivated by poverty and disenfranchisement that afflicts vulnerable targets like fishermen and local traders."[9] Sudden and severe impoverishment, especially among marginal coastal seafaring communities, makes piracy a viable way to meet basic needs. For example, the big increase in the number of piracy attacks in Indonesia's waters and ports in the past ten years may be attributed to its sharp economic downturn and domestic instability in the wake of the 1997 currency crisis. Eric Frecon has interviewed one poor migrant from a poor Indonesian kampong who puts it this way. "I became a pirate . . . to earn a living. Singapore was rich; we were poor. So, we went to pillage the areas [around] Singapore."[10]

In times of economic hardship piracy is still viable for some traditional maritime peoples. This helps to explain why most acts of piracy involve petty theft from ships in ports or anchorages. According to one study, in 2002, 77 percent of all attacks occurred in ports.[11] Economic duress also makes impoverished fishermen more vulnerable to and available for recruitment by entrepreneurial criminal organizations. Piracy will continue as long as poverty and unemployment persist.

Third, there is a small but increasing amount of piracy by organized criminal groups. This may be attributed in large part to the increasingly lucrative cargoes created by the economic dynamism of the region. There has been some increase in the kidnapping of crew members for ransom and in theft of bulk cargo. More attackers are armed, more crew members are injured, and more vessels are being hijacked. The role of organized crime in large-scale piracy is indicated by the sophisticated equipment, skilled labor, and managerial infrastructure necessary to transfer commodities on a global scale.

Fourth, all maritime piracy begins and ends on land. Whether they are poor seafarers or criminal gangsters, pirates are recruited and based on shore. Ultimately, their booty must be "fenced" on land. Whatever is taken at sea eventually arrives at a port. This requires official documentation. In the case of pirated goods, this means reliable false documentation. Officials have to be persuaded to look the other way; their corruption is essential to the routine transfer of contraband. Hence, effective antipiracy measures need more than maritime security measures; they also need close coordination with national law enforcement authorities and anticorruption agencies.

How costly is the piracy threat to shipping through the South China Sea? James Warren of the Asia Research Institute at the National University of Singapore has claimed that piracy in the (Southeast Asia) region has cost the world economy a staggering twenty-five billion U.S. dollars a year.[12] Stanley Weeks notes that "piracy raises insurance rates, restricts free trade, increases tensions between the affected littoral states, their neighbors and the countries whose flagged ships are attacked or hijacked."[13]

Coastal states have been under considerable pressure from user states to provide safe and secure navigation through the South China Sea, especially in narrow choke points such as the Malacca Strait. The coastal states, particularly Indonesia, have been described in the media as not doing enough to suppress piracy. Also, despite the clear threat that piracy appears to offer, shipowners have not taken much action to stop it. This is perhaps explained by the high cost of preventive measures. The Organisation for Economic Co-operation and Development (OECD), for example, has stated that new security measures to counter the threat of terrorist attacks will require an initial

investment by ship operators of at least US$1.3 billion and will increase annual operat-
ing costs by US$730 million.[14]

In economic terms, however, the relatively low cost of piracy may not warrant such
expensive preventive measures. A closer examination of the data on piracy shows that
the problem might not be as alarming as sometimes portrayed by the media, at least
not in economic terms. For example, in 2005 over sixty-three thousand ships sailed
through the Malacca and Singapore straits. In the same year, the IMB reported only
twelve cases of actual and attempted attacks on ships in the straits. Hence, the probability of attack in 2005 was a relatively low 0.019 percent, or nineteen out of a hundred
thousand. In 2003, in the heavily trafficked Malacca Strait—frequently referred to as
one of the most "pirate infested" seas of the world—the risk of a transiting ship being
attacked was less than 0.001 percent.

Moreover, many of these reported piracy attacks were little more than cases of petty
theft against ships at anchor in port, and most piracy victims are themselves poor fishermen and traders. Considering the relatively minor costs, many shipowners may also
be reluctant to report pirate attacks to the authorities or otherwise assist in the investigation of pirate attacks. Apart from reflecting badly on the company's image, reporting
a pirate attack may cause the victim vessel to be detained in harbor for investigation.
The cost of such delays—varying from five to twenty-five thousand U.S. dollars per
day—may easily exceed the losses incurred by a pirate attack. If suspected pirates are
arrested, crew members of the victim ship may be unable or unwilling to bear the
expense or risk of testifying at the trial.

Many low-cost antipiracy measures are available, such as equipping the superstructure
with proper locks and providing antipiracy training. However, shipowners and insurance companies have little economic incentive to implement antipiracy measures. Contrary to the popular impression from news media reports, most shipowners have not
seen piracy as a menace to international shipping. Ultimately, "repelling intruders
becomes a cost-benefit analysis for ship-owners."[15] Shipowners and shipping companies don't adopt antipiracy measures because they don't find it worth the cost.

### Arrest and Conviction of Pirates

Piracy is related to other criminal activity in and around ships and ports, and it often
overlaps other crimes. The arrest and conviction of pirates, smugglers, drug runners,
and terrorists—both politically and economically motivated—are in many ways inter-
connected. In particular, the proceeds from all of these crimes eventually end up on
land, which means that responsibility for stopping piracy must ultimately include law
enforcement authorities on land.

The range of criminal activity around seaports is extensive, including the smuggling or illicit import of illegal drugs, contraband, stowaways and aliens, restricted or prohibited merchandise, and munitions. Metropolitan areas near major seaports often have the highest rates of motor vehicle theft. Stolen cars and computers are reported among the most lucrative illegal trade from rich countries to poor countries.[16] Smuggling may also be a precondition for piracy, by providing the essential goods and services of weapons, speedboats, port access, and illegal markets to dispose of pirated goods. Hence, piracy may represent only one aspect of criminality. Widespread poverty around the Malacca Strait also generates smugglers, procurers, prostitutes, and other criminals.

Port authorities are understandably more concerned about smuggling and illegal imports—the most common maritime crimes—than about piracy. Smuggling and illegal importation occur whenever ships unload goods illegally, in areas where they are prohibited, thereby violating states' embargo or import quotas. Hence, embargoed Iraqi oil found its way to energy importers in Asia, and black-market Marlboro cigarettes evade import duties in many porous ports. It is possible that a shipper may be unaware of an illegal cargo; that is the responsibility of the cargo owner or customs broker. Given the rapid speed and volume of trade flows, it is extremely difficult to detect and detain prohibited shipments. On the contrary, there are substantial pressures on port authorities to expedite shipments across their borders, especially in large, hub ports.

Since the 11 September 2001 attacks on the United States, links between terrorism and piracy have been extensively examined.[17] However, maritime terrorist attacks or threats—that is, politically or ideologically motivated attacks against ships—have been scarce around the South China Sea. Those few that have occurred were within the territorial waters of coastal states. For example, Singapore foiled a terrorist plot in 2002 to hit visiting U.S. Navy vessels using a small boat rigged with explosives. The most notable maritime attack to date was carried out by the Abu Sayyaf Group (ASG) on *Superferry 14* in Manila Bay in February 2004; 116 people were killed or missing and presumed dead. However, it is not clear whether the attack was primarily motivated by ASG in pursuit of its political objectives. ASG was later found to have sent an extortion letter prior to the bombing, suggesting that it had been motivated by economic factors.

There are some notable obstacles to staging a successful terrorist attack in the South China Sea. Targets are less accessible at sea. A maritime terrorist attack would require very complex and expensive coordination of efforts. An attack, even if successful, could be much less visible than a terrorist attack on land. So far, there have been no terrorist attacks or hijacking attempts in the South China Sea, compared with dozens of terrorist attacks against churches, hotels, and other land-based targets. Overall, the probability of a maritime terrorist attack appears low. However, the total costs of a major blockage of vital sea-lanes like the Malacca Strait could be huge. Although they have been scarce, terrorist attacks on a ferry or cruise ship might have dramatic public impacts: the low probability times the high possible cost still makes maritime terrorism a substantial risk. To date, there has not been a clear relationship between piracy and terrorism.

Arresting and convicting pirates in the South China Sea is a major concern for nonregional countries with major shipping and naval interests, such as the United States, Japan, India, and Australia. They want to maintain freedom of navigation through the straits and sea-lanes of the South China Sea for oil tankers, containerships, and naval vessels. The South China Sea is the main thoroughfare between the Pacific Ocean and the Indian Ocean and is therefore of great strategic significance. The United States sends its warships, including aircraft carriers from its Pacific Fleet, through the South China Sea in support of military missions in the Arabian Sea and Persian Gulf. The South China Sea is the vital artery that connects America's prime Asian ally, Japan, with its Middle East energy suppliers.

Coastal states with extensive coastlines, such as Indonesia, Malaysia, Vietnam, and China, mainly want to protect their recently declared sovereign rights and resource control over exclusive economic zones (EEZs) up to two hundred nautical miles off their respective coastlines, as provided by the United Nations Convention on the Law of the Sea 1982 (UNCLOS). They have also taken on the political responsibility for controlling piracy along with their claims of economic control in their EEZs. For example, Indonesia will not allow any country or private security firm to guard international ships passing through the Malacca Strait on its side of the waterway. Ibnu Hadi, the Director for Asia Pacific and Africa Inter-Regional Cooperation at the Indonesian Foreign Ministry, has said, "Indonesia will strongly object to any security guard escorting ships in its waters. Indonesia cannot accept foreign ships escorted by foreign security guards."[18]

Coastal countries also want to assert their sovereign rights to protect tourism, fisheries, and other environmental resources in their territorial waters and EEZs. However, many coastal Southeast Asian nations want to share with international shippers the burden of providing safety of navigation. Overall, this situation presents a dilemma for user states with high concerns over piracy as to whether and how to demand accountability from the coastal states with political responsibility for maritime security where international sea-lanes traverse their territorial waters. The dilemma is complicated by other pressing concerns for countries bordering the South China Sea, such as smuggling, trafficking, poaching, and pollution.

Poaching or illegal, unreported, or unregulated fishing is perhaps a more important concern for coastal states. For centuries, the South China Sea has provided abundant fisheries offering food security and employment opportunities for coastal countries. However, as coastal urban populations have grown and as fishing technology has improved, competition for shared fish stocks has intensified considerably.

There is massive illegal fishing, in the form of unregistered foreign vessels who "pirate" the seas. Foreign fishing boats intruding in rich regional fishing grounds are especially vulnerable and attractive targets for pirates. Eduardo Santos asserts that pirates in the southern Philippines prey more on marginal fishermen than on tankers, barges, containerships, or other commercial shipping vessels. They may not only seize the fish catch; they may also rob ships of their engines, equipment, cash, and other valuables.[19] In May 2004, the director of the North Sumatra Fishery Office estimated that eight thousand fishing boats, or two-thirds of the province's fishing fleet, were not operating, because of the threat of piracy.[20] The Indonesian government has estimated that the country loses four billion U.S. dollars each year due to illegal fishing alone—several times more than the estimated cost of all pirate attacks worldwide.[21]

For some South China Sea coastal states, any proposed international coordination to combat terrorism or piracy is of lower priority than other pressing issues. These include protecting and maintaining control over newly acquired ocean resources, protecting national security, or protecting bureaucratic interests. In Indonesia, all three issues may coexist. With a coastline twice as long as the circumference of the earth, and with no more than a few dozen operating vessels to patrol its territorial waters, the Indonesian navy and marine police face a wide range of problems, including illegal fishing, illegal migration, drug trafficking, smuggling, and marine pollution.

To put this in perspective, there were only 103 incidents of piracy in Indonesian waters reported to the IMB in 2002, compared with 1,687 murders, nine thousand cases of violent theft, and eleven thousand serious assaults on land.[22] This means that piracy makes up less than 0.05 percent of Indonesia's cases of reported crime. As a direct result of these competing demands, antipiracy measures not surprisingly receive limited funding.

### Recent Developments in Antipiracy Measures and Burden Sharing

Stakeholder priorities changed substantially after July 2005, when the Joint War Committee (JWC) of the Lloyd's Market Association listed the Malacca Strait and certain areas in the southern Philippines (together with areas such as Iraq, Lebanon, and Somalia) as "prone to hull war, strikes, terrorism and related perils." As a result, marine insurance premiums were increased for vessels transiting these areas despite very strong protests by regional governments and shipowners. The JWC removed the listing in August 2006 after regional governments—with the assistance of international organizations and user states—instituted several security measures.

The JWC listing was a catalyst for several antipiracy developments. In 2003, the thirty-sixth Association of Southeast Asian Nations (ASEAN) Ministerial Meeting had issued a "Statement on Cooperation against Piracy and Other Threats to Maritime Security" but had taken little action. Subsequently, the ASEAN Regional Forum convened a meeting of maritime specialists to coordinate coast-guard action, information exchange, and investigation of piracy reports. Japan's Anti-piracy Coast Guard Program provided additional antipiracy technologies and training.

The IMB Piracy Reporting Center in Kuala Lumpur and the International Maritime Organization's (IMO's) Piracy Reporting Center in London stepped up monitoring and compliance efforts. The IMO made it mandatory for all oceangoing vessels of three hundred gross tons or more to be equipped with an Automatic Identification System (AIS) by the end of 2004. The AIS automatically sends and receives such ship information as identity, position, course, speed, and cargo information to and from other ships, aircraft, and shore installations, all integrated by satellite links. The IMB has endorsed antipiracy measures like the Secure-Ship electric fence and ShipLoc, an inexpensive satellite tracking system designed to locate ships at sea or in port by a tiny transmitter concealed on board. This would permit long-range identification and tracking of ships by anyone with authorized Internet access.

Singapore has implemented the most forceful measures to address maritime security threats. It was the first Asian port to join the U.S.-sponsored Container Security Initiative and has provided sea security teams to escort selected vessels transiting the Singapore Strait. It has restricted circulation of small craft and ferries within the port area and increased surveillance efforts by installing tracking devices on all Singapore-registered small boats to identify their locations, courses, and speeds. Together with Indonesia, it operates a radar tracking system on Batam Island to identify, track, and exchange intelligence on shipping in the Singapore Strait.

In 2003, Malaysia and Thailand started coordinated naval patrols along their joint maritime frontier. Following this, in 2004, Singapore, Malaysia, and Indonesia began coordinated naval patrols in the Malacca Strait, under the code name MALSINDO. In September 2005, the "Eyes in the Sky" initiative began, with coordinated air patrols over the strait by the three coastal states. The Philippines, meanwhile, has proposed building on its maritime border patrol exercises with Malaysia and Indonesia by formalizing a tripartite agreement to exchange information and intelligence. The increase in coordinated patrol activities has been accompanied by an increased effort to modernize regional naval and coast-guard capabilities.

Representatives of the governments of Indonesia and Malaysia have frequently asked shipping companies and the international community to share the costs of policing the Malacca Strait against pirates. Their requests, however, are received with little enthusiasm by most international actors involved—with the notable exception of Japan, which has funded a number of initiatives to provide training and resources to the law enforcement authorities in the region. Regrettably, the states that are most adversely affected by piracy—Indonesia, Myanmar, Bangladesh—can hardly afford to suppress it, whether financially, militarily, or politically. In September 2005, Indonesia and the IMO convened a meeting in Jakarta to discuss safety, security, and environmental protection in the Malacca and Singapore straits. This assembly recognized the role of burden sharing between coastal and user states, especially in the use and maintenance of international straits pursuant to article 43 of UNCLOS ("Navigational and Safety Aids and Other Improvements and the Prevention, Reduction and Control of Pollution").

Following on from this, in February 2006 the United States hosted a meeting in Alameda, California, that assembled representatives from Indonesia, Malaysia, Singapore, Australia, Germany, India, Japan, the Netherlands, Norway, the Philippines, South Korea, and the United Kingdom. (China was invited but did not attend.) While the meeting's objective was to coordinate potential user-state contributions to assist the Malacca/Singapore Strait littoral states, little progress was made on burden sharing. On the one hand, the littoral states want burden sharing to include the cost of providing safety and environmental protection services. On the other hand, international user states view burden sharing as a means of becoming more directly involved in maritime security measures to address piracy and terrorism threats.

In September 2006, Malaysia and the IMO organized a meeting in Kuala Lumpur of coastal states, major shipping nations, and shipping companies. Working groups on safety of navigation and maritime security were established to undertake projects on such issues as the removal of shipwrecks, the establishment of a hazardous and noxious-substance response center, the installation of AIS transponders on small ships, and the placement of tide, current, and wind measurement systems.

Substantial voluntary contributions have been made by China and Japan for these projects. Some have advocated toll-road or user-pays systems to help fund pollution cleanup and navigational aids. The United States and many shippers, however, oppose strongly the introduction of any fees. They prefer to see greater transparency and accountability in any use of funds for maritime safety and security. They would also like to see Malaysia and Indonesia ratify the International Convention on Maritime

Search and Rescue 1979 and the Convention for the Suppression of Unlawful Acts against the Safety of Maritime Navigation 1988 (known as the SUA Convention).

In addition, these countries are also considering becoming members of the Regional Cooperation Agreement on Combating Piracy and Armed Robbery against Ships in Asia (ReCAAP), which was initiated by Prime Minister Junichiro Koizumi of Japan in 2001. Its Information Sharing Center was established in Singapore during September 2006. Malaysia and Indonesia indicated their willingness to participate in this effort but have not yet ratified the agreement, due to sensitivities over national sovereignty.

### Persistent Problems in Controlling Piracy

Despite the recent developments in antipiracy efforts and the recent decline in piracy reports in several areas of the South China Sea, there are some persistent problems in combating piracy. Long-standing concerns include many unresolved overlapping claims and jurisdictional disputes. For example, the Spratly Islands are claimed by six countries and occupied by three of them. These territorial claims are especially important as anchors for assertions of exclusive economic zones around the disputed islands and the oil and natural gas resources they are thought to contain. With few agreed-upon boundaries in the South China Sea, countries act largely in their own self-interest. Hence, "the lack of agreed jurisdiction complicates maritime enforcement, leads to unchecked degradation of the marine environment and facilitates illegal activities at sea, including possible maritime terrorism."[23]

Second, international user states themselves have divergent security priorities. For example, recent policy of the United States in the region has been primarily driven by its global war on terrorism. It aims to achieve "maritime domain awareness"—the development of a comprehensive picture of everything that moves on the world's oceans. American security officials want to "wire" ships so that their locations, courses, speeds, cargoes, registrations, ports of departure, and ports and times of arrival can be tracked with precision, as in an air traffic control system.[24] Japan, on the other hand, is primarily interested in antipiracy measures, reflecting its acute vulnerability to any disruption of its trade and raw materials flows.

A third reason for limited progress is that many coastal states give top priority to protecting national sovereignty and controlling their recently acquired EEZ resources. The declaration of EEZs by coastal states has led to numerous overlapping and multiplying jurisdictional claims and to legal confusion over the right to exercise innocent passage through territorial seas by warships, the right to conduct military surveillance activities in the EEZ of a coastal state, and the arrest authority of states in hot pursuit of pirates in contested waters. There is general agreement that the exercise of freedom of navigation and overflight in and above EEZs should not inter-fere with the rights of the coastal state. However, there is still disagreement about when overflights become intrusive eavesdropping missions to scout the defenses of potential rivals. One tragic symptom of this disagreement was the collision between a U.S. EP-3 surveillance aircraft and a Chinese fighter jet over Chinese EEZ waters near Hainan Island on 1 April 2001, after which a political crisis ensued.

Fourth, antipiracy efforts are also greatly hindered by the "flags of convenience" sys-tem of ship registration. It is extremely easy and convenient to reregister and reflag a ship. According to former IMB director Captain Jayant Abhyankar, "One simply has to fax information as to a ship's name, ownership, tonnage, and dimensions, and a registration will be granted. The information given is not checked. Once registered, it is free to be hired for trade transport."[25] It is a system of "managed anarchy," accord-ing to Stephen Flynn, former commander in the U.S. Coast Guard and a writer on maritime security.[26] According to the International Transport Workers Federation, the flags of convenience condone poor safety, pay, and training standards. A 2001 IMO survey found over thirteen thousand cases of falsified documents of seafarers, most of whom were from Indonesia and the Philippines.[27] This provides an easy opportunity for pirates or hijackers to infiltrate a ship's crew. Having hijacked a ship, they can elude detection by reregistering it at sea for a nominal fee, thus imposing a layer of obfuscation against the search for the attackers.

Piracy carried out by organized-crime groups sometimes employs "phantom ships," operating under false identities. They may be hijacked or bought in the salvage market. They can be registered and reflagged after unloading illegal cargo. Reregistration and safety inspections are cheap, fast, and cursory in several jurisdictions. Adding to the problem is the widespread practice of most maritime shipping services to require pay-ment in hard currency on delivery. The cash-based, fast-paced, transient nature of shipping makes it an ideal medium of exchange and money laundering for criminal entrepreneurs. At one time there were thought to be twelve phantom ships operating in Southeast Asia; all but one of them were registered in Panama or Honduras.[28]

There are some simple solutions for preventing smuggling or fraudulent sale of contra-band from phantom ships. Every ship has an IMO identification number, based on its original Lloyd's registry. That number could be engraved permanently in a prominent place, so that any cargo dealer can quickly determine whether or not a suspicious vessel is in fact a phantom ship. This solution is simple, cheap, and likely to be highly effective in locating phantom vessels.

Shipowners and shipping companies are responsible for adopting antipiracy security measures, including relatively cheap physical-security measures like "safe rooms" and the installation of locks and bolts on cargo holds, in addition to satellite-based global positioning systems to track their shipments around the globe. Some shipping companies have invested in antipiracy devices like ShipLoc or Secure-Ship, or even cheaper methods, such as high-pressure water hoses or security lights. But most do not, apparently because they calculate that the risk of loss is not worth the cost of prevention.

Shippers have long-established norms of working outside national boundaries. They have to contend with import quotas, embargoes, and restrictions imposed by states for political reasons, to the commercial detriment of the shipper. Shippers may even obtain bigger profits in making prohibited goods available. In these restricted areas, it may be convenient to shipowners for their vessels to be out of radio contact or undetectable.

Another persistent problem for combating piracy is institutional insularity. A good deal of useful information about piracy is contained in the computers and files of police, coast-guard, customs, immigration, military, intelligence, and other national authorities. However, even within one national government, "information is readily available but it is locked away in 'silos' or 'stovepipes'—institutional frameworks that distribute critical information vertically but not horizontally."[29] Sharing information horizontally among governments is much more difficult. Doing so very quickly—for example, when a suspect ship is first sighted—is even more difficult.

Hence, a number of factors impede coordinated antipiracy efforts: uncertainties over legal jurisdiction, disputed sovereignty, and uncoordinated efforts at the recovery of crews, cargoes, or ships. Even when pirates are detected, hot pursuit across national boundaries has seldom been attempted. When coordinated surveillance (like the recent MALSINDO patrols) has reduced piracy attacks, pirates have generally responded by increasing their attacks in less protected areas of the region. State and market stakeholders have made only limited progress in coordinating and sustaining antipiracy security measures for the vital shipping lanes of the South China Sea.

### Conflicting Claims, Overlapping Interests

Piracy is often dramatized by the news media, spreading the impression that it is more of a problem than it really is. Piracy is difficult to define and measure. It appears to be related to other forms of crime, on land and at sea. Hence, any antipiracy response must be a coordinated effort—on land and at sea. But this coordination is difficult to achieve. As a result, there is still no effective governance, or burden sharing in the provision of security, of the sea-lanes transiting the South China Sea. Coastal states don't want to give up any sovereign controls. Shippers don't want to impose restrictions or costs on their operations. Major user states have not offered sufficient support to establish the necessary measures. The current situation is far from the highly ambitious proposal by the World Bank, the United Nations Development Program, and the IMO to construct a "Marine Electronic Highway," a shipping traffic control system similar to the global air traffic control arrangement, with comprehensive, integrated electronic information, navigation, and control systems.

Whatever their conflicting claims and mutual suspicions may be, political leaders in the coastal states are beginning to understand that they must cooperate in order to manage the increase in shipping traffic, to use the resources of the South China Sea sustainably, and to address maritime security threats, including piracy. While some progress has been made, there is as yet no durable agreement on how to share the burden for providing safety and security from piracy in the region. The nation-states of Southeast Asia that have only recently extended their sovereignty and resource claims to EEZs in the South China Sea are in no rush to negotiate them away, and shippers who traverse the busiest sea-lanes in the world are reluctant to impose any stringent or expensive security measures.

All these regional and international stakeholders share many overlapping interests—for example, in promoting safe navigation for commercial shipping. On antipiracy or anti-terrorist enforcement measures, however, they have had conflicting views. Littoral states are insistent that the process of achieving regional maritime security should be locally initiated and led. They are willing to accept external assistance, but they contend that ultimately they must have the authority and capability to provide that security. For example, Tokyo's financial contributions, technical assistance, and joint training are welcomed by the littoral states. These measures not only increase the pool of available resources for maritime security but also diversify sources of assistance, avoiding sole reliance on the United States. However, regional states and shippers have yet to put aside their individual stakeholder interests and then negotiate and implement an effective regional maritime antipiracy security system. Unfortunately, it may take an event equivalent to the 11 September 2001 attacks on the United States, a spectacular collision, or a devastating oil spill to overcome contending stakeholder interests and institutional inertia and to galvanize the political will needed for effective antipiracy security measures.

### Notes

1. William Langewiesche, *The Outlaw Sea: A World of Freedom, Chaos, and Crime* (New York: North Point, 2004), p. 1.

2. Sam Bateman, "Maritime 'Regime' Building," in *The Best of Times, the Worst of Times:*

*Maritime Security in the Asia-Pacific,* ed. Joshua Ho and Catherine Zara Raymond (Singapore: World Scientific, 2005), p. 259.

3. International Maritime Bureau [hereafter IMB], *Piracy and Armed Robbery against*

*Ships Annual Report, 1 January–31 December 2007* (2008).

4. Graham Gerard Ong-Webb, "Introduction—Southeast Asian Piracy: Research and Developments," in *Piracy, Maritime Terrorism and Securing the Malacca Straits* [hereafter *Piracy*], ed. Graham Gerard Ong-Webb (Singapore: Institute of Southeast Asian Studies, 2006), p. xviii.

5. James Boutilier, "The Best of Times, the Worst of Times: The Global Maritime Outlook 2004," in *Best of Times, the Worst of Times,* ed. Ho and Raymond, pp. 15–16.

6. United Nations, *Review of Maritime Transport 2006* (New York: Conference on Trade and Development, 2007), p. 3.

7. Ibid., pp. 4–5, 76.

8. Mark Valencia, "The Politics of Anti-piracy and Anti-terrorism Responses," in *Piracy,* ed. Ong-Webb, p. 98.

9. Adam J. Young, *Contemporary Maritime Piracy in Southeast Asia: History, Causes, and Remedies* (Singapore: Institute of Southeast Asian Studies, International Institute for Asian Studies, 2007), p. 9.

10. Eric Frecon, "Piracy and Armed Robbery at Sea along the Malacca Straits," in *Piracy,* ed. Ong-Webb, p. 71.

11. Rommel C. Banlaoi, "Maritime Security Outlook for Southeast Asia," in *Best of Times, the Worst of Times,* ed. Ho and Raymond, p. 61.

12. "Asia Piracy Costs $25 Bln a Year, Says Expert," Reuters, Singapore, 11 December 2002.

13. Stanley Weeks, "Piracy and Regional Security," in *Combating Piracy and Ship Robbery: Charting the Future in the Asia Pacific Waters,* ed. Hamzah Ahman and Akira Ogawa (Tokyo: Okazaki Institute, 2001), p. 100.

14. Organisation for Economic Co-operation and Development, *Price of Increased Maritime Security Is Much Lower than Potential Cost of a Major Terror Attack* (Paris: Directorate for Science, Technology and Industry, 21 July 2003), available at www.oecd.org/.

15. Young, *Contemporary Maritime Piracy in Southeast Asia,* p. 93.

16. Karen Kvashny, "Modern Maritime Piracy in Asia: A Case Study of Transnational Organized Crime" (dissertation, University of California, Irvine, 2003), p. 70.

17. For example, see Martin N. Murphy, *Contemporary Piracy and Maritime Terrorism: The Threat to International Security* (London: International Institute for Strategic Studies, 2007).

18. IMB, *Piracy and Armed Robbery against Ships Annual Report, 1 January–31 December 2007,* p. 39.

19. Eduardo Santos, "Piracy and Armed Robbery against Ships in the Philippines," in *Piracy,* ed. Ong-Webb, pp. 38, 46.

20. Stefan Eklöf, "Political Piracy and Maritime Terrorism: A Comparison between the Straits of Malacca and the Southern Philippines," in *Piracy,* ed. Ong-Webb, p. 52.

21. Ibid., p. 45.

22. Young, *Contemporary Maritime Piracy in Southeast Asia,* p. 86.

23. Bateman, "Maritime 'Regime' Building," p. 260.

24. Boutilier, "Best of Times, the Worst of Times," p. 23.

25. Kvashny, "Modern Maritime Piracy in Asia," p. 61.

26. "Brassed Off," *Economist,* 16 May 2002.

27. Young, *Contemporary Maritime Piracy in Southeast Asia,* p. 59.

28. Kvashny, "Modern Maritime Piracy in Asia," p. 61.

29. Boutilier, "Best of Times, the Worst of Times," p. 23.

# PART TWO

Piracy in South and Southeast Asia

# CHAPTER SIX

# The Looting and Rape of Vietnamese Boat People

BRUCE A. ELLEMAN

Soon after the end of the Vietnam War and the reunification of North and South Vietnam, large numbers of Vietnamese began to leave the country, often by boat. They were part of a movement by which from the mid-1970s onward approximately three million people fled Vietnam, Laos, and Cambodia. Of this number, most were eventually resettled, "including 1.4 million in the United States, 260,000 in China, 200,000 in Canada, 185,000 in Australia, and 130,000 in France." Perhaps half a million eventually returned to Vietnam.[1]

Many of these refugees fled by sea, and in particular from 1975 onward there was a huge maritime exodus—including many people of Chinese heritage, called the "Hoa"—from Vietnam. These maritime refugees were generally referred to as the "boat people." Soon incidents of piracy against them began to be reported in the press, at rates that grew slowly throughout the late 1970s. However, as political tension between China and Vietnam led to war early in 1979, the boat-people problem increased rapidly, and the number of boats fleeing Vietnam continued to grow through the early 1980s; for example, from May 1982 through April 1983, a total of 463 refugee boats landed in Malaysia and Thailand.[2]

The Southeast Asian countries bordering on Vietnam clearly felt threatened by this exodus. Many of the acts of piracy against the boat people appear to have been politically motivated, at least politically sanctioned, as an indirect method of deterring the flood of refugees. However, piracy of this type did not end with the diminishing of the exodus in the middle to late 1980s. By that time piracy was no longer the realm of occasional pirates but of professionals, many of whom now preyed as well on unsuspecting international shipping, thereby dramatically increasing overall cases of piracy within the region.

### The End of the Vietnam War and the Growth of Piracy

The history of Chinese immigrants in Vietnam is long, dating back thousands of years. Since Annam claimed its independence from China in 939, after a thousand years as a Chinese colony, the loyalty of the Hoa, or ethnic Chinese, has often been called into question. During the 1979 Sino-Vietnamese conflict, the Vietnamese government took many steps to mitigate what it considered the Hoa threat, although it has been pointed out that "the actions the Vietnamese admit to have taken toward the Hoa, they assert, compare favorably with those the United States took with regard to Americans of Japanese descent when America considered itself threatened by far-away Japan."[3] Many of Hanoi's actions exacerbated the boat-people phenomenon, however, indirectly fuelling the enormous increase in piracy throughout the region.

Piracy has been a major concern in Vietnamese waters for many centuries. During the early nineteenth century, for example, pirates preyed on the mainly Chinese-owned and -operated ships conducting trade between southern Vietnam (Cochin China) and Singapore. Between 1780 and 1810 (as mentioned in chapter 2), when South China was plagued by several competing pirate leagues, Tâyson rebels in Vietnam sanctioned raids into Chinese waters. Before their final defeat in 1810, pirate fleets set out each spring and summer from bases on the Sino-Vietnamese border to plunder vessels and villages between Guangdong and Zhejiang. Unable to defeat them militarily, China adopted a political solution, recruiting many of the pirates into the Chinese navy.

Often, pirates operating in the South China Sea preyed on Chinese ships involved in the lucrative Southeast Asia and East–West trade. In 1843, immediately after the end of the First Opium War in China, there was a huge surge in attacks. Perhaps confident that China was too weak to respond, Malay pirates attacked a large number of Chinese ships. Among fifty Chinese ships passing near Malaya on one occasion, "the havoc was dreadful, probably not less than twenty boats were taken and their crews (140 men at least) either murdered or sold into slavery by Malays residing under British rule."[4]

During the early 1880s, China tried and failed to halt efforts by France to turn its Vietnamese tributary into a colony. Chinese troops, under the banner of the "Black Flag," fought French troops from bases in northern Vietnam. While China's June 1885 defeat meant that control of Vietnam was ceded to France, ethnic Chinese, Hoa, who had moved there over the preceding centuries, remained. Many of these were merchants and continued to play important roles in Vietnam's economy. Such "overseas" Chinese traditionally retained Chinese citizenship, however, and the Chinese government had always insisted on a "traditional posture of extraterritoriality, by which it had asserted the right to intervene to protect the interests of its overseas citizens."[5] The political status of Chinese living in Vietnam remained unclear through the 1970s, after the end of the U.S. war.

Since the 1950s, Chinese in South Vietnam had been pressured to adopt Vietnamese citizenship, and many of them did so. But in North Vietnam, the Hoa could legally retain Chinese citizenship even while they enjoyed equal rights as Vietnamese: "We had the best of both worlds. . . . The Hoa in the north had all the rights and privileges of Vietnamese citizenship and none of its disadvantages. From about 1970 the Vietnamese had been trying to get us to become citizens, but few of us regarded it to be in our best interests. We could even vote in their elections. We were regarded as Vietnamese in all respects, except that we were not subject to the military draft."[6]

There is a long history of Southeast Asian states using pirates as political weapons. This practice was revived in the mid-1970s with the beginning of the exodus. As noted, many of the refugees were ethnic Chinese attempting to flee from Vietnamese repression; the number of ethnic Chinese involved surpassed 85 percent in some camps. These statistics suggest that the Vietnamese government "singled out" the Hoa for persecution. In fact, beginning in 1977, Hanoi tried to convince Hoa living along the border with China, who previously had been considered Chinese, to adopt Vietnamese citizenship. For those who would not declare themselves Vietnamese, the choices were stark: "Those who refused were forced to choose between returning to China or moving inland away from the border. Many of the poor preferred to return to China rather than become Vietnamese citizens."[7]

In November 1976, as Vietnam was putting pressure on the Hoa in the north, local pirates far to the south threatened boat people fleeing on the Vietnamese fishing boat *PK 504*. Turned away from Singapore, the refugees had headed north again toward Thailand and were off Songkhla when "their boat was boarded by a group of men brandishing guns. They were not in uniform but identified themselves as policemen. The refugees, who had heard of plundering and rape by pirates, defended themselves with the only ammunition available to them: the pirates got the last of the gold, worth $20,000."[8] Fortunately, these boat people eventually reached Darwin, Australia—after an eight-thousand-kilometer journey—and the refugees were allowed to remain in that country, but the "pirates" had succeeded in keeping them from landing in Thailand.

### Background to the 1979 Sino-Vietnamese Conflict

The boat-people exodus was closely linked to political events. A particular example was China's 1974 decision to dispute Vietnam's claim to the Paracel Islands, one of the first signs of increasing Sino-Vietnamese tension. In 1978, Hanoi asked to become a member of Soviet-led Council for Mutual Economic Assistance (better known as Comecon), thus allowing Vietnam to distance itself economically from China. U.S. government sources soon reported that by August 1978 as many as four thousand Soviet advisers had been sent to Vietnam. In addition, during September 1978 the Soviet Union began sending increased arms shipments to Vietnam, both by air and by sea, including "aircraft, missiles, tanks, and munitions."[9]

This dramatic improvement in Soviet-Vietnamese relations at China's expense came to fruition on 2 November 1978, when Vietnam and the Soviet Union signed a Treaty of Friendship and Cooperation. This treaty was clearly aimed at China, since the sixth clause stated that the two countries would "immediately consult each other" if either is "attacked or threatened with attack . . . with a view to eliminating that threat."[10] Reportedly, this treaty also included a secret protocol granting Soviet military forces access to Vietnam's "airfields and ports."[11] Soon after a 15 December 1978 announcement that Sino-American relations would be normalized, Vietnam attacked Cambodia. By 7 January 1979, Vietnamese forces had secured Phnom Penh.

An early indicator of Beijing's concern over the Soviet-Vietnamese treaty was voiced by *Renmin Ribao,* which warned that Moscow was using Vietnam against China as it had earlier tried (and failed) to use Cuba to exert diplomatic pressure against the United States. Beijing also warned that Moscow's ultimate goal was to bring the whole of Indochina under its control. From China's perspective, the Soviet Union could use its military relations with Vietnam to outmaneuver and outflank China.[12]

During this period of heightened tensions, the Hoa people, living primarily along the Sino-Vietnamese border but also in Vietnam's large cities in the south, became stuck in the middle. There is evidence that the Chinese government urged, perhaps even ordered, the Hoa to leave Vietnam. According to one account: "It was a big secret, but the Vietnamese were not behind it [Hoa leaving Vietnam]. They had much to lose if we left. China had much to gain and [the Chinese] were the likely instigators." Beginning in 1978, rumors were spread that if the Hoa did not return to China they would be treated "as traitors and killed when the Chinese troops arrived." That China was tacitly supporting the exodus was best shown in June 1978, when it sent ships to Haiphong and Ho Chi Minh City (Saigon) to repatriate Chinese citizens.[13]

Recalling the Hoa back to China was arguably a form of economic warfare, since they were important to Vietnam's economy. The leaders of Vietnam appear to have understood this and sought to retain valuable resources represented by the large numbers of Chinese fleeing the country. As a result, Vietnam's "navy could apparently attack the refugee boats with impunity even before they had left Vietnamese waters."[14]

In preparation for war, Beijing normalized relations with Washington on 1 January 1979. Reportedly, President Jimmy Carter even gave the visiting Deng Xiaoping

"American 'moral support' for the forthcoming Chinese punitive war against Vietnam."[15] The United States and China hoped to test Soviet resolve as to whether it would
stand by its treaty with Vietnam. In fact, to put pressure on the Soviet Union's strategic
alliance with Vietnam, Deng reportedly told Carter in January 1979 that a war between
China and Vietnam might be used to "disrupt Soviet strategic calculations."[16]

On 15 February 1979, Deng declared that China planned to conduct a limited war
against Vietnam. To prevent Soviet intervention on Vietnam's behalf, Deng warned
Moscow the next day that China was prepared for a full-scale war; in preparation for
such a conflict, China put all of its troops along the Sino-Soviet border on emergency
war alert, set up a new military command in Xinjiang, and evacuated an estimated
three hundred thousand civilians from the border. In addition, the bulk of China's
active forces—as many as a million and a half troops—were stationed along China's
border with the Soviet Union.[17]

China's military offensive against Vietnam began on 17 February 1979, when an estimated thirty thousand People's Liberation Army troops crossed the 480-mile-long
Sino-Vietnamese border at fourteen points. By 25 February, the incursion had grown
to seventy-five thousand Chinese troops out of a total of 180,000 deployed along the
border. Finally, by early March, an estimated 120,000 Chinese were facing an equal
number of Vietnamese.[18] After three weeks of intense fighting, China could claim that
it captured the capitals of three provinces—Cao Bang, Lang Son, and Lao Cai—of the
six that bordered on China. When Beijing announced a troop withdrawal on 5 March
1979, the primary goals of its offensive had yet to be achieved, and Vietnam's military
potential had not been seriously damaged. As a result, the Sino-Vietnamese border
remained tense.

To most outsiders, China's military action appeared to have been a failure. But as Deng
had announced, from the very beginning China's action against Vietnam had been limited, to test Soviet resolve. Not only were many of China's best troops stationed along
the Sino-Soviet border, but Beijing decided not to use the estimated five hundred fight-
ers and bombers it had stationed near Vietnam. Claims that China's effort was not a
complete military success generally overlook the fact that China allocated only a small
fraction of its resources to the task.[19]

By December 1979, however, Sino-Soviet tensions had increased, as a result of the
Soviet Union's invasion of Afghanistan, which outflanked China's ally Pakistan. On 19
January 1980, Beijing warned Moscow that the invasion threatened "world peace" and
"Chinese security." On 20 January Beijing announced that further Sino-Soviet negotia-
tions would be halted.[20] These events corresponded with a massive Hoa exodus from
Vietnam, during which thousands of people attempted to leave by boat.

### The 1979 Sino-Vietnamese War and the Boat-People Exodus

With the outbreak of war between Vietnam and China in 1979, the boat-people exodus increased, to include many Hoa who were party members and former officers in Vietnam's military. Hanoi's concern about Hoa loyalties grew as China prepared for war, and many Vietnamese no longer trusted their erstwhile Chinese compatriots. According to one Hoa officer who had fought alongside Ho Chi Minh and Vo Nguyen Giap: "But all the same, at a time when Vietnam was being threatened by China, the Vietnamese no longer dared have Hoa people in their military. After China's invasion they feared a second attack, this time with Hanoi as its objective, and so on February 18 (one day after China's invasion) began expelling us overseas."[21]

Of course, many non-Hoa fled Vietnam as well, primarily from southern Vietnam. Often, they were businessmen who opposed Vietnam's decision in March 1978 to crack down on black-marketeering and to centralize the economy under government control. Others left because they rejected communism and sought greater political freedom overseas. Finally, many other boat people fled Vietnam because of government repression. Often the ethnic Vietnamese refugees had little money and so were generally ignored by local fishermen and were not attacked by pirates. Sometimes locals even gave them food and water to help them reach their destinations.

As the numbers of people fleeing Vietnam increased, however, so did the flow of Hoa wealth out of the country. The cost of leaving Vietnam became very high; many Vietnamese officials eagerly sought bribes in exchange for exit visas. If a person was caught trying to leave illegally, the authorities would confiscate everything he owned. Eventually, between July 1978 and June 1979, set fees were established of about two thousand U.S. dollars per adult and $1,200 per child for permission to leave Vietnam.[22]

The first wave of boat people was accepted and assimilated by neighboring countries. However, many in those countries saw the Hoa exodus as a "mass invasion" supported by the Vietnamese government, in that it had refused to halt the flow of immigrants. Beginning in 1979, the governments of Indonesia, Malaysia, the Philippines, Singapore, and Thailand—that is, virtually the entire Association of Southeast Asian Nations (ASEAN)—stated that they would not accept any more Indochinese refugees. Piracy rates began to increase at the same time.

### Piracy as a Tool of State Policy

As earlier chapters have explained, privateers are, in effect, pirates sanctioned by state governments. While it is difficult to prove that the pirates preying on the boat people were working hand in hand with the governments of Vietnam's neighbors, certainly the increase in Southeast Asian piracy during the Hoa exodus appeared to correspond with their desire to keep additional refugees from arriving on their shores. It is important to note, therefore, that pirate attacks off Thailand increased in 1978, as the Hoa fleeing Vietnam began to outnumber the Vietnamese. By deterring mainly the Hoa boat people from coming to Thailand, the pirates might "form a first line of defence for the Thais against Vietnam." What the 1979 ASEAN announcement did, in effect, was deny protection for the boat people, thus making it "open season" for pirates to attack the Hoa. The early piratical incidents were referred to as "opportunistic attacks," but by 1982 it was estimated that "some 300 Thai fishing boats—two per cent of the Thai fishing fleet—were engaged in piracy."[23]

However cruel by Western standards, this policy of using pirates to stem the tide of Hoa refugees was quite successful: "Between 1981 and 1982, boat refugee arrivals in Thailand dropped by 62 per cent, from over 15,000 to less than 6,000, and the number of arrivals continued to decline in the following years."[24]

In 1975, refugees could often travel undisturbed. However, as more boats appeared, it became obvious to the local fishermen that many carried gold and other valuables.[25] The prospect of acquiring great wealth was as important a motive as the withdrawal of protection by the ASEAN governments, if not more. By the late 1970s, rumors were spreading that Hoa refugees leaving Vietnam were trying to smuggle their wealth out of the country in the form of gold or diamonds. For example, in 1978 a Chinese merchant from Cholon reached Malaysia with US$1.2 million in uncut diamonds, hidden in a can of lubricating oil, and declared them when departing on a plane for the United States. Another Chinese businessman declared US$200,000 in gold and $350,000 in currency. Finally, an "Indo-Chinese woman, when asked to declare her assets [on arrival in Australia], unbuttoned her blouse and proudly displayed a special corset containing $250,000 in cash, jewellery and gold."[26]

Lust for gold led to a rapid increase in piracy. Approximately one-third of the ethnically Chinese boat people—seventy-seven thousand out of 292,315—decided to head for Hong Kong, which was safer because they were "not beset with pirates" along the way. However, of those who went south, the vast majority of those who left Vietnam in small boats were attacked, some by ships marked as belonging to the Vietnam navy.[27]

Many refugee boats were attacked more than once. One statistic from 1981 indicates that 349 boats, or fully 77 percent of all of the boats that arrived in Thailand, had been attacked at least once on the way.[28] Boat attacks averaged 3.3 times per boat in 1981, and a total of "454 people were killed by pirates, 571 women were raped and 228 people, mostly girls and young women, were abducted."[29] Although no accurate figures for those drowned or otherwise killed are available, one estimate of losses, in the 10–15 percent range, would mean thirty to forty thousand people.[30]

In addition to those who left by boat over the open sea, another 250,000 Hoa crossed the border between Vietnam and China, either on foot or by boat along the coastline.[31] Little information exists on whether these immigrants encountered problems similar to those of the boat people, but the shorter distances involved gave less chance for opportunistic attacks. Also, there were not the same ethnic tensions as existed to the south, where the Vietnamese immigrants were treated as unwelcome invaders.

### Shift from Amateur to Professional Pirates

Over time, Southeast Asian piracy shifted from individual fishermen working alone to professional pirates working in unison. In the Gulf of Thailand, piracy quickly became a highly organized business, with several fishing boats, working in teams, surrounding and attacking a refugee craft. Initially they simply demanded "money, gold, earrings or bracelets," but over time the number and frequency of attacks increased: "In the '80s, refugee boats crossing the Gulf of Thailand were attacked by pirates almost two thirds of the time and each boat was boarded at least twice."[32]

Pirate attacks, especially after 1978, occurred most frequently off of Thailand, by small fishing boats that might have been attracted by what appeared to be easy pickings. Several such attacks were repulsed with guns or knives. In one such instance, "As pirates attacked his boat [referring to a noted heart surgeon named Cung], he directed the defense by encouraging the escapees to fight back with courage and persistence. The pirates finally gave up and the boat successfully landed at Pulau Bidong with only two casualties."[33]

However, the boat people did not usually have the means to repel large groups of pirates. When attacked by one set of pirates after another, before long they had nothing left to hand over. According to one account, a "fourteen-metre boat with 183 passengers was raided ten times by pirates. Women were forced to strip naked. Their clothes and bodies were thoroughly searched for gold, necklaces and other jewelry. In the second attack, the pirates used a derrick to remove the pump engine from the refugee boat. By the tenth attack, nothing of value remained, so all those wearing jeans were ordered to hand them over."[34]

There are no accurate statistics on piracy rates prior to 1981. A more critical analysis of 1981 reported that the majority of the Vietnamese boats arriving in Thailand had been attacked, most of them repeatedly: "A total of 571 deaths were reported, along with 599 rapes and 243 abductions."[35] Most of those abducted were young women and girls, who were forced to work as prostitutes. Unlike earlier attacks, however, this new wave of piracy appeared to be by professional pirates, often linked to organized crime.

As a result of this shift, Thai fishermen over time also became targets—perhaps as a means of stopping their attacks on the boat people, so that more booty would be available for the professional pirates—and in 1982 it was reported that five Thai fishing trawlers were lost to pirates every month; over a two-year period some "500 Thai fisherman had been killed by pirates."[36] Although it is difficult to determine exactly when this shift took place, clearly the "opportunistic" attacks of the late 1970s had shifted to "organized" ones by the early 1980s.

This development threatened to interfere with commercial shipping, however, and brought more international attention to the problem. Prompted by the rapid rise in attacks, which local officials seemed incapable of halting, in February 1981 the U.S. government funded a two-million-dollar antipiracy program by the Thai government, involving a Thai cutter and two spotter aircraft. This program assisted 180 ships under attack and arrested a handful of pirates, but it was only a drop in the bucket.

### International Efforts to Halt Piracy

In 1982, a larger international effort, called the Anti-Piracy Arrangement, began, with total funding of £3.6 million from a dozen countries—Australia, Canada, Denmark, France, Germany, Italy, Japan, the Netherlands, Norway, Switzerland, the United Kingdom, and the United States. "The anti-piracy unit consists of no more than three 16-metre fast patrol craft, about 5 surveillance aircraft, 3 special operation task trawlers, and roughly 130 naval personnel."[37] Although the percentage of boats attacked dropped, the number of dead and missing increased on those ships that were attacked, so there was little improvement.[38]

All U.S. Navy ships in the vicinity were required to assist boats in distress, and from 1983 through June 1989 they picked up a total of 1,380 boat people. Rear Admiral James E. Taylor assured the U.S. House of Representatives Subcommittee on Immigration, Refugees, and International Law that "having experienced the perils and rigors of sea, I'd like to assure you that naval personnel have great compassion and empathy for refugees encountered on the high seas attempting to flea [*sic*] Southeast Asia. The U.S. Navy's policies have resulted in what we consider to be an outstanding record of responsiveness, swift compassion to sea rescues in the South China Sea."[39]

Navy ships were not required to determine before providing aid if refugees were fleeing from Vietnam; "With regard to a ship encountered at sea [their duty] is to make sure that the people are not in distress, that the boat is seaworthy, that they have all the equipment that they need, that they are medically sound, and provide them whatever assistance is necessary."[40] While supporting an antipiracy policy, however, the U.S. government did not necessarily want it to be too effective, since "an effective anti-piracy programme might constitute a significant pull factor for the refugees to flee to Thailand."[41] Clearly, the existence of piracy was preventing an even greater number of people from fleeing Vietnam by sea.

Even with the continuing efforts of foreign nations, too many piracy incidents during this period went unreported. One especially egregious incident, in March 1984, involved a refugee boat holding sixty people, in which "only two twelve-year-old girls and five males survived Thai pirates' savagery."[42] Still, the overall number of piracy attacks dropped by 67 percent during one year alone, from 1,122 in 1981 to 373 in 1982, and then further to only eighty-seven in 1986. Moreover, the percentage of boats attacked dropped from 77 percent to 64, and then to 13, during these same years, and the average number of attacks per boat dropped from 2.5 to 1.7 to 1.5. Total deaths also dropped dramatically, with zero deaths in 1987 due to piracy.[43] Unfortunately, there was a temporary resurgence in 1988 and 1989, with over five hundred and 750 people killed during each year, respectively, before the Hoa exodus virtually ended in the early 1990s.[44]

One reason for the sudden increase in the number of piracy incidents during the late 1980s could have been ongoing territorial disputes between China and Vietnam. In 1988, these tensions broke into open conflict, as Chinese naval forces clashed with Vietnamese troops on the Spratly Islands. The connection may have been that in that period the Chinese and Vietnamese navies were too busy to concentrate on piracy suppression. Also, increased piracy attacks might have helped to keep ships and people out of the area, which perhaps simplified matters for the government forces in their primary tasks.

Beginning in 1989 and during the early 1990s, as well, China was heavily criticized by Western governments over the Tiananmen Square massacre; Beijing had its hands too full with internal dissent to pay much attention to Vietnam. In addition, the collapse of the Soviet empire in 1989 induced the Vietnamese government to adopt pro-business legislation during the early 1990s, producing a sudden economic upsurge. As a result of these rapid changes, many Hoa decided to remain in Vietnam. Thus, just as political events clearly had an enormous role in the origins of the boat-people exodus, political changes may have also contributed to its ultimate end.

## Conclusions

Unlike the many types of profit-motivated piracy mentioned in the previous chapters, one prime motivation—at least in the beginning—for piracy against the boat people seems have been a desire to halt an unwanted flow of refugees. Once it became clear that Hoa refugees were carrying gold and other valuables, opportunistic pirates were quickly replaced by professional pirates. Interestingly, just as the beginning of the exodus can be linked to political events, the end of the boat-people phenomenon corresponded almost exactly with the end of the Cold War. The collapse of the Soviet Union, which had been one of Vietnam's major allies, forced the Vietnamese government to reorient the nation away from state socialism and toward a market-driven economy.

This timing shows that piracy can be influenced by politics. According to Stefan Eklöf, "political factors go a long way to explain the outbreak of piracy in the Gulf of Thailand from the end of the 1970s. In the eyes of the Vietnamese government, the refugees were traitors, or at least lacking in patriotism." On the other side of the Gulf of Thailand, however, the Thai government was "more concerned about the social and economic strain that the large flow of refugees caused, and it was not a high priority to protect these refugees, especially not in international waters where most attacks occurred."[45]

This series of political changes in the early 1990s, plus Vietnam's economic reforms, meant that the skills of the Hoa, who were primarily from Vietnam's former merchant class, were suddenly in demand once again in Vietnam. The repression against the Hoa ended, and they were allowed to open businesses again. For these reasons, many Hoa decided to remain in Vietnam. The pirates, without an easy target, either quit or focused on other maritime groups, including fishermen, yachtsmen, or commercial vessels. Without a doubt, this transition during the early 1990s had a direct impact on the spectacular growth of piracy in other areas of Southeast Asia, including the Malacca Strait.

## Notes

1. W. Courtland Robinson, *Terms of Refuge: The Indochinese Exodus and the International Response* (London: Zed Books, 1998), p. 2.

2. Roger Villar, *Piracy Today: Robbery and Violence at Sea since 1980* (London: Conway Maritime, 1985), p. 34.

3. Charles Benoit, "Vietnam's 'Boat People,'" in *The Third Indochina Conflict,* ed. David W. P. Elliott (Boulder, Colo.: Westview, 1981), p. 139.

4. Nicholas Tarling, *Piracy and Politics in the Malay World: A Study of British Imperialism in Nineteenth-Century South-East Asia* (Melbourne, Australia: F. W. Cheshire, 1963), p. 207.

5. Benoit, "Vietnam's 'Boat People,'" pp. 140–44.

6. Ibid.

7. Ibid.

8. Bruce Grant, *The Boat People: An "Age" Investigation* (New York: Penguin Books, 1979), p. 18.

9. Robert S. Ross, *The Indochina Tangle* (New York: Columbia Univ. Press, 1988), p. 208.

10. *Foreign Broadcast Information Service: Soviet Union,* 6 November 1978, pp. 6–9.

11. Ramesh Thakur and Carlyle Thayer, *Soviet Relations with India and Vietnam* (New York: St. Martin's, 1992), p. 61.

12. William J. Duiker, *China and Vietnam: The Roots of Conflict* (Berkeley, Calif.: Institute of East Asian Studies, 1986), p. 80.

13. Benoit, "Vietnam's 'Boat People,'" pp. 150–52.

14. Stefan Eklöf, *Pirates in Paradise: A Modern History of Southeast Asia's Maritime Marauders,* (Copenhagen: Nordic Institute of Asian Studies, 2006), p. 30.

15. Marilyn B. Young, *The Vietnam Wars, 1945–1990* (New York: HarperCollins, 1991), pp. 309–10.

16. Ross, *Indochina Tangle,* p. 225.

17. Robert A. Scalapino, "Asia in a Global Context: Strategic Issue for the Soviet Union," in *The Soviet Far East Military Buildup,* ed. Richard H. Solomon and Masataka Kosaka (Dover, Mass.: Auburn House, 1986), p. 28.

18. Michael Clodfelter, *Vietnam in Military Statistics: A History of the Indochina Wars, 1772–1991* (London: McFarland, 1995), pp. 287–88.

19. John Blodgett, "Vietnam: Soviet Pawn or Regional Power?" in *Emerging Powers: Defense and Security in the Third World,* ed. Rodney W. Jones and Steven A. Hildreth (New York: Praeger, 1986), p. 98. The decision not to use airpower followed a pattern set during the 1969 Sino-Soviet border conflicts, when the two sides apparently agreed that an air war might too easily escalate into a nuclear confrontation.

20. Alfred D. Low, *The Sino-Soviet Confrontation since Mao Zedong: Dispute, Detente, or Conflict?* (New York: Columbia Univ. Press, 1987), p. 52.

21. Benoit, "Vietnam's 'Boat People,'" p. 140.

22. Ibid., p. 157.

23. Eklöf, *Pirates in Paradise,* p. 19, citing the Committee on Foreign Affairs (1982), p. 62.

24. Eric Ellen, ed., *Piracy at Sea* (Paris: ICC, 1989), p. 282.

25. Nghia M. Vo, *The Vietnamese Boat People, 1954 and 1975–1992* (London: McFarland, 2006), pp. 143–44.

26. Grant, *Boat People,* p. 63.

27. Eklöf, *Pirates in Paradise,* p. 30.

28. Ellen, *Piracy at Sea,* pp. 282–83.

29. Eklöf, *Pirates in Paradise,* p. 21, citing Committee on Foreign Affairs, p. 84.

30. Grant, *Boat People,* p. 81.

31. Benoit, "Vietnam's 'Boat People,'" p. 140.

32. Vo, *Vietnamese Boat People,* pp. 143–44.

33. Ibid., p. 119.

34. Grant, *Boat People,* p. 65.

35. Robinson, *Terms of Refuge,* p. 61, quoting U.S. Committee for Refugees, *Vietnamese Boat People: Pirates' Vulnerable Prey* (Washington, D.C.: February 1984), p. 6.

36. Eklöf, *Pirates in Paradise,* p. 24, citing Committee on Foreign Affairs, p. 69.

37. Villar, *Piracy Today,* p. 36.

38. Robinson, *Terms of Refuge,* pp. 167–68.

39. House Committee on the Judiciary, *Orderly Departure Program and U.S. Policy Regarding Vietnamese Boat People: Hearing before the Subcommittee on Immigration, Refugees, and International Law,* 101st Cong., 1st sess. (Washington, D.C.: U.S. Government Printing Office, 28 June 1989), p. 39.

40. Ibid., p. 89.

41. Eklöf, *Pirates in Paradise,* p. 33, quoting Richard Vine, director of the U.S. State Department's Bureau of Refugee Programs, remarks to the House Committee on Foreign Affairs (1982), pp. 5, 13–14, 71.

42. G. O. W. Mueller and Freda Adler, *Outlaws of the Ocean: The Complete Book of Contemporary Crime on the High Seas* (New York: Hearst Marine Books, 1985), p. 316, quoting "53 Missing after Attack on Boat from Vietnam," *New York Times,* 3 March 1984, p. 9.

43. Ellen, *Piracy at Sea,* pp. 282–83.

44. Robinson, *Terms of Refuge,* p. 170.

45. Eklöf, *Pirates in Paradise,* p. 30.

# CHAPTER SEVEN

# Piracy and Armed Robbery in the Malacca Strait
## A Problem Solved?

CATHERINE ZARA RAYMOND

The Malacca Strait is a narrow waterway that extends nearly six hundred nautical miles from the Andaman Sea to the South China Sea, between Malaysia and Indonesia. The strait provides a vital shipping lane for vessels sailing from Europe and the Middle East to East Asia, as well as smaller vessels on local voyages. Unfortunately, when we think of the Malacca Strait, images of a waterway infested with pirates often spring to mind.

While this image could arguably have been justified in the past, it is now rather outdated. According to the International Maritime Bureau (IMB), which produces quarterly and annual reports on piracy and armed robbery against ships, there were only three successful and four attempted attacks by pirates on shipping in the Malacca Strait in 2007.[1] This low level of piracy has continued into 2008, with the Half Yearly Report issued by the Regional Cooperation Agreement on Combating Piracy and Armed Robbery against Ships in Asia (ReCAAP) Information Sharing Center in Singapore listing only one successful attack on a vessel in the Malacca Strait and three attempted ones.[2] Considering that around ninety thousand vessels transit the strait on an annual basis, the proportion of ships being attacked in the waterway is extremely small.

With statistics such as these, one might wonder why we are still seeing the publication of articles such as one appearing in a recent issue of *National Geographic Magazine*, whose cover declares, "The Strait of Malacca, Dark Passage: Pirates Haunt It. Sailors Fear It. Global Trade Depends on It."[3] There seems to be a failure, particularly outside the region, to keep pace with the change in the frequency of pirate attacks and the scale of the problem. While piracy has certainly been a concern in the waterway in the past, with reported attacks reaching seventy-five in 2000, the number of cases has been falling since 2005, largely as a result of a number of countermeasures introduced by the three littoral states of Malaysia, Singapore, and Indonesia. This decrease in attacks was achieved despite a 10 percent increase in cases worldwide.

This chapter will discuss the reduction in pirate attacks in the Malacca Strait and how the attacks themselves have changed over the last decade. The measures attributed to the reduction will then be discussed, as well as the underlying principles and attitudes that have shaped these initiatives. Particular attention will be given as to how the issue of sovereignty, a principle of utmost importance in Southeast Asia, has impacted multilateral and bilateral cooperative efforts to address the transnational problem of piracy, including a series of International Maritime Organization (IMO) meetings convened to tackle pressing issues affecting the safety and security of shipping in the Malacca Strait. The conclusions will make recommendations regarding issues that require further action.

### The Changing Nature of Piracy in the Malacca Strait

Piracy has occurred in the Malacca Strait for hundreds of years. The October 1992 creation in Kuala Lumpur of the IMB's Piracy Reporting Center (PRC), which was tasked with, among other things, collecting data on pirate attacks around the world, started to highlight the scale of the problem in Southeast Asia. However, it was not until the late 1990s that the issue came to the attention of the international community.

This occurred primarily for two reasons. First, in 1997 the Asian financial crisis had a harsh impact on the region. It is believed that the deteriorating economic situation forced many people living in coastal areas in Indonesia and Malaysia to turn to piracy to supplement their incomes. The economic collapse also caused widespread political instability, in particular in Indonesia, making it easier for people to pursue illegal methods of income generation. Second, in the late 1990s several high-profile pirate attacks took place in the region, among them the attack on the *Petro Ranger* in 1998. This may have led to an increased tendency among shippers to report attacks, particularly attempted attacks or more minor cases.

As a result of these factors, by the late 1990s the annual number of reported pirate attacks in the strait had gone from virtually zero to seventy-five.[4] Piracy was now seen as a significant problem that required urgent attention. One year after piracy incidents peaked in the Malacca Strait, al-Qa'ida launched its attack on the Twin Towers in New York, demonstrating that ordinary means of transportation can be utilized to carry out large-scale attacks on economically important targets.

This incident prompted a reassessment of the vulnerability of the maritime sector to attack by terrorists; in Southeast Asia, the presence of pirates operating seemingly unchecked highlighted how insecure the maritime domain was. Speculation soon began as to the likelihood that the region's pirates would cooperate with regional or international terrorist groups to carry out a devastating attack on shipping.

During this period there were several different types of piracy taking place in the Malacca Strait.[5] These included robbery of vessels at sea, the hijacking of vessels, and kidnap-for-ransom attacks. Another common type of piracy takes place against vessels berthed in harbors or at anchor. However, this type of attack is unlikely to affect vessels on international voyages through the strait. The most common targets in this case would be smaller vessels that transit the coast of Indonesia or those on local voyages from, for example, Malaysia's Port Klang to the port of Belawan in Indonesia.

The robbery of a vessel by pirates usually takes place while the ship is under way, often at night, and most often between one and six o'clock in the morning. The pirates board the vessel using grappling hooks and then take any cash and valuables from the ship's safe and crew, including high-tech navigation equipment or whatever else they can seize quickly. In this type of attack the value of the stolen goods can be between ten and twenty thousand U.S. dollars.[6] The ship can be taken over for up to a few hours by from five to ten pirates, although many incidents are over within half an hour.[7] It is in this type of piracy that the most significant reduction has taken place since 2000. This may be partially due to an increased awareness on the part of crew members following the introduction of new maritime security requirements for vessels.[8]

If a vessel is hijacked, it is usually seized for a significant length of time, perhaps for several days, while the cargo is unloaded at a port selected by the pirates or transferred to another vessel. Hijacking has been less common than the former type, simple robbery, because good intelligence gathering and careful planning prior to the attack are required to ascertain the cargo and route of the vessel. A secure port to unload the stolen cargo is also needed, not to mention a willing buyer.

A variation of this latter kind of piracy is the permanent seizure of a vessel by pirates, who turn the vessel into a "phantom ship"; the key difference is that once the pirates have disposed of the vessel's cargo, they do not abandon the vessel itself. The ship is repainted and the crew dumped or killed. The ship then sails to a new port with a false name and forged documentation.[9] In recent years tugs have been favorite targets of pirates, perhaps because they do not usually have Automatic Identification System (AIS) equipment installed and yet are very valuable ships. Also, they are easier to attack, given their low freeboards. Once taken, they may be used in various maritime criminal activities, which would favor a small vessel of kinds commonly seen in ports and international waterways.

Kidnapping is the most serious form of piracy taking place in the Malacca Strait since 2001. During a kidnap, armed attackers take over the vessel and abduct two or three senior crew members, who are then held ashore pending ransom negotiations. The kidnapped crew members are usually released unharmed following payment by their employers. Ransoms demanded can range from US$100,000 to US$200,000. However, the sum of money eventually paid to the attackers following negotiations is usually substantially lower, somewhere between ten and twenty thousand U.S. dollars.[10]

Of the three 2007 attacks deemed successful by the IMB in the Malacca Strait, one was a boarding of a containership under way northwest of Pulau Perak: crew members spotted flashlights on the deck of their vessel, and when they raised an alarm a small boat was seen moving away from the ship. Another incident took place when several unlit fishing boats approached a containership while it was under way. The ship's master took evasive action to deter the suspected pirates; two were still able to board. However, the pirates were unarmed; they were detained by the ship's crew and handed over to the authorities in Singapore. The third incident was a kidnapping; according to the IMB report documenting the attack, "ten pirates armed with firearms boarded the tug towing the barge laden with steel billets. The pirates damaged all communications equipments and stole crew personal belongings and ship's documents." The pirates kidnapped the master and the chief engineer, whom they took ashore. A ransom was demanded, and eleven days after they were kidnapped, following payment of the ransom, the two were released.[11]

The details of the three incidents from 2007 reveal that two were essentially unsuccessful. Although they were classified by the IMB as "actual attacks" rather than "attempted attacks," the pirates were able neither to steal anything nor attack anyone during the incidents. Meanwhile, in the only successful case of piracy documented in the first half of 2008 in ReCAAP's Half Yearly Report, pirates reportedly attacked two fishing trawlers in the early hours of the morning while the vessels were under way. All the crew members were thrown overboard off a nearby island in Indonesia. The crews were rescued, but the trawlers have yet to be located.[12] It is likely that the vessels and their cargoes were sold on the black market.

If the overall frequency of pirate attacks in the Malacca Strait has been significantly reduced in recent years, however, kidnapping remains a worrisome threat, especially given the great danger it poses to crew members. The continued occurrence of this form of piracy, even at low levels, necessitates a reexamination of the various countermeasures that have been implemented to improve security in the Malacca Strait. The current practice is for the employers of kidnapped crews to pay ransoms for their release. It is widely acknowledged by experts in this field that not only does paying ransom encourage further kidnappings, but the ransom money often goes to finance weaponry to be used in future attacks. A policy of no negotiation with kidnappers must be adopted to make kidnapping a nonprofitable industry.

### How Piracy Was Reduced

International pressure has been exerted on the littoral states, in particular on Indonesia and Malaysia, to address the problem of piracy.[13] This effort began in 2000, when piracy attacks peaked in the Malacca Strait, and increased even more following the events of 11 September 2001 and the subsequent conclusions drawn about the possible insecurity of the maritime domain. At this time, both Japan and the United States indicated a desire to participate in enhancing security in the waterway. However, it was not until 2004 that real steps toward securing the strait were made.

There were several stumbling blocks. Malaysia and Indonesia saw the issue of piracy purely as a domestic concern to be addressed internally by each state as it saw fit. They repeatedly emphasized their desire to uphold the sovereignty of their territorial waters, which make up most of the waterway. Singapore was more willing to cooperate, on both the regional and extraregional levels. Its stand on the issue was voiced by the then deputy prime minister Tony Tan at a 2004 conference on maritime security in Singapore, during a discussion on the issue of patrolling the strait: "It is not realistic to unilaterally confine such patrols only to countries in this part of the world. . . . [W]e can do more if we galvanize the resources of extra-regional players."[14]

The concerns of Malaysia and Indonesia were heightened when Admiral Thomas B. Fargo, then commander of the U.S. Pacific Command, outlined a proposal by the United States called the Regional Maritime Security Initiative in a speech to the U.S. Congress on 31 March 2004. In his statement he remarked that "we're looking at things like high-speed vessels, putting Special Operations Forces on high-speed vessels to conduct effective interdiction in, once again, these sea lines of communication where terrorists are known to move about."[15] In response to the suggestion by Fargo, the Malaysian prime minister, Abdullah Ahmad Badawi, remarked, "I think we can look after our own area."[16]

Another disagreement that stalled cooperation was in the level of priority that should be given to addressing the problem of piracy over other, more pressing domestic issues. This applied particularly to Indonesia, which was still recovering from the Asian financial crisis of 1997, and it manifested itself in a public denial of the reported scale of the piracy problem in Indonesian waters. Another reason why Indonesia was reluctant to address the problem of piracy may have been that only 25–30 percent of the military's expenditure was covered by the military budget following the financial crisis, with the remaining funds believed to be coming from illegal activities, such as piracy.[17]

Even today, inadequate resources and a lack of funding prevent Indonesia from fully addressing the problem; according to the navy chief of staff, Admiral Slamet Soebijanto, the country is still in need of another 262 patrol ships to make up a total of 376, the amount deemed necessary to safeguard Indonesia's seventeen thousand islands.[18] In addition, of the 114 vessels that the Indonesian navy currently has, only 25 percent are believed to be serviceable at any given time.[19]

Even in its ports, Indonesia is struggling to enforce regulations that have now become an international norm: in September 2007, the U.S. Coast Guard issued a warning to the Indonesian transport ministry stating that it had found seven port terminals that did not fully comply with the ISPS Code (a set of measures designed to enhance the security of ships and port facilities that were made mandatory under the International Convention for the Safety of Life at Sea, of which Indonesia is a signatory).

### New Maritime Security Initiatives

Despite these problems, several maritime security initiatives were introduced in the Malacca Strait between 2004 and 2007. Although significant, they have arguably been constrained in their scope and capability by both the unwillingness of some of the littoral states to cooperate fully and a lack of resources. The first multilateral measure to be introduced by the three littoral states was the Trilateral Coordinated Patrol, or MALSINDO.

MALSINDO was launched in July 2004 and involved the navies of Malaysia, Indonesia, and Singapore patrolling in a coordinated fashion in their respective territorial waters. Following the introduction of this new measure, however, there was no immediate reduction in the number of pirate attacks taking place in the strait. The lack of a provision for cross-border pursuit into each of the participating states' territorial waters has been cited as the main flaw in this measure. However, cross-border pursuit would have been viewed by the participating states as an infringement of their sovereignty.[20]

Five months after the introduction of MALSINDO, an earthquake occurred off the west coast of Sumatra, Indonesia. The earthquake triggered a series of devastating tsunamis that affected most coastlines bordering the Indian Ocean. However, the areas worst hit were in Indonesia, particularly in Aceh, on the northern tip of Sumatra, an area in which many pirates were believed to be based. Some coastal villages in Aceh are thought to have lost more than 70 percent of their inhabitants, while 44 percent of the people lost their livelihoods.[21]

Reports received by the IMB in the weeks after the tsunami indicated that piracy attacks in the Malacca Strait had ceased. Even unaffected areas recorded zero attacks immediately following the disaster.[22] The significance of the impact that the tsunami seems to have had on pirate incidents in the waterway is evident in a comparison of the total attacks in 2004 with those in 2005, which show a more than 60 percent reduction, from thirty-eight to twelve.[23] However, this explanation cannot account for the continued decline in piracy from 2005 to 2007. It was predicted that "once life resumes normally in North Sumatra crime will return and with it attacks against ships."[24] Yet four years on from the disaster, when life has certainly returned to some measure of normality in the affected areas, the frequency of pirate attacks has not returned to its 2004 levels.

One explanation could be the changing political situation in Aceh. Before the tsunami, the province had been the site of a bitter twenty-six-year conflict between the Free Aceh Movement (known by its Indonesian abbreviation, GAM) and the Indonesian authorities. Around thirty-five thousand Indonesian troops and 14,700 police had been stationed in the area in an effort to suppress the GAM independence movement. However, following the tsunami both parties were brought to the negotiating table in order to discuss the disaster relief operation. This paved the way for a peace deal that was signed in August 2005.

Under the terms of the settlement, the GAM agreed to decommission its weapons and dissolve its armed wing, while the Indonesian authorities agreed to withdraw more than half of their forces from the area. As a result, around eight hundred weapons were handed in by the rebels and more than twenty-five thousand Indonesian troops left. Given that both GAM rebels and Indonesian troops had been accused of carrying out piracy, this development may well have played a part in the reduction in the number of attacks in the Malacca Strait.

The introduction in September 2005 of joint air patrols over the strait by the littoral states may have been another factor contributing to the decline in the number of incidents. The three states each donate two planes for the patrols, known as the "Eyes in the Sky" (EiS) plan. The plan permits aircraft to fly for up to three nautical miles into the twelve-nautical-mile territorial waters of the participating states; it was hoped that this measure would provide a valuable supplement to the trilateral coordinated sea patrols, which were limited to their own territorial waters.

Politically, EiS was significant because it was the first time the littoral states had been willing to put aside concerns over the sovereignty of their territorial waters and allow foreign forces across the border. This compromise included the agreement that each patrolling aircraft would have on board a representative from each of the three littoral states. Later, in April 2006 both MALSINDO and EiS were brought together under the umbrella of the Malacca Strait Patrols.

Despite its political success, EiS has been criticized as superficial and a mere reflection of the desire of the littoral states to be seen to be doing something in the face of international pressure. It is estimated that seventy sorties per week need to be carried out by the aerial patrols in order to monitor the strait effectively, 24/7. However, currently only eight are flown. There is also a lack of patrol vessels to carry out investigation and interdiction, if necessary, following the sighting of a suspect vessel by the aerial patrols.[25] It would seem that EiS's apparent success in helping to prevent any resurgence in attacks may be a function more of its deterrent effect than of its actual, practical application.

### The Regional Cooperation Agreement on Anti-Piracy

The most recent antipiracy initiative to be implemented is ReCAAP, which came into force in 2006. The agreement, which encompasses the whole region, was drafted in 2004 and required the signature and ratification of ten of the participating countries— all the members of the Association of Southeast Asian Nations, plus Japan, China, Korea, India, Bangladesh, and Sri Lanka—in order to enter into force. The aim of the initiative, which is the first antipiracy measure to be implemented on a government-to-government level, is to foster multilateral cooperation to combat the threat of piracy and armed robbery against ships. Its activity takes the forms of information sharing, capacity building, and cooperative arrangements.

A total of fourteen countries have now signed and ratified the agreement, and an Information Sharing Center, or ISC, has been set up in Singapore to facilitate communication and information exchange between member countries and to produce regular reports on pirate attacks in the region.[26] Information is exchanged between designated points of contact, or "focal points," in the member countries via a secure Web-based information-network system, on a 24/7 basis. In addition to acting as a point of information exchange, these focal points manage piracy incidents within their territorial waters, facilitate their respective countries' law enforcement investigations, and coordinate surveillance and enforcement with neighboring focal points.[27]

Nonetheless, the agreement has not yet been signed or ratified by Malaysia or Indonesia; the two countries have signaled a willingness to cooperate with the ISC, but to date no progress has been made toward securing their formal acceptances of the agreement. The lack of participation by Malaysia and Indonesia cannot help but cast doubt on its effectiveness, particularly given Indonesia's status as the most pirate-prone country in the world and both countries' strategic positions along the Malacca Strait.[28]

Although these antipiracy measures suffer from obvious and sometimes serious flaws, the continued decline in the number of pirate attacks in the waterway is testimony to their collective success, even if that success has been more in terms of improving security awareness on the part of the shippers and in deterring perpetrators. However, if piracy is to be completely eradicated in the strait—an important task, given that organized criminals are still able to carry out successful kidnappings in the waterway—

countermeasures need to become more targeted. In particular, the land bases and net-works of pirates need to be disrupted; without these, the pirates cannot launch effective attacks on the water.

### The International Maritime Organization Meetings

During this period of increased multilateral activity among the littoral states, another process has been under way at the international level, in cooperation with the IMO. The initiative was conceived by the IMO in 2004 with the aim of promoting a compre-hensive approach to security, safety, and pollution control in critical sea-lanes around the world. Known as the "Protection of Vital Sealanes" initiative, it takes as its current focus the straits of Malacca and Singapore. A series of meetings was convened under the title "Straits of Malacca and Singapore: Enhancing Safety, Security and Environ-mental Protection," the first of them in Jakarta in 2005. This was followed by another meeting in Kuala Lumpur in 2006 and then one a year later in Singapore.

These meetings are significant with regard to piracy in the Malacca Strait less for what they produced than for what they did not produce. At the start of this process there was speculation that these meetings would result in some sort of organized burden sharing of the maintenance of security in the waterway, with at least some involvement of the user states, in the form of financial or resource donation. This assumption seemed to be borne out when during the Jakarta meeting it was agreed that "a mechanism be established by the three littoral States to meet on a regular basis with user States, the shipping industry and other stakeholders with an interest in the safe navigation through the Straits of Malacca and Singapore (the Straits) . . . to discuss issues relating to the safety, *security* and environmental protection of the Straits."[29]

However, it was later stated, at the Singapore meeting, that "the scope of the Co-operative Mechanism focuses on safety of navigation and environmental protection in the Straits."[30] That is, the word "security" had been dropped from the discussions. Indeed, this more narrow focus on safety of navigation and environmental protection was reflected in the list of six projects, outlined by the littoral states during the Kuala Lumpur meeting, that are to be addressed under the framework of the Co-operative Mechanism:

(i)   Removal of wrecks in the Traffic Separation Scheme in the Straits;

(ii)  Cooperation and capacity building on Hazardous and Noxious Substance (HNS) preparedness and response in the Straits;

(iii) Demonstration project of class B automatic identification system (AIS) transponder on small ships;

(iv)  Setting up a tide, current and wind measurement system for the Straits to enhance navigation safety and marine environment protection;

(v)  Replacement and maintenance of aids to navigation in the Straits;

(vi) Replacement of aids to navigation damaged by the tsunami incident.[31]

The outcome of this process shows once again that the littoral states, in particular Indonesia and Malaysia, are unwilling to share the responsibility of maintaining security in the straits with the user states. While ad hoc contributions from user states on a bilateral basis have been accepted in the past for improving security in the waterway, there seems to be a desire at present to avoid any long-term institutionalization of the process—which, according to the Indonesian state secretary, Hatta Radjasa, would provide an opportunity for the involvement of foreign forces in securing the waterway.[32]

The outcome of the meetings also reflects the view that improving navigational safety in the straits and the protection of their marine resources is of the greatest regional concern. Although completely eradicating the piracy threat is considered a laudable goal, piracy still poses very little risk to the majority of vessels passing through the straits, while navigational safety and environmental concerns affect them all equally.

In the short term, it would seem that low levels of piracy will continue to occur in the Malacca Strait until countermeasures are developed that address the root causes of the problem and not just the symptoms. Economic development must be encouraged among the coastal areas of Indonesia and Malaysia in order to reduce unemployment, and corruption of local officials also needs to be addressed. However, antipiracy measures already in place should not be neglected; they need to be continuously developed to keep pace with the changing nature of piracy in the waterway.

It is clear from events over the past few years that maintaining the security of the straits and dealing with the problem of piracy will remain the responsibility of the three littoral states. The role of the user states will continue to be limited to ad hoc financial or resource contributions, supplemented by diplomatic pressure. Whether or not this is to the detriment of the fight against piracy in the Malacca Strait, it is most likely to remain the status quo for many years to come.

What is needed now is greater attention to regions that are considerably more insecure than the Malacca Strait. According to one maritime security expert, "while international attention was focused on the Strait of Malacca . . . the security situation in the sea lanes linking the Philippines, Indonesia and Malaysia [was] allowed to deteriorate."[33] The areas referred to are the Sulu and Celebes seas—the first of which is located in southwest Philippines, while the Celebes Sea is bordered by the Phillipine island of Mindanao to the north, Sabah and Kalimantan to the west, and Indonesia's Sulawesi Island to the south. Largely as a result of the separatist conflict taking place in

Mindanao, the areas have become "notorious for illegal maritime activities such as smuggling, piracy, and trafficking in illegal narcotics, guns and people."[34]

While the claim that the situation in these areas has been allowed to deteriorate further due to the current focus on the Malacca Strait may be to some extent unwarranted, clearly these areas have been insecure for some time and this should be addressed. Meanwhile, other parts of the world, including Bangladesh, discussed in the next chapter, are experiencing sharp increases in piracy. Lessons learned in the fight against piracy in the Malacca Strait should be applied to other regions to make these waters more secure. No longer should there be a false perception that the Malacca Strait is a "Dark Passage." Rather, it is time for it to be held up as an example to the rest of the world of how piracy can successfully be reduced.

## Notes

1. International Maritime Bureau [hereafter IMB], *Piracy and Armed Robbery against Ships Annual Report, 1 January–31 December 2007* [hereafter *Annual Report,* 2007] (2008), available at www.icc-ccs.org/. The IMB's definition of the Malacca Strait does not include the coastal waters of Malaysia and Indonesia. These are classified separately under the appropriate country.

2. ReCAAP is the Regional Cooperation Agreement on Anti-Piracy; see below for further details. ReCAAP ISC, *Half Yearly Report for 1st January 2008–30th June 2008,* available at www.recaap.org/.

3. Peter Gwin, "Dangerous Straits," *National Geographic Magazine* (October 2007).

4. IMB, *Annual Report, 1 January–31 December 2002* [hereafter *Annual Report,* 2002] (2003), p. 5, available at www.icc-ccs.org/. Figures include both attempted and successful attacks.

5. Given that most attacks in the Malacca Strait take place within the territorial waters of the littoral states, the correct term to use for the crime is "armed robbery," not piracy. However, for the purposes of this chapter, "piracy" will be used to mean both armed robbery against ships and pirate attacks.

6. Anthony Davis, "Piracy in Southeast Asia Shows Signs of Increased Organization," *Jane's Intelligence Review* (June 2004), p. 2.

7. See Catherine Zara Raymond, "Piracy in the Waters of Southeast Asia," in *Maritime Security in Southeast Asia,* ed. Chong Guan Kwa and John K. Skogan (London: Routledge, 2007), p. 66.

8. In 2004 the International Ship and Port Facility Security (ISPS) Code came into force and introduced worldwide a range of new security requirements for vessels and port facilities.

9. See Raymond, "Piracy in the Waters of Southeast Asia," p. 67.

10. See ibid.

11. IMB, *Annual Report,* 2007, p. 41.

12. ReCAAP ISC, *Report for May 2008,* available at www.recaap.org.

13. Pressure was greater on Malaysia and Indonesia rather than Singapore, because piracy was thought to originate from these two countries. Malaysia and Indonesia were reluctant to acknowledge that they had problems with piracy in their waters.

14. "Singapore Seeks Joint Patrols of Malacca Straits, involving Japan," *Asian Political News,* May 2004.

15. David Rosenberg, "Dire Straits: Competing Security Priorities in the South China Sea," *ZNet,* 13 April 2005, www.zmag.org/.

16. Sudha Ramachandran, "Divisions over Terror Threat in Malacca Straits," *Asia Times,* 16 June 2004, available at www.atimes.com/.

17. Carolin Liss, "The Challenges of Piracy in Southeast Asia and the Role of Australia," Austral Policy Forum, 07-19A, *Global Collaborative,* 25 October 2007, www.globalcollab .org.

18. "Navy Needs 262 More Warships to Safeguard Indonesian Waters," *Anatara News,* 18 September 2007.

19. Liss, "Challenges of Piracy in Southeast Asia and the Role of Australia."

20. Raymond, "Piracy in the Waters of Southeast Asia," p. 73.

21. *BBC News,* available at news.bbc.co.uk/. For the American reaction, see Bruce A. Elleman, *Waves of Hope: The U.S. Navy's Response to the Tsunami in Northern Indonesia,* Newport Paper 28 (Newport, R.I.: Naval War College Press, February 2007), available at www .usnwc.edu/press/newportpapers/documents/ 28.pdf.

22. IMB, *Piracy and Armed Robbery against Ships Annual Report, 1 January–31 December 2003* [hereafter *Annual Report, 2003*] (2004), p. 25.

23. IMB, *Annual Report, 2007,* p. 5.

24. IMB, *Annual Report, 2004,* p. 25.

25. See Raymond, "Piracy in the Waters of Southeast Asia," pp. 73–74.

26. Reports are available at ReCAAP's website, www.recaap.org.

27. "ReCAAP Information Sharing Centre," *Intertanko,* www.intertanko.com/.

28. See Catherine Zara Raymond, "Piracy in Southeast Asia: New Trends, Issues and Responses," *Harvard Asia Quarterly* 9, no. 4 (Fall 2005), p. 17.

29. IMO/SGP 2.1/1, 16 August 2007, p. 1 [emphasis supplied]. Available at www.mpa .gov.sg/.

30. Ibid, p. 3.

31. "Fact Sheet on the IMO-Singapore Meeting and the Co-operative Mechanism," *Maritime and Port Authority of Singapore (MPA),* www .mpa.gov.sg/.

32. "RI Rejects Any Effort to Internationalize Malacca Strait," Antara News, 29 August 2007.

33. Ian Storey, "The Triborder Sea Area: Maritime Southeast Asia's Ungoverned Space," *Jamestown Foundation* 5, no. 19 (2007), p. 2.

34. Ibid.

# CHAPTER EIGHT

# Piracy in Bangladesh
## What Lies Beneath?
SAMUEL PYEATT MENEFEE

Little research has been done on piracy in Bangladesh, even though in 2006 the International Maritime Bureau (IMB) labelled Chittagong the "most dangerous port in the world." Vijay Sakhuja, of the Institute of Southeast Asian Studies, surmises that "piracy in Bangladesh waters has not attracted international attention primarily due to the fact that geographically, it does not sit astride any major sea-lane" and suggests that "this factor may explain the piracy problem."[1]

Densely populated and with a high rate of poverty, Bangladesh was part of India and of Pakistan before achieving independence in 1971. Generally low lying, much of Bangladesh is occupied by the Ganges Delta, the confluence of the Padma (or Ganges), Jamuna (or Brahmaputra), and Meghna rivers. The floodplain sediments are locally known as *chars*. In the west of the country is the Sundarbans, a marshy jungle constituting one of the world's three largest mangrove forests. Some six thousand square kilometers of this forest lie in Bangladesh, with another four thousand in India.

Bangladesh is divided governmentally into six administrative divisions, three of which—Chittagong, Barisal, and Khulna—lie along the coast, running from Myanmar in the east to India in the west. Because of space constraints, they will be the focus of this chapter. Representative examples will show how each of these divisions is afflicted by piracy of varying type and intensity.[2]

### The Chittagong Division

Chittagong, a city of some 3.9 million on the banks of the Karnaphuli River, is the country's major seaport and a transit point for most of the country's exports and imports. The port possesses extensive facilities suitable for oceangoing vessels and enjoys a large regional and local trade. However, due to inadequate warehousing and poor transportation facilities, many ships are forced to wait many days before their cargoes are loaded or off-loaded. Over the past quarter-century, night attacks have targeted foreign merchant vessels visiting the port, usually involving the theft of unguarded but valuable items, such as mooring lines, zinc anodes (protecting the ship's propellers and rudder from corrosion), and ship's stores.

The history of petty theft against merchant ships visiting Chittagong goes back to at least the early 1980s. Most took place against ships already moored. For example, at around 12:30 AM on 27 October 1983, an East German vessel in the roads was robbed of four mooring lines, despite patrols by the crew. On 26 May 1986, about thirty armed intruders boarded a Danish vessel at 10:05 PM, wounding one crewman and stealing ship's stores and property. Further attacks occurred on 9 October and on 23 October, when five boats holding as many as a hundred "pirates" raided the British *Benvalla*. The intruders used poles and long hooks to board and then stole three mooring lines before the crew repelled them with pressure hoses.[3]

Over time, these attacks became more aggressive and began to take place against vessels still under way. On 5 May 1992, *Liberty Spirit* was approaching the anchorage at the mouth of the Karnaphuli when pirates armed with knives were twice repelled from the vessel's stern.[4] On 11 January 1994, *Moon Bird* was boarded by seven pirates armed with machetes; several crewmen were attacked, and ropes and equipment were stolen.[5] On 21 August 1994, *Young II* was boarded and ropes and other materials were stolen. The vessel's chief engineer and from ten to twelve of the crew were injured in the attack and had to be taken to a local hospital.[6] On 26 July 1997, at around eleven o'clock in the evening, the Danish *Star Bird* was anchored in Chittagong Roads when armed intruders boarded from two boats, forward and aft, stole three mooring ropes, one heaving line, a fire hose and nozzle, a wrench, three raincoats, and six pairs of boots.[7]

Over time, thieves became less cautious and attacked even during the day. In 1999 the Indonesian *Karya Sentosa*, which had been waiting for a berth and developed a leak, was being moved to safety when it grounded; the ship was pirated and set ablaze by individuals from the village of Gaheia.[8] At nine in the morning of 22 November 1999, a Panamanian bulk carrier was approached by a wooden boat carrying machete-wielding men, who cut a mooring line and threw it into the water.[9] Eight people in a boat approached the stern of the Thai *Laemthong Glory* off Chittagong on 17 November 2000 and boarded, stole stores, and threatened the crew when confronted.[10]

While mooring lines and ship's stores appeared in this period to be favored targets, perhaps because they were portable and extremely easy to resell, since about 1998 zinc anodes have become targets. On 16 July 1998, the Danish *Arktis Crystal*, a cargo vessel, was attacked twice from beneath the pier. Initially, the pirates fled when the crew fired a distress flare. On the second occasion, they jumped into the water alongside the vessel and attempted to remove its zincs. The men escaped, though police were able to confiscate their boats.[11] On 15 November 2000, the Malay chemical tanker *Bunga Mawar* had zinc anodes stolen from its rudder about 11:15 PM. The duty engineer heard a knocking sound at the vessel's stern; the robbers fled when the crew was alerted and mustered on deck.[12]

Occasionally these attacks have been combined with more conventional pilfering. On 6 May 2000, there were three attacks against the one Panamanian liquefied petroleum gas (LPG) tanker *Gaz Lion,* anchored in the port. At two o'clock that morning small boats were seen approaching the tanker, but the deck watch repelled them. An hour later, robbers boarded, pursued and threatened the deck watch with knives, and stole a mooring line. At 4:00 AM there was a third assault, in which two or three zinc anodes were stolen from the rudder: "The Master reported the attacks to port control but the naval vessel observed patrolling did not respond."[13]

The year 2000 was one of the worst years on record for maritime crime against ships visiting Chittagong. On 25 January 2000, for example, the Slovenian tanker *Daihung* was boarded by armed intruders;[14] there were other attacks on 10, 13, and 25 May.[15] The early morning of 20 June 2000 saw the Indian bulk carrier *Chettinad Glory* boarded at 2:45 by six armed men, who threatened the duty seaman and broke open the rope store before fleeing.[16] There were five attacks in July, six in August, three in September, and five in October.[17]

Ships visiting Chittagong adopted more rigorous security measures. On 1 August 2001, at thirty minutes after midnight, six pirates attempted to board a containership from a motorboat but desisted when searchlights were shone on them. On 25 November, at around 3:15 AM, twelve men with long knives boarded a tanker anchored off Kutubdia Island but escaped when the alarm was sounded and the crew mustered. On 14 December, men with knives boarded a chemical tanker, cut three mooring lines, and lowered them into the water, but then fled in their boats when the watch sounded the alarm and shore personnel fired warning shots.[18]

Since ships had become so successful in fighting off attacks, the thieves adopted a different technique. On 12 June 2002, a party of line handlers assisted a chemical tanker to pay out more line fore and aft. When the vessel was fast, its crew observed that hundred-meter lengths had been cut out of both lines, which had then been respliced so that the theft would not be immediately noticed. Other thieves did not attack the ships but waited to attack crew members on shore. On 8 July, the third officer of a cargo ship in Berth 3 was assaulted when he left the vessel at ten in the evening to check its draft: "Seven persons armed with long knives attempted to grab the mates [*sic*] gold chain and watch and dislocated his arm requiring him to be hospitalized. Master reports this was the third robbery attempt since his arrival at Chittagong."[19]

Figures gathered by Chairman Shahadat Hossain of the Chittagong Port Authority (CPA) showed that there were fifty-eight petty thefts in the port in 2003.[20] After years of ignoring these attacks, the local police and coast guard finally began to pay attention to the problem. On 14 July, when *Chilean Express* and *Blue Sea* were raided in the Outer Anchorage near Patenga Point, the coast guard dispatched two vessels, causing the pirates to throw their goods and arms overboard and sink their boat; seven thieves were arrested and turned over to the Patenga police.[21]

The next year, fifty-two petty thefts were reported at the port, a slight improvement.[22] However, on 4 July 2004, a cargo ship was boarded at 1:30 in the morning. The crew mustered, and the pirates fled empty-handed; the coast guard and port control were unable to respond to the incident due to bad weather. On 7 November, about seven in the evening, a gang of a hundred looted the South Korean cargo vessel *Amazon*, which had arrived at the port to be scrapped; only five people were arrested. The same day, a gang of about a dozen thieves armed with knives and swords boarded a bulk carrier at 11:30 PM. Despite distress rockets fired at them by the crew, they were able to steal ship's stores and escaped in a motorboat.[23]

In 2005, the number of petty thefts dropped again, to twenty-eight.[24] That year, on 9–10 August at about nine o'clock in the morning, the coast guard and navy seized five high-powered boats filled with alleged pirates. The men had attacked the tug *Radwan* as it was towing a tanker in for scrapping at Sitakundu. Looted electronic items and cables were later recovered from the pirates, forty-four of whom were apprehended aboard by the coast guard, with another ten picked up by the navy as they fled.[25]

According to Shahadat Hossain of the CPA, during the first six and one-half months of 2006 a total of twenty-seven petty thefts occurred in the port, representing an increase over the previous year.[26] No further incidents were reported in August, but there were eight in September and seven in October. On 24 November, a bulk carrier was robbed at about 4:00 AM, when fifteen pirates with knives boarded the vessel and bound two of the crew: "Three watchmen broke into the bosuns store." Once an alarm was raised, the thieves jumped overboard with ship's stores, walkie-talkies, and cell phones.[27]

Attacks continued during 2007, but some ships successfully fought back. For example, on 1 June 2007: "Approximately 40 robbers armed with long knives and steel bars boarded the vessel. The alarm was raised; and the crew mustered and closed all access doors. The master fired rocket flares, picked up the anchor, and [proceeded] at full speed to open sea. The crew caught two robbers and the others jumped overboard and escaped in their speedboats with the ship's stores. The port control and coast guard were informed. A coast guard patrol boat arrived for investigation and took the two robbers for interrogation."[28]

Most recently, on 13 February 2008, at around 3:15 AM, the containership *Kota Tegap* was boarded by a dozen pirates armed with knives and a revolver: "The robbers overpowered the deck watchman, took over his intercommunications microphone and tied him to the winch. They . . . unlocked the aft mooring stores, and stole two mooring ropes and two lifebuoys. They also broke open the $CO_2$ room and dry provision store. . . . When the robbers tried to open the general deck store, they were spotted by a deck watch keeper who raised the alarm and alerted the bridge."[29]

In addition to attacks on foreign vessels, thieves also have targeted local fishing boats and trawlers. On 6 February 2003, the *Bangladesh Observer*'s correspondent noted: "In many cases piracy was not reported to the police. The miscreants are active in the river belt of the Megha stretching from Satnal to Haimchar."[30] On 7 April 2003, robbers looted goods from a trawler in the Meghna River, seriously injuring three boatmen.[31] An attack on eight fishing boats on 27 July 2003 at Compagnionj upazila (subdistrict) in Noakhali District resulted in twelve injuries.[32] On 4 August, fifteen to twenty thieves in a speedboat attacked a fishing vessel near Char Ababil; six fishermen were beaten and stabbed.[33] On 19 August, eight boats on the Meghna were looted, causing local fishermen to call for "deployment of river police in the Meghna from Satnal to [the] Haimchar area where the pirates are active now-a-days."[34]

A particularly gruesome incident involved the fishing boat *Kawsar* on 27 October 2003, allegedly as a punishment for the crew's having reported an earlier robbery. The pirates attacked the trawler near Sonadia Island, forced the fishermen into the ship's ice chamber and nailed it shut. Nurul Haque, the sole survivor, hid in a barrel. The police subsequently seized the trawler, a speedboat used in the piracy, and the boat's driver; the "municipal chairman of Maheshkhali Island was identified to be the owner of both the boats, police said."[35] The police arrested five pirates, who then led the police to their weapons, at Jhilanga. The police and pirates exchanged at least forty gunshots, and one of the arrested pirates, named Kalu Mia, died in "cross fire" as he tried to escape.[36] The Cox's Bazar police superintendent, Toufiq Uddin, told the press that those seized confessed that they were "professional sea robbers." After taking the *Kawsar* they had transported the looted fish to Kastrurighat and sold them the next day for ninety-two thousand *taka* (BDT).[37]

As this short account indicates, the number and intensity of pirate attacks in and around Chittagong have increased over time. Many of the petty thefts at the port are focused on removable equipment, like mooring lines and zinc anodes, that is not of immediate use to the thieves but has resale value, suggesting the existence of a network of buyers. These operations coexist with attacks on fishing vessels, which are also found in other divisions, such as Barisal.

**The Barisal Division**

The numerous forested areas near Bhola and Hatia in the Barisal Division are perfect hideouts for pirates. There are many small inlets surrounded by dense jungles where pirates can take refuge. Local fishermen stay away from these areas, since even the "coast guard patrols cannot fully protect them." The rise of piracy here mirrors an increase in local fishing, with most attackers operating at night and targeting lone trawlers. The fishermen are aware of the danger but have little choice: "'They sneak up on our vessels, often while we sleep,' says Ratan, whose nets and equipment had been stolen on the water. 'At least fifteen or twenty of them jumped out of their boat, against only eight of us. We know that if we're quiet and cooperative, they may only beat us, but they will let us go. If we try to be brave, then we won't stand a chance at surviving.'"[38]

In the past, local fishermen were hesitant to report piracy attacks; indeed, many cooperated with the robbers out of fear, while others became paid informants. "'In Shonapur, even the imams are involved with dacoits [robbers],' says fish trader Mohammad Selim. 'For nearly all of us, we would have to leave this area if we wanted to openly talk about Mizan [a group of pirates].'" The lack of cooperation from locals has been a continuous hindrance to the police and coast guard operations in the area.[39]

Most commonly, fishing nets, which can cost up to Tk 1.5 lakh (that is, 150,000 *taka*, about two thousand U.S. dollars), are stolen at gunpoint and sold to *delals* (middlemen) in Bhola. Gangs also steal fishing boats and sell them back through *delals* at a fraction of their original cost. Occasionally, the *delals* steal the money and do not return the boat; Mohammad Shahjahan had four vessels stolen this way. "There are hundreds of people involved in these things and they are backed by powerful political leaders; we have no defense against them. . . . Coast guard patrols come now and then, but it's nowhere near enough."[40]

Piracy is seasonal, preying on fishing boats during the height of the fishing season. For example, on 3 November 1994, pirates boarded a loaded trawler off the coast of Patuakhali in the Bay of Bengal, bound the thirteen crew members, threw them into the bay, and stole the vessel.[41] In early December, four speedboats with about thirty pirates aboard surrounded the fishing boat *Aliya* and two other fishing boats near Barguna. The pirates, armed with automatic weapons, made the fishermen jump into the sea, blew up the engines of two of their own boats, and escaped with *Aliya* and its catch, valued at fifty thousand U.S. dollars. At least fourteen fishermen drowned, according to two survivors.[42]

On 19 January 2003, seven or eight pirates looted cash and valuables from twelve trawlers on the Agunmukha River before vanishing in a speedboat.[43] Fishermen aboard the FB *Mayer Doa* returning from their fishing grounds at night on 10 March were attacked near Rumparchar by pirates who stole nets and valuables.[44] On 2 April 2003, "a daring trawler dacoity was committed in 3 fishing trawlers in the Bay near Pathergata. . . . [A] gang of pirates with firearms attacked them and looted fishing nets and other valuables worth about Tk 500,000. The pirates also beat up the fishermen."[45] On 7 May, some twenty-seven trawlers in the bay were boarded by armed pirates off Andar Char, losing their catch, nets, and other valuables. Eleven fishermen who attempted to resist were thrown into the sea; seven drowned, and four were rescued by other fishermen.[46]

On 6 July 2003, pirates who had previously taken four fishermen hostage exchanged gunfire with police on the Chora Meghna Arpangsia River. Two of the criminals were killed, and their captives were rescued from two trawlers abandoned when the robbers fled into the forest.[47] On 14 July there occurred attacks against two fishing vessels in the Bay of Bengal near Barolbaria of Patharghata upazila by a gang of from twenty to thirty; eight fishermen were seriously injured in the attack, in which fish, valuables, and cash were looted.[48]

As a result of this surge of attacks, the Phorghata trawler owners association "complained that for the last few months piracy in the Bay has been increased in an alarming proportion due to [an] absence of Coast Guard."[49] A similar attack was reported by the Trawler Owners Association on 18 July 2003, near Laldiarchar, with fish and the vessel's engine being stolen and four fishermen injured.[50] On 19 July 2003, police intercepted a gang as it moved toward a trawler grounded near Molongchora. A gun battle resulted; about eighty rounds were fired over the next hour before six of the eight robbers were captured.[51] However, sometimes the police cooperate with the thieves; in September 2003, five policemen were arrested during naval operations against pirates on the Meghna for "allegedly collecting tools from fishermen in association with pirates."[52]

Even when police are not trustworthy, the thieves do not always escape. During October 2003 it was reported that "four alleged pirates were caught by people at Mirzakalu Bazar in Charfession upazila while they were selling goods looted from fishermen." When the local police tried to release them, "Some local people led by local Union Parishad Chairman Jasim informed higher police officials. Borhanuddin thana then arrested the pirates and lodged a case."[53]

These events led to a police crackdown, and on or about 18 November 2003 Faruk Sarder, the leader of the Faruk Bahini gang, was allegedly killed during a gun battle with police on the Meghna River; his body was washed away downstream.[54] On the night of 30 November, Abdus Salam Kahn and other local fishermen surrounded a pirate vessel that was preparing to rob a trawler on the Bay of Bengal. This led the Galachipa police to arrest eleven pirates from various villages in Kalapara upazila.[55]

Faced with increased police patrols, the pirate gangs are becoming better equipped. As the *Daily Star* (Chittagong) noted in August 2004, a group called Shiraj Bahini would attack "fishermen and traders, loot their cash and valuables. . . . After committing the crime the pirates fled away towards Lalmohon with the booty by a white colour speed-boat." Apparently, "police fail to catch them due to the absence of speed-boats" and "cannot take action against them because of their location outside the district."[56]

In response to the increased threat of robbery, the fishermen have banded together for safety. Nonetheless, eight fishing trawlers seeking shelter from a storm on 4 October 2004 were attacked by about forty pirates in three fast trawlers a hundred kilometers south of Patharghata. In a two-hour fight, some seventy fishermen were injured, four with gunshot wounds.[57] On the night of 1–2 November, "more than 100 trawlers were reported looted . . . on the Meghna River estuaries of Manpura, Tazmuddin, Daulatkhan of Bohia, and Dhal Char. In one case, a fisherman fought back and detained some of the pirates, whereupon 20 pirate boats responded with a looting spree. About 50 local fishermen have been reported abducted for ransom."[58] Similarly, on 23 April 2005, a dozen fishing trawlers were attacked in the Meghna estuary near Burhanuddin upazila, injuring at least eleven fishermen: "Police and fishermen report that over 50 fishing trawlers have been looted, 15 trawlers hijacked, and at least 100 fishermen injured in such attacks over the past month. The recent increase in attacks corresponds to the approaching fishing season. Sources state the pirates mainly belong to two rival gangs."[59]

Police attempts to halt maritime crime are temporary at best, Sisyphean at worst. As one gang is arrested, others move in and take its place. In July 2004, for example, it was reported "that, despite recent high-profile arrests of river pirate gangs preying on local traders and fishermen, other gangs rapidly move into areas where arrests have been made. In the Meghna River estuary 183 trawlers have collected red flags as tokens that they have paid 'tolls' to local bandits, who effectively rule the area. At least 10 fishermen have been killed, 60 injured, and 120 abducted while 110 trawlers have been hijacked for non-payment of the tolls during the past year."[60]

In February 2006, police conducted an operation against the pirate Bachchu Majhi and his group, the Bachchu Bahini. A raid on a relative's house in Chittagong eventually led to the pirate's apprehension at the Chittagong port labor colony. "Upon his arrest, Bachchu told the police that he would hand over his arms cache, which was hidden in a char [Boyar Char shoal]. 'When we went to recover the arms, other members of his group attacked us. Bachchu got away from us and was killed in the crossfire.'"[61]

Alauddin, the forty-year-old leader of the Alauddin Bahini, was also wanted in connection with fifteen incidents of murder or piracy. On 15 August 2006, police received a tip that he was robbing fishing trawlers in the Meghna River off Boyar Char. They found from thirty to thirty-five pirates boarding a trawler, and during a firefight the pirates fired about 250 rounds and the police about seventy-five. The gang fled into the jungle, leaving Alauddin mortally wounded: "Hundreds of people, mostly fishermen, brought out jubilant processions on the riverbanks . . . on hearing about the death of one who was a dread to them."[62]

By 2008, there were at least three major groups of pirates in the Bhola region. The Mizan group took its name from the alleged leader, a "tea-stall owner hailing from Shonapur. . . . Local police have raided his home several times to no avail."[63] The Kamal group was damaged by a police and coast guard operation on 4 February 2008, which resulted in a gun battle on Bashongbhanga Char and the capture of ten pirates. Although Kamal, the leader, escaped, it was noted that "piracy operations have all but stopped in the region[;] . . . this is usually the case after a group has been arrested. Invariably, the pirates return to work as soon as they feel safe again." In fact, Mofiz Keramat of Shonapur, one of those arrested, claimed they were scapegoats, set up by the ex–union *parishad* (UP) chairman Mintu of Dholigournagar upazila. The accusation of UP chairmen being involved in piracy is not a new one in the area. Local journalists claim that at least ten current and former chairmen are involved in collecting tolls from the pirates in exchange for protection: "The arms on the boats belonged to Chairman Mintu. If you bring him here, I can accuse him to his face," said Mofiz.[64]

### The Khulna Division

Khulna Division, to the west, includes the port of Mongla, through which 20 percent of the country's trade passes.[65] Many of the attacks here mirror those taking place in or near Chittagong. On 27 January 1996, for example, the tug *Dynamic* was towing three waterman lash barges from the anchorage when thieves boarded and stole eleven mooring lines.[66] On 18 September two years later, the cargo ship *Ots Uranus,* from Cyprus, was raided in the anchorage by fifty pirates armed with long knives. The intruders threatened the crew and stole ship's equipment and supplies.[67]

The year 2000 was particularly bad. On 4 January the Vietnamese bulker *Ariel* was boarded by armed pirates and a crewman held hostage while equipment was stolen.[68] The Russian general cargo vessel *Ardeal* was boarded on 1 May 2000, and six armed intruders from a wooden boat held a watchman hostage before fleeing.[69] On 12 November, from twenty to twenty-four thieves from four wooden boats tried to board the Saudi Arabian cargo vessel *Ibn Qutaibah*. The crew and shore guards prevented that, but zinc anodes were stolen from the ship's hull.[70] On 23 December, the Panamanian

*Marblue* was pirated by three men with knives who stole eighty meters of welding cable and sixty meters of pipe.[71]

There were at least seven incidents in the port over the course of 2001. On 17 April, for example, a bulk carrier at mooring buoy six was boarded in the early hours by thieves who broke open the manhole cover into the steering-gear flat and stole engine spares, mooring lines, and vessel stores. A cement carrier was hit at 8:00 PM on 31 May; ten robbers with knives assaulted a watchman when he found them lowering mooring line into a small boat.[72]

On 15 March 2002, a bulk carrier anchored in the Pusur River suffered two attacks. At 7:55 that morning, armed pirates stole a wire rope. Slightly over an hour later, three armed robbers boarded from a small boat by means of the anchor chain and tried to steal mooring lines. They attacked the chief officer with knives but jumped overboard and escaped when assistance came. A cargo vessel was robbed of zinc anodes welded to its stern on 29 July while waiting at the mooring buoy; the same crime occurred on another vessel there on 20 August. On 22 August 2003, an LPG carrier was obstructed in its passage of the Pusur River by ten men in small fishing boats who attempted to board, even after the master increased the ship's speed. On this occasion, the coast guard responded within thirty minutes and escorted the carrier the rest of the way to port.[73]

The resource-rich mangrove forests of the Sundarbans are also found in Khulna. These consist of many small islands and mudflats, separated by a network of tidal waterways that are particularly difficult to patrol. The Forestry Department controls fishing activities, which generally take place between about mid-October and mid-February. Fishermen from Chittagong and other areas of the country catch fish and dry them on the beaches. The *bawalis*, woodcutters of the area, "collect Nipa Palm *(golpata)*, which is used for making roofs and mats" from November to January. "During this period they live in groups on large boats as [a] precaution against pirates."[74]

Not surprisingly, here too the fishing season corresponds closely with piratical activities. Forestry "Department officials and employees work in a very insecure environment as the ill-equipped forest guards are no match for the 15 or more organized groups of heavily armed pirates and bandits who rule the roost in the forest."[75] Although pirates initially focused on petty theft, they have branched out into kidnapping fishermen or hijacking trawlers and holding them for ransom. The 28 November 2000 kidnapping of sixty-five Indian fishermen from thirteen trawlers at the mouth of the Thakurani River, in the Indian Sundarbans, may have been carried out by Bangladeshi pirates. The captives were taken to an isolated island in the Bay of Bengal; five were released, and a ransom of 500,000 rupees (US$11,000) was demanded for the rest. The abandoned boats were recovered.[76] It is not uncommon for a fisherman or a trawler to be captured and held for ransom repeatedly.

On the evening of 18 December 2002, "Forest guards and Indian pirates traded gunfire for over two hours . . . at Harindanga canal of the Sundarbans. . . . [The] guards captured five Indian pirates including their ringleader Kanai Mondol."[77] A *Bangladesh Observer* article of 23 February 2003 discussed the serious violence in the Sundarbans border region: "Over 15 armed groups of pirates[,] both local and outside the border [ten were reported to be Indian], control the entire Satkhira forest range of the Sundarbans subjecting thousands of fishermen and bawalis for extortion, loot and harassment."[78] Between 4 January and 14 February 2003, some 150 individuals were kidnapped for ransom.[79]

On 3 March 2003, passengers aboard a salt-laden trawler on the Chittagong–Khulna route were assaulted by a gang that stole salt, fuel, and cash, stabbing five people in the process—one of whom was thrown in the river;[80] the *Daily Star* reported in early July that "hardly a day goes by" in the Sundarbans "without incidents of piracy, robbery or poaching." In response to this threat, the government launched Operation GOLDEN TIGER on 12 July 2003 with a six-hundred-man task force composed of personnel from the coast guard, navy, the Bangladesh Rifles and Ansars (both paramilitary forces), police, and the Village Defence Party (an auxiliary force under the Ministry of Home Affairs). "Ten ships and a number of speedboats have been requisitioned to carry out the joint operation," the purpose of which was to flush out pirates and smugglers.[81]

Attacks continued during the summer months, long after the fishing season was over. In July 2003, five fishing trawlers were "suddenly attacked by the pirates near Narikelbaria of Pathergata upazila of the district." A dozen fishermen were injured.[82] Locals reported in August that "ten groups of pirates were engaged in plunder. The groups often engaged in infighting for domination in the area."[83] On 23 December, Marabhola police killed Ali Ahmed, alleged leader of a pirate gang that had attempted to loot the outpost.[84]

On 2 January 2004, ten Bengalis who "went to the Sundarbans for a trip by engine boat" were kidnapped at gunpoint near Pashurrola by Indian pirates. "Later, the gang released two boatmen . . . on condition that they would come back to the Maloncha River . . . with the ransom money within three days."[85] On 13 March, pirates belonging to Motaleb Bahini kidnapped two fishermen from Kalichchar Canal. A ransom of Tk 1 lakh (100,000 *taka*) was demanded within two days, or the hostages would be killed.[86] Three fishermen abducted on 13 August from the Firingi area by the Baro Bhai gang had a Tk 7.5 lakh ransom set, payable within a week. On the 22nd, a rescue attempt resulted in an hour-long shootout; "the police had to return empty handed, as they could not enter the forest in the face of heavy firing of the pirate gang."[87]

Several subsequent police drives were launched. One involving the Bangladesh Rifles was scheduled for late August, but the threat of a major attack apparently led to the hostages' release, and they reached the Munshiganj police outpost on 30 August 2004.[88] Although these efforts had some impact, *New Age* reported in August 2005 that pirates kidnapped ninety-eight Borguna fishermen from seven trawlers in the Shala Canal, Sundarbans, where they were riding out a storm in the Bay of Bengal. Nets and valuables worth Tk 10 lakh were looted, and a Tk 5 lakh ransom was demanded.[89]

Clashes between local pirates and coast guard have continued to intensify. On 5 July 2006, a patrol vessel challenged a boat carrying fifteen or sixteen people at Nakelbaria, near Dublar Char. Without stopping, the craft opened fire on the coast guard patrol vessel. Two pirates were killed and four injured in the hour-long gunfight that ensued.[90] On 1 December, "a joint team of Rab [properly RAB, for Rapid Action Battalion] and Coastguard clashed with the members of Sumon Bahini on the estuary of the Pashur near Mongla Port . . . leaving three—a coastguard, a Rab member and a pirate—dead." Four days later, Jamal, the second in command of the group, was captured in Barisal, and on the basis of his statement, RAB members raided the Sukuchi area in the Sundarbans, recovering arms and ammunition.[91]

During 2007, the number of robberies continued, and the percentage of kidnap-for-ransom attacks appeared to increase. On 8, 11, and 12 July 2007, "pirates looted fishing nets and fish worth over Tk 5 million from twenty-eight trawlers and kidnapped over a hundred fishermen for ransom." Later that month, they kidnapped four and wounded five others from two trawlers in Kotar Kadar Canal. One of the boats was hijacked along with hilsa fish worth Tk 300,000.[92] As recently as 29 December 2007, eleven men fishing in the Bay of Bengal were abducted by pirates of Baki Billah Bahini, who took them to their hideout in the Sundarbans and demanded a Tk 1 million (US$1,500) ransom. On 1 January 2008, the Bangladesh Rifles, acting on a tip, chased the kidnappers in the Kalindi River and encircled their boats near Kalir Char about an hour before noon. An hour-long gun battle ensued, in which about 450 rounds were expended. Five pirates were killed and two others wounded, and all eleven captives were freed.[93] One of the wounded pirates disclosed "that pirates belonging to Masum Bahini, Raju Bahini, Motaleb Bahini and Baki Billah Bahini are regrouping again to increase their strength in the Sundarbans to counter law enforcers' drive."[94] In early April 2008, Sundarbans forest officials acknowledged the problem was worsening but also claimed that "some 484 pirates and smugglers along with arms and ammunition" had been arrested in the region during the preceding four years alone.[95]

## Conclusions

There is very little empirical data regarding Bangladeshi piracy, but press accounts reveal a richer vein of attacks than might be suggested by the published maritime reports of thefts from vessels at Chittagong and Mongla. The type and intensity of these activities vary widely within this fairly small region, from the pilfering of ship's supplies and fittings, such as mooring lines and zinc anodes, to the theft of fish and nets, and finally to the hijacking of trawlers and the kidnapping of fishermen for ransom. Maritime crime appears to be part of Bangladesh's social and political fabric; the overattention to attacks on international shipping has perhaps masked both the severity and extent of the domestic problem throughout that country's coastal regions.

Bangladesh does not sit astride a major international shipping route, as Indonesia does, but if local piracy remains unchecked, it could easily mushroom and lead to increased national and regional instability. Attacks that affect international trade arise in milieus in which local piracy is viewed as a successful business. Attacks on simple fishing boats in Bangladesh might in time grow to piracies against supertankers, as happened most recently with piracy off Somalia.

For years, piracy and maritime crime in and around Bangladesh have been grossly underreported. Information is now appearing for the first time about the pirates' organization, politics, methods, and motivations, but much additional research is needed to understand their impact. If the international community does not educate itself about localized occurrences of maritime and riverine crime, it will remain unprepared for the hidden shoals and reefs around it—"what lies beneath."

---

### Notes

1. Vijay Sakhuja, "Chittagong: A Pirate's Paradise," *Opinion Asia,* www.opinionasia.org/Chittagong.

2. Rajshahi and Dhaka are "inland" but have major rivers running through them. Sylhet is less relevant.

3. Eric Ellen, ed., *Piracy at Sea* (Paris: ICC, 1989), pp. 258–68.

4. Anti-Shipping Activity Message [hereafter ASAM] 1992-22, *Federation of American Scientists,* www.fas.org/.

5. ASAM 1994-3, available at www.fas.org/.

6. ASAM 1994-38, available at www.fas.org/.

7. ASAM 1997-63, available at www.fas.org/.

8. ASAM 1999-91, available at www.fas.org/.

9. ASAM 1999-120, available at www.fas.org/.

10. ASAM 2000-395, available at www.164.214.12.145/; *International Chamber of Shipping/International Shipping Federation* [hereafter ICS/ISF], www.marisec.org/.

11. ASAM 1998-46, available at www.fas.org/.

12. ASAM 2000-396, available at www.164.214.12.145/; www.marisec.org/.

13. ASAM 2000-69, available at www.164.214.12.145/.

14. *Individual Country Reports: Reported Attacks 2000,* ICS/ISF, www.marisec.org/.

15. ASAMs 2000-67, -68,-78, available at www.164.214.12.145/.

16. "SIS: Recent Incidents of Piracy," *Euronet/Internet,* www.euronet.nl/; *Reported Attacks 2000;* ASAM 2000-117, available at www.164.214.12.145/.

17. *Reported Attacks 2000;* ASAM 2000-337, available at www.164.214.12.145/.

18. ASAMs 2001-230, -315, -343, available at www.164.214.12.145/.

19. ASAMs 2002-168, -188, available at www.164.214.12.145/.

20. "CPA to Protest Ranking of Ctg [Chittagong] Port as Most Dangerous," *Daily Star* (Chittagong), 28 July 2006.

21. "Merchant Vessel Attacked by Pirates near Patenga: 7 Held," *Bangladesh Observer,* 16 July 2003, p. 16. See also "7 Pirates Held by Coast Guards," *Bangladesh Observer,* 18 July 2003, p. 3.

22. "CPA to Protest Ranking of Ctg Port as Most Dangerous."

23. ASAMs 2004-178, -184, -212, -274, and 2005-9, -28, available at www.164.214.12.145/.

24. "CPA to Protest Ranking of Ctg Port as Most Dangerous."

25. "54 Pirates Arrested," *New Age* (Dhaka), 10 August 2005, www.newagebd.com/; ASAM 2005-258, available at www.nga.mil/portal/.

26. "CPA to Protest Ranking of Ctg Port as Most Dangerous."

27. ASAMs 2006-59, -61, -98, -126, -156, -157, -189, -210, -245, -283, available at www.nga.mil/portal/.

28. ASAMs 2007-43, -147, -274, available at www.nga.mil/portal/.

29. ASAM 2008-95, available at www.nga.mil/portal/.

30. "Piracy in Fishing Boats at Meghna River Rampant," *Bangladesh Observer,* 6 February 2003, p. 6.

31. "Villager Shot to Death, 25 Injured by Dacoits in Mymensingh: Pirates Attack Trawler in Meghna at Char Jabbar, Tk 5 Lakh Looted," *Bangladesh Observer,* 10 April 2003, p. 6.

32. "Murder, Rape, Looting, Dacoity, Snatching Common Affair: Anarchism Created by Robbers, Terrorists in Noakhali Char Areas," *Bangladesh Observer,* 1 August 2003, p. 6.

33. "Govt Blamed for Failing to Check Terrorism: Dacoity at Fish Depot in Raipur, Tk 70,000 Looted," *Bangladesh Observer,* 10 August 2003, p. 6.

34. "Pirates Active at Patherghata, Satnal to Haimchar," *Bangladesh Observer,* 25 August 2003, p. 6.

35. Roland Buerk, "'Pirates' Kill Bangladesh Crew," *BBC News,* news.bbc.co.uk/.

36. "3 including Constable Injured, Arms Recovered: Pirate Killed in Gun Battle with Police in Cox's Bazar," *News from Bangladesh,* 6 November 2004, www.bangladesh-web.com/.

37. Ibid.; "'Pirate' Gang Lord Killed in 'Crossfire,'" *Daily Star Web Edition,* 4 November 2004.

38. Naeem Huque, "Pirates of the South," *New Age* (Dhaka), www.newagebd.com/.

39. Ibid.

40. Ibid.

41. ASAM 1995-6, available at www.fas.org/.

42. ASAM 1995-84, available at www.fas.org/.

43. See "Piracy Loot Cash, Valuables from 12 Trawlers in Patuakhali," *Bangladesh Observer,* 22 January 2003, p. 6.

44. "4 Fishermen Thrown into Sea, Tk 5 Lakh Looted: Dacoity in Fishing Trawlers Rampant in Bay," *Bangladesh Observer,* 17 April 2003, p. 6.

45. "Trawler Dacoity in Bay," *Bangladesh Observer,* 4 April 2003, p. 16.

46. International Chamber of Commerce, *Piracy and Armed Robbery against Ships: Annual Report, 1 January–31 December 2003* (London: International Maritime Bureau, 2004); ASAM 2003-164, available at www.164.214.12.145/.

47. "Dacoity on Highways, in Rural Areas Rampant in Country-side," *Bangladesh Observer,* 10 July 2003, p. 6.

48. "Dacoity in 2 Fishing Trawlers, Tk. 2.50 Lakh Looted near Barguna," *Bangladesh Observer,* 19 July 2003, p. 6; "Dacoits Loot Worth Tk 5 Lakh in Barguna," *Bangladesh Observer,* 25 July 2003, p. 6.

49. "Dacoits Loot Worth Tk 5 Lakh in Barguna," p. 6.

50. "Dacoity Committed in Fishing Trawler," *Bangladesh Observer,* 27 July 2003, p. 6.

51. "Police, Robbers Trade Fire in Narsingidi, Ctg: Engineer, Dacoit Shot Dead, Several Injured," *Bangladesh Observer,* 24 July 2003, p. 6.

52. "4 Pirates Caught by People in Bhola," *Daily Star Web Edition,* 20 October 2003.

53. Ibid.

54. "Notorious Pirate Gang Leader Faruk Killed?"*Daily Star Web Edition,* 24 November 2003.

55. "Bid to Commit Robbery Foiled: Eleven Held," *Daily Star Web Edition,* 1 December 2003.

56. "Tk 50,000 Fish Looted by Pirates," *Daily Star Web Edition,* 15 August 2004.

57. ASAM 2004-250, available at www.164.214 .12.145/.

58. ASAM 2005-10, available at www.164.214 .12.145/.

59. ASAM 2005-145, available at www.nga.mil/ portal/.

60. ASAM 2004-188, available at www.164.214 .12.145/.

61. "Pirate Gang Leader Killed in 'Crossfire,'" *New Age* (Dhaka), 27 February 2006.

62. "Pirate Killed, 7 Cops Hurt in Mid-river 'Gunfight' in Bhola," *New Age* (Dhaka), 16 August 2006.

63. Huque, "Pirates of the South."

64. Ibid.

65. The other 80 percent goes through Chittagong. Mongla is about eight kilometers from Khulna, the third-largest city.

66. ASAM 1996-1, available at www.fas.org/.

67. ASAM 1998-58, available at www.fas.org/.

68. *Reported Attacks 2000.*

69. Ibid.; ASAM 2000-37, available at www.164 .214.12.145/.

70. ASAM 2000-397, available at www.164.214 .12.145/; *Reported Attacks 2000.*

71. *Reported Attacks 2000.*

72. ASAMs 2001-126, -168, available at www.164 .214.12.145/.

73. ASAMs 2002-74, -216, -217, and 2003-236, available at www.164.214.12.145/.

74. *Banglapedia,* s.v. "Bawali," banglapedia .search.com.bd/.

75. "Coast Guard in Action to Flush Out Criminals from Sundarbans," *Daily Star Web Edition,* 14 July 2003.

76. ASAM 2001-3, available at www.164.214 .12.145/; "Pirates Kidnap 65 Fishermen in Eastern India," *Independent Online,* 28 November 2000.

77. *Sustainable Development Network Program,* 21 December 2002, www.sdnbd.org/.

78. "Coast Guard in Action to Flush Out Criminals from Sundarbans."

79. "Abduction of Fishermen, Bawalis Rampant: Indian Pirates Create Reign of Terror in Sundarbans," *Bangladesh Observer,* 23 February 2003, p. 6.

80. "Dacoity on Dhaka–Ctg Road Rampant: Cash of Bus Passengers Looted near Chandina," *Bangladesh Observer,* 11 March 2003, p. 6.

81. "Coast Guard in Action to Flush Out Criminals from Sundarbans."

82. "Tk 1.50 Lakh Looted from 5 Trawlers in Barguna," *Bangladesh Observer,* 30 July 2003, p. 16.

83. "4 Dead in Clash among Sundarbans Pirates," *Bangladesh Observer,* 9 August 2003, p. 6.

84. "Pirate Killed in Gunfight with Cops," *Daily Star Web Edition,* 25 December 2003.

85. "Indian Pirates Kidnap 10 Bangladeshis from Sundarbans," *Daily Star Web Edition,* 3 January 2004.

86. "Tiger Kills Fisherman, 2 Others Abducted by Pirates in Sundarbans," *Daily Star Web Edition,* 15 March 2004.

87. "Pirates Release Abducted Fishermen in Sundarban," *News from Bangladesh,* 1 September 2004, www.bangladesh-web.com/.

88. Ibid.

89. "Pirates Kidnap 98 Fishermen," *New Age* (Dhaka), 10 August 2005.

90. "2 Pirates Killed, Four Injured in Sundarban," *New Age* (Dhaka), 7 July 2006.

91. "13 Firearms Seized from Sundarbans," *Daily Star Web Edition,* 6 December 2006. This account is slightly different from "Coastguard Killed after Encounter with Pirates," *Daily Star Web Edition,* 3 December 2006. See also

"Coastguard Killed after Encounter with Pirates," Bangladeshnews.com, 3 December 2006; and "Encounter with Pirates: Rab Member's Body Recovered from Pashur," *Daily Star Web Edition,* 5 December 2006.

92. "Pirates Kidnap Fishermen, Loot Their Hilsa Catch from Sundarbans," *Financial Express* (Dhaka), 25 July 2007.

93. "Five Pirates Die in Gunfight with BDR," *Daily Star* (Chittagong), 2 January 2008.

94. "Pirate Gangs in Sundarbans Unite against BDR Drive," *Daily Star Web Edition,* 26 January 2008.

95. "Timber, Valuables Worth Tk 250m Seized," *Financial Express* (Dhaka), 3 April 2008.

# CHAPTER NINE

# Confronting Maritime Crime in Southeast Asian Waters
## Reexamining "Piracy" in the Twenty-first Century
SAM BATEMAN

There is nothing new about maritime crime in Southeast Asia. It has a long history, and the maritime criminals of today are mainly descendants of the marauders, pirates, and bandits of yesteryear. However, changes to the extent and nature of maritime crime have occurred over the years. The decline in fish stocks and loss of access to traditional fishing grounds, along with general economic problems, have led to unemployment and loss of income in coastal villages throughout the region. This has, in turn, forced some villagers to turn to piracy, sea robbery, and other forms of maritime crime. However, these villagers are often just "foot soldiers" organized by opportunistic businessmen or criminal gangs.

Most criminal groups—including so-called pirates—engage in several different types of criminal activity. There is no strict demarcation between people involved in piracy and those involved in other forms of maritime crime. Many are nonprofessional criminals, such as fishermen and traditional barter traders, making money in such low-level crime as smuggling cigarettes from Indonesia to Malaysia to avoid paying excise taxes. The networks involved are not large, and they tend to be family or village oriented. Smuggling has been going on for generations and continues to the present day, especially where people on both sides of modern borders share ethnic and family ties.

Transnational organized crime has also increased across Southeast Asia. Processes of globalization, convenient international travel, information processing, electronic transfers of funds, and ready access to secure communications have facilitated transnational crime just as much in Southeast Asia as they have elsewhere in the world. Due to the archipelagic geography of the region and the difficulties of policing sea routes and maritime borders, the sea is the main medium for the illegal movement of people and goods. Hence, organized crime in Southeast Asia invariably has a significant maritime dimension.

"Legitimacy" for maritime crime is sometimes provided by political or religious causes, as well as by the developments in globalization that might facilitate transnational collusion between radical groups and separatist movements. What might have been purely local causes in the past can now more readily take on global dimensions. In many instances also, colonial lines of demarcation cut across traditional family and ethnic groupings. Much of today's illegal activity at sea, particularly smuggling and the illegal movement of people, is "illegal" only by virtue of contemporary, rather than traditional, border controls and trade regulations.

Recent concerns with maritime crime in Southeast Asia have been with piracy and armed robbery against ships. Such activities have provoked international interest as they are assessed as threats to the free movement of shipping and seaborne trade. They have also led to speculation that because piracy and sea robbery occur in the region, there could be a higher risk of maritime terrorist attack. However, there are few grounds to conflate piracy and maritime terrorism.[1] Also, in hindsight, it may be argued that the risks posed by piracy and sea robbery to international shipping in the region have been exaggerated.

The focus on measures to reduce risks of piracy and sea robbery in the region has served to distort the picture with maritime crime more generally. It ignores the links between different kinds of maritime crime and the fact that the perpetrators of different criminal activities at sea are often one and the same. It has also led to a concentration on patrolling at sea, which at best is a deterrent measure, rather than on policing on shore. This chapter examines the "bigger picture" by examining all forms of maritime crime in Southeast Asia, rather than just focusing on piracy and sea robbery, and suggests some possible actions to deal with the entire range of maritime crime.

## Maritime Crime in Southeast Asia

People in the coastal villages of Sumatra, Java, Malaysia, the Riau Islands, and the Sulu Archipelago have a tradition of what is regarded by modern standards as maritime criminality. They have long been involved in piracy, smuggling, and trafficking in commodities and people. International borders in these areas were unknown in the past, although there would have been long-standing recognition of where limits of traditional lands, waters, or rights existed.

The practices of smuggling, trafficking, and seeking employment away from home areas have not stopped merely because colonial and postcolonial administrations have established national borders. In addition, in many areas, the people on both sides of a modern border—for example, between Sumatra and Peninsular Malaysia, or between Sabah and the southern Philippines—may be closely related, speak the same language, and have far more in common with each other than with administrations in faraway national capitals.

There is still a tradition of unregulated cross-border movement by local people wherever border demarcation is uncertain and means of enforcing it are weak. For example, a family group wishing to visit relatives across the sea may not bother about the formality of border controls, and it may, understandably, take "gifts" along. Much of this activity is generally harmless, but it can assume more dangerous proportions, particularly when drugs or arms are involved.

Smuggling and the movement of people both have long histories in Southeast Asia. They are frequently regarded as extensions of historical trading arrangements between neighbors that are still conducted through the barter system. They are particularly prevalent in the Sulu Sea area and the Malacca Strait. Effective bilateral or trilateral cooperation in the area appears limited. There are difficulties in intercepting and arresting people engaged in smuggling and illegal border crossings.

Smuggling in the Sulu Sea has been increasing rapidly, particularly from the Philippine side. It involves cigarettes, illegal immigrants, sex trafficking, drugs, and other valuable commodities. There is also widespread smuggling of subsidized diesel fuel and kerosene from Malaysia to Indonesia, particularly through Penang.[2] Other smuggled goods include alcohol and motorcycles. Traditional fishermen might undertake the smuggling, but the real masterminds are located on shore and keep themselves at arm's length from illegal activity.

Illegal people movement in the region may be either short-term (for family reunions or other social visits) or long-term, mainly to seek work. Malaysia is particularly concerned about illegal migration by sea across the Malacca Strait from Indonesia and down the strait from Thailand, Myanmar, or Bangladesh.[3] People with strong and longstanding traditional family links across the Malacca Strait and the Sulu Sea moving across colonial boundaries do not regard themselves as illegal immigrants. There is much traditional movement of people by sea between the southern Philippines and Sabah, as well as between Sumatra, Malaysia, and southern Thailand. These movements may be exploited by both criminal and terrorist groups.

Registration of aliens is a significant problem in the Philippines, where there are many Indonesians, particularly on islands around Mindanao. There are known links between these people and smuggling and terrorist activities. The Philippines also has illegal immigrants from China and India who may be involved in the sale of smuggled goods, financial crimes, and other forms of criminality. All types of smuggling in the

Philippines are interrelated. Cross-border regulation (including the regulation of ferry traffic), particularly in the Sulu Sea region, is weak. People move illegally into the Philippines from East Kalimantan through Sandakan and the Sulu Archipelago to Zamboanga and elsewhere in Mindanao, and from Manado in North Sulawesi through the Greater Sunda Islands to General Santos and Cotabato in Mindanao.

### Drug and Arms Trafficking

Trafficking in drugs by sea remains a major source of income for many transnational, organized criminal groups. Myanmar remains the major source country for opiates—principally heroin—in Southeast Asia, but small amounts are also produced in Laos.[4] Cannabis is trafficked in the region, especially to Malaysia. Sometimes this has involved land routes but more frequently transfers at sea or simply floating the product ashore. Cannabis is also widely smuggled in the Philippines. The New Peoples' Army is active in cultivating cannabis, especially in the northern Philippines.

There is an increasing problem in the region with the manufacture and trafficking in methamphetamines ("ice") and other amphetamine-type stimulants (ATSs) from Myanmar and other Asia-Pacific countries, including China, India, and North Korea. "Ice" has replaced heroin as the most lethal drug in the region, and its manufacture and use are increasing. *Shabu* (crystalline methamphetamine hydrochloride or, also, "ice") is the major drug of choice in the Philippines, with factories in the central Philippines, mainly resourced from China or Taiwan. This is a worrying trend, because the physiological impact of "ice" is far more serious than those of heroin, cocaine, cannabis, ecstasy, or other ATSs. Ephedrine and pseudoephedrine, which are major precursor chemicals for the manufacture of methamphetamines and other ATSs, are manufactured in China and India and are moved mostly by sea.

Small-arms trafficking in Southeast Asia is "an integral part of broader transnational crime that includes terrorism, drug trafficking, money laundering, piracy and human trafficking."[5] Small arms are widely available in the region, and trafficking by sea is the preferred means of movement. Past conflicts in Indochina have provided major sources of small arms and light weapons. Thefts of weapons from military bases and police stations are common, particularly in Indonesia and the Philippines, and small arms are manufactured both legally and illegally in the region, particularly in the Philippines.

Due to its geographical characteristics, its role in the Cambodian conflict, and its relatively open society, Thailand is "an ideal point of origin and transit in the trafficking of small arms."[6] Because of the troubles in Aceh, GAM was a major recipient of small arms and light weapons smuggled across the Malacca Strait from Thailand.

Arms have also flowed to the Tamil Tigers (LTTE) in Sri Lanka through southern Thailand.[7] A former Indonesian military officer was arrested in the United States in 2006 in connection with arms smuggling to the LTTE in Sri Lanka.[8] Sri Lanka remains concerned about Indonesia as a conduit for the smuggling of firearms from southern Thailand to the LTTE.

The Philippines has plenty of weapons available. These include domestically produced small arms and weapons stolen or "sold" from the armed forces of the Philippines. The domestic arms-manufacturing industry produces weapons both legally and illegally, with some illegal exports to criminal groups in Japan and Korea. The trade is managed by criminal syndicates and is largely carried by sea in containers rather than by small boat. A common route for terrorists, firearms, and explosives coming into Indonesia from the Philippines, through Sabah, is via Palu in Central Sulawesi and then to Surabaya in Java (probably by boat) or onward to Jakarta or other destinations in Indonesia.

The proliferation of small arms and light weapons is a major factor underpinning the incidence of maritime crime in Southeast Asia. Illegal trafficking occurs across the Malacca Strait and the Andaman Sea from southern Thailand into Aceh, Bangladesh, India, and Sri Lanka, and it is also prevalent into and out of the Philippines. Measures to control trafficking in small arms might assist in reducing the violence of acts of piracy and sea robbery. Given the proliferation of small arms and light weapons in Southeast Asia, it is not surprising to find that pirates and armed robbers are making greater use of them.[9]

### The Threat of Illegal Fishing

Illegal, unregulated, and unreported fishing has become a serious problem in the region, especially for Indonesia. With the depletion of fish stocks in the region, many coastal villagers have lost their basic means of livelihood and are tempted into illegal activity. The devolution of powers to regional governments in Indonesia has reduced central oversight of fisheries enforcement.[10]

The fishing industry in Malaysia is more developed than that in Indonesia. As the fish stocks in the area are depleted, Malaysian fishermen are tempted to cross into Indonesian-claimed waters to exploit the fish stocks there, using their larger vessels and more sophisticated techniques. This exposes them to harassment, extortion, and arrest by Indonesian law-enforcement officials, who may be acting corruptly, even engaging in "bush justice." The experience of the Hutan Melintang fishing community suggests that the rate of these predations, robbery and informal detentions of Malaysian fishermen and fishing vessels by Indonesian law-enforcement personnel, has not declined.[11]

Illegal activity could involve the village or district *tauke* (towkay) system. Tauke is a Chinese (Hokkien dialect) word for "boss" or "business proprietor." Within each *kampong* (village or settlement), there is a recognized business leader, and the taukes manage the local fishing and other production sharing systems in Malaysia, Indonesia, and elsewhere in Southeast Asia, including Aceh and the Riau Islands. Taukes are invariably of Chinese ethnicity, reflecting the long involvement of ethnic Chinese in managing fishing activities in the Malacca Strait.[12] The masterminds behind smuggling and other illegal maritime operations are usually taukes; they use the local villagers as "foot soldiers," thus keeping themselves at arm's length from the illegal activity.

While the tauke is not necessarily the headman of the kampong, he effectively controls the "business" activities undertaken in the kampong. Some—but certainly not all—taukes have criminal associations, and they become the links through which more sophisticated organized crime might operate in, for example, people smuggling, cigarette or diesel-fuel smuggling, illegal fishing, or piracy. It is very difficult to counter the criminal role of a tauke, who has a very powerful position in the kampong and acts as the link between the poor and the wealthy, the fishermen and the businessmen, and possibly the criminals and the military.

**Piracy and Armed Robbery at Sea**

Many types of maritime crime may be increasing, including smuggling of goods and people, but piracy and armed robbery against ships in Southeast Asia have actually gone down significantly in recent years. For example, the "phantom ship" phenomenon—when a ship is hijacked, given a false identity and documentation, and sold or used for further trading—has been largely solved with the introduction of "ship identification numbers" and "continuous synoptic records" by the International Maritime Organization (IMO). Because of these international reforms, it has become much more difficult to give a ship a false identity.

As mentioned above, the number of reported piracy attacks in the region has trended steadily downward from 2004 to the present. The table shows the number of attacks (actual and attempted) in Southeast Asia for each year from 2001 to 2008. The large number of attacks in the earlier years in the table may be attributed to two main factors. First, it may have been a consequence of the economic downturn of the late 1990s, with more people turning to sea robbery for income. Second, several high-profile pirate attacks in the late 1990s might have drawn increased attention to piracy, which in turn may have led to increased reporting of incidents.

Reservations should be noted about the statistics from the International Maritime Bureau (IMB). On the one hand, there could be some underreporting of attacks. Both

*Piracy in Southeast Asia: Actual and Attempted Attacks 2001–2008*

| LOCATION | 2001 | 2002 | 2003 | 2004 | 2005 | 2006 | 2007 | 2008 | TOTAL |
|---|---|---|---|---|---|---|---|---|---|
| Cambodia/ Vietnam | 8 | 12 | 15 | 4 | 10 | 3 | 5 | 11 | 68 |
| Indonesia | 91 | 103 | 121 | 94 | 79 | 50 | 43 | 29 | 610 |
| Malacca Strait | 17 | 18 | 28 | 38 | 12 | 11 | 7 | 2 | 133 |
| Malaysia | 19 | 14 | 5 | 9 | 3 | 10 | 9 | 10 | 79 |
| Philippines | 8 | 10 | 12 | 4 | 0 | 6 | 6 | 7 | 53 |
| Singapore Strait | 7 | 5 | 2 | 8 | 7 | 5 | 3 | 6 | 43 |
| Thailand | 8 | 5 | 2 | 4 | 1 | 1 | 2 | 0 | 23 |
| Myanmar/Burma | 3 | 0 | 0 | 1 | 0 | 0 | 0 | 1 | 5 |
| South China Sea | 4 | 0 | 2 | 8 | 6 | 1 | 3 | 0 | 24 |
| TOTAL | 165 | 167 | 187 | 170 | 118 | 87 | 78 | 66 | 1038 |

*Source:* IMB, *Piracy and Armed Robbery against Ships – Annual Reports 2008;* ReCAAP Information Sharing Centre, *Annual Report 2008.*

the IMB and the IMO have noted reluctance by some shipmasters and shipowners to report incidents, due to concern that an investigation might disrupt the ship's schedule and increase insurance premiums. Also, attacks on local craft, such as fishing boats, barges, and small barter vessels, may not be reported to the IMB.[13] This underreporting might, for example, partly explain the lack of reported attacks in the Philippines in 2005, as shown in table 1.

On the other hand, overreporting is also possible. Many incidents constitute either unsuccessful attempts to board or petty theft—of such small items as paint, mooring lines, or outboard motors—from vessels in port or at anchor. These may previously have gone unreported but are later reported due to the publicity given to this form of maritime crime and greater awareness of the reporting channels available. The IMB statistics may also be inflated by the propensity of ships to report any close approach by a small craft as an "attempted attack" and by the lack of follow-up by the IMB to determine whether an attack was in fact actual.[14]

There are several reasons for the improved situation. National and regional responses, including increased patrolling and surveillance, have been important, although operations at sea have a mainly deterrent effect; few pirates or sea robbers are actually caught at sea. Tighter government control and local policing ashore are other factors that have contributed to the improved situation. In addition, there is greater awareness generally in the shipping industry of the importance of security, following the introduction of the International Ship and Port Facility Security Code by the IMO in 2002, and its coming into force in 2004.

The vast majority of attacks in the region are on vessels at anchor, in port, or entering or leaving a harbor. For example, of the seventy-eight actual and attempted attacks in 2007, fifty-two were against vessels that were not at sea. These attacks are usually of a minor nature and are best countered by more effective policing by port authorities, including active patrolling of ports and anchorages. Some international involvement, through assistance with building the capacity of local authorities, may be useful.

Most high-value seaborne trade in Southeast Asia is carried in larger vessels transiting the region, whereas the majority of successful attacks occur almost entirely on small vessels. In fact, most attacks are on smaller, more vulnerable vessels carrying trade within the region or on local fishing and trading vessels, or cruising yachts. Larger vessels gain considerable protection from their size and speed. Most modern merchant ships engaged in international trade travel in excess of fourteen knots, and it is both difficult and dangerous for small craft to attempt to approach them at such speeds.

With the exception of insecurity in some ports and anchorages, such as in Bangladesh, piracy and sea robbery in the region appear to be under control. The measures taken by regional countries both at sea and on shore have largely been effective—again, with exceptions, and although policing generally against maritime crime could still be improved. There are no grounds for the operational involvement of nonregional countries in providing security at sea against piracy and sea robbery in Southeast Asia. Nevertheless, contributions from nonregional countries would assist in building the capacity of regional countries to provide security in ports, anchorages, and littoral waters.

### Maritime Terrorism

In Southeast Asia, the vulnerability of the maritime sector to attack by terrorists has been of concern due to the economic importance of the sector, the incidence of piracy and sea robbery in the region, and the presence of terrorist groups with either histories of attacking maritime targets or intent to launch such attacks. Also, as target hardening occurs on land, maritime targets might become more attractive to terrorist groups.

Possible scenarios in Southeast Asia range from the highly speculative and most unlikely to the credible.[15] The more spectacular scenarios tend to be based on inadequate knowledge of the operating environment. Most commonly postulated is the notion that the Malacca and Singapore straits could be physically blocked. The traffic separation scheme (TSS) is 0.6 nautical miles wide in the vicinity of One Fathom Bank, off Port Klang in the Malacca Strait, and this is often identified as an area where the strait could be blocked. However, the distance from coast to coast outside the TSS is much greater and would still allow the passage of most vessels. The most likely cause of a diversion of traffic away from the straits would be a collective sense by the shipping community that the straits were insecure, which in turn would be more likely due to a threat like sea mining than to the physical blocking of passage.

The more catastrophic scenarios highlight possible attacks on liquefied natural gas or liquefied petroleum gas tankers, either through the planting of devices on board or by the use of a tanker as a mobile weapon to strike secondary targets. Such attacks seem improbable, due to the technical complexities involved and the opportunity and expertise required. Notwithstanding, its potential is given disproportionate focus, due to the results such an attack might produce.

The main maritime terrorist threat in the region is usually seen as coming from al-Qaʻida and its associated groups in Southeast Asia, particularly Jemaah Islamiyah and the Abu Sayyaf Group (ASG). These groups have camps in the southern Philippines, where they train together and share expertise. Group members routinely move between Sabah, Indonesian Borneo, and these camps by speedboat, local craft, and ferries. The ASG in the Philippines has already shown that it can conduct bomb attacks against ships. It claimed responsibility for the *Superferry 14* attack;[16] it was also blamed for the bomb attack on the ferry *Dona Ramona* in August 2005, as the ship was about to depart from Zamboanga.[17]

These attacks show that ferries, and potentially cruise liners, are vulnerable to attack. With passenger ships and ferries, it is not so much the bomb that might do the damage but rather the fire and panic that could follow an explosion among so many people in a confined space.[18] Measures to defeat attacks against ferries are a national responsibility, involving, for example, better screening of passengers and their luggage and enhanced security on board.

The potential for cooperation between pirates and terrorists is often overstated in writings that emphasize possible linkages between pirates and terrorists.[19] Piracy and maritime terrorism might involve a similar modus operandi by the attackers, but piracy is conducted for private ends, while terrorism has political motives. In assessments of the risk of maritime terrorism, pirates have been seen as having skills and expertise that might be attractive to a terrorist group, but these are not particularly specialized, and they are readily available. There are many former naval personnel, fishermen, and commercial seafarers in Southeast Asia with knowledge and experience that could be used by a terrorist group.

### Regional Solutions to Maritime Crime

Rather than seeing in isolation each of the different types of maritime crime mentioned in the preceding sections, the real challenge is to understand their root causes and choose appropriate responses in a more holistic manner. Measures to control maritime crime in the region should not be focused solely on piracy prevention or the risks of maritime terrorism. Measures should recognize the interests of all stakeholders and encompass other illegal activities at sea, such as the prevention of trafficking in arms, drugs, and people, as well as the operational dimensions of maritime safety, search and rescue, and marine environmental protection.

There are relatively few agreed maritime boundaries in Southeast Asia. Of the nearly sixty maritime boundaries in the region, less than 20 percent have so far been settled. Indonesia is one regional country that has very assiduously pursued agreements on maritime boundaries with its neighbors. In sharp contrast, the Philippines has no agreed maritime boundaries with any of its neighbors. Very few exclusive economic zone (EEZ) boundaries have been drawn in the region. The lack of maritime boundaries complicates enforcement against crimes at sea generally, while the lack of EEZ boundaries specifically makes enforcement against illegal fishing difficult.

Little progress is being made. Reaching agreement on outstanding maritime boundaries is both necessary and difficult. Trilateral, perhaps multilateral, negotiations are required, because some end points must be agreed among three or more countries.[20] Regional countries should move expeditiously to resolve existing maritime boundary disputes to ensure that jurisdiction can be exercised properly at sea. If boundaries cannot be resolved, countries should be prepared to enter into provisional arrangements for the maintenance of law and order in disputed areas without prejudice to their positions in the boundary negotiations. In particular, bilateral agreements between neighboring countries are essential for the reduction of illegal migration and smuggling.

Because most likely maritime boundaries lack historical bases, local cultural, social, and economic circumstances must also be recognized in border areas. Freedom of traditional movement and trade should be respected in agreed border-control arrangements, rather than simply classifying these activities as smuggling or illegal people movement.

### National Maritime Law Enforcement

Maritime jurisdiction and enforcement are extremely complex issues, particularly where maritime boundaries are not agreed upon. This is a special problem in key regional hot spots for maritime crime, such as the Malacca and Singapore straits and the Sulu and Celebes seas. Crimes at sea are often transnational, with more than one national jurisdiction involved. A state's criminal jurisdiction can vary with the ownership of the vessel and the exact location of the crime. This might be as a flag state over vessels flying its flag, as a coastal state over waters under national jurisdiction, as a port state over vessels in its internal waters, as an archipelagic or straits state, as a state of nationality of people or organizations engaged in illegal activities, or as a state exercising jurisdiction on the high seas as permitted by international law.

Regional countries face difficulties in combating illegal activities at sea, due to a shortage of trained personnel, a lack of modern equipment, the obsolescence or inadequacy of much national legislation, and the weak maritime law-enforcement capability of national agencies.[21] Problems also arise from the lack of interagency coordination and duplication of effort between agencies; some regional countries, notably Indonesia and the Philippines, have a number of different agencies dealing with some areas of maritime security without adequate arrangements for coordination. Last, any form of investigation or intelligence collection in the coastal areas where criminal networks exist will be fraught with difficulties, including personal risk to the police involved.

Indonesia, as the largest archipelagic state in the world, is very much aware of the extent of its maritime interests and of the needs to protect its maritime sovereignty and maintain law and order at sea. However, its efforts have been thwarted by the lack of capacity to conduct security operations and by the lack of coordination between the various government agencies that have responsibility for various aspects of maritime enforcement. At least ten agencies have been identified as involved in maritime security management, nine of them authorized to conduct law enforcement at sea.[22] The situation has been further complicated since the collapse of the Suharto government by government reforms, including the autonomy laws that involve devolution to provincial governments of authority, including some responsibility for law enforcement at sea. J. N. Mak considers that "the Indonesian decentralization process has led not only to more autonomy for agencies such as the military and the police, but also to a greater lack of accountability."[23]

Malaysia has been most successful in recent years in dealing with piracy and sea robbery. It has largely overcome the difficulties of maintaining law and order in a large and diverse maritime area that includes parts of the Malacca Strait, the South China Sea, and the Sulu and Celebes seas around east Malaysia. Unresolved obstacles to Malaysia's security efforts include the lack of a full suite of maritime boundaries around east Malaysia and of an EEZ boundary with Indonesia in the Malacca Strait. The lack of the latter boundary means that what Indonesia might regard as enforcement against illegal fishing by Malaysian vessels might be seen as piracy by Malaysia.

The Philippines is a large archipelagic country, one that faces major problems in providing and maintaining control in its more remote island groups, particularly in the south. Numerous small inlets and islands and a weak navy and coast guard add to the difficulties of providing an acceptable level of maritime security. The Philippines is particularly concerned about the illegal trade in small arms and light weapons, illegal migration, piracy, cross-border kidnappings, and smuggling of narcotics, as well as pre-cursor chemicals for narcotics and explosives.[24] Fighting maritime crime is a task mainly for the Philippine coast guard, although that service suffers in the competition for resources with other elements of the armed forces.

### Multilateral Law Enforcement

Considerable progress has been made in Southeast Asia over recent years in developing regional responses to the threats of piracy and sea robbery, although cooperative measures to deal with other forms of maritime crime are less well developed. Cooperative operational arrangements in the Malacca and Singapore straits, such as MALSINDO (Malaysia, Singapore, Indonesia) to coordinate naval patrols, the "Eyes in the Sky" project to provide cooperative air surveillance, and a joint coordinating committee to oversee these arrangements, are well established. However, the littoral states, especially Indonesia and Malaysia, remain firm that user states are to have no roles in patrolling the straits.[25] Embryonic operational cooperation is also developing in the Sulu and Celebes seas among Indonesia, Malaysia, and the Philippines. However, problems of governance, interagency coordination, and the lack of resources remain, especially in Indonesia, the Philippines, and Thailand.

Another significant development is the IMO-sponsored meeting process on security, safety, and environmental protection arrangements in the Malacca and Singapore straits. This began with the Jakarta meeting in September 2005 and continued with meetings in Kuala Lumpur in September 2006 and in Singapore in September 2007. The process provides a regular forum for dialogue among stakeholders, comprising the littoral countries, the user states, relevant international organizations, and the international shipping industry. A recent meeting, in Singapore, agreed to establish a "Cooperative Mechanism" for navigational safety, security, and environmental protection in the straits—a forum for regular dialogue, a committee to coordinate and manage specific projects, and a fund to receive and manage voluntary financial contributions from the shipping industry and user states.[26]

The ASEAN Chiefs of National Police meetings deal with the preventive, enforcement, and operational aspects of cooperation against transnational crime, including piracy and all forms of smuggling, as well as matters relating to terrorism. However, the sharing of information and joint operational policing activity against maritime crime in the region remain underdeveloped. This is partly due to a lack of trust and common accord between ASEAN countries and their dialogue partners, especially where issues of sovereignty or domestic sensitivities over organized crime and corruption may be involved. This is often the case, as transnational crime investigations can easily conflict with the ASEAN principle of "non-interference in the internal affairs of one another."[27] Interstate cooperation against crime invariably requires some surrendering of sovereignty. Also, in some countries, corrupt officials are directly or indirectly involved in the criminal activities and will be reluctant to risk exposure through inquiries by external investigators. The lack of extradition treaties between regional countries is another fundamental problem.

Despite much rhetoric, there has been some hesitancy at the "Track One" level in dealing too specifically with transnational organized crime in Southeast Asia. At the "Track Two" level, the Council for Security Cooperation in the Asia Pacific (CSCAP) has had working groups and study groups dealing with various aspects of transnational crime. These groups have produced at least two memorandums dealing with transnational crime that have helped in drawing attention to particular issues.[28]

### Problems of Securitization and Governance

Piracy and sea robbery have largely been "securitized" in the region, tending to become matters of national security.[29] The threats have become the medium for new initiatives for collective and common security. But in effect, securitizing the problems of transnational crime has elevated them to the political level, where grand statements can be made but little action occurs. As Ralf Emmers has observed, ASEAN "has failed to act upon the issue of transnational crime due to domestic factors, including the role of corruption, vested interests and a lack of resources, but also because of its own consensus model and inbuilt resistance to institutional reforms."[30] The ASEAN principle, already mentioned, of mutual noninterference might be added to this list of factors.

Securitizing the threat has also led to an environment of increased military spending, whereby capabilities are acquired ostensibly to fight terrorism and piracy but actually for purposes more purely military. Developing countries in the region should be pursuing programs to drive down poverty and social unrest and to remove root causes of piracy and terrorism, but they are being pressed instead to increase defense spending to provide greater security, especially at sea. These militarized approaches have high opportunity costs and set back development initiatives that might alleviate root causes of criminal activity and social unrest. A law-enforcement response to maritime crime is preferable to one based on the projection of military power.

Lack of good governance is evident both in the causes of a breakdown in law and order at sea and in the inability of governments to deal with disorder when it occurs. It seems that the farther away the seat of national government, the greater the problems of governance, including graft and corruption. These factors lead to increased maritime crime. For example, the barter trade between the southern Philippines and neighboring countries is unregulated; considerable quantities of dutiable goods are smuggled across borders; there is no patrolling of any strength in border areas; appropriate security leg-islation and regulations are not in place; and there is no effective national system for tracking small vessels used for criminal activity or stolen from other jurisdictions.

Levels of governance over particular areas prone to criminal activities are other factors that have influenced the extent and nature of maritime crime in Southeast Asia. For example, between the world wars American authorities appear to have exercised fairly effective control in the Sulu Archipelago. More recently however, lower standards of governance have led to an apparent upsurge in maritime crime in this area, notably armed robbery, kidnappings, and smuggling. Social unrest, nationalism, and political extremism, as well as porous and inadequately controlled maritime borders, add new dimensions to the situation.

## Conclusions

A reexamination of the contemporary situation with piracy and sea robbery in South-east Asia has often shown that the same people are involved in piracy and other illegal activity at sea, however different the offenses involved. They range from local fishermen or unemployed villagers to the onshore criminal infrastructure supporting piracy and maritime crime, to the offshore financiers, facilitators, and beneficiaries of such activi-ties. Countries outside the region, like the United States, have tended to promote mili-tary solutions to the problems of piracy and sea robbery when more emphasis should probably be placed on civil law enforcement against maritime crime generally.

Rather than seeing piracy and sea robbery in isolation, these crimes should be regarded as part of a continuum of maritime crime that also includes the various types of smug-gling, illegal fishing, and unlawful pollution of the marine environment. For this rea-son, the prevention of maritime crime is primarily a matter of civil law enforcement onshore rather than one requiring a military response at sea. Piracy and sea robbery attacks should be subject to the same criminal investigation procedures as other forms of criminal activity.

Of course, greater efforts are required to promote cooperation to deal with transna-tional organized crime in the region. Some areas that need attention are

- Improvement in security in ports, anchorages, and port approaches, where the vast majority of incidents of sea robbery occur

- Adoption of stronger measures to control trafficking in small arms and light weapons in the region

- Governance and interagency coordination, particularly in Indonesia, the Philippines, and Thailand

- Investigation of the onshore infrastructure supporting maritime crime, as well as the financing, facilitation, and beneficiaries of maritime crime

- Resolution of maritime boundaries within the region as soon as possible, to ensure that jurisdiction can be exercised at sea.

If sea boundaries cannot be resolved, provisional arrangements for law enforcement in the disputed areas should be entered into on a bilateral basis and without prejudice to the boundary negotiations.

The developing countries of the region, particularly the large archipelagic states of Indonesia and the Philippines, lack the capacity to deal with maritime crime in the extensive waters under their national jurisdictions, including in ports and anchorages. They have other priorities of poverty alleviation and development and should not be encouraged to increase expenditure on military forces at the expense of other forms of development. They require assistance in building their capacities to deal with maritime crime, but this should be directed more toward civilian agencies concerned with maritime crime and port security than toward the military. Finally, there remains a fundamental need for international cooperation to redress the underlying causes of piracy and maritime criminality in the region, such as depressed social conditions, poverty, and unemployment.

## Notes

Some parts of this chapter are based on field research and interviews in Kuala Lumpur, Jakarta, Manila, and Singapore in October–November 2006, conducted by the author and Mr. John McFarlane, visiting fellow at the Strategic and Defence Studies Center, Australian National University, for the Australian Strategic Policy Institute. Mr. McFarlane's input is gratefully acknowledged.

1. Adam Young and Mark J. Valencia, "Conflation of Piracy and Terrorism in Southeast Asia: Rectitude and Utility," *Contemporary Southeast Asia* 25, no. 2 (August 2003), pp. 269–83.

2. Diesel fuel is a very profitable commodity to smuggle from Malaysia to Indonesia. At this stage, due to subsidies, the price of diesel in Malaysia is about an eighth that in Indonesia. As a result, there is a healthy diesel-smuggling operation from Peninsular Malaysia to Sumatra. Malaysian-based Taiwanese fishing boats and Malaysian fishing vessels are believed also to refuel other fishing vessels at sea.

3. Sumathy Permal, "Trafficking in the Strait of Malacca," *Maritime Studies* 156 (September/October 2007), p. 6.

4. Some 90 percent of the world's opium is grown in Afghanistan, mainly in Helmand Province. However, most of this product, in the form of heroin, is trafficked through Iran, the Caucasus, Central Asia, and the Middle East into Russia and Europe. It appears that very little Afghan heroin is trafficked into Southeast Asia and beyond.

5. Rizal Sukma, "The Problem of Small Arms in Southeast Asia: An Overview," in *Small Is (Not) Beautiful: The Problem of Small Arms in Southeast Asia,* ed. Philipe Jusario Vermonte (Jakarta: Center for Strategic and International Studies, 2004), p. 9.

6. Thitinan Pongsudhirak, "Small Arms Trafficking in Southeast Asia: A Perspective from Thailand," in *Small Is (Not) Beautiful,* ed. Vermonte, p. 60.

7. Ibid., pp. 67–68.

8. Brian White, "Six Indicted in Arms Brokering for Tamil Tigers and Indonesia," Associated Press, 29 September 2006.

9. See Sam Bateman, Catherine Zara Raymond, and Joshua Ho, *Safety and Security in the Malacca and Singapore Straits: An Agenda for Action* (Singapore: Institute of Defence and Strategic Studies, May 2006), pp. 25–26.

10. Dirhamsyah, "Maritime Law Enforcement and Compliance in Indonesia: Problems and Recommendations," *Maritime Studies* 144 (September/October 2005), p. 9.

11. J. N. Mak, "Pirates, Renegades, and Fishermen: Reassessing the Dynamics of Maritime Piracy in the Malacca Straits," in *Australia and Its Maritime Interests: At Home and in the Region,* ed. Andrew Forbes (Canberra: Sea Power Centre–Australia, 2008) pp. 161–180.

12. John G. Butcher, *The Closing of the Frontier: A History of the Marine Fisheries of Southeast Asia, c. 1850–2000* (Singapore: Institute of Southeast Asian Studies, 2004), pp. 80–83.

13. Mak, "Pirates, Renegades, and Fishermen."

14. According to the IMB, the feeder containership *Sinar Merak* was attacked on 22 January 2007 in the Malacca Strait after leaving Belawan for Singapore. However, subsequent investigations by Singapore security agencies revealed that the two persons found on board the *Sinar Merak* were actually innocent Indonesian fishermen, survivors of a small craft that had been run down by the containership as it maneuvered aggressively to avoid a suspected attack. Nevertheless, the IMB continues to show this incident as an actual attack in the Malacca Strait. ReCAAP Information Sharing Centre, *Report for January 2007* (Singapore), p. 11.

15. See Sam Bateman, "Maritime Terrorism: Issues for the Asia-Pacific," *Security Challenges* 2, no. 3 (October 2006), pp. 77–92.

16. *Superferry 14* sank in February 2004 near Manila after a bomb explosion and fire on board. It constitutes the most serious act of maritime terrorism so far in terms of loss of life, with 116 people killed or missing. Other attacks on ferries in Southeast Asia include the February 2000 bombing of the Philippine ferry *Our Lady Mediatrix,* which killed forty people, and the December 2001 bombing of the Indonesian ferry *Kalifornia,* which

killed ten. John F. Bradford, "The Growing Prospects for Maritime Security Cooperation in Southeast Asia," *Naval War College Review* 58, no. 3 (Summer 2005), p. 67.

17. "Ferry Blast Injures 30 in Southern Philippines," *New York Times,* 28 August 2005.

18. See Sam Bateman, "Ferry Safety: A Neglected Aspect of Maritime Security?" IDSS Commentaries 31/2006 (Singapore: Institute of Defence and Strategic Studies, 3 May 2006).

19. For example, Graham Gerard Ong, "Ships Can Be Dangerous, Too: Coupling Piracy and Terrorism in Southeast Asia's Maritime Security Framework," in *Piracy in Southeast Asia: Status, Issues, and Responses,* ed. Derek Johnson and Mark Valencia (Singapore: Institute of Southeast Asian Studies, 2005), pp. 45–76.

20. When several countries are opposite or adjacent to each other, a boundary between any two of them will inevitably intersect the claim of another country. This is the situation in most seas of Southeast Asia and in the Gulf of Thailand. A commonly applied principle is to terminate the agreed boundary near the point of intersection (a theoretical tripoint), leaving the precise position of the point to subsequent trilateral negotiations. Victor Prescott and Clive Schofield, *The Maritime Political Boundaries of the World,* 2nd ed. (Leiden, Neth.: Nijhoff, 2005), p. 312.

21. The situation in Indonesia is discussed in detail in Dirhamsyah, "Maritime Law Enforcement and Compliance in Indonesia."

22. Ibid., table 1, p. 3.

23. Mak, "Pirates, Renegades, and Fishermen."

24. Jesse M. Pascasio, "Developing a Subregional Maritime Security Arrangement" (paper, Fourth Meeting of CSCAP Study Group on Capacity Building for Maritime Security Cooperation, Kuala Lumpur, 27–28 May 2006), p. 3.

25. Ary Hermewan, "Malacca Coast Patrol to Stay Local," *Jakarta Post,* 26 August 2007.

26. "Milestone Agreement Reached on Cooperation over the Straits of Malacca and Singapore," IMO Briefing 29/2007, 18 September 2007.

27. Amitav Acharya, "Preventive Diplomacy: Concept, Theory and Strategy," in *The Next*

PIRACY AND MARITIME CRIME 153

Stage: Preventive Diplomacy and Security Cooperation in the Asia-Pacific Region, ed. Desmond Ball and Amitav Acharya, Canberra Papers on Strategy and Defence 131 (Canberra: Strategic and Defence Studies Centre, Australian National Univ., 1999), p. 106.

28. "The Relationship between Terrorism and Transnational Crime," CSCAP Memorandum 7, July 2003; and "Trafficking of Firearms in the Asia Pacific Region: The Way Ahead: Building on Regional Cooperation," CSCAP Memorandum 9, May 2004. Track One encompasses formal intergovernmental activities, involving ministers and officials, while Track Two activities are nongovernmental, involving academics, private sector representatives, and nongovernmental organizations. Officials are often involved in Track Two activities, but they do so under the polite fiction that they are acting in a private or nonofficial capacity.

29. The process of *securitization* has its origins in the Copenhagen School of Strategic Studies and the writings of such people as Barry Buzan and Ole Waever. It relates security to survival and establishes five categories of comprehensive security: military, environmental, economic, societal, and political. Ralf Emmers, "ASEAN and the Securitization of Transnational Crime in Southeast Asia," *Pacific Review* 16, no. 3 (2003), pp. 419–38.

30. Ibid., p. 420.

# PART THREE

Piracy in Africa

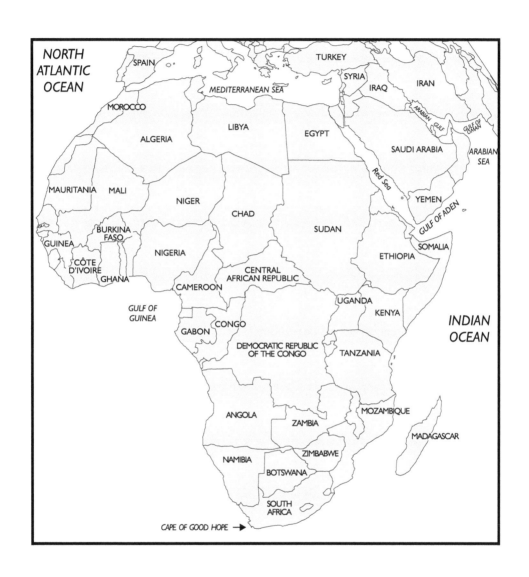

# CHAPTER TEN

# President Thomas Jefferson and the Barbary Pirates

ROBERT F. TURNER

Thomas Jefferson was fundamentally a man of peace, known for his observation that "if there be one principle more deeply rooted than any other in the mind of every American, it is, that we should have nothing to do with conquest."[1] In 1823, President Jefferson denounced "the atrocious violations of the rights of nations, by the interference of any one in the internal affairs of another."[2]

This was radical thinking for the time; for example, when war with England seemed imminent near the end of Jefferson's tour as secretary of state, he proposed what today would be termed "economic sanctions" as an alternative to force. In a letter to Tench Coxe, he wrote: "As to myself, I love peace, and I am anxious that we should give the world still another useful lesson, by showing to them other modes of punishing injuries than by war, which is as much a punishment to the punisher as to the sufferer. I love, therefore, . . . [the] proposition of cutting off all communication with the nation which has conducted itself so atrociously. This, you will say, may bring on war. If it does, we will meet it like men; but it may not bring on war, and then the experiment will have been a happy one."[3]

However, when facing the threat of uncontrolled piracy along the Barbary Coast, he reacted very differently. Jefferson's problem with the Barbary pirates during the early nineteenth century was exacerbated by a long history of European weakness during which payments of tribute and ransoms promoted a growth industry of terrorism. The Barbary regencies had preyed upon European commerce—and were generously rewarded for having done so—for two centuries before the United States arrived on the scene as an independent actor.[4] The revolutionary victory deprived American ships of the protection of the British flag—like other European powers, the British were paying tribute to secure unmolested transit on the high seas. This lack of protection, combined with the increase in American commerce and the fact that American merchant ships "carried not an ounce of shot" to defend themselves, made the new nation's commerce particularly attractive for plunder.[5] Jefferson's response to the Barbary threat was to use the nation's new naval forces to face down and destroy the pirate threat.

### The Barbary Threat

So long as the American colonies were a part of the British Empire, their commercial vessels were protected from attack by the annual tribute London was paying the Barbary states. However, ratification of the 1783 Treaty of Paris recognizing America brought that protection to an end. In October 1784, the American merchant brig *Betsy* was seized on the high seas and taken with its crew of eleven to Morocco.[6]

Lacking both a naval force to protect American commerce and the ability to compel the American states to furnish the necessary funds to provide for a navy, the Continental Congress, deciding to follow the European lead, authorized eighty thousand U.S. dollars to "negotiate peace" with Morocco to obtain the release of the prisoners.[7] Not surprisingly, two weeks after a ransom was paid and the crew of *Betsy* was freed, cruisers from Algiers seized two other American vessels, with twenty-one hostages. More soon followed. The conditions of imprisonment were such that by the time peace was purchased in 1796, only eighty-five of the 131 American hostages imprisoned in Algiers remained alive.[8]

As word spread across the North African coast that the Americans had signed a treaty to pay tribute to Algiers, the other Barbary states quickly threatened to prey upon American vessels unless they received equally generous treatment.[9] Particularly troublesome in this regard was Yusuf Karamanli, pasha (or bashaw) of Tripoli, who had seized power upon the death of his father in 1796. Six years earlier, Yusuf had murdered his older brother Hasan, and he now held the family of his eldest brother Hamet—who had been out of the country at the time of their father's death—as hostages to dissuade the rightful heir from returning and asserting his claim to power.[10]

The few surviving historical accounts suggest that Yusuf Karamanli was "feared and hated" in Tripoli;[11] one American diplomat who dealt with him extensively described him as "a large, vulgar beast," "a bully," and "a cur who can be disciplined only with the whip."[12] One of Yusuf's first acts as bashaw was to sign with the United States on 4 November 1796 a treaty of "firm and perpetual peace and friendship," which was ratified with the unanimous (23–0) advice and consent of the Senate on 7 June 1796.[13] Article 10 of this treaty specified that no "periodical tribute or farther payment is ever to be made by either party."[14] Article 12 provided that in the event of a dispute neither party would resort to arms but that the dispute would be submitted to the dey of Algiers for binding resolution.[15]

Documents referenced in the treaty acknowledged a receipt of a one-time payment of forty thousand Spanish dollars, assorted watches, rings, and fancy cloth.[16] Additionally, there was a "note" in which the U.S. government promised that each new consul appointed to represent the United States in Tripoli would bring twelve thousand Spanish dollars and specified quantities of artillery, anchors, pine and oak boards (wood being scarce in the desert), and other valuable commodities.[17] This, of course, provided a strong incentive for the bashaw to quarrel with any American diplomat, as an excuse to declare him persona non grata and set the stage for a successor with a new installment of treasure.

In July 1797, James Leander Cathcart was appointed American consul to Tripoli, and William H. Eaton became consul at Tunis. Despite the clear provisions of the treaty, the bashaw expressed displeasure that other Barbary leaders received nicer gifts. He suggested that if further tribute were not forthcoming, he would find it necessary to declare war. The threats intensified during the summer of 1799 and continuing into 1800.

In January 1801, the bashaw again threatened to cut down the flagpole in front of the American house—the method by which war was formally declared—and in February he formally repudiated the "perpetual" treaty of 1796 and demanded as an alternative to war a new treaty accompanied by US$250,000 plus an annual tribute of $50,000. Soon thereafter, Cathcart was informed by a messenger, "The door of the palace is closed to you until you pay the Bashaw his due."[18] The bashaw wrote personally to the American president lamenting the absence of new gifts and stating that "if only flattering words are meant without performance, every one will act as he finds convenient."[19]

Finally, on 10 May 1801, the bashaw announced that he was declaring war against the United States, and four days later the flagpole at the U.S. consulate was chopped to the ground. Washington did not learn of the declaration of war for more than a month, as there was no wireless radio, intercontinental telegraph, or air transportation to relay such information. However, as the bashaw would soon learn, the election of 1800 was not a positive development for the future of piracy along the Barbary Coast.

### Thomas Jefferson: A New Sheriff in Town

The problem of the Barbary pirates was not new to Thomas Jefferson, who took office as the nation's third president on 4 March 1801. He had dealt with it as George Washington's first secretary of state (1790–93); even before that, under the Articles of Confederation, as minister to France (1784–89), he had listened to shocking accounts of the barbaric treatment of American merchant seamen enslaved in North Africa. Jefferson had been frustrated that nothing could be done to help them, and while in Paris he had exchanged several letters with Secretary for Foreign Affairs John Jay, the U.S.

minister to Great Britain, John Adams, and others on this issue. In a 15 December 1784 letter to Jay, however, Adams argued that those who thought "it would be more manly to fight them" had "more spirit than prudence."[20] In another letter, he reasoned that it was not "good economy" to spend "a million annually to save one gift of two hundred thousand pounds."[21]

Jefferson too took an economic approach but understood there was more involved than money. He explained: "The question is whether their peace or war will be cheapest? But it is a question which should be addressed to our Honor as well as our Avarice? Nor does it respect us as to these pyrates only, but as to the nations of Europe. If we wish our commerce to be free and uninsulted, we must let these nations see that we have an energy which at present they disbelieve. The low opinion they entertain of our powers cannot fail to involve us soon in a naval war."[22]

On several occasions Adams suggested that he might prefer Jefferson's approach were it possible to protect American commerce by force, but, as he noted, the new nation had no navy and probably lacked the political will to persevere in such a policy. On 3 July 1785, he wrote Jefferson: "The policy of Christendom has made cowards of all their sailors before the standard of Mahomet. It would be heroical and glorious in us to restore courage to ours. I doubt not we could accomplish it, if we should set about it in earnest; but the difficulty of bringing our people to agree upon it, has ever discouraged me."[23]

These debates continued into the Washington administration, when Jefferson called for a military response.[24] As early as 1786, he had favored trying to "effect a peace" with the Barbary pirates "through the medium of war," arguing that paying tribute was beneath the dignity of the new nation and would contribute to disrespect by others that might ultimately lead to war with a European power. In Jefferson's view, both "justice and honor" favored a military response.[25]

Washington agreed with Adams that it was wiser simply to follow the European practices. But as the years passed, it became increasingly clear that the problem could not be solved by buying "perpetual" treaties of peace, as these adversaries lacked honor and would merely respond to payoffs with increased demands. Jefferson believed that giving presents to the Barbary powers was "money thrown away," as "there is no end to the demand of these powers, nor any security in their promises."[26]

In 1786, Jefferson proposed a collective treaty with European states as a means of deterring or defeating armed aggression by the Barbary pirates against international commerce.[27] He explained that "the object of the convention shall be to compel the piratical States to perpetual peace, without price"—that is to say, without paying ransom—and "to guarantee that peace to each other."[28]

Jefferson proposed that each party to the treaty authorize its minister to the court of Versailles to participate in a committee for effecting the treaty, with decisions to be made by majority vote. He suggested further that the group first direct its joint actions against Algiers, the strongest of the Barbary regencies: "When Algiers shall be reduced to peace, the other piratical States, if they refuse to discontinue their piracies, shall become the objects of this convention either successively or together, as shall seem best."[29] Although the scheme was well received in parts of Europe, it ultimately failed, because under the Articles of Confederation the American Congress lacked the legal power to compel the states to supply the necessary funds to sustain such a commitment. Indeed, it was in part to rectify shortcomings in the Articles that the Philadelphia Convention was convened in 1787 to write the Constitution.

Jefferson, like so many of his contemporaries, believed that a nation wishing to be free and live in peace had to be able to defend itself and be willing to protect its rights. The issue was not whether we preferred war or peace but whether we would have the option of peace, lacking a credible ability and willingness to defend our rights. In a 1793 letter to James Monroe, he wrote: "I believe that through all America there has been but a single sentiment on the subject of peace and war, which was in favor of the former. The Executive here has cherished it with equal and unanimous desire. We have differed perhaps as to the tone of conduct exactly adapted to the securing it."[30]

Like President Washington, Jefferson believed that "the power of making war often prevents it, and in our case would give efficacy to our desire of peace."[31] He understood that war could result both from our own wrongs and from the wrongs of other states, and emphasized to President Madison that "it has a great effect on the opinion of our people and the world to have the moral right on our side."[32]

His strategy was set forth eloquently in a 1785 letter to John Jay, now secretary of state for the Continental Congress: "Justice . . . on our part, will save us from those wars which would have been produced by a contrary disposition. But how to prevent those produced by the wrongs of other nations? By putting ourselves in a condition to punish them. Weakness provokes insult and injury, while a condition to punish it often prevents it. This reasoning leads to the necessity of some naval force, that being the only weapon with which we can reach an enemy. I think it to our interest to punish the first insult: because an insult unpunished is the parent of many others. We are not at this moment in a condition to do it, but we should put ourselves into it as soon as possible."[33]

### Jefferson's Decision to Use the U.S. Navy to Defeat the Barbary Pirates

Jefferson's success in the election of 1800 gave him the opportunity to try the policy of "peace through strength" that he had been advocating throughout his government career. According to his own handwritten notes, his cabinet meeting of 15 May 1801 was devoted to a discussion of whether two-thirds of the new American navy—created by Congress during the Adams administration—should be sent to the Mediterranean to protect American merchant ships. The cabinet unanimously concurred in the desirability of the expedition and also agreed that if, upon arrival at Gibraltar its commander, Captain Richard Dale, learned that war had been declared against the United States, he was to distribute his forces "so as best to protect our commerce & chastise their insolence—by sinking, burning or destroying their ships & Vessels wherever you shall find them."[34]

Captain Dale was a superb choice to head the squadron sent to the Mediterranean, having distinguished himself as first lieutenant to John Paul Jones aboard *Bonhomme Richard.* Tasked with the assignment on 20 May 1801, he departed Hampton Roads on 1 June and reached Gibraltar a month later. (Captain Dale was given the honorary title of "commodore," because he commanded more than one vessel at the same time.)

Reflecting Jefferson's strong commitment to morality and enhancing the rule of law in international relations, Dale was given strict orders to treat any prisoners with compassion, "humanity," and "attention."[35] Shortly thereafter, Cathcart was instructed by Secretary of State Madison to refrain from initiating any negotiations, so that the bashaw would have to make the first move. Madison thought this would discourage any expectations of obtaining "the smallest contribution . . . as the price of peace."[36]

Historians report that the squadron "made a good impression on the Barbary Coast."[37] When it appeared off Tripoli on 24 July "the Pasha was a good deal disturbed and anxious to treat for peace."[38] One week later, the American schooner *Enterprise*, commanded by Lieutenant Andrew Sterrett, won a decisive victory in a three-hour battle with a larger Tripolitan cruiser without a single American casualty.[39]

Unfortunately, for reasons that are beyond the scope of this chapter, when Jefferson reported on Lieutenant Sterrett's engagement in his first annual report to Congress he misrepresented the facts and gave the impression that the absence of congressional authorization for the mission left the squadron with only the power to fend off attacks on American ships.[40] The consensus view of Jefferson's cabinet was that the president needed no specific statutory authority to fight a war initiated or declared by a foreign state.[41]

Indeed, Congress does not appear to have even been formally notified of the dispatch of two-thirds of the nation's navy into harm's way for more than six months, although there is no evidence of any effort to keep the mission a secret and it was widely reported in the press. Nor, for that matter, is there evidence that Congress was unhappy about not having been asked to authorize the initial deployment. While Congress did subsequently enact a variety of statutes authorizing the use of force as requested by Jefferson, few members seemed to view this minor confrontation against pirates as requiring a formal declaration of war. The primary effect of Jefferson's misstatement to Congress has been to mislead future generations of scholars.[42]

### The "Two Years' Sleep" and General William Eaton

A very important lesson to be drawn from Jefferson's war with the Barbary pirates is the importance of strong military leadership. After some initial successes, Commodore Dale returned to Washington in April 1802, just prior to the end of the enlistment period of his crew, and a new squadron—under the command of Captain Richard Morris—was dispatched to the Mediterranean with orders to wage war against Tripoli. Morris had all the social graces and ran a happy ship, but he had no stomach for war in North Africa. Indeed, he did not even set eyes on Tripoli for more than a year, though he had been instructed to blockade the state.

Finally, on 7 June 1803, Morris went ashore under a white flag to talk with the bashaw. Yusuf demanded US$250,000 plus twenty thousand a year and reimbursement for all of the costs of the war. Lacking any authority to negotiate, Morris returned to Gibraltar, where he learned that the frustrated Jefferson had relieved him of command. A board of inquiry later found Morris guilty of gross negligence and recommended that he be court-martialed. Rather than approving the recommendation of the board, the president—who referred to the period as the "two years' sleep"—simply fired Morris and replaced him with William Eaton.[43]

If Captain Richard Morris showed little courage or initiative, William Eaton made up for it in spades. The forty-one-year-old protégé of Timothy Pickering—who had served as secretary of state during the Adams administration—had served as consul at Tunis from 1798 until 1803. He was, to say the least, not disposed to kowtow to Yusuf Karamanli or any other Barbary tyrant. Indeed, he viewed his negotiating instructions under the Adams administration as so offensively weak that he wrote the secretary of state and suggested that his role might be better filled by a slave: "If we will have peace at such a price, recall me, and send a slave, accustomed to abasement, to represent the nation."[44]

More than a century before the more famous British army lieutenant Thomas Edward Lawrence—"Lawrence of Arabia"—achieved legendary status promoting revolution in Iraq and Saudi Arabia, William Eaton learned the languages and culture of North Africa and attired himself in flowing Arab robes, inspiring those who served under him to follow him and making converts of people who at first dismissed him as an impractical dreamer. One biographer reports that Eaton "spoke at least four Arab dialects without an accent."[45] First Lieutenant P. N. O'Bannon, commander of a Marine detachment that followed "General" Eaton (as he was hereafter known, though his highest actual army commission, before his consulship had been as a captain) into war, wrote: "Wherever General Eaton leads, we will follow. If he wants to march us to hell, we'll gladly go there."[46]

When in early 1801, as noted above, the bashaw of Tripoli sent his army commander, a renegade Scotsman named Lisle, to inform Consul Cathcart that the door of the palace was closed to him until the bashaw was given "his due," Eaton had been present, and what happened next has been described by one of his biographers: "The bullying was more than William could tolerate. 'Lisle,' he said, addressing him in English, 'if any harm comes to Mr. Cathcart, I give you my solemn, personal word of honor that I shall hunt you down, put a noose around your neck and hang you from the nearest palm tree. If I can, I shall do it with the aid of the United States Army and Navy. If possible, I shall also enlist the services of the Royal Navy, which has grown tired of the blustering of a traitor. But, if necessary, I shall do it alone!'"[47]

On 1 August 1802—a year to the day after Lieutenant Sterrett won his naval victory—William Eaton achieved a similar success without a single ship under his command by simply announcing in Tunis, without the slightest authority, that Tripoli was in a state of blockade. Afraid of a run-in with American warships, merchant shipmasters simply refused to accept cargo bound for Tripoli. When Commodore Dale, who had returned to the United States, learned of this initiative he strongly approved. Eaton later wrote the Speaker of the House of Representatives in Washington: "I kept the enemy three months in a state of blockade when we had not a ship of war within three hundred leagues from his port; his chief commerce and whole supplies of provisions depending on Tunis."[48]

### Forming Alliances with Your Enemy's Enemy

Eaton's greatest achievement was originally suggested by James Cathcart—an incredible land attack against Tripoli, to be led by Yusuf's exiled elder brother Hamet. It reflects an important understanding about incentive structures: if one wants to get the bashaw of Tripoli to make concessions, success is more likely if the bashaw perceives that he has something valuable at risk should the quarrel go badly. Cathcart and Eaton proposed to locate the bashaw's elder brother, Hamet Karamanli, and signal Yusuf that if he did not immediately make peace and release all American hostages he risked losing his job and perhaps his life to the rightful heir to the throne.

Eaton first raised the idea of using Hamet to put pressure on Yusuf with Secretary of State Madison in a letter dated 5 September 1801. In 1803, he returned to the United States to plead his case in person. It is clear that Jefferson and Madison approved the idea of making some use of Hamet, at least in general terms, but they apparently sought to keep what in a more recent era would be called "plausible deniability" and so left much of the detail to Eaton's discretion. Historians who have examined the record are divided over whether Jefferson or Madison knew of and actually approved what ultimately occurred. While several writers assert that the Hamet expedition was specifically approved by Washington, Jefferson's biographer Merrill Peterson argues that the president "refused to endorse" Eaton's "audacious plan . . . to lead a motley insurrectionary army overland against Tripoli."[49] Historian Henry Adams may have captured the reality in noting that Eaton's orders were "vague."[50]

Whatever Jefferson's intention, near the end of 1803 Eaton was appointed naval agent for the United States on the Barbary Coast and was promised forty thousand dollars to further some sort of operation involving Hamet. In furtherance of Eaton's plan, Commodore Barron instructed Lieutenant Isaac Hull to lead a group of Marines to accompany Eaton to Alexandria, Egypt, to try to locate Hamet. Hull and his party were instructed to "disguise the true object" of their mission, pretending to be on leave. In late February, Eaton made contact with Hamet and offered to assist him in regaining his throne, promising a sum of money as well to secure Hamet's cooperation. The two entered into a "convention" that provided in part: "The government of the United States shall use their utmost exertions so far as comports with their own honor and interest, their subsisting treaties and the acknowledged law of nations, to reestablish the said Hamet Pasha in the possession of his sovereignty of Tripoli."[51]

While some historians have observed that this agreement exceeded Eaton's instructions, it is difficult to interpret the actual language used as committing the United States to do anything it did not conclude to be in its "interest." In addition to initiating a covert operation with Hamet, to gain the cooperation of Tunis Eaton quietly promised its chief minister a payment of ten thousand dollars if the operation succeeded. This idea too apparently originated with James Cathcart.

The dozen Americans then put together a motley band of roughly five hundred Arab and Greek mercenaries from about a dozen countries, and in early March 1805 the party set out on a five-hundred-mile march across the Western Desert to Tripoli. As it traveled, the force grew to between six hundred and seven hundred fighting men, with roughly another five hundred family members and "camp followers" bringing up the rear.

Eaton's leadership skills were frequently put to the test during the arduous trip. As food and water supplies dwindled and the heat took its toll, there were demands for additional payments and threats of desertion. Eaton at one point cut off rations to the Arabs to end a threatened mutiny, and when Hamet refused to continue Eaton marched off into the desert without him—to be joined by a frustrated Hamet two hours later. The situation worsened on 15 April, when the force arrived at Bomba to find that the promised American warships had not arrived. However, *Argus* arrived early the next morning, and the next day *Hornet* brought additional food and military supplies.

On 25 April the band completed the sixty-mile march from Bomba to Derne, the second-largest city in Tripoli, and learned that two-thirds of the city inhabitants were ready to welcome Hamet as their rightful leader. Knowing that the town was defended by a force of eight hundred and that Yusuf's army was about to arrive from Tripoli, Eaton sent a message to the governor under a flag of truce offering terms in the hope of avoiding further bloodshed. Receiving in reply a message saying, "My head or yours," Eaton's force commenced an attack.[52] The governor fled, and Eaton's army soon took the city. Days later, Yusuf's army of twelve hundred arrived from Tripoli and attacked Eaton's army, but after Eaton's men demonstrated the accuracy of American cannon fire, Yusuf's men quickly lost their stomach for war. Eaton's army was prepared to move on Tripoli with the support of offshore American naval fire when his entire operation was undermined from Washington.

From the start, one of the strongest critics of Eaton's plan was Colonel Tobias Lear, the U.S. consul in Algiers, who believed that Hamet was simply too weak to be a viable ally against Yusuf and that the long march across the desert could not possibly succeed. Government leaders in Washington had no way of following Eaton's progress and did not know that Commodore Edward Preble was doing a brilliant job of putting pressure on Tripoli. Indeed, Preble's blockade was so effective that the Barbary pirates had been shut down completely for months. But at the end of October 1803, the frigate *Philadelphia* ran aground off Tripoli in strong winds and was captured by the pirates.

News of this setback was a shock to Jefferson and no doubt contributed to the decision to authorize Lear to pursue a diplomatic solution in Tripoli. In fact, three months after it was captured, *Philadelphia* was burned in a daring raid, led by Lieutenant (later Commodore) Stephen Decatur, in which scores of pirates were killed without a single American fatality and only one American sailor was slightly wounded. Professor Forrest McDonald notes: "Lord Admiral Horatio Nelson, the greatest sailor of the entire era of fighting sail, called Decatur's raid 'the most bold and daring act of the age.'"[53] But by the time news of Decatur's heroic escapade reached Washington, Lear had already been authorized to seek a negotiated peace.

On 11 June 1805, *Constellation* arrived off Derne with a message from Commodore Rodgers informing Eaton that a peace treaty had been signed on 5 June by Lear and Yusuf. Eaton was ordered to withdraw all the Christians and Hamet's party immediately; the Arab mercenaries were to be left ashore, abandoned to their fate. Historians disagree about whether they were thereafter immediately slaughtered or allowed to return home, but this aspect of the operation was hardly a high point of American honor.

Even though his operation was terminated before achieving total victory, Eaton's bold adventure had a great influence on the outcome of the war. Two days passed between the arrival of *Hornet* with authorization for Lear to begin negotiations and Yusuf Bashaw's signing of a peace treaty aboard *Constitution*. Six months earlier, before Eaton's expedition with Yusuf's brother, the Spanish consul in Tripoli had sent word to Lear that the United States could probably negotiate a favorable treaty. By the time Yusuf learned of Eaton's expedition, Yusuf was genuinely concerned and therefore even more willing to negotiate. When Lear presented a draft peace treaty, Yusuf agreed immediately to sign it, asking only the addition of one article promising that Eaton would be withdrawn immediately and would no longer provide any support to Yusuf's domestic enemies.[54]

The treaty was unprecedented in the relations of Western nations with the Barbary pirates. Even before Lear's arrival, the bashaw had reduced the price of peace from three million dollars to sixty thousand, but when Lear presented him with a draft that provided for no payment and no annual tribute it was promptly accepted. The treaty provided for the immediate exchange of all prisoners; since the bashaw held three hundred Americans while the Americans had only one hundred Tripolitans, Lear agreed to a payment of sixty thousand dollars for the difference.[55] The treaty further provided that in the event of future war, prisoners would be exchanged rather than enslaved and that the party holding more prisoners would be compensated at a fixed rate, depending upon each prisoner's rank.[56]

Additional provision was made for the punishment of Tripolitan ship commanders who subjected any American to abuse or plundered property.[57] On 12 April 1806—only hours before President Jefferson's sixty-third birthday celebration—the Senate gave its consent to ratification by a vote of twenty-one to eight. President Thomas Jefferson quickly ratified the treaty.

Conclusions

In retrospect, Jefferson and Madison may have erred in undermining Eaton's bold adventure, although any difference in the final outcome probably would not have justified the additional loss of life that might have accompanied an attack on Tripoli. Scholars have speculated that Lear could have had a treaty without paying Yusuf sixty thousand dollars for the release of the three hundred American prisoners, and they are quite possibly right. Had President Jefferson and Secretary of State Madison been in possession of more timely and accurate information about the situation in the

Mediterranean, and had they been able to communicate on a real-time basis with
Eaton and Lear, perhaps they would have taken a firmer stand.

Although bitter and feeling betrayed, Eaton returned to the United States as a hero and
for many months was feted at receptions around the nation. The Massachusetts legisla-
ture granted him ten thousand acres in what is now Maine, and Congress voted to settle his account equitably and to grant a small sum as well to Hamet. When Congress
learned of the details of the covert operation that contributed to the peace, the only
criticism voiced was that Hamet had been treated shabbily—although he had obtained
the release of his wife and family from Yusuf pursuant to the treaty of peace—and that
the abandonment of the Arab mercenaries might make it more difficult to recruit such
forces in the future should that ever become desirable.

But it is noteworthy that no one in Congress criticized the administration for sending
two-thirds of the American navy to attack foreign ships without notifying Congress.
More broadly, this American venture sent shock waves across Europe and throughout
the other Barbary states. Later in the Second Barbary (or Algerine) War, Stephen
Decatur was sent back to the Mediterranean with a squadron to demand that Algiers
abandon its efforts to extract tribute from the United States. When the dey asked for
time to consider the demand, Decatur responded: "Not a minute." The dey thereupon
accepted the American demand—his concession was quickly followed by those of the
other Barbary states. Emboldened European leaders quickly announced their own
refusal to continue paying tribute, and centuries of terror on the high seas soon came
to an end.[58]

Jefferson was correct that deterrence should be the ultimate goal, but he also observed,
"An insult unpunished is the parent of many others."[59] If there is one lesson to be
learned from Jefferson's success against the state-sponsored Barbary pirates, it is the
importance of creating appropriate disincentives. In this case, persuading Yusuf
Karamanli that his own interests were at stake made a crucial difference. In the final
determination, deterring pirate leaders is the only way to ensure the end of piracy.

---

**Notes**

This chapter is based in part upon an earlier essay
by the author that appeared under the title "State
Responsibility and the War on Terror: The Legacy
of Thomas Jefferson and the Barbary Pirates" in
*Chicago Journal of International Law* 4 (2003), pp.
121–40.

    1. Jefferson to William Short, 28 July 1791, in
*The Papers of Thomas Jefferson,* ed. Julian P.

Boyd and Ruth W. Lester (Princeton, N.J.:
Princeton Univ. Press, 1982), vol. 20, pp.
686–88.

    2. Jefferson to James Monroe, 24 October 1823,
in *The Writings of Thomas Jefferson,* ed. Andrew A. Lipscomb and Albert Ellery Bergh
(Washington, D.C.: Thomas Jefferson

Memorial Association, 1903), vol. 15, pp. 477–78.

3. Jefferson to Tench Coxe, 1 May 1794, in ibid., vol. 9, pp. 284–85. Later, as president, Jefferson sought to stave off war by persuading Congress to enact the Embargo Act of 1807.

4. Merrill D. Peterson, *Thomas Jefferson and the New Nation* (New York: Oxford Univ. Press, 1970), pp. 310–11.

5. For increase in American commerce, Ray W. Irwin, *The Diplomatic Relations of the United States with the Barbary Powers, 1776–1816* (Chapel Hill: Univ. of North Carolina Press, 1931), p. 101. For "ounce of shot," Stanley Lane-Poole, *The Story of the Barbary Corsairs* (New York: G. P. Putnam, 1890), p. 274.

6. Peterson, *Thomas Jefferson and the New Nation,* pp. 310–11.

7. Ibid., p. 311.

8. Joel S. Sorkin, "The Piratical Ensigns of Mahomet," *National Review,* 28 March 1986, pp. 50, 52.

9. Lane-Poole, *Story of the Barbary Corsairs,* p. 275.

10. For useful background on this period, see Gardner W. Allen, *Our Navy and the Barbary Corsairs* (New York: Houghton Mifflin, 1905), pp. 88–89, and Francis Rennell Rodd, *General William Eaton: The Failure of an Idea* (n.p.: Minton, Balch, 1932), p. 59.

11. Donald Barr Chidsey, *The Wars in Barbary: Arab Piracy and the Birth of the United States Navy* (New York: Crown, 1971), p. 60.

12. Samuel Edwards, *Barbary General: The Life of William H. Eaton* (Englewood Cliffs, N.J.: Prentice Hall, 1968), p. 84.

13. "Treaty of Peace and Friendship," art. 1, 8 Stat 154, 154 (1797). Also, see *Journal of the Executive Proceedings of the Senate of the United States of America, 1789–1805* (7 June 1797), available at memory.loc.gov/.

14. "Treaty of Peace and Friendship," art. 10.

15. "In case of any dispute arising from the violation of any of the articles of this treaty, no appeal shall be made to arms; nor shall war be declared on any pretext whatever. But if the consul residing at the place where the dispute shall happen, shall not be able to settle the same, an amicable reference shall be made to the mutual friend of the parties, the Dey of Algiers, the parties hereby engaging to abide by his decision." Ibid., art. 12.

16. Receipt available at Yale Law School, Lillian Goldman Law Library, *The Avalon Project: Documents in Law, History, and Diplomacy,* avalon.law.yale.edu/18th_century/bar1796t.asp.

17. Note available at *Avalon Project,* avalon.law.yale.edu/18th_century/bar1796t.asp.

18. Edwards, *Barbary General,* p. 86.

19. Irwin, *Diplomatic Relations of the United States with the Barbary Powers,* p. 97.

20. Allen, *Our Navy and the Barbary Corsairs,* p. 35.

21. Irwin, *Diplomatic Relations of the United States with the Barbary Powers,* p. 46.

22. Jefferson to John Page, 20 August 1785, in *The Papers of Thomas Jefferson,* ed. Julian P. Boyd, Mina R. Bryan, and Elizabeth L. Hutter (Princeton, N.J.: Princeton Univ. Press, 1953), vol. 8, pp. 417–19.

23. John Adams to Jefferson, 3 July 1785, quoted in Allen, *Our Navy and the Barbary Corsairs,* pp. 36–37.

24. See, for example, Thomas Jefferson, *Report [to Congress] on American Trade in the Mediterranean* (28 December 1790), in *The Papers of Thomas Jefferson,* ed. Julian P. Boyd, Ruth W. Lester, and Lucius Wilmerding, Jr. (Princeton, N.J.: Princeton Univ. Press, 1971), vol. 18, p. 423.

25. Irwin, *The Diplomatic Relations of the United States With the Barbary Powers,* p. 47. See Jefferson to John Adams, 11 July 1786, in *The Papers of Thomas Jefferson,* ed. Julian P. Boyd, Mina R. Bryan, and Fredrick Aandahl (Princeton, N.J.: Princeton Univ. Press, 1954), vol. 10, p. 123.

26. Jefferson to Wilson Cary Nicholas, 11 June 1801, in *The Writings of Thomas Jefferson,* ed. Paul Leicester Ford (New York: G. P. Putnam, 1897), vol. 8, pp. 62–63.

27. See William Kirk Woolery, *The Relation of Thomas Jefferson to American Foreign Policy* (Baltimore, Md.: Johns Hopkins Univ. Press, 1927), pp. 29–33.

28. Thomas Jefferson, "Proposals for Concerted Operation among the Powers at War with the Piratical States of Barbary," November 1786, in *Writings of Thomas Jefferson,* ed. Lipscomb and Bergh, vol. 17, pp. 145–46.

29. Ibid., pp. 147–48.

30. Jefferson to James Monroe, 28 June 1793, in *The Papers of Thomas Jefferson,* ed. John Catanzariti and Eugene R. Sheridan (Princeton, N.J.: Princeton Univ. Press, 1995), vol. 26, p. 392.

31. Jefferson to George Washington, 4 December 1788, in *The Papers of Thomas Jefferson,* ed. Julian P. Boyd, William H. Gaines, Jr., and Joseph H. Harrison, Jr. (Princeton, N.J.: Princeton Univ. Press, 1958), vol. 14, p. 328. This letter was mistakenly dated 4 November 1788 by Jefferson, who corrected his error in a subsequent letter of 5 December 1788 (ibid., p. 336). See also Jefferson to James Monroe, 11 July 1790, reprinted as "Whatever enables us to go to war, secures our peace" in *The Papers of Thomas Jefferson,* ed. Julian P. Boyd and Lucius Wilmerding, Jr. (Princeton, N.J.: Princeton Univ. Press, 1965), vol. 17, p. 25.

32. Jefferson to James Madison, 19 April 1809, in *Writings of Thomas Jefferson,* ed. Lipscomb and Bergh, vol. 12, pp. 273–74.

33. Jefferson to John Jay, 23 August 1785, in *Papers of Thomas Jefferson,* ed. Boyd, Bryan, and Hutter, vol. 8, pp. 426–27.

34. Samuel Smith to Richard Dale, 20 May 1801, in *Naval Documents Related to the United States Wars with the Barbary Powers,* ed. Claude A. Swanson (Washington, D.C.: U.S. Government Printing Office, 1939), vol. 1, pp. 465–67.

35. Allen, *Our Navy and the Barbary Corsairs,* p. 93; Rodd, *General William Eaton,* p. 73.

36. Irwin, *Diplomatic Relations of the United States with the Barbary Powers,* p. 113.

37. Rodd, *General William Eaton,* p. 77.

38. Allen, *Our Navy and the Barbary Corsairs,* p. 95.

39. This encounter was at the heart of Jefferson's 8 December 1801 report to Congress in his first annual message, but Jefferson's portrayal of Lieutenant Sterrett's orders was both at odds with the decision of his cabinet the previous March and clearly contrary to the actual orders found in naval records. See Robert F. Turner, "War and the Forgotten Executive Power Clause," *Virginia Journal of International Law* (1994), vol. 34, p. 903.

40. For a general discussion of Jefferson's reasons, see ibid., pp. 910–15. See Thomas Jefferson, *First Annual Message to Congress* (8 December 1801), quoted in ibid., pp. 910–11.

41. See Turner, "War and the Forgotten Executive Power Clause," pp. 912–13.

42. Among the dozens of scholars who have relied upon Jefferson's first annual message to Congress as evidence that Commodore Dale sailed to the Mediterranean with very limited authority, see generally Forrest McDonald, *The Presidency of Thomas Jefferson* (Lawrence: Univ. Press of Kansas, 1976), p. 61; Rodd, *General William Eaton,* p. 80; Lane-Poole, *Story of the Barbary Corsairs,* p. 276; and Chidsey, *Wars in Barbary,* p. 75.

43. Henry Adams, *History of the United States of America during the First Administration of Thomas Jefferson* (New York: Scribner's, 1889), vol. 2, p. 137; Peterson, *Thomas Jefferson and the New Nation,* pp. 798–99; Chidsey, *Wars in Barbary,* pp. 83–84.

44. Chidsey, *Wars in Barbary,* p. 68.

45. Edwards, *Barbary General,* p. 5.

46. Ibid., p. 3; Eaton's highest government rank had been captain in the Army, but he acquired the "courtesy" title as a result of his exploits in North Africa.

47. Ibid., p. 86.

48. Irwin, *Diplomatic Relations of the United States with the Barbary Powers,* p. 110.

49. Peterson, *Thomas Jefferson and the New Nation,* p. 799. But compare Irwin, *Diplomatic Relations of the United States with the Barbary Powers,* p. 143.

50. Henry Adams, *The Formative Years: A History of the United States of America during the Administrations of Jefferson and Madison* (London: Collins, 1948), vol. 1, p. 283.

51. Allen, *Our Navy and the Barbary Corsairs,* p. 231.

52. Rodd, *General William Eaton,* p. 233.

53. McDonald, *Presidency of Thomas Jefferson,* p. 78.

54. Irwin, *Diplomatic Relations of the United States with the Barbary Powers,* p. 152. According to Adams: "Immediately upon hearing that his troops had failed to retake Derne, he entered into negotiations with Tobias Lear, the American consul-general at Algiers, who had come to Tripoli for the purpose; and on this occasion the Pasha negotiated with all the rapidity that could be wished. [On] June 3, 1805, he submitted to the disgrace of making peace without being

expressly paid for it" (Adams, *The Formative Years,* vol. 1, p. 285).

55. "Treaty of Peace and Amity," art. 2, 8 Stat 214 (1805).

56. Ibid., art. 16.

57. Ibid., art. 6.

58. John W. Foster, *A Century of American Diplomacy: Being a Brief Review of the Foreign Relations of the United States, 1776–1876* (New York: Houghton Mifflin, 1900), pp. 207–208; Lane-Poole, *Story of the Barbary Corsairs,* p. 291.

59. Jefferson to John Jay, 23 August 1785, in *Papers of Thomas Jefferson,* ed. Boyd, Bryan, and Hutter, vol. 8, pp. 426–27.

# CHAPTER ELEVEN

# The Limits of Naval Power
## The Merchant Brig *Three Sisters,* Riff Pirates, and British Battleships

ANDREW LAMBERT

This chapter examines a nineteenth-century British response to piracy on a major Mediterranean trade route. While the Riff pirates were only a minor irritant, Britain could not stop them without deploying a significant naval and military force ashore, an option that risked opening the complex and dangerous issues connecting Britain, France, and Spain with Morocco, Algeria, and Gibraltar—issues the British preferred to leave alone. The only other naval response, catching the pirates red-handed and administering local chastisement, proved inconclusive.

Between 1846 and 1856, eight ships were attacked off the Moroccan Mediterranean coast—six British, one French, and one Prussian: *Ruth,* 30 March 1846 (crew escaped); *Three Sisters,* 2 November 1848 (crew escaped); *Violet,* 5–6 October 1851; *Flora* (Prussian), December 1852; *Cuthbert Young,* 21 June 1854 (crew escaped); *Jeune Dieppois* (French), 8 April 1855; *Lively,* 2 May 1855 (crew escaped); and *Hymen,* 14 May 1856. In addition, a large number of Spanish coasters and boats were taken. A similar surge of piracy in 1834–35 had been ended by the military intervention of the Moroccan sultanate.[1]

The British, French, and Prussian governments considered a range of naval and military options, but the problem was ultimately resolved once again by Moroccan forces. In part this outcome reflected mutual forbearance by London and Paris, for whom Morocco served as a vital buffer between French-occupied Algeria and the strategic British base at Gibraltar. One enduring lesson of this case study is that because pirates—like all other people—must live on the land, it is on the land that they must often be stopped; naval power alone is not sufficient to fight piracy.

## The Riff Pirates

The Riff coast—the Mediterranean coast of Morocco, roughly between Ceuta and Melilla, on Cape Tres Forcas—was an obvious location for pirates, since it was isolated, extremely poor, and yet close to attractive markets. Most Riff (Berber) tribes found smuggling more attractive than piracy, and the governor of Gibraltar was only too pleased to welcome the cargoes they carried.[2] Many of the small sailing vessels that worked along the shore were smuggling weapons into Algeria or tobacco and other luxury goods into Spain. They hugged the shore to evade Spanish coast guards and the French navy.[3] Not a few of these ships were owned by and operated out of Gibraltar, as Spain and France recognized. Even late in the nineteenth century the Riffs were happy to seize the occasional Spanish smuggler.[4] Riff fishing boats, forty feet by six feet, rowing up to sixteen oars, were large enough for smuggling and localized piracy. Sailing ships passing the Strait of Gibraltar to enter the Mediterranean were liable, if they did not keep north of the island of Alboran, to find themselves taken up by a southerly current and becalmed close by the Guelaya Peninsula, within easy range of Bu Gafar rowing boats and the heavily armed men who owned them. The Banu Bu Gafar depended on fishing and coastal trade for their livelihood. In the 1830s the French occupied Algeria, disrupting coastal trade, and the Spanish stepped up their attacks on Riff coastal shipping. This removed an obvious outlet for commerce and threatened the seafaring population. The Spanish attacks would be extended to fishing boats and small craft in 1854, paralyzing the Moroccan coast. Half the piratical attacks occurred at this time. Although there was no direct link between Spanish activity and piracy, the seized vessels were not owned by the Bu Gafar; nonetheless, the Spanish presence remained a significant factor. Cut off from opportunities for legitimate trade, they found temptation hard to resist.

The Bu Gafar who attacked the ship *Ruth* were one of many tribes on this coast collectively known as Riff pirates. They towed their prizes to one of the narrow beaches between Cape Tres Forcas and Azanen Bay before stripping them of cargo, equipment, and recoverable metals and burning the hulks. If a crew was taken, so much the better, since its members could be ransomed through the European representatives at Tangier—rather than the distant Moroccan government. However, as noted, the crews from four of the six British ships taken between 1846 and 1856 did not wait to be attacked but escaped by boat. Together with the essentially commercial nature of the ransom process, this suggests that other factors might have been operating, that perhaps the crews colluded with the pirates.

When the inevitable naval vessel turned up to recover a captured ship or simply bring down righteous indignation upon the locals, it soon discovered an uncomfortable truth. The British had little knowledge of the area, lacking accurate maps and reliable charts. The Bu Gafar villages were almost impossible to locate, often out of sight and invulnerable to bombardment, as were their boats, which the Riff buried in the sand or hid in caves. The coast was dominated by cliffs, a marked advantage for the defenders in a firefight.[5] The same vantage point enabled the Riffs to spot approaching warships with their excellent telescopes and then to use signal fires to communicate orders.

Once they had spotted a likely target, the Riff pirates had sufficient arms to capture their prize. In particular, they possessed the locally manufactured long-barrel Riff musket.[6] A rather chastened naval report of 1846 noted: "The Reef [Riff] musket will carry half as far again as an English musket and the Reefians are good marksmen & known to be the most warlike and daring race in Morocco."[7] Nor were their weapons restricted to muskets: in 1848, the steam sloop HMS *Polyphemus* came under fire from a well handled cannon, which the sultan of Morocco had sent for use against the Spanish.

While the depredations of the Riff pirates were on the whole small in scale and irregular, the sultan proved unable to deal with them. Britain preferred not to press the issue, having no desire to add to Morocco's problems or to give France an excuse to act on a coast close to Gibraltar. Consequently, the standard British response to incidents of piracy in the strait was to send a warship, recover the prize, and chastise the insolent barbarians.

In May 1846, when the Riff captured the British merchant brig *Ruth,* the governor of Gibraltar dispatched the brig HMS *Fantome,* under the command of Commander Frederick Nicolson. On 12 May 1846, Nicolson located the pirates near Cape Tres Forcas, where they had dragged the ship ashore to plunder the cargo. Nicolson landed, drove the pirates off the beach, and recovered *Ruth,* along with part of the cargo. Several pirates were killed, while the British lost one dead and eight wounded.

Nicolson's zeal was rewarded; he was promoted to captain, his first lieutenant became a commander, and prize money was distributed among the crew. However, his commander in chief on the Mediterranean station, Admiral Sir William Parker, was not impressed. The operation had been brave and resolute, but as *Ruth* was a "valueless wreck . . . I cannot but regret that a conflict for the possession of it was risked, as the habits of the Moors were not only known, but the consequences of attempting it anticipated." It would have been far better, he was convinced, to have demanded restitution through the proper authorities.[8]

The contrast between Nicolson's bloody action and Parker's cautious reserve was significant. An old hand on the international stage, Parker understood that armed force was a tool of limited utility in such situations. Whatever Nicolson might have thought, the

Riff pirates had probably congratulated themselves on driving off the infidel and having retained most of their ill-gotten gains.

When pressed for compensation for *Ruth,* the sultan professed his inability to punish
the Riffs. The British were anxious not to put pressure on Morocco while the French
war with Abd al Qadir in Algeria was still in progress. Then the local Moroccan governor intervened, inflicting enough "punishment" to satisfy John Drummond Hay, the
British consul at Tangier. However, the sultan was officially warned that should any
more such acts occur the British would take measures into their own hands.[9] Basing a
steam warship at Gibraltar provided the navy with a superior instrument to meet the
pirate challenge. Steamers could ignore wind and tide, approach the coast at speed,
and select the best position for coastal bombardment or use their large paddle-box
boats for amphibious warfare.

### The Capture of the Brig *Three Sisters*

On 31 October 1848, the Liverpool-registered merchant brig *Three Sisters* left Gibraltar
for Malta, loaded with baled fabrics and a large quantity of gunpowder. The Canadian-
built, 134-ton vessel was owned by the master, mate, and other small investors. Normally engaged in the Liverpool–Demerara trade, *Three Sisters* was out of its normal
routine.[10] Furthermore, it was not insured. The consignee was the Gibraltar firm of
James Glasgow and Company.

On 2 November 1848, *Three Sisters* was attacked by several boats from the Riff coast.
When the pirates opened fire, the crew tumbled into a boat and rowed out to sea. The
pirates towed *Three Sisters* ashore. The crew, picked up by a passing merchant ship the
next morning, reached Gibraltar on the 7th. Significantly, the governor's first concern
was to establish that their cargo had been legitimate. Once that had been attested by the
consignees, General Sir Robert Wilson, the governor of Gibraltar, referred the case to
Drummond Hay, expecting him to make representations to the Moroccan government,
and requested Commander James McCleverty of *Polyphemus* to convey that message to
Tangier.

McCleverty refused, instead proceeding immediately to the scene of the crime.[11] Early
the following morning *Polyphemus* ran into Al Khoyamich Bay, then cruised east
toward Cape Tres Forcas. On the morning of 8 November 1848, as he cleared Cala
Tramontana, McCleverty sighted the prize, pulled up on the beach and surrounded
by seven Riff boats, below prominent cliffs occupied by an estimated five hundred
armed men.

*Polyphemus* steamed into range, and the pirates opened fire, only to be driven from
their positions by well directed grapeshot, canister, and musketry. When the Riffs fell

back, a boarding party managed to weigh the brig's anchor, and *Polyphemus* began to tow it out to sea. The Riffs opened fire with a small cannon, which the sloop could not counter, and renewed musketry. Five sailors were wounded. In the face of a numerous, well armed enemy, McCleverty abandoned his original intention of landing to burn the pirate boats, determining that they were not worth the inevitable loss of life, and carried on with his prize to Gibraltar.[12]

The brig had been stripped "of all her sails, running ropes and in fact every portable thing on deck. The hold was broken open and a large part of the cargo . . . taken out."[13] On arrival at Gibraltar, it was discovered that the pirates had unloaded 850 kegs of gunpowder and a considerable quantity of cloth. They had not troubled themselves with four hundred barrels of herring, fifteen hogsheads of tobacco, two tons of cocoa, or twenty tons of coal.

The news of the *Three Sisters* affair found Admiral Parker tied up by the interminable, distressing politics of Naples and Sicily. He had no ships to spare and knew that his next move would be eastward to the Aegean, to support Turkey, not westward to chastise a few Riff plunderers. From the *Ruth* incident he knew that the sultan would disclaim responsibility, and he rejoiced that *Three Sisters* had been recovered. He praised Commander McCleverty for ignoring the governor's orders to contact Drummond Hay and for deciding not to land.[14] As this incident showed, the British, with a steam sloop stationed at Gibraltar, could respond quickly, catching culprits red-handed before any other power could act. The last thing they wanted was French military "help" to control Moroccan pirates, as the pretext for an invasion of the sultanate.

### Napier's Mission to Resolve the Trade Dispute

The foreign secretary, Lord Palmerston, was anxious to read the Riffs a lesson.[15] He took advantage of the fact that the Admiralty had ordered the Royal Navy's Western Squadron south to reinforce the Mediterranean Fleet, in response to a French buildup. Palmerston, who had directed Lord Auckland, First Lord of the Admiralty, to deploy the squadron to support his demands in the claims of a British trading firm, Redman Brothers, now belatedly added the pirate question to the mission.[16] The *Three Sisters* incident only complicated the situation: the trade dispute might be resolved by blockading major ports, like Mogador (modern Essaouira, on the Atlantic coast) and Tangier, but Riff piracy required local action.

The Admiralty had a good understanding of this coast, and Auckland evinced no enthusiasm for offensive operations: "The season of the year is not favourable to an attack upon Mogador, and the Riff coast is scarcely under the control of the Emperor [sultan], and operations there as likely to be profitless and dangerous; but perhaps something may be done with light steamers, to show the barbarians of that coast that they are amenable to punishment."[17] As Auckland informed the commander of the Western Squadron, Vice Admiral Sir Charles Napier:

> 1st You must endeavour to sweep the coast with light craft from Tetuan to Melilla, and destroy all boats. I fear, however, that from the nature of the coast this would be a very difficult and hazardous operation, and it would be probably very unprofitable
>
> 2nd You might attempt the blockade of the ports on the Western Coast. I fear at this season of the year it would be impossible to do this effectually.
>
> 3rd You might knock Tangiers or Mogador to pieces; but this would be violent, and not to be thought of for a first proceeding.

Auckland favored applying pressure by sending a powerful force to Mogador, but this would not solve the Riff question.[18] Little wonder the official orders were vague: Napier was left to chastise the pirates, if he thought it possible and the means at his disposal adequate. His discretion was carefully constrained by the overriding political imperative to avoid war or any occasion for other powers to act. In the course of a morale-boosting endorsement of Napier's abilities, longtime friend and supporter Palmerston demonstrated that the obscure mission statement had originated in the Foreign Office. Indeed Palmerston was "perfectly content" to "wait till the spring brings better weather" rather than run any risks with Napier's warships.[19]

For the moment, the squadron was trapped at Spithead by southerly gales. Napier saw an opportunity to reinforce his claim to the prestigious Mediterranean command, which would soon be vacant.[20] There was an opening for his preferred methods of rapid, decisive action, and there was danger in prolonged routine: "I hope to be allowed to make short work with the Moors if they are saucy and refuse satisfaction. Blockading is slow punishment at this season of the year, and an uncertain one."[21]

Although obliged to rein in Napier's enthusiasm, Auckland took care to be positive: "I am satisfied that you could and would bring the Moors to reason with strong means, but we must try gentle means in the beginning, backed by strong appearances."[22] Napier was quickly in his stride, requesting charts of Tangier and Mogador to supplement official reports.[23] Auckland warned that the Atlantic coast was too dangerous for sustained operations between November and April, while the inhospitable Riff coast, in the Mediterranean, could only be approached by steamers (which could readily escape the danger of embayment or grounding on a lee shore) and offered few obvious points for an attack.[24]

Arriving at Lisbon on 4 January 1849, Napier opened communications with Drummond Hay at Tangier. From the information sent by the Admiralty he concluded: "It appears to me best to leave the Line of Battle Ships at Gibraltar, take all the small craft and marines and destroy every boat on the Riff coast. . . . I don't much like establishing a blockade on the west coast because it would create alarm, and give them time to prepare against an attack."[25] Rather than risk a long, boring, and forgettable blockade, Napier would have his powerful flagship towed up to the walls of Mogador and with its guns batter them down. He asked Drummond Hay for information on the defenses of Tangier. This was not the approach Drummond Hay favored; he reported that the sultan would give way to an appropriate show of force.[26]

Unfortunately for Napier, Lord Auckland died suddenly just before the New Year. This left the Admiralty to be administered by the First Naval Lord, Vice Admiral Sir James Dundas, a desk admiral whose limited seagoing experience was compensated for by a central role in Liberal party politics. Auckland's planned drive for overall economies was pursued after his death without much thought for the wider consequences. To reduce three thousand men from the estimates Napier's squadron was to be abolished before the end of March—so much for operations on the Riff coast in May. The run-down began on 11 January, when the battleship HMS *Rodney* was ordered home to pay off "immediately."[27] It was in question whether Napier could do anything before his force evaporated. Sir Francis Baring was appointed First Lord on 16 January but took control only after being reelected to his seat in the House of Commons on 6 February.[28] In the meantime, the Admiralty remained devoted to routine—not that Napier antici-pated much when Baring returned, the two men having been electoral rivals at Portsmouth fifteen years before.

Depressed by the loss of his patron Auckland, Napier sailed for Gibraltar on 18 January 1849. He arrived on the 27th after a rough passage that mirrored his mood. The next mail brought worse news. The Admiralty had canceled a projected visit to Santa Cruz de Tenerife, directing him to call at Madeira and then return to Lisbon "without delay." A private letter from Dundas came as a hammer blow: Admiral Parker would be given a second tour as commander in chief in the Mediterranean. To make matters worse, he added, "You will not attempt anything against Morocco without further orders and this I know is the wish of Sir F Baring and the Government."[29] Baring, the new First Lord, would continue his predecessor's cautious approach—he had no intention of ordering Napier to act—and he had far less tact. Reappointing Parker was highly unusual but was perfectly logical; the Mediterranean remained tense, and Parker had shown a remarkably astute touch.

On the 31st Napier opened a private correspondence with Baring, reporting that Drummond Hay was to call upon him in Gibraltar and that when he did, they would concert plans for operations on the Riff and Atlantic coasts.[30] He sent another letter to Baring and Palmerston, asking for the Mediterranean command.[31] Napier and Drummond Hay met on the flagship, after which Drummond Hay departed in the steam frigate HMS *Sidon* to make a final demand on the Moroccan foreign minister at Laraiche to settle the Redman affair. Aware of the alarm spreading through the Moroccan ports, Napier happily stoked up these fears, ostentatiously retaining two battleships returning home from the Mediterranean. Not that he intended to act—the passage to Gibraltar had cemented his conviction that an effective blockade of the Moroccan Atlantic ports would be impossible. Once *Sidon* returned from Laraiche, he would see what could be done against the Riff. So far he had kept his cards close to his chest; "I do not believe it is thought here that we have any designs upon them, so much the better."[32] Clearly the Admiralty had other ideas; on 1 February Napier was ordered to "repair *forthwith* to Spithead."[33]

With the Admiralty utterly uninterested in Moroccan issues, Napier would have to be quick.[34] Fortunately, his ostentatious display of armed might brought the Moroccans to heel within a week. Their consul boarded the flagship at Gibraltar on 4 February, accepting binding arbitration of the Redman claim; Napier noted "he evidently appears in a very great fright and the arrival here of the *Rodney* and *Vanguard* [the homebound units he had held in the theater] has not tended to tranquilize him." Anxious to secure a quick settlement, Napier rejected the governor of Gibraltar's attempt to get involved and sent a ship to Tangier to get Drummond Hay's opinion.[35] The Admiralty approved his detaining the battleships, "under the peculiar circumstances."[36] The sudden shift in Tangier's policy, as it proved, reflected French anxieties: fearing the British might seize Moroccan territory, especially on the Riff coast close to Algeria, Paris had urged the sultan to concede. Napier was equally anxious to settle, the Atlantic coast in winter offering precious few openings for punitive action.

Hoping for further enlightenment, Napier told Baring he would send one, perhaps two battleships back to Britain and soothed any fears of costly campaigns: "To do that it must be done properly and effectually and with a good force so as to make one business of it from one end of the coast to the other. They are a bad set and deserve severe chastisement."[37] He shared another intelligence coup about the Riffs with Dundas: "I hear they are a warlike set and good shots, if they take prisoners they murder the aged and R—— the young, so I have no chance of the latter operation." At least a new governor of Gibraltar had replaced the "much detested" Wilson.[38]

The same day, the Admiralty demanded he send the planned reinforcements to Parker's overstretched Mediterranean fleet and return home with the rest of his squadron. Dundas revealed the reasons why in his private letter: "Reduction is the master now. . . . We are anxious to cut down our numbers of men . . . and relieve other ships."[39] On the 10th Napier reported that the Redman affair had been resolved and apologized to Parker the following day for detaining *Prince Regent* to support his own diplomacy. The

Moroccans had accepted arbitration by two Gibraltar merchants, who promptly reduced Redman's claim from US$17,000 to $10,000, criticizing his calculations and his paperwork. Napier surmised that "the Moors knew the merchants very well and having many transactions with them they most probably would favour the Moorish Government."[40]

### The Napier Mission and the Riff Pirates

Having resolved the primary issue, the trade dispute, Napier felt he could, notwithstanding his impending return to Portsmouth, focus on the secondary question, Riff piracy. It was a complex problem, since the Riff pirates were numerous, well armed, and resourceful. Even with his extensive experience of amphibious warfare and steam operations, Napier could see few opportunities. He agreed with Parker that the job required a powerful force of steamers and troops, and he hoped the new governor, General Sir Robert Gardiner, would lend some troops. Even so, the weather was too rough and changeable for significant coastal operations, and he found nothing to lift his spirits in the latest Admiralty dispatches: "They expect I am gone to Madeira and Dundas says we will be in England by April and do not mention one word about Mr Redman or the Riffs."[41] Little wonder he took care to seek the foreign secretary's endorsement, and Palmerston was happy to oblige: "You have acted in this matter with perfect good judgement."[42]

Everything depended on the weather, since he would need a light westerly wind for amphibious operations on the pirate coast.[43] On the evening of 17 February 1849, he embarked five hundred soldiers of the 34th Regiment on *Sidon*, a paddle-wheel frigate he had designed specifically for amphibious warfare. Royal Marines from the battleships *St. Vincent, Vanguard,* and *Powerful* boarded the paddle steamers *Stromboli, Gladiator,* and *Polyphemus,* accompanied by the screw steamers *Reynard* and *Plumper.* With his flag in *Sidon,* Napier led the squadron to sea at eight that evening, making for Cape Tres Forcas.

Napier went more in hope than expectation, but ready to act if it proved possible to attack the pirates. Delayed by a minor collision, the squadron arrived off the cape at 2:00 PM the following day but could not find anything to attack: "The only way I can see of punishing these people is by landing in the long days when the corn is ripe and setting fire to it and seizing the cattle if you can find them (their huts are not worth destroying) and informing them why you have done so. . . . When I went to the Riff country I did expect to have found something tangible to attack, but whether knowing that we were [from] Gibraltar they had removed their boats into the country or not, I really do not know, and where their towns or even great villages [are] I do not know either, but suppose they must be in the interior."[44]

Indeed, some advised him to land and strike inland, but Napier was too familiar with the habits of mountain dwellers from his time in the Lebanon to entertain any such plan.[45] Well aware that he was responsible for the safety of his men, the ships under his command, and the reputation of his country, Napier had the moral courage to resist the temptation to take risks. Heavily equipped British troops stood no chance of getting to grips with the Riffs in such hostile terrain. It was better not to run the risk of defeat, the moral and political consequences of which would have been very embarrassing. Parker backed his decision.[46]

The Admiralty was delighted: "You exercised a sound discretion in abstaining from any aggressive act upon the Riff coast." Palmerston agreed: "You have acted, on this occasion, with your usual good judgement."[47] Yet the following day, the Board of Admiralty criticized his decision to wait for an east wind rather than use steamers to tow the fleet into the Atlantic, "as their Lordships had expressed their anxiety to have the squadron home."[48] As Dundas admitted, "It is very desirable we should pay off all the ships ordered home before the 31st March otherwise we shall be much bothered with our estimates, the reduction to 40,000 men commencing that day."[49]

Having assessed the possibilities, Napier prepared to bring his squadron home.[50] Although it approved his handling of the Redman negotiations, the Admiralty was desperate to pay off the battleships before the end of March and send the smaller ships to relieve foreign stations.[51] Before leaving he discussed future operations with Drummond Hay, along with the recommendation that *Polyphemus* should visit the Riff coast more often and might be replaced with a more discreet screw steamer.[52] He was still waiting for an east wind to leave Gibraltar when the governor of Melilla sent word late on 26 February that the Riff tribes wanted to make reparation for *Three Sisters*. Once again, it seemed, the presence of a powerful force had hastened the diplomatic process. Napier put little faith in such protestations, but the Riffs were evidently "much alarmed," so he decided to discuss the matter with Drummond Hay at Tangier.[53]

The Riffs offered to pay compensation of twenty thousand U.S. dollars through the governor of Melilla, if the sultan approved. Napier asked Drummond Hay to seek the sultan's endorsement, but Drummond Hay refused, claiming he had no authority and arguing that requiring the sultan's approval was merely a device to waste time. Napier disagreed, but he had to leave the Mediterranean, thereby handing the Riff question to Drummond Hay.[54] This was not what Drummond Hay wanted to hear. He needed Napier's fleet at Gibraltar to provide leverage with the Moroccan authorities, and he suddenly produced new information on the pirates.[55] The governor of the province, he reported, had provided details of the local boat fleet and of where the pirates hid their craft. This time it was Napier's turn to be unimpressed, fearing the communication had been designed to lure him into a trap. Without more concrete intelligence he could not remain.[56] Drummond Hay responded with news of an engagement between a Spanish steamer and some Riff boats off the Zaffarine Islands. Eleven pirates had been killed. The Riffs, he observed, were always promising to keep the peace, but their promises were never fulfilled. The Bu Gafar were responsible, they had from fifteen to twenty boats at Wad Garet (Ras Baraket), the entire coast contained between eighty and a hundred. Drummond Hay ended with the brief, telling observation: "The crops have failed this year from want of water."[57]

In his official report Napier stressed that he had more confidence than Drummond Hay did that the Riffs meant to pay compensation; he implied that the consul was more concerned to control negotiations than to advance British commercial interests, a point Sir Robert Wilson had made the previous month.[58] If Drummond Hay trusted the Moroccan governor, Napier did not. He believed the governor and the Moroccan consul at Gibraltar were in league, the latter buying large quantities of gun flints "and probably wish[ing] to lure me into a snare." His views were based on a new intelligence source, a Gibraltarian smuggler who had been a prisoner of the pirates. Napier closed an increasingly testy working relationship by informing Drummond Hay that he would not refer any future Riff offers to him, "as you have declined interfering."[59]

The following day, 16 March 1849, Napier left Gibraltar for Britain, because "Mr Hay did not think proper to make any communication to the Sultan, my staying any longer was therefore useless so that I will not be an Ambassador yet."[60] This was no idle bluster. Napier had settled a far larger diplomatic question, the Syrian crisis of 1840, to the satisfaction of his friend Palmerston. Napier understood the linkage between force, coercion, and diplomacy as well as any living man, and with more time and better weather he might have made a difference in this instance. As it was, economic pressures, adverse weather, and Napier's report persuaded Palmerston "that if negotiations have failed demonstrations would best be postponed till the season would enable us to do whatever might be useful or necessary."[61] The same day the Admiralty turned those thoughts into orders: "I am to acquaint you that my Lords approve of the steps you have taken, but that as some months must elapse before any retaliatory measures can be taken they desire that you will not delay your return to England, unless there is a certainty of bringing the negotiations to an immediate close."[62]

On reflection, Palmerston supported Drummond Hay's decision not to seek government endorsement of the Riff compensation offer. He believed the only options were to hold the sultan responsible and make him pay or to punish the Riffs without reference to the sultan, and "under present circumstances the first of these courses does not seem to be expedient."[63]

### The End of the Napier Mission

Napier struck his flag on 9 April, soon after arriving at Spithead. The squadron was broken up. The demands of economy and the dictates of common sense had closed a chapter in the history of Riff piracy. The only time the Royal Navy had a force on the coast capable of punishing the pirates, it had been denied the opportunity to act. Britain now preferred to look for a diplomatic or commercial solution to the pirate problem. The cost and risk attached to the alternatives were simply too high.

The rationale for this apparently pusillanimous policy lay far from the Riff coast or the Moroccan court. As Napier and Parker emphasized, chastising the Riffs would require a significant amphibious force, at least a thousand troops and six or eight large, steam warships, and it would take time. Under existing circumstances the British simply did not have the time, or the ships, to do the job. The international scene remained complicated and unsettled: no one knew what would become of post-Orléans France, or post-revolutionary Italy, while the growing menace of Russian pressure on Turkey drew the focus ever eastward. These factors explained why Napier had been sent to deal with an issue on Sir William Parker's station. Beyond the Mediterranean, Britain faced more problems. The Schleswig-Holstein conflict of 1848–50 threatened another vital interest, access to the Baltic; Palmerston threatened to send Napier's squadron to raise the Danish blockade of the German coast.[64]

In addition, Britain's dire economic situation forced the ministers to cut the navy by three thousand men and pay off Napier's ships. When set against such problems, small-scale piracy was hardly a priority, especially as the Moroccans had already given way on the trade dispute, and the French threat had receded with the fall of the Orléans dynasty. Palmerston's long-term policy was to enhance the power of the Moroccan government, leaving the sultan to impose order in the Riff, keep the country independent, and ultimately enter Britain's informal empire of trade and capital.

While the empire was a valuable segment of the nineteenth-century British economy, it was never dominant. The empire accounted for approximately 25 percent of the market in most sectors. The most dynamic sector of the economy was the export of capital, by 1890 almost £100 million annually, much of it invested outside the empire. This sector was intimately linked to the financial services and commercial support systems of the City of London. The preeminence of the City of London in world finance was reflected in British dominance of world shipping and related services.[65] Morocco joined this system in the 1850s.

Evidence of Morocco's value came in the form of an offer of space at the 1851 Great Exhibition, an offer the sultan politely declined. However, within three years frequent changes in the Moroccan tariffs, the sultan's attempt to pay an indemnity levied by

France in 1844, and attempts by his ministers and agents to enrich themselves prompted further complaints from the British merchants at Gibraltar. British imports had been halved by changes in the Moroccan tariff, from £300,000 in 1848 to £145,000 in 1850, and although they had recovered by 1852 Morocco remained in breach of the Anglo-Moroccan Treaty. In August 1853, Foreign Secretary Lord John Russell refused to accept a Moroccan ambassador until the issue had been resolved.[66] Russell's implied threat, one that he scarcely troubled himself to veil, was to leave Morocco exposed to French and Spanish predation. Against this backdrop—powerful naval forces lay just beyond the horizon—Drummond Hay drew up the draft for a commercial treaty.

In 1854, new tariffs were established to the satisfaction of Britain. By this stage Morocco had earned British goodwill. When the Crimean War had broken out in 1854, the sultan had promptly barred Russian warships, privateers, and prizes from his ports and agreed to supply an additional thousand bullocks at a low export duty to feed the British troops passing through Gibraltar. Significantly, he had not extended this favor to French Algeria. Morocco was also an important link in British trade with sub-Saharan Africa, although this was in decline.[67] However, British trade was hampered by high duties levied at home on the main Moroccan export, wax. Also, reliance on Jewish middlemen provided obstacles, since the status of Moroccan Jews frequently changed.[68] After interminable delays, Drummond Hay's treaty, suitably amended, was signed on 9 December 1856. Morocco abandoned monopolies and barriers to imports and fixed a maximum export duty of 10 percent. These terms provided greater stability and security for British capitalists and merchants. In this way, Morocco joined Britain's informal empire only months after the Riff pirates seized what proved to be their last British ship.[69]

### The Resolution of 1856

Although the pirates escaped retribution in 1849, long-term economic development and the growth of British informal control meant their days were numbered. Yet they did not choose to go quietly. In April 1850 Palmerston returned to the charge, urging the Admiralty to send a punitive expedition, but there were more pressing issues and no spare ships.[70] On 5 October 1851, Riff boats captured the brigantine *Violet* off Point Botoya on Azanen Bay. The cargo of maize was plundered, some of the crew were killed, others ransomed. General Gardiner dispatched HMS *Janus*, a small paddle sloop, under the command of Lieutenant Richard Powell, from Gibraltar on 17 October 1849.

Powell arrived off the Riff coast the following day. At two o'clock that afternoon, he found the Spanish vessel *Joven Emilia* hauled up the beach and entirely stripped in a deep bay some four miles west of Cape Tres Forcas, probably Cala Tramontana. Powell rowed ashore under heavy musketry fire, dispersing the locals and destroying some of their boats, while ten-inch shells from his main battery guns proved to be particularly effective. He went back the next day to complete the lesson. On the 20th Powell discovered the charred frames of *Violet* on a beach three miles farther to the west. Once again the Riff opened fire. Powell landed for a second time, intending to destroy their boats, only to find himself heavily outnumbered. The landing party was driven back to its boats with eight wounded, Powell among them. Although two pirate boats had been destroyed, he saw many more hidden in the sand or drawn up in caves.[71]

Despite Palmerston's anxiety to send a large expedition, Sir Francis Baring did not think anything could be done.[72] The Royal Navy was, as ever, spread very thin, and there were more pressing tasks than punishing past acts of piracy, especially after the French had once again bombarded Tangier, threatening the balance of power at the strait. When Admiral Parker detached a powerful steamer he did so to uphold British interests should the French seize Moroccan territory.[73] Captain Henry Giffard, in command of HMS *Dragon,* retrieved four survivors from *Violet's* crew while Powell recovered from his wounds. Then *Dragon* and *Janus* returned to survey the pirate coast. Predictably, they were fired at.[74]

In 1852, Admiral Parker reflected on the Riff problem as he left the station for the last time: "I presume it would be difficult to raze villages, or burn crops, without involving a period of more than one day on shore. Whatever is attempted should be done effectually, and a little well executed would, perhaps, produce a better result than an attack on a larger scale, whereby we might be subjected to much loss of life; but I really think they ought to be punished in some degree."[75] This would be a major undertaking for any fleet. In truth, as a late-Victorian historian of the navy admitted, "it does not appear that any adequate reprisals were ever carried out against the offenders."[76] Instead Foreign Secretary Lord Malmesbury preferred to coerce the Moroccans into solving the problem, following a line that his friend Palmerston had laid out, threatening to treat the area as independent.

The British did not employ a large force against the Riff, because that would open the door to other powers.[77] Nor were the British alone in their frustration. In 1852, the Riff plundered the Stettin merchant ship *Flora* after it ran aground, but the German Navy was unable to respond at the time. Finally, on 7 August 1856, Admiral Prince Adalbert anchored the large paddle-wheel corvette *Danzig* off Cape Tres Forcas and landed a sixty-man punitive expedition. In a four-and-a-half-hour engagement he learned a painful lesson, one his British friends would have recognized only too well. Adalbert was one of seventeen wounded; another seven were killed. Naval vessels could not command the respect of the locals, absent the manpower and equipment to control the beach.[78]

Before the prince's foolhardy venture, however, the Moroccan government had taken decisive action. The sultan sent an army of eight thousand troops, led by Abd el Malek, the tough and determined local governor, into Bu Gafar territory. He burned their boats and their villages, imposed fines, seized livestock, and took hostages for future good behavior.

This assertion of authority meant the sultan would have to take responsibility for Riff piracy, and the French demanded seven thousand dollars in compensation for the plundered vessel *Jeune Dieppois*. In a local initiative of April 1856, Consul Drummond Hay met Riff chieftains on the Melilla border, conducting the meeting in Arabic, the second language of both parties (the Riff spoke a Berber dialect). Although they exchanged handshakes, Drummond Hay had no illusions. This was wise. The seizure of yet another British vessel, *Hymen,* on 14 May 1856 led Drummond Hay to demand action, and the Moroccan army returned, inflicting further punishment on the Bu Gafar. The sultan also paid compensation for *Hymen.*

That was the end of significant Riff piracy until, late in the century, central authority collapsed yet again and the Riffs returned to their old trade.[79] As a late-nineteenth-century British chronicler of the Sharifian Empire confessed, the Riff were happy to plunder any weak vessel that came close enough, and as long as Moroccan and foreign governments preferred to pay ransom and accept cash settlements, they would continue to do so. "All the good excuses in the world about upsetting the balance of power, or fear of embroiling Europe in war, will not, in the eyes of the Moors, explain the supine policy adopted with this 'sick man of the West.'"[80]

## Conclusions

While Riff piracy was a nuisance, any heavy-handed attempts by the British to suppress the pirates risked inviting the French to take further action—action that would endanger British strategic interests in the Strait of Gibraltar and the commercial and political dominance that was to be enshrined in the Anglo-Moroccan Treaty of 1856. Britain's informal empire could deliver improved trade and influence only if a relatively powerful Moroccan central government imposed order on the provinces and ensured the "Open Door" commercial treaty was carried into effect.[81]

Above all, the cost of dealing with the pirates directly would have been excessive. To impose order on a numerous, well armed, and dangerous population reduced to poverty, rendered violently anti-Christian by decades of colonial warfare with Spain, and not infrequently starving would have required a major military expedition supported by a large naval squadron. The human cost would have been high and the diplomatic problems grave. Such an operation would be, in effect, an invasion and conquest, albeit avowedly short-term. It would be expecting a good deal of France to stand by while the British subjugated the Riff coast on the promise of subsequent withdrawal. After all, that was precisely what the French had promised the British when they landed in Algeria in 1830! The alternative naval response, instituting regular patrols, would have been uneconomical. Instead, the British responded to attacks by sending warships to recover seized ships and punish the pirates for specific incidents.

It suited British interests to support and encourage the Moroccan government to deal with the problem by increasing central control over the turbulent tribesmen. That some of these "piratical" captures may have been collusive, part of a smuggling network that linked Spain, Algeria, Gibraltar, and Morocco, made any other response inappropriate. An effective Moroccan customs system, with low tariffs and adequate policing, would ultimately be the best solution to Riff piracy.

## Notes

1. C. R. Pennell, "Dealing with Pirates: British, French and Moroccans, 1834–56," *Journal of Imperial and Commonwealth History* 22, no. 1 (1994), pp. 54–83.

2. C. R. Pennell, "The Maritime Trade on the Northern Moroccan Coast in the Early Nineteenth Century," *Morocco* 1 (1996), pp. 86–88.

3. C. R. Pennell, "The Geography of Piracy: Northern Morocco in the Mid-nineteenth Century," *Journal of Historical Geography* 20 (1994), p. 275.

4. Budgett Meakin, *The Moorish Empire* (London: S. Sonnenschein, 1899), p. 271–72.

5. *Morocco*, Geographical Handbook Series BR 505 (London: Naval Intelligence Division, December 1941 [vol. 1]; October 1942 [vol. 2]). See vol. 1, pp. 73–76, for a thorough description of this coast.

6. Pennell, "Geography of Piracy," p. 276.

7. Pennell, "Dealing with Pirates," p. 63.

8. Parker to Drummond Hay, 5 June 1846, reprinted in Augustus Phillimore, *Life of Admiral of the Fleet Sir William Parker* (London: Harrison, 1880), vol. 3, p. 59.

9. Pennell, "Dealing with Pirates," p. 60.

10. *Lloyd's Register of [British and Foreign] Shipping,* the annual London publication describing, classifying, and registering all merchant ships according to physical structure and equipment, meant to enable underwriters, ship brokers, and shipowners to assess commercial risk more accurately and thereby negotiate marine insurance rates. The 1848, 1849, and 1850 entries give the same ownership and route.

11. Secretary to the governor of Gibraltar to Consul Drummond Hay, 7 November 1848; Messrs. Glasgow to Sir Robert Wilson, 7 November 1848; McCleverty to Sir Robert Wilson, 7 November 1848; all Foreign Office [hereafter FO] 174/58.

12. William L. Clowes, *The Royal Navy: A History* (London: S. Low, Marston, 1901), vol. 6, pp. 361–62.

13. McCleverty to Drummond Hay, 9 November 1848, FO 174/58.

14. Parker to Lord Auckland, 11 December 1848, in Phillimore, *Life of Admiral of the Fleet Sir William Parker,* vol. 3, p. 441.

15. This section is largely based upon G. Elers-Napier, *The Life and Letters of Admiral Sir Charles Napier* (London: n.p., 1862), vol. 2, pp. 200–204.

16. Auckland to Lord John Russell, 13 September 1848, Russell MS Public Records Office [hereafter PRO] 30/20/7D f57-8, The National Archives [hereafter TNA]; Auckland to Napier, 1 November 1848, Napier MS

British Library Additional Manuscripts [hereafter Add.] MS 40,023 f320. Redman Brothers was a British trading firm in Mazagan that suffered extensive trading losses when its grain export licenses were suddenly withdrawn, leaving it with wheat that it could not sell.

17. Auckland to Parker, 13 December 1848, in Phillimore, *Life of Admiral of the Fleet Sir William Parker,* vol. 3, p. 443.

18. Auckland to Napier, 25 November 1848, in Elers-Napier, *Life and Letters of Admiral Sir Charles Napier,* vol. 2, p. 196.

19. Palmerston to Napier, 5 December 1848, in ibid., pp. 197–98.

20. Napier to Lord John Russell, 23 October 1848, PRO 30/20/7D f172-3, asking for the prime minister's support on naval and party grounds.

21. Napier to Auckland, 25 November 1848, Add. 40,041 f150.

22. Auckland to Napier, 26 November 1848, Add. 40,023 f348.

23. Napier to Auckland, 27 November 1848, Add. 40,041 f150.

24. Auckland to Napier, 28 November 1848, Add. 40,023 f352 and 354.

25. Napier to Auckland, 9 January 1849, Lisbon, Add. 40,041 f169.

26. Napier to Captain Hamilton (Admiralty Secretary), 16 January 1849, and Napier to Baring, 31 January 1849, in Elers-Napier, *Life and Letters of Admiral Sir Charles Napier,* vol. 2, pp. 199–200; Napier to Drummond Hay, 19 January 1849, Add. 40,041 f174.

27. Admiralty to Napier, 11 January 1849, Admiralty [hereafter ADM] 2/1607, p. 242.

28. Dundas to Napier, 16 January 1849, Add. 40,041 f171; Dundas to Napier, 6 February 1849, Add. 40,041 f177.

29. Admiralty to Napier, 22 January 1849, ADM 2/1607, pp. 154–55; Dundas to Napier, 22 January 1849, Add. 40,041 f172.

30. Napier to Baring, 31 January 1849, Add. 40,041 f174.

31. Napier to Baring and Palmerston, 31 January 1849, Add. 40,041 f175-6.

32. Napier to Dundas, 31 January 1849, Add. 40,041 f176.

33. Admiralty to Napier, 1 February 1849, ADM 2/1607 f280.

34. Napier to Drummond Hay, 6 February 1849, Add. 40,041 f181.

35. Napier to Drummond Hay, 4 February 1849, Add. 40,041 f179; Napier to Admiralty, 6 February 1849, received 15 February, ADM 1/5596, papers on the Redman negotiations.

36. Admiralty to Napier, 16 February 1849, ADM 2/1607, p. 339.

37. Napier to Baring, 6 February 1849, Add. 40,041 f183.

38. Napier to Dundas, 6 February 1849, Add. 40,041 f184.

39. Admiralty to Napier, 6 February 1849, ADM 2/1607, p. 297; Dundas to Napier, 6 February 1849, Add. 40,041 f177.

40. Napier to Admiralty, 10 February 1849, received 23 February, ADM 1/5596; Napier to Parker, 11 February 1849, Add. 40,041 f186; Napier to Drummond Hay, 11 February 1849, Add. 40,041 f189.

41. Napier to Parker, 11 February 1849, Add. 40,041 f186.

42. Napier to Palmerston, 11 February 1849, Add. 40,041 f188; Admiralty to Napier, 2 March 1849, ADM 2/1607, pp. 262–63, quoting Foreign Office to Admiralty, 28 February 1849, regarding Napier's 10 February 1849 report on the Redman claim.

43. Napier to Dundas, 16 February 1849, Add. 40,041 f191.

44. Napier to Palmerston, 21 February 1849, Add. 40,041 f195.

45. Napier met Drummond Hay off Beirut in 1840, during those operations. John D. Hay, *A Memoir of Sir John Drummond Hay: Sometime Minister of the Court of Morocco* (London: J. Murray, 1896), p. 30.

46. Parker to Napier, 9 March 1849, Add. 40,023 f380.

47. Admiralty to Napier, 6 March 1849, ADM 2/1607, p. 369. The dispatch reached Napier on 9 March 1849, ADM 50/251.

48. Admiralty to Napier, 7 March 1849, ADM 2/1607, p. 376.

49. Dundas to Napier, 9 March 1849, Add. 40,041 f203.

50. Napier to Baring, 20 February 1849, Add. 40,041 f197.

51. Admiralty to Napier, 24 February 1849, ADM 2/1607, pp. 348–49; Dundas to Napier, 25 February 1849, Add. 40,041 f192; Napier to Baring, 25 February 1849, Add. 40,041 f201.

52. Napier to Drummond Hay, 26 February 1849, still at Gibraltar, Add. 40,041 f205; Napier to Dundas, 4 March 1849, Add. 40,041 f207.

53. Napier to Baring, 27 February 1849, Add. 40,041 f206.

54. Napier to Drummond Hay, 4 March 1849, Add. 40,041 f208.

55. Napier to Dundas, 9 March 1849, Add. 40,041 f209.

56. Napier to Drummond Hay, 11 March, Add. 40,041 f211.

57. Drummond Hay to Napier, 14 March 1849, ADM 1/5596.

58. Napier to Admiralty, 15 March 1849, received 25 March, ADM 1/5596; Wilson to Napier, 6 February 1849, Add. 40,041 f181.

59. Napier to Drummond Hay, 15 March 1849, Add. 40,041 f212.

60. Napier to Baring, 16 March 1849, ADM 50/251; Napier to Baring, 17 March 1849, Add. 40,041 f215.

61. Palmerston to Baring, 19 March 1851, Baring MS N13. 10.

62. Admiralty to Napier, 19 March 1849, ADM 2/1607, p. 397.

63. Foreign Office to Admiralty, 31 March 1849, ADM 1/5599.

64. Holger Hjelholt, *British Mediation in the Danish-German Conflict 1848–1850* (Copenhagen: Munksgarrd, 1966), vol. 2, p. 82.

65. The standard account of this process is P. J. Cain and A. G. Hopkins, *British Imperialism: Innovation and Expansion 1688–1914* (London: Longman, 1993), see esp. pp. 125–77.

66. P. G. Rogers, *A History of Anglo-Moroccan Relations to 1900* (printed in London but unpublished), pp. 162–63.

67. J. B. Williams, *British Commercial Policy and Trade Expansion 1750–1850* (Oxford, U.K.: Clarendon, 1972), pp. 91, 93.

68. Ibid., pp. 304–305.

69. Meakin, *Moorish Empire,* pp. 399–414, provides an interesting late-nineteenth-century perspective.

70. Palmerston to Admiralty, 17 April 1850, TNA FO 17456.

71. Powell to Sir William Parker, 22 October 1851, FO 174/56.

72. Baring to Palmerston, 13 November 1851, Palmerston MS Southampton University GC/BA 305.

73. B. Greenhill and A. Giffard, *Steam, Politics and Patronage: The Transformation of the Royal Navy 1815–54* (London: Conway Maritime, 1994), pp. 187–91.

74. Giffard's report to Parker, 11 January 1852, FO 174/56.

75. Parker to Drummond Hay, 7 April 1852, in Phillimore, *Life of Admiral of the Fleet Sir William Parker,* vol. 3, p. 707.

76. Clowes, *Royal Navy,* vol. 6, pp. 361–62.

77. Rogers, *History of Anglo-Moroccan Relations to 1900,* p. 161.

78. L. Sondhaus, *Preparing for Weltpolitik: German Sea Power before the Tirpitz Era* (Annapolis, Md.: Naval Institute Press, 1997), p. 57.

79. Pennell, "Geography of Piracy," p. 280.

80. Meakin, *Moorish Empire,* pp. 272–73.

81. D. C. M. Platt, *Finance, Trade and Politics in British Foreign Policy 1815–1914* (Oxford, U.K.: Clarendon, 1968), p. 86.

# CHAPTER TWELVE

# Guns, Oil, and "Cake"
## Maritime Security in the Gulf of Guinea
ARILD NODLAND

Nigeria, the most populous country in Africa, is at the center of an unprecedented rise in piracy and maritime crime. During 2007, for example, the International Maritime Bureau (IMB) reported forty-two attacks against international shipping and offshore installations.[1] Nigeria illustrates better than anywhere else in Africa that financial good times have a downside. The vast riches brought by oil have not benefited large segments of the population, especially in the oil-producing region of the Niger Delta. Corruption, theft, pollution, maladministration, unemployment, and bad governance have created levels of frustration and aggression that increasingly have resulted in attacks on shipping and offshore petroleum activities. Those who have been left stranded by decades of oil bonanza have lost patience and have decided to take matters into their own hands.

Nigeria is a focal point of international attention because in terms of maritime security it is in a league of its own. Africa's largest oil producer has the dubious honor of topping the Gulf of Guinea's list of acts of piracy and armed robbery against ships. Out of 178 reported attacks between 2003 and 2007, 137 took place in or just off Nigeria (see figure 1).[2] Altogether some 237 foreigners and dozens of Nigerians were kidnapped in sixty-seven separate incidents in the coastal states of the delta region in 2006 and 2007 alone;[3] of these, ninety-eight were foreign sailors or rig workers kidnapped at sea.[4] As a direct result of these attacks, in December 2007 Liberia and Norway raised their International Ship and Port Facility Security (ISPS) Code security levels from I to II for ships operating in Nigerian coastal waters and ports; the Panama Maritime Authority followed suit on 22 January 2008. To date, no other country in the Gulf of Guinea has been given quite the same treatment by international maritime authorities.

As capital continues to pour into Nigeria and other gulf states, security must increase for foreign as well as domestic investments. Current maritime surveillance and security

## FIGURE 1
*Gulf of Guinea: Piracy and Armed Robbery against Ships, 2003–2007*

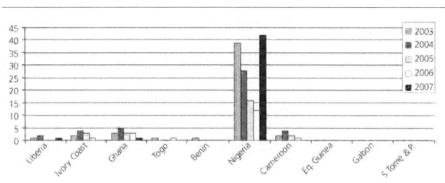

*Source:* International Chamber of Commerce, *Piracy and Armed Robbery against Ships: Annual Report 1 January–31 December 2007* (London: International Maritime Bureau, 2008), pp. 5–6.

provisions are not efficient, in large part due to the lack of strength, unity, or cohesion of Nigerian and other naval forces in the region. In the words of one African affairs specialist: "No country on the Gulf has a naval force worthy of the name."[5] In response, local and regional arrangements, such as cooperation among naval commanders of certain gulf states, have been initiated to address the growing security challenge. A more recent proposal is the "Gulf of Guinea Guard Force," the brainchild of Nigeria's president, Umaru Musa Yar'Adua, who envisages a regional naval force built and trained with American assistance.[6] In addition, the establishment of AFRICOM, the U.S. Africa Command, is a clear sign that interest in the continent, especially the Gulf of Guinea, reaches far beyond African borders.

### Nigeria: A Blessed Country

Nigeria is the largest country on the Gulf of Guinea, a stretch of water defined by Cape Palmas in Liberia to the west and Cape Lopez in Gabon in the south. In between are a number of coastal countries, including the Ivory Coast, Ghana, Togo, Benin, Nigeria, Cameroon, and Equatorial Guinea. In the gulf itself is the small island republic of São Tomé and Príncipe. These ten countries are commonly called the "gulf states."

In recent years, the Gulf of Guinea has increasingly become an important supplier of fossil fuels. International demand, especially from the United States and China, for a steady flow of oil and gas is rapidly changing the region's—in fact all of Africa's—geostrategic significance. The "scramble for Africa's oil" has put the continent back on the map, and since 1990 oil firms have invested more than US$20 billion in exploration and production activity in Africa. Another fifty billion dollars, it was estimated in 2007, will have been spent by the end of this decade.[7] With increased strategic importance comes a steady flow of foreign firms wanting to reap the benefits of the economic boom. Bankers, oil executives, restaurateurs, furniture dealers, and commodity investors are all investing in the Gulf of Guinea. Most of them rely on shipping to carry their goods to and from gulf ports.

Thousands of men and women also work on oil rigs off the gulf's coastline, especially that of Nigeria, which is the country most affected by the security problems of the kinds that have often followed similar booms in developing nations. A web of pipelines stretches thousands of kilometers across the mangrove swamps of the delta, interrupted here and there by gas flares sending orange flames into the air. The pipelines sometimes burst; sometimes they are plundered by gangs of youths trying to get rich fast in the lucrative oil-theft trade, locally known as "illegal bunkering." Either way, large quantities of crude are spilled into the swamps, rivers, and creeks, where local villagers are trying to eke out meager livings from fishing and farming. In October 2006, the World Wildlife Fund reported that up to 1.5 million tons of oil had been spilled in the delta over the past fifty years—the equivalent of an *Exxon Valdez* disaster every twelve months.[8]

Ken Saro-Wiwa, the former leader of the Movement for the Survival of the Ogoni People (MOSOP), once stated, "Nigeria was full of inflation, corruption, injustice, armed robbery, maladministration, drug-trafficking, hunger, knavery, dishonesty and plain stupidity . . . [b]ut it is still a blessed country."[9] This one, brilliant sentence sums up the hopes and potential of a great nation, while at the same time recognizing its many obvious flaws and shortcomings. It also reflects the people's view that they have been shortchanged and polluted long enough—a conviction that, as we shall see, is a key reason why so many ships are attacked and why so many oil workers have been abducted, especially in the Niger Delta.

Trying to understand, much less explain, the complexity of the roots of the conflicts of the Niger Delta could easily become the work of a lifetime, but as John Ghazvinian has put it, "as with most human conflict, its causes can be boiled down to money, land and ethnic rivalry."[10] Big egos, pollution, and poor governance are also factors. There are plenty of just causes for political activism in the delta, but the line between grievance and greed is thin. Crime, community activism, and political militancy often go hand in hand.

The Niger Delta is made up of nine states, with 185 local government areas, and it has a population of twenty-seven million (see figure 2). It has forty ethnic groups, speaking some 250 dialects spread across five to six thousand communities and settlements. About 1,500 of those communities play host to oil-company operations of one kind or another. Many of these communities receive compensation for the use of their land. But others do not, thus creating constant friction not only between the communities and the petroleum multinationals but also among neighboring villages and different ethnic groups—or "tribes," in Nigerian parlance.

Injustice, real or imagined, becomes a fact of life when the bounty of oil is doled out. Since oil exploration started in the late 1950s, hundreds of billions dollars have been squandered, mismanaged, or plundered by corrupt government officials at all levels. The rewards for holding political office are huge. Politicians for decades have jockeyed for positions, power, access to federal and state budgets, and lucrative local business deals. Meanwhile, local constituents have had to make do with mud huts and Stone Age squalor in Ogbainbiri, Fishtown, and other villages in Nigeria's southeastern corner. Although the delta produces all of the nation's oil and gas and generates 80 percent of federal revenue, its people live without electricity or clean, running water. Roads have fallen in disrepair, due to decades of neglect; education and access to medical services are patchy at best.

**FIGURE 2**
*Nigeria: The States of Delta Region*

1. Abia
2. Akwa Ibom
3. Bayelsa
4. Cross River
5. Delta
6. Edo
7. Imo
8. Ondo
9. Rivers

Hopes were once high that the oil industry would benefit the communities of the Niger Delta, but the oil business is a practical— some say cynical—as well as a high-tech one. Rather than training a local workforce, international oil firms have found it cost-effective to bring in foreign professionals and, with them, modern air-conditioned facilities, tennis courts, and swimming pools, all surrounded by razor wire and armed guards. The resulting contrast between riches and staggering poverty is a recipe for disaster.

Unemployment numbers in the petroleum heartland are formidable, and the Nigerian government gives them as the main reason why there is so much crime and militancy. Unemployment is, of course, another significant factor of underlying instability. Frustrated and marauding young men roam the streets of Port Harcourt or cruise the waterways in the mangrove swamps of the delta in canoes or fast aluminum craft bristling with guns, scouting for the next easy target.

But the core of the problem goes beyond joblessness and relates to such fundamental issues as the question of who owns the oil, endemic corruption, and the never-ending political tugs-of-war between political elites in the capitals of the oil-producing states and the faraway federal center, Abuja. By March 2005 the country's problems had become serious enough to prompt the U.S. National Intelligence Council to identify the possibility of an "outright collapse of Nigeria."[11]

Luckily, it has not come to that quite yet. If Saro-Wiwa's cautious optimism is anything to go by, Nigeria will muddle through, as it has done many times before. No one has the stomach for another civil war like the one that ravaged Biafra from 1967 until 1971. However, the growing maritime security challenge of piracy in the Niger Delta is of enormous contemporary concern, and it is forcing Nigeria to respond.

### Nigeria's Maritime Security Challenges

Mariners and petroleum workers in Nigerian waters labor under difficult, sometimes dangerous, circumstances and must be constantly concerned about being kidnapped for ransom. *Oyibos*—foreigners—are, however, not the only ones concerned about insecurity on the seas. According to Nigeria's director of fisheries, Mr. Akinshola Amile, piracy attacks on Nigerian fishing vessels have steadily increased from four reported attacks in 2003 to more than 107 in 2007; fifty attacks were recorded in January 2008 alone, of which twenty took place within a week, resulting in the deaths of ten sailors (see figure 3).[12]

The Nigerian government is well aware of these problems and struggles to cope with the increasing maritime crime rate. At least fifteen soldiers attached to the Niger Delta

FIGURE 3
*Attacks on International Shipping and Offshore Oil Facilities, 2007–2008*

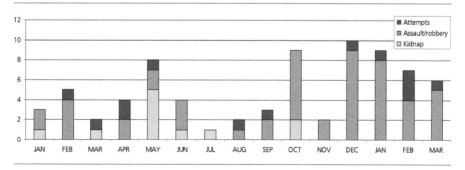

*Source:* Bergen Risk Solutions, "Maritime Security in Nigeria," *Quarterly Review,* no. 4 (April 2008), p. 6.

Joint Military Task Force died between June 2007 and January 2008 in Bayelsa State alone while attempting to maintain peace and security along the creeks and waterways of the state.[13] Many Nigerian police officers have become increasingly reluctant to serve in the delta, and many marine police stations have been looted and sacked by bandits or suspected militants.[14] In Lagos, where security of the water channels is the sole responsibility of the Nigerian Ports Authority and the marine police, lack of adequate equipment and logistics tend to impede effective policing.[15]

Maritime workers are becoming increasingly impatient. In December 2007, the Agricultural and Allied Workers Union of Nigeria (AAWUN) condemned the increasing attacks on members' fishing vessels by pirates and called on both the federal and Lagos State governments to protect them. "No fewer that 44 members of our union have been killed during such attacks," said an AAWUN official in December 2007. Stolen goods were estimated to be valued at about ₦120 million (US$960,000) over a two-year period.[16] As a result of such losses, the Nigerian Trawler Owners Association went on strike in February 2008, withdrawing over 170 fishing boats off the fisheries in protest.[17]

International shipping and offshore facilities have also felt the consequences of the increase in maritime crime. Bergen Risk Solutions, a Norwegian risk-management consultancy, recorded twenty-two attacks on foreign marine assets in the first three months of 2008, which is a clear increase over the previous year, when the fifty-three attacks were carried out during the entire year, at that point an all-time high.[18] While far from reassuring, greater information about these attacks will allow seafarers to mitigate the risk of attack by avoiding the most dangerous areas or by employing greater deterrence if they have to venture into high-risk zones.

Fortunately, the attacks appear to follow distinct geographical patterns and so should be reasonably easy to avoid. Lagos, the area off Escravos and Benin River (Delta State), and Bonny River (the stretch of water leading from Bonny Island to Port Harcourt in Rivers State) are the three areas worst affected recently by maritime attacks. Bonny River has seen a drastic increase in robbery and armed assault since October 2007, partly because many criminals have been chased out of Port Harcourt, the oil capital, by a government security offensive launched in August 2007.

There are also significant differences in the nature of acts of piracy in the Lagos area and the Niger Delta. Whereas Lagos incidents clearly are executed by small-time bandits motivated purely by financial gain—many attacks hardly qualify as piracy, and many would-be robbers go back overboard at the sight of a sturdy sailor—maritime raids in the delta often have more determined, political, and violent dimensions. Also, while kidnap for ransom has been commonplace in the delta, it is virtually nonexistent in Lagos. Attacks in the Niger Delta are also better coordinated and often entail the use of numerous fast attack craft, explosives, and heavy weapons, such as .50-caliber machine guns and rocket-propelled grenades.

From the pirates' perspective, the chance of success is higher in the delta than in Lagos; to date only one attack has occurred outside the thirty-five-nautical-mile mark in the delta, none more than twenty nautical miles off Lagos.[19] In addition, most attacks, especially in Lagos, take place at night. The most popular targets are berthed or drifting vessels, barges, fixed installations (like oil rigs), or floating production storage and offloading vessels (FPSOs) and floating storage and offloading vessels (FSOs)—converted oil tankers serving as storage/drilling ships.

Many of the attacks in the Niger Delta have been attributed to politically motivated militants, but Nigeria also has more than its fair share of criminals. This dangerous cocktail of political activism and crime has led to a sustained string of attacks that have posed a constant, indeed increasing, risk over the last five years. In August 2007, Port Harcourt, home of the petroleum industry and capital of the oil-rich Rivers State, saw the worst fighting in years as criminal gangs went on a rampage. The situation was defused only after Nigerian government forces launched a massive counteroffensive and rebels and politicians agreed to open talks. So far the talks have yielded few results, other than driving attackers from their normal hunting grounds on shore toward the more vulnerable and easy targets at sea, a transition that has helped to blur even further the lines between true insurgents and simple criminals.

### The Niger Delta Insurgency

Attacks on international firms in Nigeria's petroleum heartland can broadly be divided into three categories: attacks by political militants, by criminal thugs, and by community activists. The lines between these groups are thin, often overlapping. An attacker may one day kidnap an oil worker to buy a nice car, the next day he may join a raid by a militant group, and on the third he might hijack an oil rig to generate cash for his tribal chief—or to get jobs, a new hospital, or a generator for his village.

Although banditry and community-related issues are assessed to be the main driving forces behind attacks, over the last couple of years the political insurgents have received the most attention (see figure 4). Among the main groups are the Movement for the Emancipation of the Niger Delta (MEND), the Joint Revolutionary Council, the Niger Delta Vigilante, and the Niger Delta People's Volunteer Force (NDPVF).[20] These groups—or better, networks—have not only carried out their fair share of attacks but have done so with great fanfare.

FIGURE 4
*Attacks on Foreign Firms in the Niger Delta, 2007*

DUE TO COPYRIGHT RESTRICTIONS
SOME OR ALL IMAGES ARE NOT INCLUDED

Used by permission.

MEND, the most notorious of the groups, first appeared on 10 January 2006, when it simultaneously kidnapped four foreign oil workers at gunpoint from Shell's offshore EA oil field and blew up the Trans Ramos crude-oil pipeline in Bayelsa State, cutting supplies to the Forcados export terminal by a hundred thousand barrels per day. In the year that followed, MEND was especially astute in combining armed action and a skillful media campaign that drew international attention to the group's cause. By using armed force but justifying its actions as legitimate grievances of the delta's impoverished population, MEND became—and still is, some argue—the leading factor in guerrilla war in the area.

The group has fragmented since it first appeared, but "the cause" is very much alive and well. The core demands are the release of jailed militant leaders, including MEND leader Henry Okah, who was arrested in Angola on 3 September 2007; the demilitarization of the Niger Delta; the immediate payment of US$1.5 billion compensation from Shell—approved by the Nigerian National Assembly—covering four decades of environmental degradation; and local control of resources, up to and including secession from the Nigerian federation.[21]

In a media statement on 24 June 2007, shortly after his release from jail, NDPVF leader Alhaji Mujahid Dokubo-Asari said, "My next move is that I will continue the agitation for the convocation of a Sovereign National Conference which I believe is the only solution to the problem confronting us. . . . Nigeria is a nation founded on falsehood and fraud. How can such a nation stand?"[22] Asari's demand for independence for his Ijaw ethnic group—the largest in the delta—is, of course, unlikely to be granted, since it might result in civil war. Ijaw control of oil revenues is in direct conflict with the ambitions and wishes of most other peoples and states of the Nigerian federation—not to mention the Nigerian federal government, which gets the lion's share of its revenue from the delta's oil.

Asari's hostile rhetoric subsided after he was invited to be part of an eighteen-man peace-broker team appointed by the federal government in September 2007.[23] As he came under the wing of Yar'Adua's administration, the previously vocal militia leader denounced kidnapping of foreign workers and dismissed MEND leader Jomo Gbomo as a common thug. In retaliation, Jomo called Asari a sellout and a traitor.

The squabble among the major leaders of the delta's militant movements reveals crucial flaws in their collective quest for the betterment of "their" people. The delta's armed struggle is, at best, fragmented. At worst, it is a hodgepodge of conflicting interests in which personal feuds, ulterior motives, and enormous egos stand in the way of any meaningful progress toward peace. Couple all this with greed and criminal agendas, and any real attempt at bringing prosperity and stability to the region remains a long way off.

Short of independence and war, the more realistic aims of the Niger Delta's political activists are to retain larger shares of revenues so that local living conditions can be improved. Better roads and medical services, more jobs, lower pollution, less corruption, more clean running water, and a steady supply of electricity are among their key, and understandable, demands. Any improvements in this situation will be especially felt by sailors and oil workers, who have had to face a constant risk of being robbed or—if they are particularly unlucky—being taken hostage and held for ransom.

The federal government has made several strategic and tactical efforts to come to terms with the delta's unrest. Ex-president Olusegun Obasanjo was lauded by international observers for his credible anticorruption campaign and his 27 March 2007 launch of a "Long Term Master Plan" to address the delta's problems. However, it will take considerable time before any such plan can hope to have a significant impact.

Obasanjo's efforts have been followed up by the current regime of President Yar'Adua, who took office on 29 May 2007. Yar'Adua, immediately after his inauguration, announced that he would convene a Niger Delta Summit on 4 June 2007 to address the delta's problems once and for all. As of early August 2008, however, the summit had still not been held, and responses to government peace and prosperity initiatives have been, unsurprisingly, mixed. As a sign of initial goodwill, MEND and other groups declared a cease-fire on 3 June 2007, to give the new government time to negotiate. But they abandoned the cease-fire after only one month, unimpressed with achievements to that point.

Despite countless cease-fires since then, attacks on international assets have not only continued but increased, especially at sea. One possible explanation for this rapid increase can be found in the following passage from the *Nigerian Tribune:* "21-year-old Ekene Ibebuka, a Port Harcourt–based secondary school drop-out . . . disclosed that he received ₦2.4 million [US$20,000] in one of the kidnapping operations in Port Harcourt, where two expatriates were abducted by his late Prince Igodo–led militant group. When asked if he was into kidnapping of expatriates to express his disgust at the neglect of the Niger Delta region, Ekene retorted, 'No! (In pidgin English) Nothing concern me for that side. I do [*sic*] everything (kidnapping) to help myself and to live fine.'"[24]

Criminality and get-rich-fast attitudes will remain significant challenges to shipping and other international operations and investments until Nigerian security forces, perhaps with the help of loyal militias, can crack down on the criminal gangs. Or until the fundamental causes of unrest—unemployment, corruption, pollution, etc.—are addressed. These things will probably not happen any time soon. In the meantime, the Nigerian navy has had to shoulder the burden of trying to restore order.

### The Nigerian Navy on the Spot

Faced with such daunting social, economic, and political problems, the Nigerian navy—the country's main provider of maritime security, along with the Niger Delta Joint Task Force and the marine police—is clearly struggling to maintain law and order in the nation's territorial waters. Pressure to improve Nigeria's maritime security comes from the very top echelons of the Nigerian government, and there is certainly no lack of determination or good intentions within the security forces themselves.

The Nigerian navy command structure consists of the Naval Headquarters in Abuja and two operational commands, headquartered in Lagos and Calabar.[25] Two other operational bases are at Warri and Port Harcourt. In addition, five to seven "forward operating bases" have been established to cope with piracy and the militant threat. When the navy celebrated its fifty-first anniversary in 2007, Rear Admiral Peter Shola Adeniyi (Commanding Officer, Eastern Naval Command) said in a speech that "the Navy has done its utmost and lived up to expectation despite some constraints. With the limited resources at our disposal, we've been able to work as expected of us. We have been policing and securing our resources in the deep sea effectively." Realizing, perhaps, that this did not reassure anyone, he argued that if the navy were given more resources, such as more platforms, it would "do more than it is already doing." His concerns were echoed by Admiral Ekpenyong Okpo (retired), who stated that "the Navy is on course, but the problem . . . is that it does not have enough boats to patrol the Niger Delta."[26]

The admirals have a point. The navy is seriously underresourced. The fleet consists of some fifteen vessels, six helicopters, and a number of small inshore patrol crafts—far too few for the daunting task of stabilizing the Niger Delta. The service's performance and operational capability is described by an anonymous international maritime security consultant in this way: "Due to a combination of the following the Nigerian navy cannot offer a credible deterrent: Lack of planned and preventive maintenance, lack of spare parts, lack of adequate training (such as coxswain and seamanship skills); lack of fuel; weapon systems are not well maintained and ammunition can be in short supply/ badly maintained."[27]

To increase maritime security in the Niger Delta, President Yar'Adua convened on 13 June 2007, soon after his inauguration, a meeting in Warri, in the western delta. The governors of the three main oil-producing states—Bayelsa, Delta, and Rivers—met with the top brass of Nigeria's security forces, including the commander of the Niger Delta Joint Task Force, Brigadier General Lawrence Ngubane, and navy captain Mufutau Ajibade, commanding officer of Warri Naval Base, to determine how best to ensure the early return of the oil multinationals to abandoned oil fields. Yar'Adua told Governor Timipre Silva-Sam of Bayelsa State, Dr. Emmanuel Uduaghan of Delta State, and Mr. Celestine Omehia of Rivers State that the country could not survive the endless closure of the facilities.

Good intentions alone, however, simply will not solve the problem. Despite efforts at negotiating with local armed groups and sending security forces after those who do not cooperate, attacks have increased, not decreased. Nigerian as well as foreign naval security experts agree on one thing: the country's security forces are not ready to offer a credible maritime deterrent in the face of increasingly confident waterborne criminals and militants.

As a result of the security crisis in the Niger Delta, the International Maritime Organization (IMO) issued on 10 February 2008 a warning that if the safety of Nigeria's territorial waters continued to be threatened, no foreign vessels would be allowed to load crude oil or gas.[28] To make things worse, there has been reliable evidence of collusion between criminals and senior navy commanders, especially in the trade of stolen oil. President Yar'Adua and his administration need all the help they can get to improve the situation. Foreign countries, including the United States, are the most likely sources of this help.

## U.S. Africa Command: What Is Its Role in the Gulf of Guinea?

In its last few years, the George W. Bush administration, in seeking to diversify American energy supplies, purposefully labored to reduce American dependence on Middle Eastern oil. The U.S. focus on the Gulf of Guinea has increased significantly for that reason, as well as in the aftermath of the 11 September 2001 attacks and the subsequent invasion of Iraq. On 6 February 2007, the Bush administration announced its intention to create a new unified combatant command, U.S. Africa Command, or AFRICOM. Its aim is to promote American national security objectives in Africa and its surrounding waters.

The military involvement of the United States on the continent was previously divided among the U.S. European Command (EUCOM), Central Command (CENTCOM), and Pacific Command (PACOM). The new command's area of responsibility includes all African countries except Egypt. AFRICOM was launched as a subunified command under EUCOM on 1 October 2007 and was made fully operational as a stand-alone command on 1 October 2008.

The justification for AFRICOM is Africa's growing strategic importance to U.S. interests, as noted by analysts and American policy makers in recent years. Among those interests, according to Congressional Research Service, are "Africa's role in the Global War on Terror and potential threats posed by uncontrolled spaces; the growing importance of Africa's natural resources, particularly energy resources; and ongoing concern for Africa's many humanitarian crises and armed conflicts."[29] Several African nations have been courted with aid and training programs, with one objective in mind: to encourage them to welcome an increased U.S. presence on the continent. According to official U.S. sources "the President's intent is to have AFRICOM located on the African continent where it can best interact with partner nations."[30]

The problem is that only a few countries—among them, Liberia—want American military bases on their soil, even though many, in security terms, could use a helping hand. Currently, AFRICOM is headquartered at Kelley Barracks in Stuttgart, Germany. On 19 November 2007, Nigeria formally announced that it would not host AFRICOM.[31] The government made its position official as President Yar'Adua met with state governors and federal lawmakers. Nigeria is also, at least publicly, against the U.S. command's basing its headquarters anywhere in West Africa.

Nigeria's rejection of AFRICOM is grounded in its desire to appear independent of outside influence, even though cooperation with the United States on many levels is desired, required, and already implemented. For example, Exercise MARITIME SAFARI–LAGOS 2008, a joint maritime surveillance training exercise involving the Nigerian navy and air force and the U.S. Navy, was held 22–28 February 2008.[32] According to Nigerian defense officials, the exercise focused on search and rescue procedures, aircraft maintenance, and best practices in improving maritime safety.

Another sign of Nigeria's willingness to accept American presence, short of bases, is its participation in the African Partnership Station, a naval assistance program under the AFRICOM rubric. An agreement was reached at the beginning of November 2007 that granted Washington a naval presence in this strategically important region for the purpose of training and humanitarian aid.[33]

Notwithstanding Nigeria's need for, indeed welcome of, U.S. support, Yar'Adua's government has to balance its maritime security needs with the country's other domestic interests and with its obligations to other important partners, like China, which is a key supporter and financier of federal government projects. In addition, Nigeria's large Muslim population could find U.S. "interference" hard to accept. Also, U.S. involvement in Nigerian affairs can be interpreted as meddling and as a sign of Nigerian weakness and caving into foreign ambitions, which touches upon the issue of national pride.

One illustration of how sensitive this latter issue can be appeared in a December 2007 editorial in the *Vanguard,* a widely read Lagos newspaper: "Recently, the Americans pompously expressed their interest in establishing a military base in Nigeria to protect its interests, especially stable crude oil supply. Its efforts at total control of Nigeria's security could not have been better put. These actions demonstrate U.S. government's contempt for Nigeria." Some Nigerian military leaders have stated that they "would be finished as a force" if they let U.S. forces roam freely.[34] In early May, following pressure from Africans, Washington publicly dropped its plans for a new headquarters on the continent. Instead, the United States will place staff there as needs arise. AFRICOM already uses thirteen offices of defense cooperation at American embassies in African capitals. The offices will be renamed "offices of security cooperation," according to military newspaper *Stars and Stripes.*[35]

In the face of African resentment, President Bush worked hard to convince the continent's leaders of the nation's good intentions. In addition to a much-publicized tour of Africa in February 2008, the Bush administration spent billions of dollars on humanitarian assistance. For example, by the end of its first five-year phase, in September 2008, the President's Emergency Plan for AIDS Relief, better known as PEPFAR, had spent US$18.8 billion, mainly in Africa. President Bush asked Congress for another thirty billion for the next five years. This silent campaign of humanitarian assistance is, according to the newspaper the *Economist,* "doing good, quietly."[36] Still, the U.S. government is not handing out something for nothing. There is a strategy behind the expanding generosity of the United States toward Africa, and a central goal of this strategy is to secure U.S. access to energy resources.

As for Nigeria, American concerns are spelled out in the 5 February 2008 annual threat assessment of the Director of National Intelligence: "Persistent insecurity in Nigeria's oil-producing region, the Niger Delta, poses a direct threat to U.S. strategic interests in sub-Saharan Africa."[37] AFRICOM's greatest challenge is to balance the need for access to oil with a policy that does not offend Nigeria and other countries in the Gulf of Guinea. Statesmanship, tact, persistence, and wisdom are required on both sides of the Atlantic in order to address constructively the security dilemma in Nigerian waters and the wider Gulf of Guinea. Just maintaining the status quo—or worse, letting Nigeria slip even farther into chaos—is in no one's interest.

## Conclusions

"To understand politics in Nigeria," writes Marvin Zonis of the University of Chicago, "you have to know about 'cake.'" "Cake" refers to resources controlled by the government: revenues, jobs, infrastructure projects, access to universities, public-sector employment.[38] Cake is what the criminal gangs, community pressure groups, and political militants in the Niger Delta are after, and also, to a far lesser extent, Lagos small-time bandits. Cake is what corrupt government officials have been unscrupulously shoving by the truckload into their foreign bank accounts—or dishing out to loyal supporters and friends. Many gangs and militant groups have been used to intimidate opponents by cynical political thugs in their quests for power, position, and more cake.

In turn, these politicians have looked the other way when the gangs have committed their shady deeds. "Political connections have helped these gangs to commit criminal offenses with near-total impunity," writes Human Rights Watch in a recent report;[39] "While Nigeria's military intervened in August [2007] to halt the escalating inter-gang bloodletting, Nigeria's federal government and the police have completely failed to address the root causes of the violence—not one Rivers State politician has been investigated or held to account for directly fomenting the state's epidemic of gang violence."[40] On 5 April 2008, a notorious gang leader stated to the *Niger Delta Standard*, "I, Ateke Tom, made Dr. Peter Odili [former Rivers State governor] and Mr. Rotimi Amaechi [the current governor] in 1999 when they were nobody."[41]

Against this backdrop, there is little reason for optimism with regard to Niger Delta security. The problems of the delta, indeed of Nigeria, are mainly systemic—including corruption, bad governance, rampant poverty, unemployment, and criminal connections far into the offices of senior politicians and naval commanders.[42] All of these problems contribute to an environment that is less than conducive, to put it mildly, to stability and prosperity. In addition, there has recently appeared an unhealthy penchant for getting rich fast, avoiding the tedium of patient effort and hard work. This attitude seems to have overwhelmed too many young men in the delta. Even the patient Ogonis, of whom Saro-Wiwa once was a leader, are detecting rumblings among their youth. The current MOSOP leader, Ledum Mitee, during October 2007 was particularly concerned that his followers were beginning to emulate the violent behavior of the Ijaws.[43]

The true causes of insecurity in Nigerian waters have to be considered at three levels, all of which will contribute to a continuing poor security environment in the near to distant future. At the micro level, there are the scores of frustrated and testosterone-driven young men who, as mentioned above, simply want to "help [themselves] and to live fine." At the national level, there are the many systemic shortcomings. At the macro level, that of international politics and law, Nigeria needs to balance its security needs and U.S. courtship with the interests of other significant players—notably China, the country's large Muslim population, and other states that might resent American meddling in the region's internal and regional affairs. None of these three parameters are likely to change significantly in the near term. Meanwhile, until these problems are solved, foreign as well as Nigerian mariners and oil workers will be left to juggle their own security risk management as best they can.

## Notes

Additional research was contributed by Ms. Ingrid Mellingen and Mr. Odin Hjellestad.

1. Bergen Risk Solutions [hereafter BRS], a Norway-based risk management firm, reported fifty-three attacks during the same period. The numbers compiled by BRS are higher than IMB's, as some attacks are, for various reasons, not reported to the bureau. BRS numbers also include attacks on such fixed offshore objects as oil rigs and FPSOs, barges, and FSOs.

2. International Chamber of Commerce, *Piracy and Armed Robbery against Ships: Annual Report 1 January–31 December 2007* (London: International Maritime Bureau, 2008), pp. 5–6.

3. BRS, "Niger Delta Security: Monthly Report," 11 January 2008. The four coastal states most affected are Delta, Bayelsa, Rivers, and Akwa Ibom. Rivers State is by far the worst.

4. BRS, "Maritime Security in Nigeria," *Quarterly Review,* no. 1 (July 2007), p. 14, and "Maritime Security in Nigeria," *Quarterly Review,* no. 3 (January 2008), p. 11.

5. Quoted in Daniel Morris, "The Other Oil-Rich Gulf," *National Interest Online,* www.nationalinterest.org/.

6. *This Day* (Lagos), 2 February 2008, available at www.thisdayonline.com/.

7. John Ghazvinian, *Untapped: The Scramble for Africa's Oil* (Orlando, Fla.: Harcourt, 2007), p. 7.

8. Ibid., p. 19.

9. Martin Meredith, *The State of Africa: A History of Fifty Years of Independence* (London: Free Press/Simon & Schuster, 2006), p. 576.

10. Ghazvinian, *Untapped,* p. 19.

11. National Intelligence Council, *Mapping Sub-Saharan Africa's Future: Conference Summary* (Washington, D.C.: March 2005), p. 16.

12. *Daily Sun* (Lagos), 13 March 2008, available at www.sunnewsonline.com/.

13. *Nigerian Tribune* (Ibadan), 5 January 2008, available at www.tribune.com.ng/.

14. *The Punch,* 5 January 2008, www.punchng.com/.

15. *Minutes of the 2nd Port Facility Security Officer (PFSO) Forum* (Lagos, Nigeria: Lagos Maritime Security Zone, 6 December 2007).

16. *Vanguard* (Lagos), December 2007, available at www.vanguardngr.com/.

17. *This Day* (Lagos), 13 February 2008, available at allafrica.com/stories/200802130730.html/.

18. BRS, "Maritime Security in Nigeria," *Quarterly Review,* no. 4 (March 2008). The trend of increasing attacks continued in the second quarter. As of 30 June 2008 BRS had recorded forty maritime security incidents that year.

19. BRS, "Maritime Security in Nigeria," *Quarterly Review,* no. 5 (July 2008). On 19 June 2008 armed men in three boats attacked Shell's deepwater Bonga field, approximately sixty-five nautical miles off the coast of Bayelsa State. The attackers, probably associated with MEND—a militant group—opened fire on a drilling ship (FPSO) and three supporting vessels.

20. The NDPVF was most active in 2004 and 2005, when its leader, Alhaji Mujahid Dokubo-Asari, declared war on the federal government and foreign oil firms. Asari was arrested in September 2005 and charged with treason. He was released on 14 June 2007 as a peace gesture by recently elected President Yar'Adua. MEND, which had been demanding Asari's release from the day it first emerged, on 10 January 2006, may be considered a successor organization to the NDPVF. There is also a myriad of smaller groups throughout the region.

21. Michael Watts, "Petro-insurgency or Criminal Syndicate? Conflict and Violence in the Niger Delta," *Review of African Political Economy* 34, no. 14 (December 2007), p. 646; Jomo Gbomo (MEND spokesman), e-mail to author, 21 October 2007.

22. *Daily Champion* (Lagos), 24 June 2007, available at allafrica.com/.

23. Nigerians-abroad.com.

24. *Nigerian Tribune* (Ibadan), 20 June 2007, available at intellibriefs.blogspot.com/.

25. *Nigerian Navy Official Website,* www.nigeriannavy.gov.ng/.

26. *Vanguard* (Lagos), 5 June 2007, available at allafrica.com/.

27. E-mail to author, 2 July 2007.

28. *Guardian* (Lagos), 11 February 2008, available at www.guardiannewsngr.com/.

29. U.S. Library of Congress, *Africa Command: U.S. Strategic Interests, and the Role of the U.S. Military in Africa* (Washington, D.C.: Congressional Research Service, 7 December 2007), available at www.fas.org/.

30. *United States Africa Command,* www.africom.mil/.

31. *International Herald Tribune,* 19 November 2008, available at www.iht.com/.

32. Nigerians-abroad.com.

33. Reuters (Dakar), 12 November 2007, available at africa.reuters.com/.

34. *Vanguard* (Lagos), 3 December 2007, available at allafrica.com/.

35. Charlie Coon, "AFRICOM Halts HQ Plan; Will Phase In Staff," *Stars and Stripes,* Mideast edition, 4 May 2008, available at www.stripes.com/.

36. "Doing Good, Quietly," *Economist,* 16 February 2008, p. 44.

37. Available at www.fas.org/.

38. Marvin Zonis, Dan Lefkovitz, and Sam Wilkin, *The Kimchi Matters: Global Business and Local Politics in a Crisis-Driven World* (Chicago: Agate, 2003), p. 19.

39. "Politics as War: The Human Rights Impact and Causes of Post-election Violence in Rivers State, Nigeria," *Human Rights Watch* 20 (March 2008), no. 3, p. 57.

40. Ibid.

41. *OyibosOnline: The Expat's Guide to Nigeria,* www.oyibosonline.com/.

42. "Conviction of Admirals Confirms Navy Role in Oil Theft," IRIN News Agency, UN Office for the Coordination of Humanitarian Affairs, 6 January 2005, available at www.irinnews.org/.

43. Ledum Mitee, interview by author, Port Harcourt, 3 October 2007.

# CHAPTER THIRTEEN

# Fish, Family, and Profit
## Piracy and the Horn of Africa
GARY E. WEIR

The frightening increase in piracy off the coast of Somalia since the turn of the present century demonstrates just how fast this kind of threat can emerge and how severe the difficulties involved in understanding and subduing it can be. Since 1992, in fact, there have been 3,583 piratical attacks worldwide. According to the United Kingdom's House of Commons Transport Committee: "This represents an increase from 1993 to 2005 of 168%. In the same period, 340 crew members and passengers died at the hands of pirates, and 464 received injuries. In 2005 alone piracy resulted in over 150 injuries and assaults and over 650 crew members were taken hostage or kidnapped."[1] Recent assaults on Japanese and French vessels near Somalia and the military response by the latter in April 2008 demonstrate the lasting significance of this problem and the complexity of its roots.[2]

Given the definition of piracy crafted in the United Nations Convention on the Law of the Sea 1982 (UNCLOS), most activity characterized by that name over the past decade actually comes far closer to armed robbery than actual piracy.[3] In Malaysia and Indochina, traditional hotbeds of this practice, most incidents reported by the International Maritime Bureau (or IMB, a division of the International Chamber of Commerce, or ICC) actually take place at the pier, while the ship rests at anchor, or in territorial waters, a distinction often not made in gathering the statistics.

The nature of this definitional problem in its Somali form presents a contrast with the historical Asian paradigm. Pursuit, seizure, and deprivation at sea in waters bordering the Gulf of Aden and in the Indian Ocean fall more clearly than the Asian events into the UNCLOS definition of piracy. This kind of lawlessness has always presented political and international complexities, made more difficult by national jurisdictions, corporate motives, and the scattered geography of the broader Asian region. In the Horn of Africa, part of the considerable expanse patrolled by U.S. Naval Forces, Central Command and Combined Task Force 150, the geography and the jurisdictional difficulties, while not simple, do not present the same level of complexity.

The proximity of politically unstable nations or territories has regularly emerged as both cause of and *permission* for armed robbery or piracy at sea.[4] The northeast and eastern coasts of Somalia, at the Horn of Africa, have caught the attention of the IMB, which reported a very "alarming rise" in what it called piracy beginning in midsummer 2005. Somalia's internal unrest, its lack of government control, and the authority of local clan warlords have created a favorable climate for maritime crime, one that often gives thieves and pirates *permission* to act freely.

The IMB has called for a combined response and solution—that is, international naval assistance, especially along the Somali coast. It also initially encouraged merchant masters and navigators to observe a coastal approach limit of at least fifty nautical miles. The threat to international commerce extends to cargo and container ships, oil tankers, and even United Nations food and medical supply ships. In the Gulf of Aden, in the Indian Ocean, and off the Somali coast, the uncontrolled activity of maritime criminals also presents a threat to the traffic that supports American forces in Iraq. However, in evaluating the event statistics collected by the IMB, one needs to remember that profitability and the safety of business interests drives the ICC, making it eager both for peace and for someone to bear most of the cost for piracy countermeasures.

In September 2001, a group of nations agreed to form Combined Task Force (CTF) 150 in response to UN Security Council Resolution 1373, which committed them to regional patrols as part of the global war on terrorism. The task force members include the United States, Pakistan, Australia, Great Britain, France, and Netherlands, among others. The French very early began escorting UN World Food Program ships into Mogadishu.[5]

### Background to Piracy in Somalia

Historically, the IMB request for combined assistance resonates with the nineteenth-century American experience against privateers and pirates based in northern Africa and the Caribbean Sea. Two hundred years ago, the United States needed logistical bases so that its armed forces could operate in the Mediterranean, thousands of miles from home. As the nineteenth century dawned, British-held Gibraltar became an essential logistical base for U.S. operations during the Barbary Wars. In that same conflict, the loan of shallow-draft vessels from the Kingdom of Sicily also enabled the U.S. Navy to operate in shallow waters to enforce a blockade of Tripolitan ports. In this war, cooperation with local authorities and collaboration with allied navies made success possible. This formula brought success once again when the U.S. Navy worked closely with the Royal Navy in the 1820s against Caribbean piracy.[6]

During that same century and on the other side of the world, the Italians, French, and British controlled the Horn of Africa. The latter nation took the lead, due to the authority of the Royal Navy and the proximity of both imperial India and the presence of a British resident authority in Aden. Thus, the United Kingdom effectively exerted control over the strategically significant Somali Basin and the Gulf of Aden, at the southern entrance to the Red Sea. A formal protectorate emerged as British Somaliland, with the governing authority in nearby Aden administering British interests through 1905.

British authority in the area survived World War I, and the presence of significant air and naval power through the 1920s permitted the United Kingdom to sustain its position there. Losing control for just a short time to Italy during the East African campaign in 1940 and 1941, British forces once again asserted imperial authority and retained control of the region until both independence and unification with Italian Somaliland gave birth to the Somali Republic in 1960. This infant democracy lasted only nine years before succumbing to a coup and the dictatorship of General Muhammad Siad Barre, who initially established very close ties with the Soviet Union within the context of the Cold War. His loyalties later shifted when neighbor and traditional enemy Ethiopia allied itself with the Soviet Union.

Control over local waters provided a foundation for the local economy and the only hope of prosperity. Siad Barre maintained a small maritime force to protect the enormously rich fisheries in Somali waters, to sell (at a profit) fishery licenses to foreign companies, and to monitor access to regional ports that served the import and export trade through this strategic region south of the Red Sea and Suez. The humble Somali maritime force guarded these resources and also restricted the traditional regional tendency toward piracy and maritime crime. But when the Siad Barre regime collapsed in 1991, everything changed.

The evaporation of the Siad Barre regime opened the door to a period of instability. The naval task force associated with United Nations peacekeeping operations in Somalia (UNOSOM I and II) between 1991 and 1995 managed to monitor effectively the considerable maritime traffic through the important lanes of passage off the Horn of Africa. These routes historically cater to ships moving from Africa into the Gulf of Aden–Red Sea area. In most cases ships passed fairly close to the Somali coast to effect more economical passages. For each large modern merchant bottom that plies these waters one can also find many more ships traditional to the region carrying cargo along routes regularly employed for centuries. Many of these vessels are the large cargo dhows so common in those waters.

Before unrest closed destinations or made calls too risky, a number of Somali ports regularly played host to ships moving through this portion of the Indian Ocean. These included Kismaayo, El Aolde, Merca, and El Maan. Mogadishu played this role as well until it was closed to foreign vessels in 1995. When the United Nations forces left in 1995, Somalia had no effective government, could not continue monitoring the waters off its coast, and descended into a period of clan warfare.[7]

### Piracy and Economic Survival

The chaotic situation ashore and the damage inflicted on the country's economy and infrastructure had a very significant effect at sea. For many of the coastal village communities, offshore fishing represented a regular and significant livelihood. These small businessmen and their families depended completely on the rich fishing off the Somali coast as a source of treasure going back generations. In these cases the fishermen operated from small dhows, wooden canoes or boats, or more recently modern small boats, such as motorized fiberglass skiffs. They would use traditional techniques, for the most part gathering their catch using nets and then off-loading the take for sale upon returning to shore.[8]

The collapse of the Somali central government in 1995 opened the region to uncontrolled foreign exploitation. Large commercial fishing vessels began working off the Somali shoreline and very often inside the country's territorial waters and traditional domestic fishing areas. These large-scale fishing ships dwarfed the boats of the local fishing fleet and placed in danger a coastal subsistence economy based on traditional fishing practices.[9] The high-seas piracy problem emerged from this context.

When violence first erupted between these conflicting interests in 1995, it came as a surprise to no one. Many pirates armed themselves with weapons, which were easily available due to the struggle for power among the Somali clans. Somalia's 2,060-mile-long coastline was soon considered to be one of the "world's most dangerous stretches of water because of piracy."[10] By 2002, the IMB was reporting that the number of attacks had jumped from 335 in 2001 to 370 in 2002 and had increased its rating for the risk of attack from "possibility" to "certainty."[11]

### Piracy and the Absence of Government Authority

The first incidents between 1995 and 2000 occurred when Somali fishermen boarded foreign vessels and accused them of fishing illegally. The local fishermen sought immediate compensation for catches taken in their traditional fishing areas. These actions occasionally took the form of efforts by local clan militias seeking to control their neighborhoods ashore and to coordinate actions against the foreign interlopers at sea. Many groups who boarded foreign vessels in this manner frequently referred to themselves as a "coast guard," protecting Somali waters and resources. In some cases this self-proclaimed coast guard took the vessels in question back to Somali ports, holding their cargoes and crews for ransom in compensation for lost revenue.

Foreign interests responded not by withdrawing but by arming the crews of their ships, hiring security forces, or bargaining with the local warlords or clan leaders for fishing "licenses." The latter came at prices high enough to make those documents a rather lucrative source of income for the clans ashore. Of course, the clans had no legal authority to offer licenses of any kind, but no central government existed to set the entire problem in a national context with legal agreements and effective enforcement power.[12]

In the months immediately after the fall of the Siad Barre regime, both the Republic of Somaliland in the northern, formally British imperial, territory, and the Puntland Autonomous Region, formed in 1998, attempted to exert control and supervision of fishing and territorial waters. Both had rudimentary coast guards and dabbled in the lucrative business of fishing licenses.

To the south the internal strife and the offshore issues produced a different result. The clans fought over the right to control Mogadishu and took over the basic revenue sources usually reserved for central governments. Some clan warlords controlled the airports, others the maritime facilities and customs revenue, and still others focused on the profitable business of selling fishing licenses of dubious legality. Piracy, as an independent and openly illegal enterprise, developed only slowly, because clan leaders did not wish to have their licensing businesses interrupted.

Central Somalia has produced the most aggressive forms of piracy—well organized, clan related, and determined. In this region, traditionally called the Mugdug, poverty has reigned as long as memory serves, and the region's lack of resources has permitted it to escape the attention of the other regional clan warlords. For this area, the fishing industry provides virtually the only means of income.[13] Thus the people of the Mugdug suffered most from the foreign exploitation of the coastal fishing grounds. When clashes began between local fishermen and the commercial fishing ventures, no clan interests or presumptive central authority intervened to prevent uncontrolled escalation.

In the dangerous environment of the Mugdug, legitimate efforts to limit both foreign exploitation of Somali resources and the growth of various related, profitable, but often illicit businesses collectively transformed themselves into a full-fledged venture in modern piracy. The developing piracy ring, initially acting under the direction of the Habir Gedir subclan of the Hawiye clan, emerged as a major threat to Horn of Africa commercial interests in 2004 under the leadership of Mohamed Abdi Afweyne. Under

Afweyne's leadership, the organization flourished; the town of Harardhere became the ring's headquarters and gave its name to this potent enterprise. In spite of the transition to piracy, an important part of the justification, openly trumpeted by those involved, remained the need to protect from foreign exploitation Somali resources and the popular livelihood of coastal communities. The ring, portraying any fees collected or cargoes expropriated as legitimate products of the defensive effort, used the national turmoil and economic suffering as political and cultural cover for its illicit activities.[14]

When the Harardhere ring made the leap to high-seas piracy and much larger commercial vessels as victims, it naturally used the traditional tools available to Somali fishermen, with a bit of tactical refinement. Its skiffs, frequently seen in international press coverage, were employed because of the availability of small motorized boats of fiberglass construction with styrofoam cores. These boats litter the coastline, and the local fishermen, from among whom the Harardhere ring recruited its members, knew how to use them.

By 2004 the pirates began to use multiple skiffs in their work. A larger skiff provided room for provisions that might sustain a pirate crew, just as it would a fishing party, for up to two weeks, and at a range of two hundred nautical miles. It could also carry food and water, as well as providing the means and space for storing and repairing fishing nets, reflecting the more traditional occupational habits of the crew. In looking for targets, these fishermen-turned-pirates identified their prey visually. Thus, a patrol vessel or potential victim could hardly tell the difference at distance between a pirate and a legitimate fisherman.

In approaching any vessel two smaller skiffs, each with a crew of four or five, would place themselves astride the vessel, one to starboard and the other to port, with the larger skiff astern in pursuit. The pirates then placed one or more of their number on board the target vessel to intimidate the crew and clear the way for the rest of the boarding party, which would bring the captured vessel to port with the skiffs in tow. (In many recent cases CTF 150 patrols intercepting seized ships have first destroyed the towed skiffs to make sure the pirates remained on board and could not slip away.)[15]

Implemented in early 2005, this technique has resulted in some failures but also in some disturbing successes. The latter include the capture of MV *Feisty Gas,* a compressed-gas transport, in April 2005 and MV *Torgelow* the following October.[16] These major attacks as well as an attempt to take the cruise ship *Seabourne Spirit* in November 2005 drew international media attention, a warning to mariners from the IMB, and a response from international naval forces in the area. The IMB advised all merchant masters to keep their vessels two hundred nautical miles away from the Somali coast. The merchantmen most vulnerable tended to operate at ten knots or less, in daylight, with no emergency broadcast capability and no security force on board. Moving into Somali territorial waters proved especially dangerous, since the American component of CTF 150 could not operate within the twelve-mile limit.

All three episodes also brought up the legal and tactical issue of onboard armed security. *Seabourne Spirit* carried Gurkhas, former military personnel, as security, and this fact played a role in the vessel's ability to resist seizure. The masters and shipping companies did not favor arming the crew, however, and professional onboard security added expense. For many shipowners these measures also seemed to increase the likelihood of more violent clashes with pirates. The only other option seemed increasing the size of the crew to enable more effective ship security, enhance lookout capability, and reduce the debilitating effect of fatigue. The latter had become a critical factor, because the crew had to perform security functions in addition to its regular duties.[17]

**Enter Combined Task Force 150**

The presence of CTF 150, especially after the *Seabourne Spirit* incident, prompted a change in pirate habits. The Harardhere group began using captured low-value vessels as mother ships for the skiffs. In this they sought the advantage of surprise, by appearing to be part of the normal commercial traffic of the region.

In one case the U.S. Navy responded to an alert from the IMB in Kuala Lumpur that pirates had in this way (unsuccessfully) assaulted MV *Safina Al Bisarat,* a bulk carrier outside the two-hundred-nautical-mile safety zone off Somalia's central eastern coast. U.S. Central Command responded by sending the guided-missile destroyer USS *Winston S. Churchill* (DDG 81) to investigate. The warship located the dhow responsible for the attack, chased it down, and boarded it, after firing some warning shots by way of persuasion. The boarding party detained sixteen Indian nationals and ten Somali men. The Indians claimed that the Somalis had seized their dhow six days before near Mogadishu and had used it since to surprise and capture victims. The Navy investigated the incident and discussed with international authorities the proper disposition of the men taken from the dhow.[18]

Ships assigned to the patrol area of Somalia had repeated encounters with pirates.[19] USS *James E. Williams* (DDG 95) assisted the North Korean crew of MV *Dai Hong Dan* in regaining control of its vessel after pirates seized its bridge in October 2007. The Koreans had kept control of both the steering gear and the engines, and with the assistance of the American vessel they successfully assaulted the pirates on the bridge. At the same time another American destroyer pursued a Japanese vessel reportedly hijacked by pirates off Somalia. As if to demonstrate the extent of the danger in these waters, the destroyers USS *Arleigh Burke* (DDG 51) and USS *Porter* (DDG 78) responded to a call for help from MV *Golden Nori,* a Japanese chemical tanker seized off the Socotra Archipelago near the Horn of Africa on 28 October 2007. When the destroyers drew near the captured ship, *Porter* used its main battery to destroy the skiffs being towed astern. *Arleigh Burke* then received permission from the tenuous transitional government of Somalia to enter territorial waters to subdue the ship. The Navy continued to track *Golden Nori* until the pirates abandoned it on 12 December.[20]

Somali national instability, of which maritime crime is one of the worst by-products, inevitably came into direct contact with the war in Iraq. In 2005, the IMB reported a rise in maritime lawlessness in the Arabian Sea. In spite of the proximity of warships, the ICC reported two attacks off the Basra oil terminal, two more at buoy anchorages, and another five in Iraqi waters on 19 and 20 November. In each case the perpetrators injured and robbed the crew and made away with arms, cash, personal property, and, occasionally, some rather advanced technologies.[21] In some Somali episodes the IMB and other sources have reported the use of fast pursuit craft against commercial targets as far as a hundred nautical miles out to sea. Virtually all reports confirm the use of sophisticated small arms and rocket-propelled grenades, as well as crude weapons. This activity represents a threat to life, property, and free navigation of the sea at the southern end of an area of great concern to the U.S. Navy Central Command and Combined Task Force 150.

The advent of the Council of Islamic Courts (CIC) in 2006, capable of confronting the clans and warlords, presented the prospect of Somalia as a haven for terrorists but not for pirates. While some of the more radical members of the courts supported al-Qaʻida and had little love for the United States, they had even less love for high-seas piracy, which they declared immoral. This produced a challenge to Somali pirates when during 2006 the CIC briefly managed to reopen the port of Mogadishu without pirate interference to gather port-entry fees and other profits. However, the CIC's influence over piracy lasted only a very short time. A transitional-national-government force and the Ethiopian National Defense Force brought the brief reign of the council to a close and introduced uncertainty once again.

**The Way Ahead**

On 22 April 2008, France, the United Kingdom, and the United States called for a United Nations resolution to support the nations determined to fight piracy off Somalia. Only one week before, the French armed forces had captured six Somali pirates who had seized the French-owned luxury yacht *Le Ponant* and held the crew of twenty-two for a week, hoping for ransom. The French government had the pirates taken to France for interrogation. Apparently undeterred, another contingent of pirates took a ship moving through the region from Dubai on 21 April; in addition, the Spanish navy went off in pursuit of a seized Spanish tuna boat taken with a crew of twenty-six off the Somalia coast. The French ambassador to the United Nations, Jean-Maurice Ripert, commented to the press that his country had no desire to endanger the law of the sea; the French, Americans, and the British, he said, simply wanted a mandate from the United Nations to take action against piracy in the name of the international community.[22] He explained, "The idea is to give a mandate, to call on states of the U.N. to tackle piracy by organizing patrols, reacting to acts of piracy, to take as many preventative measures as possible."[23]

In response to the increased threat of piracy off Somalia, on 2 June 2008 the UN Security Council adopted Resolution 1816, with the consent of Somalia—which, the resolution observed, "lacks the capacity to interdict pirates or patrol and secure its territorial waters." This resolution authorized foreign naval vessels to enter Somali territorial waters for an initial period of six months, which could later be lengthened by mutual agreement. This resolution also allowed foreign naval vessels to use "all necessary means" to repress acts of piracy and armed robbery at sea, consistent with relevant and existing provisions of international law.[24]

This resolution may result in stopping the pirates, but it does not address the underlying factors that created them in the first place. In looking for a solution, we need to recall the history of the problem. The Somali situation emerged from the exploitation of traditional fisheries and the inability of local fishermen to preserve their resources and livelihood. Thus, the long-term solution to this problem must go beyond traditional coalitions, formal alliances, the power of regional neighbors, and the destruction of individual targets. An international framework of common applicable law, common enforcement, and common policy must extend beyond regional boundaries and political borders.[25]

Rather than reinventing the wheel, building upon existing successful civilian fisheries agreements might present the best model for not only strengthening those agreements but also extending them to provide greater security against maritime crime.[26] Developed in this way, the collaboration would feel inclusive, mostly civilian, and military only in a minimal sense. In Asia, the forms of cooperation developed by the South Pacific Forum Fisheries Agency, whose members have already agreed to enforcement collaboration, would certainly provide the basis for a framework that would address piracy and armed robbery at sea.[27]

In the immediate region of Somalia, concerned nations might look to the Regional Commission for Fisheries (RECOFI). This association counts among its members Bahrain, Iran, Iraq, Kuwait, Oman, Qatar, Saudi Arabia, and the United Arab Emirates.[28] Its objectives include the development, conservation, and management of marine resources and the promotion of aquaculture. At the same time RECOFI has decided to regulate fishing methods and gear as well as the seasons for fishing and the extent of the catch.

Many of RECOFI's primary concerns and goals address the issues of central control and national sovereignty that triggered the so-called coast-guard actions off Somalia by local fishermen. The lack of such control has generated a pool of unemployed and desperate candidates ripe for recruitment into the pirate crews that have turned the Horn of Africa and the Gulf of Aden into such dangerous places. RECOFI has also embraced the need "to keep under review the economic and social aspects of the fishing industry." Regardless of its present nature, large-scale and increasingly deep-ocean piracy in Somalia originated from the desire of poor communities to save their livelihoods. In its present form RECOFI cannot entirely address the problem at hand, but it can certainly provide a framework upon which to build. Many other agreements exist that might serve the same purpose, and they touch every part of the world ocean.[29]

For their part, navies can inform and support locally enforced regional frameworks built upon agreements like RECOFI and upon the progress made in previous years by the Piracy Reporting Center in Malaysia, and its supporting organizations, created in 1992. Any framework must include all nations affected, regardless of political perspective or bilateral commitments. The same common civilian and commercial interests that lead nations to agree on fisheries management will help to address maritime crime.

More practical policy responses might include enabling both local authorities and corporate countermeasures. Naval forces can provide mine countermeasure vessels, should criminals lay mines in choke points or ports. Navies should also offer to increase or enhance exercises, training, and cooperation to assist regional or secondary maritime forces in undertaking these tasks. Naval experience with unmanned aerial vehicles (UAVs) and ship security systems can help the spread of best practices in the use of methods suggested by the International Maritime Organization, such as the Inventus UAV, ShipLoc, and Secure-Ship. These measures would dovetail well with the strategy of supporting a regional framework.

Any effort to explore a more global framework would obviously require more multinational naval involvement. Addressing the Seventeenth International Seapower Symposium on 21 September 2005 at the Naval War College, in Newport, Rhode Island, Admiral Michael Mullen, U.S. Navy, then the Chief of Naval Operations, began to explore the possibilities open to global navies: "As we combine our advantages, I envision a 1,000-ship Navy—a fleet-in-being, if you will, made up of the best capabilities of all freedom-loving navies of the world. . . . This 1,000-ship Navy would integrate the capabilities of the maritime services to create a fully interoperable force—an international city at sea."[30] For some naval historians the admiral's statements seemed timely indeed. The Combined Operations Project led in 2005–2006 by the Contemporary History Branch of the U.S. Naval Historical Center had examined the nature of effective naval coalitions and their ability to address the varied threats on the high seas. In each of the case studies, conducted by American, Canadian, Australian, and British historians, communication and trust emerge as paramount. Without the trust engendered by effective, well trained liaison officers, and frequent collaborative exercises at sea, combined operations can quickly become exercises in futility.

Deliberate, frequent, and regular contact allowed his commanding officers to broker the mutual understanding that served Vice Admiral Lord Nelson so well two centuries ago. This dynamic has become even more necessary today, given the potential contemporary barriers of language, culture, technology, and operational experience. The history of recent combined operations repeatedly speaks to these critical but often overlooked personal aspects. In short, history suggests that in naval operations as well as in international, civilian maritime policy, "you cannot surge trust."[31]

Human relations emerge strongly as the primary asset or resource needed to bring peace and enforcement to the maritime commons, including the Horn of Africa. Commodore James Stapleton, Royal Australian Navy, the naval component commander in the international military response to violence in East Timor in 1999, once made this very point in reflecting on the reasons for success in that operation. The naval component of the multinational United Nations task force supporting Operation STABILISE achieved a very high level of interoperability. Effective communication and division of labor brought to the effort in East Timor the kind of success currently sought off the Somali coast.

In a 2004 oral interview by the author, referring to the commanding officers of the ships under his temporary command for Operation STABILISE, Stapleton recalled that "they'd all come from a major exercise that was called off, the one that I was going to go to. So they'd had time in company and they'd worked with [USS] *Mobile Bay* before, they'd worked with [HMS] *Glasgow* . . , they'd worked with [HMNZS] *Te Kaha*. . . . I'd worked with these ships before, I knew the COs, I knew the capabilities of each of the ships. So we'd worked together pretty much for a lot of the time."[32] Combining proved relatively easy, as the relationships remained fresh and current and drew on strong common experience: "It was very much a one-on-one . . . with every country, but the way I spoke to them and the operation order for communications, the operation order for the flying program . . . , was the standard NATO signal which they all have."[33]

It was necessary to take measures consciously designed to build and renew the human network among ships and people, a relationship that cannot have the flavor of a single nation alone: "[I had people] from each country on my staff. . . . I had a Frenchman on my staff, I had a Canadian or two, engineers. I had New Zealanders. This became a problem for me then about classification, and what I could leave lying around . . . [i]ssues like that. And what was privileged information, and what wasn't. . . . It does make problems, but if you don't manage it, and I didn't have those guys and girls on my staff, for sure, then the coalition thing doesn't work."[34]

All this had to become as natural as the first cup of coffee in the morning, a fit so well engineered over time, socially and professionally, that it could become second nature:

> You hear people say, "I'm an Australian," but people in Australia still know what you mean when you say "I'll have a brew," a coffee, "I'll have a NATO standard" (that's white and two [sugars]). Maybe that's because that reflects my age . . . and I did a lot of training in the UK. So I knew NATO, and I know the publications. But if you're using ATP, the tactical publications, you can talk to any navy in the world, because everyone's got Allied Tactical Publications. You can also use international codes. So it was never really an issue about integration. . . . Everybody just fitted in.[35]

History strongly suggests that very often, ignoring these experiences, we have placed our emphasis elsewhere or viewed naval personnel simply as extensions of platforms and technologies. We must recognize that the cultural expectations shaping naval careers have long militated against the role the international community needs many officers to play—the very role that can make combined action against Somali piracy most effective.[36]

As the first decade of the twenty-first century comes to an end, the Horn of Africa needs more than ever officers who can play these roles. A three-million-dollar ransom was paid in early January 2009 to free the Saudi supertanker *Sirius Star* from Somali pirates;[37] in response to that event, on 8 January Vice Admiral William Gortney, the commander of Naval Forces, U.S. Central Command, and of the Combined Maritime Force, announced the creation of Combined Task Force 151, dedicated exclusively to antipiracy operations.[38] Four days later Commodore Stapleton's homeland announced that it would join other international forces, including those of the United States and China, in the new mission against pirates in the Gulf of Aden and near the Horn of Africa.[39] A force adequate to address the symptoms of piracy seems near. What will the cure look like?

If navies intend to help keep the ocean open in an age of regional instability, piracy, and terrorism, combined operations regularly informed by professional historical per-spective must become a permanent and essential part of naval practice. Addressing piracy in a way that goes beyond simple retaliation has proved very difficult. Recent historical experience in Asia suggests the ingredients of a possible solution to modern maritime crime, a solution that while naturally displaying the difficulties of crafting a working formula, shows promise.

Malaysia and China have traditionally opposed combined antipiracy patrols in the Asia-Pacific region, and their unsuccessful effort to collaborate raises a significant question. Are patrols the answer to piracy? Given that Asian maritime crime mostly occurs at the pier or at anchor, many navies openly question the efficacy of patrols. The Royal Malaysian Navy recently noted that ships, on average, actually report attacks about ten hours after the event. By that time, a responding patrol cannot help, as the criminals might be anywhere.[40]

Patrols address the symptoms but not the cause. If regional agreements on fisheries management form the basis for comprehensive security agreements to protect resources and regional economies, navies will have to play a variety of high- and low-profile roles to enable the agreements to take hold. Not all of the measures taken to ensure a safe, healthy, and shared ocean will take the form of overt naval action. Some still await definition and may recall times past when a modest naval presence directly advanced local economic interests in many and varied ways.[41] In the end, the solution to piracy is as local as the lost livelihood of a pirate recruit in one of the Harardhere camps along the Somali coast, and as global as Admiral Mullen's international city at sea. If we can see the connection and act on it, the region can once again find both the rule of law and a way to sustain itself.

---

## Notes

1. United Kingdom, House of Commons Transport Committee [hereafter Transport Committee], "Piracy," *Eighth Report of Session 2005–06,* HC 1026, 6 July 2006, p. 3.

2. "Somali Pirates Seize French Yacht," *BBC News,* 4 April 2008, available at www.bbc.co.uk. The French armed forces pursued the pirates during the second week of April 2008, seized them, and released the hostages; the pirates will shortly go on trial for the act. Since this seizure, the French have captured fifty-seven pirates in the waters off Somalia. Most are still awaiting trial in France. Some journalists have reported that the French released an undetermined number to Somali authorities in Puntland. In recent days, at this writing, the United States has entered into an agreement with Kenya to turn over for trial any pirates it seizes. Daniel Sekulich, "France Captures Pirates as Kenya Agrees to Prosecute Suspects," Modern Day Pirate Tales: Notes on the World of Piracy from Journalist Daniel Sekulich, posted 28 January 2009, piratebook.blogspot.com/.

3. The United Nations Convention on the Law of the Sea 1982 (UNCLOS), and article 101, defining piracy, can be found at www.intfish.net/treaties/losc7.htm.

4. Transport Committee, "Piracy," p. 15.

5. UN Security Council Resolution 1373, available at www.state.gov/; "CTF 150," *U.S. Naval Forces Central Command–U.S. Fifth Fleet–Combined Maritime Forces,* www.cusnc.navy.mil/.

6. Michael Crawford, "Wars and Conflicts of the United States Navy," *Naval Historical Center,* www.history.navy.mil/wars/.

7. "Somalia: UNOSOM I" and "Somalia: UNOSOM II," *United Nations,* www.un .org/Depts/DPKO/Missions/.

8. "Global and Marine Ecosystems: Somalia," *World Resources Institute: EarthTrends Environmental Information,* earthtrends.wri.org/.

9. Transport Committee, "Piracy," pp. 15–17.

10. Jeni Bone, "Piracy Costs Maritime Industry $16bn+," Seabreeze.com.au.

11. "Pirate Warning for Somalia's Coastline," *Somaliland Times,* 3 February 2003, available at www.somalilandtimes.net/.

12. *People's Daily,* english.people.com.cn/; Transport Committee, "Piracy," p. 17, para. 53; Ali M. Koknar, "Terror on the High Seas," Securitymanagement.com, June 2004; "The Ship Security Plan," MaritimeSecurity.com.

13. For conditions in the Mugdug see, for example, *ReliefWeb,* www.reliefweb.int/.

14. Andrew McGregor, "The Leading Factions behind the Somali Insurgency," *Jamestown Foundation,* www.jamestown.org/; "ONI Civil Maritime Analysis Department," *National Geospatial-Intelligence Agency,* www .nga.mil/; Donald J. Puchala, "Of Pirates and Terrorists: What Experience and History Teach," *Contemporary Security Policy* 26, no. 1 (April 2005), pp. 1–5.

15. For example, see the action of *Porter* in 2007 near the Horn of Africa: "U.S. Destroyer Pursuing Hijacked Ship in Somali Waters, Military Says," www.cnn.com/; also, "Pirates Attack UAE Ship off Somalia," asia.news .yahoo.com/. Many such instances can be found on the websites of the major international news organizations, such as CNN and BBC; Puchala, "Of Pirates and Terrorists," p. 5.

16. Most of the episodes mentioned here can be explored in greater depth by searching on the term "piracy" at www.imo.org, the site of the International Maritime Organization (IMO), and by reviewing the regular piracy warnings of the International Chamber of Commerce, at www.icc-ccs.org/imb/overview .php.

17. Koknar, "Terror on the High Seas"; "The Ship Security Plan"; Puchala, "Of Pirates and

Terrorists," p. 5; Transport Committee, "Piracy," pp. 20–22.

18. Jim Krane, "U.S. Navy Seizes Pirate Ship off Somalia," Associated Press, available at www.boston.com.

19. "U.S. Navy Ships Return Fire on Suspected Pirates," Navy.mil, 18 March 2006, story NNS060318-01.

20. "Crew Wins Deadly Pirate Battle off Somalia," Cnn.com, 30 October 2007.

21. International Maritime Bureau, *Weekly Piracy Report for 15–22 November 2005,* www .icc-ccs.org/.

22. "France, U.S., UK Draft Somalia Piracy Resolution," Reuters, 22 April 2008, available at www.reuters.com; "Pirates on French Yacht Captured," Aljazeera.net, 11 April 2008.

23. "France, U.S., UK Draft Somalia Piracy Resolution."

24. "Security Council SC/9344," *United Nations,* www.un.org/.

25. Sam Bateman, "Regional and International Frameworks for Maritime Security Cooperation," *APAN: Asia-Pacific Area Network,* 29 November 2005, www.apan-info.net/.

26. Ibid.

27. Prof. M. J. Peterson, University of Massachusetts, Amherst, e-mail to author, 30 November 2005.

28. "Regional Fisheries of the World," *Food and Agriculture Organization of the United Nations,* www.fao.org/.

29. "RECOFI Objectives," *International Fisheries Law and Policy Portal,* www.intfish.net/.

30. Adm. Michael Mullen, USN, "Remarks as Delivered for the 17th International Seapower Symposium, Naval War College, Newport, RI," Navy.mil, 21 September 2005.

31. Dr. Steven Harris of the Directorate of History and Heritage, Canadian Forces senior historian, coined this phrase during one of the Combined Operations Project's analytical sessions in Canberra, Australia, in July 2005.

32. Commodore James R. Stapleton, RAN, interview with Gary E. Weir, 14 December 2004, copy in author's possession. USS *Mobile Bay* (CG 53) is an Aegis guided-missile cruiser, HMS *Glasgow* (D 88) a guided-missile destroyer, and HMNZS *Te Kaha* (F 77) a frigate.

33. Ibid.

34. Ibid.

35. Ibid.

36. While a 21 July 2008 report in *USA Today* describes recently successful collaborative arrangements between the U.S. Navy and local authorities to restrict piracy and maritime crime in Asian waters, it notes the difficulty of implementing similar solutions in Africa, because of the absence of a legitimate, empowered Somali government. Citing the IMO, reporter Donna Leinwand states, "African waters account for 56% of all pirate attacks, spiking from 27 attacks in the first half of 2005 to 64 attacks since January." If order does not return to Somalia in the near future, it may be that only a regional arrangement can provide the authority to bring enforcement to the Horn of Africa.

37. "Q&A: Somali Piracy," *BBC News,* 9 January 2009, available at news.bbc.co.uk/.

38. "New Counter-piracy Task Force Established," Navy.mil.

39. "Australian Warship Could Be Sent to Indian Ocean in Piracy Purge," *Australian,* 12 January 2009.

40. Andrew Forbes, Deputy Director (Research), Sea Power Center–Australia, e-mail to author, 28 November 2005.

41. "France, U.S., UK Draft Somalia Piracy Resolution"; "Pirates on French Yacht Captured." Piracy figures were up 20 percent in the first quarter of 2008: "Piracy Figures Up by 20% for First Quarter of 2008," *ICC Commercial Crime Services,* www.icc-ccs.org/.

# Conclusions
BRUCE A. ELLEMAN, ANDREW FORBES, AND DAVID ROSENBERG

Piracy has deep historical and cultural roots; it has flourished for millennia. Whether high-value sea robbery by organized criminal groups or low-value petty theft by impoverished seafarers, piracy is related both to changing economic conditions, such as poverty, industrialization, and urbanization, and political conditions, including a government's legitimacy and ability to maintain law and order.

There are many different types of piracy: simple robbery at sea; absconding with a cargo; and even taking control over a ship, reflagging it, and then attempting to sell the vessel intact, as a "phantom ship." Sometimes pirates actively seek out specific ships to attack, while in other instances they wait for unsuspecting vessels to approach within striking distance.

Pirates seek opportunities to exploit differences in the value of goods from one region to another. This happened during Britain's eighteenth-century attempts to regulate trade with its colonies in North America and during the nineteenth-century opium trade between India and China. Organized criminal groups resort to piracy when it is more profitable than such other means of enrichment as drug trafficking or smuggling. In the thirteen American colonies, many people were eager to buy cheap goods from privateers. This was also the case among early Southeast Asian pirates, who preyed on the lucrative West–East opium trade and then sold the higher-quality Indian opium to local buyers.

Piracy can thrive in the waters off land areas where law and order is absent. Another causal factor is economic or political upheaval, such as the end of a war. This happened after the First Opium War, World Wars I and II, and the Cold War; in each case economic activity increased, but naval patrols by the major belligerents decreased. The end of the U.S. war in Vietnam led to another predatory form of piracy, aimed at the mass migration of people from Vietnam. These pirate attacks were largely ignored by regional governments, which hoped to stem the flow of refugees.

Europe was the focus of economic development and growth in the eighteenth and early nineteenth centuries; the Barbary pirates, accordingly, preyed on Mediterranean shipping. The Asia-Pacific region has now become the driver of global economic growth, and as a consequence, the South China Sea and adjoining waters, including the Malacca Strait, have assumed greater importance. Pirates working from locations like Somalia can also take advantage of sea routes running along their coastlines to attack commercial ships.

Piracy hot spots have included East Asia and the South China Sea, South and Southeast Asia, and Africa. Some of these hot spots, such as the Sulu region, have long histories of local piracy; others, like the Gulf of Thailand, do not. This suggests that history and culture are not the only major determinants of piracy. In general, rather, as targets of opportunity increase, piracy increases. Once opportunistic piracy has proved highly profitable, organized criminal groups may move in, push out the original perpetrators, and attempt to make even greater profits. Eklöf observes that "the relationship between the opportunistic local pirates in the southern Malacca Strait region and the (criminal) syndicates thus seems to be symbiotic rather than competitive, thereby perpetuating piracy in the region and adapting it to changing external circumstances."[1]

In other cases, pirates have been associated with active political rebellions against central governments, as in the case of the Taiping pirates in China. Somali pirates have claimed nationalist motives; they say they are fighting to defend the nation's fishing interests. Nigerian pirates have claimed to be standing up against the oil companies and the Nigerian government to reclaim long-lost tribal rights.

This concluding chapter is structured around four distinct but interrelated themes: factors that encourage piracy, issues related to the international shipping industry, the roles of shipowners, and the responses of multilateral naval forces. It ends with an examination of how navies might be better used in the future to manage this growing problem.

### Factors Encouraging Piracy and Maritime Crime

The location of a criminal attack determines whether it is an act of piracy or simply a maritime crime, within the jurisdiction of a particular country. This legalistic distinction, of course, is meaningless to the victim. Traditionally, piracy included almost any theft on the water, even along a country's coastline or on its rivers, which explains why many medieval cities were located far inland. From the eighteenth century onward, however, "maritime crime" was considered to take place in territorial waters out to three nautical miles, with piracy occurring beyond three nautical miles on what was by then called the "high seas." Territorial waters progressively extended outward to the current twelve nautical miles. With the 1994 entry into force of the United Nations Convention on the Law of the Seas 1982, twelve-nautical-mile territorial waters and two-hundred-nautical-mile "exclusive economic zones" were codified, with some countries arguing that international waters—or high seas—had decreased correspondingly.[2] Notwithstanding this new codification of ocean usage and sovereign rights, many countries make boundary claims or attempt to enforce security requirements that far exceed what is allowed under international law.[3]

Historically, pirates have most often operated from small islands or archipelagoes immediately adjacent to major shipping lanes; indeed, they may originally have been legitimate members of local maritime communities. Pirates value the geographic importance of access to ports, straits, and the sea lines of communication through them. Although located close to shipping activity, pirate havens on land can be extremely hard to find and therefore to police. One response of the international community to the general difficulties of locating, identifying, and prosecuting pirates on land, especially if local governments decline to act, is to use navies to catch pirates in the act of committing crimes at sea. When pirates have been captured by international forces, it has usually been at sea, and most often during piratical raids gone wrong. However, such a policy is expensive; the most cost-effective approach remains improving police work ashore.

As several of the case studies have emphasized, ports and adjacent waters are the most likely places for maritime crime. The widespread petty theft in the port of Chittagong, Bangladesh, is a case in point. Such acts might be perpetrated by a variety of individuals or groups on an opportunistic basis. Thefts in waters farther removed from the port imply a familiarity with boats and navigation, skills usually associated with seafarers or fishermen.

Pirates may also scout targets in ports. For example, in China during the 1920s, pirate leaders would select targets in port and even travel in the ships they planned to attack—often paying first-class fares—so they could observe their workings. Such detailed preparations could result in pirates' hijacking the entire ship, robbing the passengers of their valuables, and ransoming the ship and passengers for huge sums. This practice became so widespread that some ships were pirated many times.

Other danger areas are shipping lanes through international straits. Several case studies included here show how pirates take advantage of narrows to attack ships, especially the Malacca Strait and the Strait of Gibraltar. Pirates also take advantage of ambiguities of jurisdiction, waters where boundaries have not been delimited or where naval or maritime forces—such as coast guards or marine police—do not normally operate. The piracy attacks against the Vietnamese "boat people" during the 1970s and 1980s fit this category. Remote or peripheral waters between various Southeast Asian countries also afford opportunities for piracy. For example, in early June 2008 there was an attempted pirate attack on a cattle transport steaming from the Philippines to Australia. It took place in Indonesian waters about seventy miles south of Balut Island, an area that was not routinely patrolled.[4]

Motivations for piracy or maritime crime are most often related to economic deprivation, in the case of opportunistic crime, or a cultural or lifestyle choice, in the case of organized criminal gangs acting for material gain. Sudden and severe impoverishment, especially among marginal seafaring communities, makes piracy a viable way to meet basic needs. For example, the rapid increase in the number of piracy attacks in Indonesian waters and ports after 1997 may be attributed to that nation's sharp economic downturn and domestic instability in the wake of the regional currency crisis. Similarly, decline in global fisheries and encroachment on local grounds may lead to unemployment in the fisheries sector and thus a turn to opportunistic maritime theft.

The decline and impoverishment of traditional coastal villages also motivates unemployed seafarers to turn to sea robbery. Eklöf notes, "The roots of contemporary piracy in the southern Malacca Strait region can be found in the rapid social and economic change, due to the expansion of global capitalism that over the past decades has affected the region and which is particularly obvious in the spectacular growth of Batam on the southern side of the Singapore Strait."[5] This helps to explain why most acts of what is called piracy actually involve petty theft from ships in ports or anchorages. Economic duress also makes impoverished fishermen more vulnerable to and available for recruitment by entrepreneurial criminal organizations. In some instances, captured sailors have been forced to become pirates.

Piracy can flourish when maritime commerce grows faster than government's ability to protect it. This was dramatically shown in the early eighteenth century, when privateers ignored peace treaties to continue preying on Spanish and Portuguese "treasure ships" coming from the New World. In Southeast Asia, it was common for political leaders to hire mercenaries to raid shipping and enemy villages; such raids were considered integral parts of warfare. In China, by contrast, pirates wanted the state to be "strong enough to provide sufficient order for the flourishing of commerce and yet weak enough to preclude close administrative control along every inch of the coast. This situation may have afforded an ideal backdrop to their activities."[6] During the 1990s, a similar phenomenon reoccurred in China, which became the "world's biggest market for smuggled goods" until the government began to "crack down on pirate activity in order to be regarded as a legitimate trading nation."[7]

An important issue when considering the case studies in this monograph is the evolution of the nation-state and the modern international-relations system. As some of the earlier historical examples show, a rudimentary international system and the existence of colonial empires made internal control within some countries problematic, thereby allowing piracy to occur and restricting solutions to piracy in other countries to naval action. The dissolution of empires from the end of World War I to the 1960s and the creation of the United Nations after World War II, combined with the growing recognition of the nation-state and the state's "right" to self-defense, have all impacted how the international community responds to piracy.

Clearly, a law-enforcement response to opportunity attacks caused by poverty is neither a long-term nor a viable solution. Where seafarers, fishermen, or farmers are unemployed, long-term solutions are antipoverty programs and policies that encourage economic growth and development. If the local government is unable to fund such programs, the international community can provide aid on a bilateral or multilateral basis. If economic motivation for opportunistic attacks can be alleviated thereby, any residual piracy can be more easily managed by law enforcement.

Against organized criminal gangs, a law-enforcement response is warranted but requires political will to act, sufficient funding to staff law-enforcement agencies with enough trained personnel, and an adequate legal system under which alleged perpetrators can be brought to justice. Again, if the local government is unable to respond in this way, the international community can assist through financial support, training, and equipment.

However, there will be situations where local governments do not wish to act or proposed solutions will require considerable time to take effect. The international community might then commit naval forces to assist local forces or act unilaterally, in an attempt to "solve" the problem. As shown in certain case studies, such interventions have generally occurred on land, destroying bases and exterminating pirates. Nowadays, such actions run counter to international law, limiting what external powers can do. Furthermore, it should be recognized that any action by external navies is by definition a response to the symptom and not the underlying cause.

### The International Shipping Industry

As many of the case-study authors have noted, the solutions to piracy and maritime crime are land based and involve law-enforcement agencies. This is because of the fairly obvious fact that pirates and criminal gangs operate and live on land and sell their stolen goods on land. There are no simple solutions: different policies are required to match the differing motivations of those committing acts of piracy or maritime crime.

As the volume and velocity of world trade increase, the targets and opportunities for piracy and maritime crime also increase. Since it is predominantly international shipping that is being attacked, it is useful to outline the size of the industry, the regulatory framework within which it operates, and actions being taken by shipowners to protect their ships from attack.

Over 80 percent of the world's merchandise trade by volume moves by sea; in 2007 this trade reached 8.02 billion tons, carried in 1.12 billion deadweight tons of shipping. The majority of the world merchant fleet in that year was made up of oil tankers and carriers. Oil tankers accounted for about 408 million tons (36 percent), bulk carriers about 391 million tons (35 percent), containerships about 145 million tons (13 percent), general cargo carriers about 105 million tons (10 percent), and other ships about 69 million tons (6 percent).[8]

The regulatory regime relating to international shipping has evolved over time, with a broad framework of five major stakeholders (and categories of stakeholders): the International Maritime Organization (IMO), the shipping industry, flag states, port states, and coastal states. The IMO is a specialized agency of the United Nations responsible for maritime issues, in charge of conventions and binding treaties, codes, advisory resolutions (some countries, but by no means all, have adopted these into their domestic legislation), and nonbinding guidelines. The IMO provides regulatory oversight of international shipping in maritime safety, marine pollution, liability and compensation, cargoes, marine technology, marine environment, navigation, lifesaving, search and rescue, radio communications, and training and certification.

Prior to World War I, only maritime states granted flags to shipping, but article 273 of the Versailles Peace Treaty of 1919 allowed landlocked states to have "flags," as well, and this concession was carried on, through the Geneva Convention on the High Seas 1958, into the United Nations Convention on the Law of the Sea of 1982 (UNCLOS). The flag state is that in which the ship has been registered, and it has primary responsibility for the conduct of the ship. The IMO requires flag states to check regularly all ships under their registries, ensuring that all carry appropriate charts and navigational instruments and that their crews are adequately trained.

Over the past forty years there has been an increasing tendency for shipowners to move their ships to "open registries" (that is, open to owners of any nationality) or "flags of convenience," rather than their own national flags. Shipowners may use four criteria to determine which flag to choose:

- What crewing levels and conditions are required by the flag state?

- What are the individual tax, commercial tax, and financial laws in the flag state?

- How well does the flag state enforce maritime safety conventions?

- What level of naval protection can it offer?

The answers to the first two questions in particular can affect operating costs and therefore profits. But poor enforcement of safety conventions by some flag states and a rise in the number of flags of convenience have led to increased control by port states.

Accordingly, in 1982 the European Economic Community, concerned about failure to comply with maritime conventions, developed and signed the Paris Memorandum of Understanding on Port State Control. Port states are concerned with the condition of ships calling at their ports, the possibility of accidents, the risk that incompetent crews might endanger ships or ports, and the living conditions of foreign crews. UNCLOS allows coastal and port states to make laws for the good conduct of ships in their territorial seas, and these states increasingly have used articles relating to safety and pollution to develop strong control regimes.

At the instigation of the United States, the international community, through the IMO, began considering in November 2001 how to improve the security of maritime transport worldwide. The result, in December 2002, after twelve months of deliberation, was a set of amendments to the International Convention for the Safety of Life at Sea (SOLAS) 1974. A new chapter was added (SOLAS chapter XI-2, "Special Measures to Enhance Maritime Security"), and the International Ship and Port Facility Security (ISPS) Code was introduced, coming into effect on 1 July 2004. The ISPS Code established a framework of preventive security for ships and ports, involving security assessments and port- and ship-security plans. Other chapters of SOLAS were revised to focus on seafarer training and screening to improve the physical security of international trade.

Finally, the coastal state, through whose waters vessels transit en route to destinations in other nations, is emerging as a stakeholder in international shipping. At a minimum, a coastal state must provide for the safety of shipping in its waters by providing navigational aids and charts, but it is unclear whether it must also protect shipping transiting its EEZ. This is the nub of the argument over the "security" of the Malacca Strait between the littoral (coastal) states of Indonesia, Malaysia, and Singapore, on the one hand, and on the other, "user countries" like Japan and the United States. These coastal states have undertaken a number of initiatives that user states have been generally reluctant to support (though Japan has been funding navigational aids and the like in the region since the late 1960s, and the United States has funded twelve radar stations along the Malacca Strait).[9]

In July 2004, after years of bilateral patrols, Malaysia, Singapore, and Indonesia began to coordinate antipiracy patrols in the Malacca Strait, in an arrangement known by the acronym "MALSINDO." On 11 November 2004, eight out of the ten members of the Association of Southeast Asian Nations, plus China, Japan, South Korea, India, Sri Lanka, and Bangladesh, adopted the Regional Cooperation Agreement on Combating Piracy and Armed Robbery against Ships in Asia (ReCAAP).[10] This entity differs from the International Maritime Bureau's Piracy Reporting Center (discussed below), in that it is not connected with shipping companies or insurance firms. ReCAAP allocated funds to set up an independent reporting agency in Singapore to monitor piracy attacks.[11] Further, in September 2005 Malaysia, Singapore, and Indonesia initiated "Eyes in the Sky," coordinated air patrols over the strait.

Such multilateral initiatives require the fusing of seldom-standardized information from diverse sources. Admiral Harry Ulrich, U.S. Navy, as commander of NATO Naval Forces Europe in 2006, showed how that can be accomplished successfully. Admiral Ulrich began stitching together a network of shore-based sensors ringing the Mediterranean and the International Maritime Organization's Automatic Identification System (or AIS, discussed below): "Almost overnight, NATO went from tracking dozens of ships on the Mediterranean to thousands, and instead of getting the data sometimes up to 72 hours late, now the contacts were being tracked in 1 to 5 minutes— to an accuracy within 50 feet on the Earth's surface." By the time Ulrich retired at the end of 2007, he had enlisted in the effort thirty-two countries throughout the Mediterranean, the North Atlantic, along the west coast of Africa, around the Black Sea, and in the Pacific.[12]

Such a system's strength is a function of its reach: the more countries that join, the larger the shared operational picture. A sea-traffic-control regime of this type can give local coast guards and naval patrols the information they need to monitor suspected pirates and deter them. However, it cannot possibly deter all pirate attacks; shipowners and shipmasters must also intensify their efforts.

### The Roles of Shipowners and Shipmasters

Given this regulatory environment, what actions have the shipowners taken to protect their ships, crews, and cargoes? The most concrete measure against piracy undertaken by the shipping industry was the creation by the IMB of the Piracy Reporting Center (PRC) in Kuala Lumpur in Malaysia in 1992. The PRC was meant to be the first point of contact for a shipmaster wishing to report an actual or attempted attack, or suspicious activity; the IMB could then initiate a response. A stated aim of the PRC is to raise awareness within the shipping industry of piracy, and it works closely with various governments and law-enforcement agencies, including in the sharing of information.

The IMB also provides practical advice to shipmasters transiting pirate-infested waters or entering ports where criminal activity is known to occur. Masters are advised to brief their crews before heading into dangerous waters and tell them what measures will be taken (as contained in the ship-security plans required under the ISPS Code). Such steps might be lighting all blind spots and dark areas, patrolling the weather deck regularly and in pairs, adopting a timetable for reports, and exerting increased vigilance when watches change. The IMB recommends that ships noting suspicious activity "increase speed," "commence evasive manoeuvres," and "use bow wave and stern wash to prevent the small boats approaching close to the ship." If a pirate "mother ship" is sighted, a vessel should "move away from it," "steam away from land," and "head into the sea," which "makes it more difficult for boats to come alongside."[13]

In practice, however, the best way for a ship to counter piracy is to avoid areas where pirates are operating. Masters advised by shipowners or the IMB that particular areas are dangerous, especially at night, do best to avoid them altogether or transit only during the day. However, this can be costly, and shipowners may refuse to authorize a detour or delay. If pirates do attack, the master and crew need to know what to do, and that requires planning and training. Also, however useful the IMB's advice, the trend in the international shipping industry toward minimum crew sizes militates against its effective implementation.

Most attacks in Southeast Asia, and in the Malacca Strait in particular, occur against ships that are berthed or at anchor. Hence, port authorities have a major responsibility to improve physical security in their ports, as the ISPS Code requires. The code also requires that all people working in a port undergo security vetting and carry special identification, to hinder pirates from scouting for targets.

At sea, maintaining a constant watch is the most important means of keeping pirates from boarding unnoticed. A ship that detects pirates before they board can try to outmaneuver them. Physical barriers, barbed wire or even electric fencing, can slow attackers down. (An example of electric fencing is the IMB-recommended Secure-Ship, a nonlethal electrified barrier, with a nine-thousand-volt pulse, surrounding the whole ship.)[14] Crew members can use water hoses or "sonic boom" guns to try to keep boats at bay or cut thrown grapnel lines to prevent pirates from boarding. In addition, "some simple weapons have also been found to be most effective, particularly the use of ships' signal cartridges and very light pistols. Empty beer bottles filled with sand which can be stacked on deck ready to hurl at intruders are also extremely effective."[15]

If pirates succeed in getting on board, the next line of defense comprises double-locked doors, especially to the bridge, engine room, communications room, and steering machinery room. However, most ships have many doors and hallways leading to the most important areas of the ship, and it is difficult to double-lock them all. Ordinary padlocks usually do not last long in salt air, and can be cut open with a pair of wire cutters; electronic key-card systems might help. If the pirates do gain access to the control areas, the master and crew are usually instructed by the owners not to resist further. This applies especially to the use of firearms; pirates are probably better armed, and the crew might be injured or killed if they fight back. Shipowners are also concerned that if a pirate is killed during an attack, revenge attacks on that line might result.

Before that point, however, as soon as pirates board the ship, the crew can activate the ship's security-alert system, a silent alarm that sends a message warning the shipowner and other authorities that something has happened. A well known example is ShipLoc, a cheap satellite-based tracking system that shipping companies can access via the Internet to monitor the locations of their ships. The device is a small, waterproof unit with a transmitter, GPS receiver, battery pack, and flat antenna. If activated, it cannot be detected by anyone on board the ship or vessels nearby.[16]

But the shipowner, receiving the warning (possibly relayed by some other nation), must verify that an attack is under way before advising the flag state, and the flag state must then advise the coastal state, which would take action. There may be long delays. More important, there is no guarantee that any relevant authority will receive the signal; or that if received it will be recognized as valid among thousands of false signals that are sent; or that if a signal is received and verified, the coastal state will respond with adequate naval forces.[17]

The last point above raises a key issue. However effective the performance of the crew, the owners, alarm systems, information-sharing centers, and the like, in a given instance, the question remains: Is there a naval, coast guard, or police vessel in the vicinity that is able to respond in a timely and meaningful manner? Often there is not.

One option is the use of private security guards. A number of firms, usually staffed by retired soldiers or seamen, offer security services. But putting guards on all merchant ships is very expensive. Captain Jayant Abhyankar, the former deputy director of IMB, sounded a cautionary note: these security personnel, he observed, "are well intentioned, eager, dedicated, aggressive, and very sharp—but we tell them not to expect to make a living on it. Shipowners just cannot afford them. And if someone gets shot and killed, all hell would break loose; it's a nonstarter, except in extremely rare circumstances."[18]

Notwithstanding, the deputy commander of Combined Task Force 150, Commander Keith Winstanley, Royal Navy, has urged owners to be proactive in the security of their ships:

> We're not ceding the waters of the Gulf of Aden to pirates, and where we can be there and give support, we are doing that. But we can't be everywhere at once and I would ask and urge the international shipping community just to check and verify that they are content that they are taking every possible action themselves to reduce the chances of piracy. That might mean something that costs money, such as private security. Ultimately, that's a question for the individual companies, as is whatever instructions they give to their masters in the event of coming across piratical attacks. But speed, manoeuvre and communication rather than stopping at the first shot would be my advice.[19]

That said, and in part because the use of private security guards to repel pirates might under certain circumstances be illegal—they have no legal authority to act in another country's waters—it will frequently be up to navies to respond to the piracy threat.

### Naval Responses to Piracy

Many of the case studies here show how difficult it is for individual ships, or even states, to fight piracy effectively, as it is a transnational crime. One of the most cost-effective options is to get help from the international community. Illustrations include Britain's efforts to assist Morocco and U.S. assistance to Nigeria. A more recent example of bilateral naval cooperation was the short-term agreement in 2002 between the U.S. Navy and the Indian Navy to guard American merchant ships carrying "high value" goods through the Malacca Strait and the Indian Ocean: "According to the bilateral arrangement, U.S. naval ships patrolled the seas in Southeast Asia, while the Indian Navy concentrated on the Bay of Bengal and the Indian Ocean."[20] However, it is extremely unlikely that such a bilateral arrangement could be maintained for very long over the objections of coastal states.

The historical examples in this work show quite clearly that international cooperation is the best way to manage a piracy threat if it cannot be contained on land. This can be done in a variety of ways, from state building to international naval patrols, to convoys. But international participation is crucial, since pirates can otherwise exploit national and sea boundaries to evade pursuit and capture. Naval forces need first of all to coordinate their surveillance and patrol efforts to detect and capture pirates and ultimately to deter piracy.

Presuming the existence of at least fragmentary maritime surveillance systems in all maritime jurisdictions at the national level, if a ship security alert is received, what happens? In theory, the coastal state makes an appropriate response, with a coast guard vessel, its marine police, or its navy. But in practice this does not always occur. Shipmasters often do not report attacks for up to ten hours, by which time, from an enforcement perspective, little can be done. Sending a vessel to intercept the merchant ship so long after the fact might waste time and resources.

If the coastal state learns of an attack in progress and is willing to respond, can its vessels get to the merchant ship in time? Unless the ship is being hijacked, the pirates will be on board only a short time, and again, responding by sending a ship may achieve little. The coastal state would have to base its forces near piracy hot spots, but if it did, it is more than likely that pirates would attack shipping even farther away. The final theoretical option is to keep response vessels always at sea, but this is very expensive.

If a response vessel is dispatched and comes upon the merchant ship while the attack is under way what can it do? If it is a warship, it will have to dispatch sailors in a fast boat either to seize the pirate vessel or retake the merchant ship. Helicopters might also be used to rappel sailors onto the deck of the captured ship. The sailors would have to be armed and be given explicit rules of engagement, so they know the bounds within which they can proceed. In contrast, if the response vessel belongs to a coast guard or marine police force, it may be small enough to put its party on board the pirate vessel or merchant ship directly.

Personnel of any response vessel must operate under the domestic law of the coastal state, so that they can take the alleged pirates into custody and return them to shore to face legal action. This aspect is often forgotten in debates about external forces intervening in another state's waters—they have no legal jurisdiction there and may therefore be committing a crime themselves. Increased awareness of the maritime domain is required.

### Increasing Maritime Domain Awareness

How serious is piracy? The U.S. Navy's Chief of Naval Operations, Admiral Michael Mullen, has asserted that "piracy is a global threat to security because of its deepening ties to international criminal networks, smuggling of hazardous cargoes, and disruption of vital commerce."[21] But most regional countries affected by piracy do not see it as a major criminal or terrorist threat, especially if it is international shipping that is at risk, not their own. Consequently, their efforts to halt piracy have to date been limited. For many coastal states, the annual cost of controlling piracy outweighs direct economic losses from it.

Global trade is predicted to increase over the next decade, so there will be a requirement for greater levels of maritime safety and security. This especially applies to the rapidly growing seaborne trade of developing countries now joining the export-led industrial revolution in Asia. If the international community commits its collective navies to antipiracy operations, a number of operational issues will need to be considered to ensure the response is up to the task. These issues include an adequate surveillance system, agreed rules of engagement for intercepting and boarding suspect vessels, and legal powers to apprehend suspected pirates for eventual court action.

Clearly, maritime surveillance is the key to gaining a better understanding of what is happening on the oceans, but currently, systems are not integrated within each country, let alone at regional or global levels. A country's navy may have a "common operating picture" (to use the U.S. term) of where its forces are at sea, and, if tasked with the responsibility, may have an idea where merchant ships are; if further tasked with coastal surveillance, it may know what other types of vessels are in its waters. Departments of transport or shipping should know what international shipping is in their waters or proposes to enter their nations' ports; flag states should know the location of all vessels in their registries. To generate a comprehensive maritime surveillance picture, all these disparate "inputs" must be integrated.

Such integration is not easy. Naval information is often classified, while international shipping data are often held as confidential. Reporting protocols invariably use different computer systems, with incompatible software. Then there are issues of privacy: What, if any, information can be released to third parties? Who might be allowed access to consolidated data? How are countries grappling with these issues? Canada and Australia operate joint intelligence centers that fuse information from a variety of sources into one comprehensive picture. Canada does this in two "marine security operations centres," while in Australia the Border Protection Command's Australian Maritime Information Fusion Centre, using the Australian Maritime Identification System, collects, collates, stores, analyzes, and redistributes information related to the detection, tracking, and threat assessment of vessels operating in or approaching Australian waters. The center tracks ship identity, crew, cargo, location, course, speed, and intended port of call. Both the Canadian and Australian systems are constrained as to disclosure of information by national privacy legislation.

The United States has promulgated a "maritime domain awareness" (MDA) policy aiming to "wire" every ship so that it can be identified and tracked throughout its journey, as is done in global air traffic control.[22] MDA aims to require each ship at sea to emit a signal identifying its name, country of origin, and route. This would permit "surveillance of activities at sea" and "intelligence-gathering on the background to the movements and presences identified."[23] When a ship is attacked by pirates, an emergency signal would report its location and what kind of danger it faced.

The 2005 U.S. National Strategy for Maritime Security had as its stated goal to "promote global economic stability and protect legitimate activities while preventing hostile or illegal acts within the maritime domain," including the Taiwan and Malacca straits.

Aside from MDA, this initiative also called for seven other plans to address threats from "piracy, international criminal activities such as illegal immigration and drug trafficking, and environmental degradation."[24] In 2007, all three U.S. sea services issued *A Cooperative Strategy for 21st Century Seapower,* which calls for "significantly increased commitment to advance *maritime domain awareness* (MDA)" with the goal of "promoting the rule of law by countering piracy, terrorism, weapons proliferation, drug trafficking, and other illicit activities."[25]

While these statements concern domestic American national and maritime security issues, the long-term goal of MDA is to expand its capacities to numerous countries. What the United States proposes in these policies is not new to the international shipping industry, which has been monitoring the locations of its vessels for many years. For example, under SOLAS, international ships of greater than five hundred gross tons must be fitted with an Automatic Identification System, which allows for the identification and tracking of these vessels. Equipped ships can exchange information—including identification, position, course, and speed—with other nearby ships and traffic systems in congested waters and ports. However, the security benefits of AIS are mixed. In theory, a hijacked ship could be traced anywhere in the world using AIS; in practice, however, because the signal is transmitted to everyone, any vessel nearby can locate the transmitting ship. There have been instances in the Malacca Strait, and possibly off Somalia, where pirates have used a ship's AIS signal to locate it; accordingly, some ships switch off their AISs in dangerous waters, defeating the whole purpose.

In further development of the ISPS Code, in 2008 the IMO introduced the Long Range Identification and Tracking (LRIT) system. When fully implemented this satellite-based system, to be fitted on all SOLAS-compliant ships, will enable countries to identify and locate all vessels transiting their waters, particularly those intending to enter port. It has already been accepted that flag states will be able to access the data from their ships anywhere in the world, while port states will be able to do so following declaration by a ship of intention to enter an LRIT-designated port. Debate continues as to whether and when a coastal state would be given access to this information for ships transiting its waters but not intending to enter one of its ports.

It is important to remember that these automated systems and the plethora of stations monitoring them and sharing their data will generate information only on legitimate, convention-compliant shipping; they will not be recording the locations of pirate vessels. Therefore, other means are required to identify pirates. Often, this is managed by fusing data from coastal radars or aerial surveillance, sometime satellites, with those on legitimate shipping; the anomalies are suspicious vessels and need to be monitored. But even so, very small craft cannot generally be "seen" by satellite or be detected by coastal radars. Given this limitation, it is an open question whether a global system is necessary or achievable. Should instead the aim be to encourage the creation of robust regional systems, linking countries under IMO arrangements or port-state memorandums of understanding? Such an approach would necessarily increase the monitoring roles of port and coastal states.

Given some adequate arrangement for tracking and monitoring international shipping, the next problem is appropriate multinational response to reported pirate attacks. In 2006, Admiral Mullen announced a plan to create a "thousand-ship navy," subsequently renamed the "Global Maritime Partnership," to promote global maritime security by cooperating to confront common problems such as arms smuggling and terrorism, piracy, human trafficking, drug smuggling, and other organized criminal activity.[26] It is not clear that the rest of the world agrees with this "threat assessment," however self-evident from an American perspective. But this reluctance does not negate the general thrust of increased naval cooperation and the benefits that may accrue from it.

The priority now given to naval cooperation is actually nothing new; it is a continuation of the practice evolved over centuries, and it is based on existing, long-term regional arrangements.[27] Various structures already exist for naval cooperation, ranging from bilateral arrangements to such regional, multilateral protocols as the Five Power Defence Arrangements, the Western Pacific Naval Symposium, and the newly created Indian Ocean Naval Symposium, as well as formal treaty obligations under NATO. Implicit in many of these arrangements are harmonization or standardization of procedures, interoperability where possible, joint exercises and training, personnel exchanges, and visits. All these activities serve to enhance naval capacity and skill levels while encouraging countries to operate together.

However, asymmetry of forces could be a problem. Historically, pirates and privateers were likely to have ships of the same sizes and capabilities as the merchant vessels they were attacking and the naval forces that responded to them. But now there are major disparities in characteristics among merchant vessels, warships, and the craft—often very small, fast boats—commonly used by pirates. It is not clear that naval vessels are any longer the appropriate platforms for response; in many cases they are too large and their weapons are inappropriate to the situation. Warships (which can stay on station longer than other vessels and have superior firepower) may be more appropriate for the deterrence of piracy than interception. Perhaps for this reason, many states are creating coast guards to protect their rights and interests in their EEZs. The recent focus on piracy off Somalia shows what can happen when a "failed" state loses control over its sovereign waters.

### The Situation off Somalia

The current situation off Somalia shows how complex antipiracy suppression operations can become. Hijackings are frequent in these waters, one of the world's busiest and most important sea-lanes. During 2008, Somali pirates reportedly attacked 111 ships and were able to seize forty-two.[28] In June 2008, the United Nations Security Council passed a resolution authorizing the use of force against pirates in Somalia's territorial waters. It gave warships the power to intervene in piracy attacks on the high seas under UNCLOS, but warships must work with local law enforcement—Somali authorities, in this case—for subsequent prosecution.

The need for this multinational force was dramatically illustrated in September 2008 when pirates hijacked the Ukrainian cargo ship *Faina* off the central coast of Somalia. What commanded international attention was not the ship's crew but its cargo: thirty-three Russian battle tanks and other heavy weapons, nominally intended for the Kenyan army but probably destined for southern Sudan. U.S., Russian, and British warships surrounded the Ukrainian vessel, and NATO antipiracy patrols escorted UN food aid shipments.

Since Resolution 1772, adopted on 20 August 2007, the Security Council has passed many resolutions dealing with piracy and armed robbery off the coast of Somalia. On 7 October 2008, the UN Security Council passed Resolution 1838, calling upon states interested in the security of maritime activities to "fight piracy on the high seas off the coast of Somalia by deploying naval vessels and military aircraft."[29]

The Security Council has not traditionally drawn a clear distinction between piracy and armed robbery, condemning both activities. Yet in Resolution 1816 it decided that states cooperating with the Transitional Federal Government of Somalia may enter the territorial waters of Somalia for "repressing acts of piracy and armed robbery at sea, in a manner consistent with such action permitted on the high seas with respect to piracy under relevant international law," and "use, within the territorial waters of Somalia[,] . . . all necessary means to repress acts of piracy and armed robbery."[30] States acting within territorial waters to combat piracy could draw their lawful authority from this resolution, even though such action is not supported by UNCLOS.

It is also notable that Resolution 1838 calls upon states "interested in the security of maritime activities to take part actively in the fight against piracy on the high seas."[31] By contrast, article 101 of UNCLOS states that it is a "duty to co-operate in the repression of piracy" and requires "all states," not just those with particular commercial interests, to cooperate to the fullest possible extent in the repression of piracy. The Security

Council's call to arms, therefore, is a more limited request, obliging only states with stakes in maritime security to fight piracy off Somalia actively.

To date, the Security Council resolutions have been ineffective. Even as an international armada surrounded *Faina,* pirates attacked three other vessels in Somali waters. In particular, on 16 November 2008 pirates seized the very large crude carrier (VLCC) *Sirius Star,* releasing it only after receiving a three-million-dollar ransom. This incident caused quite a shock to the shipping industry, since this was the first VLCC hijacked for ransom and had reportedly been located by the pirates through its AIS signal. *Sirius Star* sat off the Somali coast surrounded by warships, but no navy had the authority to recapture the ship. The ship was released in January 2009, only after the owners paid the ransom. The inadequacy of international laws regulating piracy means that captured alleged Somali pirates have either been set free or sent to Kenya for trial, since there is no legal system in Somalia that can try them.

Embarrassingly, the *Sirius Star* attack occurred when a large number of warships were in those waters precisely to prevent such a thing. These naval forces are acting under a UN Security Council resolution, but there is no unified command plan. In early January 2009 it was announced that Combined Task Force 151 (CTF 151) would be created to conduct antipiracy operations. It has been given authority to act in Somali waters by no fewer than four Security Council resolutions, plus agreements with Kenya to prosecute any pirates captured.[32]

Somali piracy has created an unprecedented international response, including ships from the United States, Europe, India, Australia, Japan, Russia, China, and Malaysia. For example, on 8 April 2009, Somali pirates hijacked the U.S.-flagged ship *Maersk Alabama* and took ship captain Richard Phillips hostage. Four days later, Navy SEAL sharpshooters from the USS *Bainbridge* killed three pirates in a successful nighttime rescue.[33] The Somali pirates were clearly not deterred by the U.S. Navy, and on 18 November 2009 attacked *Maersk Alabama* again, but this time were fought off by private guards armed with guns and a high-decibel sonic emitter. China has also sent two Frigates and a supply ship to the Horn of Africa, and has pledged to regain control of the cargo ship *De Xin Hai,* which was seized by Somali pirates on 19 October 2009. According to the International Maritime Bureau, of the 359 reported attacks or attempted attacks so far this year, 195 could be attributed to Somali pirates.[34] These developments show the pressing need for a Global Maritime Partnership.

However, patrol areas are vast, and the fundamental question remains: Should the waters be patrolled, or should the merchant ships be convoyed? That is, should the ships themselves be protected, not the ocean? Under international law, warships can convoy and protect only ships of their respective nations' flags, unless another flag state gives approval; it was this very issue that resulted in the 1856–60 Sino-British Arrow War. At present, some shipping lines have decided to reroute their traffic away from the Somali coast by sending them around the Cape of Good Hope, adding considerably to costs and causing extensive delays in delivery.

While external powers are deciding on whether to commit navies to the Gulf of Aden, shipowners are reportedly negotiating ransoms. Most often, shipowners bargain with the pirates over their ransom demands and then eventually pay—meaning the pirates win. This success merely motivates others to join their ranks. The root problem—a lawless state, in the case of Somalia—not only continues but may grow worse.

### Responding to Maritime Crime and Piracy in the Twenty-first Century

Piracy has existed for as long as people have used the sea. National navies were initially created as a method for managing piracy. Today, coast guards and marine police may also be involved.

Ultimately, successful antipiracy measures require flag states and coastal/port states to be willing and able to take action. A crime against a ship on the high seas is subject to the jurisdiction of the flag state, according to its own criminal laws. An attack on a ship exercising the right of passage in territorial seas is a crime under the laws of the coastal state, which needs to seize the attacking vessel and arrest the offenders. Meanwhile, an attack against a ship alongside in port, at anchor in port, or anchored in internal waters is within the jurisdiction of the port state, even if a foreign ship is involved.

Almost every country has made maritime piracy and sea robbery a crime, and numerous intergovernmental and industry initiatives have urged states to adopt antipiracy measures. Criminalization alone, however, has not solved the problem. States have been reluctant to search for pirates for numerous reasons, including the cost of antipiracy patrols, the suspicions of neighboring countries, and the persistence of unsettled territorial claims. By contrast, modern pirates may be highly mobile, and can be equipped with sophisticated navigational equipment and powerful weapons.

Despite these difficulties, several antipiracy measures are in place, including improved ship registration and identification systems (such as ShipLoc); the IMB's Piracy Reporting Center, which has been supplemented by such regional antipiracy agreements as ReCAAP; and coordinated antipiracy patrols like MALSINDO. In many regions, such as the Malacca Strait, coastal states have made fighting piracy a priority and have achieved substantial progress.

Success in piracy suppression will ultimately require coordinated efforts by states and shipowners. Almost all the many proposals for international cooperation are voluntary.

They take time to build, and none are likely to be effective in all situations. For the foreseeable future, therefore, maritime security advocates will need to remain firm in their commitments to a comprehensive range of policies—national and multinational, on land and at sea—if they hope to control piracy.

The international community can increase cooperation in a number of areas to manage piracy. It can ensure that the ISPS Code is enforced by flag states and port states. It can create a global surveillance system for international shipping. It can ensure that ships can alert authorities if attacked. It can ensure that piracy alerts are promptly reported to the appropriate flag-state and port-state authorities. It can ensure that maritime forces have the legal authority to respond and are prepared to do so when necessary. It can encourage affected countries to enact domestic legislation under which pirates can be tried. However, when these efforts fail, as they clearly have off Somalia, naval force will inevitably be called upon as the weapon of last resort.

## Notes

1. Stefan Eklöf, *Pirates in Paradise: A Modern History of Southeast Asia's Maritime Marauders* (Copenhagen: Nordic Institute of Asian Studies, 2006), p. 159.

2. The United States holds the view that a country's EEZ is still "international waters," but not all countries agree with this interpretation. The 1 April 2001 collision of a U.S. EP-3 reconnaissance plane and a Chinese fighter jet is just one example of how these differing views can lead to tension.

3. Stuart Kaye, *Freedom of Navigation in the Indo-Pacific Region,* Papers in Australian Maritime Affairs (Canberra: Sea Power Centre–Australia, 2008).

4. Warwick Stanley, "Pirates Attack Cattle Ship Bound for Western Australia," Couriermail.com, 11 June 2008, available at www.news.com.au/.

5. Eklöf, *Pirates in Paradise,* p. 58.

6. Dian H. Murray, *Pirates of the South China Coast, 1790–1810* (Stanford, Calif.: Stanford Univ. Press, 1987), p. 154.

7. Martin N. Murphy, *Contemporary Piracy and Maritime Terrorism: The Threat to International Security,* IISS Adelphi Paper 388 (London: Routledge, 2007), p. 39.

8. United Nations, *Review of Maritime Transport 2008* (New York: Conference on Trade and Development, 2008), pp. xiii, 33.

9. Richard Halloran, "Pirates Off, Perchance?" *Washington Times,* 23 November 2008.

10. Indonesia and Malaysia have not ratified ReCAAP.

11. Guo Xinning, *Anti-terrorism, Maritime Security, and ASEAN-China Cooperation: A Chinese Perspective,* Trends in Southeast Asia Series 15 (2005), p. 18.

12. Thomas P. M. Barnett, "To Make Sea Traffic Transparent," *Washington Times,* 30 September 2008, p. 19.

13. "Advice to Masters," *ICC Commercial Crime Services,* www.icc-ccs.org/.

14. Ibid., "Securing Your Ship."

15. Roger Villar, *Piracy Today: Robbery and Violence at Sea since 1980* (London: Conway Maritime, 1985), p. 67.

16. "Securing Your Ship."

17. Thomas Timlin, *The Use of SOLAS Ship Security Alert Systems,* Working Paper 154 (Singapore: S. Rajaratnam School of International Studies, 2008), pp. 3, 4, 11, 15.

18. John S. Burnett, *Dangerous Waters: Modern Piracy and Terror on the High Seas* (New York: Dutton, 2002), pp. 106–107.

19. David Osler, "'We Are Not the Solution' to Piracy, Says Somalia Coalition Navy Chief," *Lloyd's List,* 25 September 2008.

20. Vijay Sakhuja, "Sea Piracy in South Asia," in *Violence at Sea: Piracy in the Age of Global Terrorism,* ed. Peter Lehr (London: Routledge, 2006), p. 32.

21. Murphy, *Contemporary Piracy and Maritime Terrorism,* p. 85, citing Admiral Mullen's remarks to the Seventeenth International Seapower Symposium.

22. U.S. Homeland Security Dept., *The National Plan to Achieve Maritime Domain Awareness* (Washington, D.C.: October 2005), available at www.dhs.gov/. For MDA generally, see Steven C. Boraz, "Maritime Domain Awareness: Myths and Realities," *Naval War College Review* 62, no. 3 (Summer 2009), pp. 137–46.

23. Murphy, *Contemporary Piracy and Maritime Terrorism,* p. 74.

24. Bernard D. Cole, "Clipper Ships to Carriers: U.S. Maritime Strategy in Asia," in *Asia Looks Seaward: Power and Maritime Strategy,* ed. Toshi Yoshihara and James R. Holmes (Westport, Conn.: Praeger Security International, 2008), pp. 60–62.

25. Reprinted in *Naval War College Review* 61, no. 1 (Winter 2008), pp. 7–19, available at www.usnwc.edu/press. The quoted phrases are found on pages 17 and 13, respectively, of the document as reprinted (emphasis original).

26. Murphy, *Contemporary Piracy and Maritime Terrorism,* p. 74.

27. Chris Rahman, *The Global Maritime Partnership: Implications for the Royal Australian Navy,* Papers in Australian Maritime Affairs 24 (Canberra: Sea Power Centre–Australia, 2008), p. 7.

28. "Pirates Seize Two Ships off Somalia," *Boston Globe,* 27 March 2009.

29. UN Security Council Resolution 1838, 7 October 2008, S/RES/1838 (2008).

30. UN Security Council Resolution 1816, 2 June 2008, S/RES/1816 (2008).

31. In Resolution 1816, the language used by the Security Council was "States interested in the use of commercial maritime routes off the coast of Somalia."

32. Cdr. James Kraska and Capt. Brian Wilson, "Fighting Piracy: International Coordination Is Key to Countering Modern-Day Freebooters," *Armed Forces Journal,* available at www.armedforcesjournal.com/.

33. Coincidentally, *Bainbridge* was named after a veteran of both Barbary wars. Jay Bahadur has concluded that off Somalia "there were 68 successful pirate hijackings in 2009, compared with 49 one year earlier." "Heroes in a Land of Pirates," *New York Times,* 4 January 2010.

34. Walter Saltmarsh, "Pirates Widen Range, Straining Naval Patrols," *New York Times,* 19 November 2009.

## Bibliography

Adams, Henry. *History of the United States of America during the First Administration of Thomas Jefferson*. New York: Scribner's, 1889.

———. *The Formative Years: A History of the United States of America during the Administrations of Jefferson and Madison*. London: Collins, 1948.

Ahman, Hamzah, and Akira Ogawa, eds. *Combating Piracy and Ship Robbery: Charting the Future in the Asia Pacific Waters*. Tokyo: Okazaki Institute, 2001.

Alabaster, Ernest. *Notes and Commentaries on Chinese Criminal Law and Cognate Topics*. London: n.p., 1899.

Allen, Gardner W. *Our Navy and the Barbary Corsairs*. New York: Houghton Mifflin, 1905.

Anand, Ram P. *Origin and Development of the Law of the Sea*. The Hague: Nijhoff, 1983.

Antony, Robert J. *Like Froth Floating on the Sea: The World of Pirates and Seafarers in Late Imperial South China*. Institute of East Asian Studies China Research Monograph. Berkeley: Univ. of California, 2003.

———. *Pirates in the Age of Sail*. New York: W. W. Norton, 2007.

Baker, John C., and David G. Wiencek. *A Cooperative Monitoring Regime for the South China Sea: Satellite Imagery, Confidence-Building Measures, and the Spratly Islands Disputes*. Westport, Conn.: Praeger, 2002.

Ball, Desmond, and Amitav Acharya, eds. *The Next Stage: Preventive Diplomacy and Security Cooperation in the Asia-Pacific Region*. Canberra Papers on Strategy and Defence 131. Canberra: Strategic and Defence Studies Centre, Australian National Univ., 1999.

Bateman, Sam, Catherine Zara Raymond, and Joshua Ho. *Safety and Security in the Malacca and Singapore Straits: An Agenda for Action*. Singapore: Institute of Defence and Strategic Studies, May 2006.

Biddulph, John. *The Pirates of Malabar*. London: Smith, Elder, 1907.

Blyth, Ken. *Petro Pirates: The Hijacking of the Petro Ranger*. With Peter Corris. St. Leonards, Australia: Allen and Unwin, 2000.

Booth, Ken. *Law, Force and Diplomacy at Sea*. London: Allen and Unwin, 1985.

Bourgerie, Raymond, and Pierre Lesouef. *Palikao (1860): Le Sac du Palais d'Été et la prise de Pékin*. Paris: Economica, 1995.

Boyd, Julian P., Mina R. Bryan, and Fredrick Aandahl, eds. *The Papers of Thomas Jefferson*. Princeton, N.J.: Princeton Univ. Press, 1954.

Boyd, Julian P., Mina R. Bryan, and Elizabeth L. Hutter, eds. *The Papers of Thomas Jefferson*. Princeton, N.J.: Princeton Univ. Press, 1953.

Boyd, Julian P., William H. Gaines, Jr., and Joseph H. Harrison, Jr., eds. *The Papers of Thomas Jefferson*. Princeton, N.J.: Princeton Univ. Press, 1958.

Boyd, Julian P., and Ruth W. Lester, eds. *The Papers of Thomas Jefferson*. Princeton, N.J.: Princeton Univ. Press, 1982.

Boyd, Julian P., Ruth W. Lester, and Lucius Wilmerding, Jr., eds. *The Papers of Thomas Jefferson*. Princeton, N.J.: Princeton Univ. Press, 1971.

Boyd, Julian P., and Lucius Wilmerding, Jr., eds. *The Papers of Thomas Jefferson*. Princeton, N.J.: Princeton Univ. Press, 1965.

Bruyneel, Mark. *Comparison of 2002 Figures of the International Maritime Bureau*. London: International Maritime Bureau Piracy Reporting Center, 19 April 2003.

Burnett, John S. *Dangerous Waters: Modern Piracy and Terror on the High Seas*. New York: Dutton, 2002.

Butcher, John G. *The Closing of the Frontier: A History of the Marine Fisheries of Southeast Asia c. 1850–2000*. Singapore: Institute of Southeast Asian Studies, 2004.

Cain, P. J., and A. G. Hopkins. *British Imperialism: Innovation and Expansion 1688–1914*. London: Longman, 1993.

Callanta, Cesar V. *The Limahong Invasion*. Philippines: Pangasinan Review, 1979.

Carse, Robert. *The Age of Piracy.* London: Robert Hale, 1957.

Catanzariti, John, and Eugene R. Sheridan, eds. *The Papers of Thomas Jefferson.* Princeton, N.J.: Princeton Univ. Press, 1995.

Chesneaux, Jean, ed. *Popular Movements and Secret Societies in China, 1840–1950.* Stanford, Calif.: Stanford Univ. Press, 1972.

Chidsey, Donald Barr. *The Wars in Barbary: Arab Piracy and the Birth of the United States Navy.* New York: Crown, 1971.

Clarke, Frank G. *The History of Australia.* London: Greenwood, 2002.

Clodfelter, Michael. *Vietnam in Military Statistics: A History of the Indochina Wars, 1772–1991.* London: McFarland, 1995.

Clowes, William L. *The Royal Navy: A History.* London: S. Low, Marston, 1901.

Clune, Frank, and P. R. Stephensen. *The Pirates of the Brig* Cyprus. London: Rupert Hart-Davis, 1962.

Commonwealth of Australia. *Select Committee on a Certain Maritime Incident: Report.* Canberra: Senate Printing Unit, 2002.

Constable, Nichole, ed. *Guest People: Hakka Identity in China and Abroad.* Seattle: Univ. of Washington Press, 1996.

Course, A. G. *Pirates of the Western Seas.* London: Frederick Muller, 1969.

Croizier, Ralf. *Koxinga and Chinese Nationalism: History, Myth and the Hero.* Cambridge, Mass.: Harvard Univ. Press, 1997.

Curwen, C. A. *Taiping Rebel: The Deposition of Li Hsiu-ch'eng.* London: Cambridge Univ. Press, 1977.

David, Gregory S. *Piracy in Southeast Asia: A Growing Threat to the United States' Vital Strategic and Commercial Interests.* Quantico, Va.: Marine Corps Command and Staff College, 2002.

Davis, Sir John Francis. *China, During the War and Since the Peace.* Wilmington, Del.: Scholarly Resources, 1972.

Dillon, Dana R. *Piracy in Asia: A Growing Barrier to Maritime Trade.* Heritage Foundation, 22 June 2000.

Dinstein, Yoram, and Mala Tabory, eds. *International Law at a Time of Perplexity: Essays in Honour of Shabtai Rosenne.* Boston: Nijhoff, 1989.

Dubner, Bary Hart. *The Law of International Sea Piracy.* Leiden, Neth.: E. J. Brill, 1980.

Duiker, William J. *China and Vietnam: The Roots of Conflict.* Berkeley, Calif.: Institute of East Asian Studies, 1986.

Dupont, Pascal. *Pirates d'aujourd'hui.* Paris: Editions Ramsay, 1986.

Earle, Peter. *The Pirate Wars.* New York: St. Martin's, 2003.

Edwards, Samuel. *Barbary General: The Life of William H. Eaton.* Englewood Cliffs, N.J.: Prentice Hall, 1968.

Eklöf, Stefan. *Pirates in Paradise: A Modern History of Southeast Asia's Maritime Marauders.* Copenhagen: Nordic Institute of Asian Studies, 2006.

Elers-Napier, G. *The Life and Letters of Admiral Sir Charles Napier.* Vol. 2. London: n.p., 1862.

Elleman, Bruce A. *Waves of Hope: The U.S. Navy's Response to the Tsunami in Northern Indonesia.* Newport Paper 28. Newport, R.I.: Naval War College Press, February 2007.

Ellen, Eric, ed. *Piracy at Sea.* Paris: ICC, 1989.

———, ed. *Shipping at Risk: "The Rising Tide of Organized Crime."* Paris: ICC, 1997.

Ellen, Eric, and Donald Campbell. *International Maritime Fraud.* London: Sweet & Maxwell, 1981.

Elliott, David W. P., ed. *The Third Indochina Conflict.* Boulder, Colo.: Westview, 1981.

Forbes, Andrew, ed. *Australia and Its Maritime Interests: At Home and in the Region.* (Canberra: Sea Power Centre–Australia, 2008).

Ford, Paul Leicester, ed. *The Writings of Thomas Jefferson.* New York: G. P. Putnam, 1897.

Foster, John W. *A Century of American Diplomacy: Being a Brief Review of the Foreign Relations of the United States, 1776–1876.* New York: Houghton Mifflin, 1900.

Fox, Grace. *British Admirals and Chinese Pirates, 1832–1869.* Westport, Conn.: Hyperion, 1973.

Gao Zhihua. *Zheng Chenggong xinyang.* Hefai: Huangshan shushe, 2006.

Ghazvinian, John. *Untapped: The Scramble for Africa's Oil.* Orlando, Fla.: Harcourt, 2007.

Gottschalk, Jack A., and Brian P. Flanagan. *Jolly Roger with an Uzi: The Rise and Threat of*

*Modern Piracy.* With Lawrence J. Kahn and Dennis M. LaRochelle. Annapolis, Md.: Naval Institute Press, 2000.

Graham, Gerald S. *The China Station: War and Diplomacy 1830–1860.* Oxford, U.K.: Clarendon, 1978.

Grant, Bruce. *The Boat People: An "Age" Investigation.* New York: Penguin Books, 1979.

Greenberg, Michael D., et al. *Maritime Terrorism: Risk and Liability.* Santa Monica, Calif.: RAND, 2006.

Greenhill, B., and A. Giffard. *Steam, Politics and Patronage: The Transformation of the Royal Navy 1815–54.* London: Conway Maritime, 1994.

Grotius, Hugo. *Mare Liberum: The Freedom of the Seas, or the Right Which Belongs to the Dutch to Take Part in the East Indian Trade.* Translated by Ralph Van Deman Magoffin. New York: Oxford Univ. Press, 1916. Published in the original Latin in 1608.

Gullick, J. M. *Adventures and Encounters: Europeans in South-East Asia.* Kuala Lumpur, Malaysia: Oxford Univ. Press, 1995.

Guo Xinning. *Anti-terrorism, Maritime Security, and ASEAN-China Cooperation: A Chinese Perspective.* Trends in Southeast Asia Series 15. 2005.

Hay, John D. *A Memoir of Sir John Drummond Hay: Sometime Minister of the Court of Morocco.* London: J. Murray, 1896.

Herrmann, Wilfried A. *Asia's Security Challenges.* Commack, N.Y.: Nova Science, 1998.

Hjelholt, Holger. *British Mediation in the Danish-German Conflict 1848–1850.* Copenhagen: Munksgaard, 1966.

Ho, Joshua, and Catherine Zara Raymond, eds. *The Best of Times, the Worst of Times: Maritime Security in the Asia-Pacific.* Singapore: World Scientific, 2005.

Hourani, George F. *Arab Seafaring in the Indian Ocean in Ancient and Early Medieval Times.* Beirut: Khayats, 1963.

Hsu, Immanuel C. Y. *China's Entrance into the Family of Nations: The Diplomatic Phase, 1858–1880.* Cambridge, Mass.: Harvard Univ. Press, 1960.

Hudson, H. *Northern Approaches.* Canberra: Australian Government Publishing Service, 1988.

Human Rights Watch. *Politics as War: The Human Rights Impact and Causes of Post-election Violence in Rivers State, Nigeria.* New York: March 2008.

Hurd, Douglas. *The Arrow War: An Anglo-Chinese Confusion, 1856–1860.* London: Collins, 1967.

Hympendahl, Klaus. *Pirates Aboard! Forty Cases of Piracy Today and What Bluewater Cruisers Can Do about It.* New York: Sheridan House, 2003.

International Chamber of Commerce. *Piracy and Armed Robbery against Ships: Annual Report, 1 January–31 December 2003.* London: International Maritime Bureau, 2004.

———. *Piracy and Armed Robbery against Ships: Annual Report, 1 January–31 December 2004.* London: International Maritime Bureau, 2005.

———. *Piracy and Armed Robbery against Ships: Annual Report, 1 January–31 December 2006.* London: International Maritime Bureau, 2007.

———. *Piracy and Armed Robbery against Ships: Annual Report, 1 January–31 December 2007.* London: International Maritime Bureau, 2008.

Irwin, Ray W. *The Diplomatic Relations of the United States with the Barbary Powers, 1776–1816.* Chapel Hill: Univ. of North Carolina Press, 1931.

Jen Yu-wen. *The Taiping Revolutionary Movement.* New Haven, Conn.: Yale Univ. Press, 1973.

Ji Guoxing. *SLOC Security in the Asia Pacific.* Center Occasional Paper. Honolulu, Hawaii: Asia-Pacific Center for Security Studies, 2000.

Johnson, Captain Charles. *Lives of the Most Notorious Pirates.* Edited with an introduction by Christopher Lloyd. London: Folio Society, 1962.

Johnson, Derek, and Mark Valencia, eds. *Piracy in Southeast Asia: Status, Issues, and Responses.* Singapore: Institute of Southeast Asian Studies, 2005.

Jones, J. R. *The Anglo-Dutch Wars of the Seventeenth Century.* New York: Longman, 1996.

Jones, Rodney W., and Steven A. Hildreth, ed. *Emerging Powers: Defense and Security in the Third World.* New York: Praeger, 1986.

Karraker, Cyrus H. *Piracy Was a Business.* Rindge, N.H.: Richard R. Smith, 1953.

Kaye, Stuart. *Freedom of Navigation in the Indo-Pacific Region.* Papers in Australian Maritime Affairs 22. Canberra: Sea Power Centre–Australia, 2008.

Kemp, P. K. *Prize Money: A Survey of the History and Distribution of the Naval Prize Fund.* Aldershot, U.K.: Gale and Polden, 1946.

———. *The Oxford Companion to Ships and the Sea.* New York: Oxford Univ. Press, 1988.

Kvashny, Karen. "Modern Maritime Piracy in Asia: A Case Study of Transnational Organized Crime, Doctoral Dissertation in Criminology, Law, and Society." University of California Irvine, 2003.

Kwa Chong Guan and John K. Skogan. *Maritime Security in Southeast Asia.* London: Routledge, 2007.

Lane-Poole, Stanley. *The Story of the Barbary Corsairs.* New York: G. P. Putnam, 1890.

Langewiesche, William. *The Outlaw Sea: A World of Freedom, Chaos, and Crime.* New York: North Point, 2004.

Lehr, Peter, ed. *Violence at Sea: Piracy in the Age of Global Terrorism.* London: Routledge, 2007.

Lilius, Aleko E. *I Sailed with Chinese Pirates.* 1930. Hong Kong: Oxford Univ. Press, 1991.

Lindley, Augustus. *Ti-Ping Tien-kwoh: The History of the Ti-Ping Revolution.* Vol. 1. New York: Praeger, 1970.

Lintner, Bertil. *Blood Brothers: The Criminal Underworld of Asia.* New York: Palgrave Macmillan, 2003.

Lipscomb, Andrew A., and Albert Ellery Bergh, eds. *The Writings of Thomas Jefferson.* Washington, D.C.: Thomas Jefferson Memorial Association, 1903.

Little, Benerson. *The Sea Rover's Practice: Pirate Tactics and Techniques, 1630–1730.* Washington, D.C.: Potomac Books, 2005.

Liu Fang, ed. *Qingdai Aomen zhongwen dang'an huibian* [Collection of Chinese archives from the Qing dynasty in Macao]. Aomen: Aomen jijinhui chuban, 1999.

Lloyd, Christopher. *William Dampier.* London: Faber and Faber, 1966.

Low, Alfred D. *The Sino-Soviet Confrontation since Mao Zedong: Dispute, Detente, or Conflict?* New York: Columbia Univ. Press, 1987.

Lucie-Smith, Edward. *Outcasts of the Sea.* New York: Paddington, 1978.

Mann, Michael. *China, 1860.* London: Michael Russell, 1989.

Marr, D., and M. Wilkinson. *Dark Victory.* Sydney: Allen and Unwin, 2003.

Marsden, Reginald G. *Documents Relating to Law and Custom of the Sea.* Vol. 1, *1205–1648.* London: Navy Records Society, 1915.

McDonald, Forrest. *The Presidency of Thomas Jefferson.* Lawrence: Univ. Press of Kansas, 1976.

Meakin, Budgett. *The Moorish Empire.* London: S. Sonnenschein, 1899.

Meier, Dirk. *Seafarers, Merchants and Pirates: In the Middle Ages.* Translated by Angus McGeoch. Woodbridge, Suffolk, U.K.: Boydell, 2006.

Meredith, Martin. *The State of Africa: A History of Fifty Years of Independence.* London: Free Press/Simon & Schuster, 2006.

Miller, Harry. *Pirates of the Far East.* London: Robert Hale, 1970.

Mueller, G. O. W., and Freda Adler. *Outlaws of the Ocean: The Complete Book of Contemporary Crime on the High Seas.* New York: Hearst Marine Books, 1985.

Murphy, Martin N. *Contemporary Piracy and Maritime Terrorism: The Threat to International Security.* IISS Adelphi Paper 388. London: Routledge, 2007.

Murray, Dian H. *Pirates of the South China Coast, 1790–1810.* Stanford, Calif.: Stanford Univ. Press, 1987.

Neumann, Charles, ed. *History of the Pirates.* London: Oriental Translation Fund, 1831.

Norman, L. *Sea Wolves and Bandits.* Hobart, Australia: J. Welch and Sons, 1946.

Ong-Webb, Graham Gerard, ed. *Piracy, Maritime Terrorism and Securing the Malacca Straits.* Singapore: Institute of Southeast Asian Studies, 2006.

Ortzen, Len. *Stories of Famous Sea Raiders.* London: Arthur Barker, 1973.

Pennell, C. R., ed. *Bandits at Sea: A Pirates Reader*. New York: New York Univ. Press, 2001.

Peterson, Merrill D. *Thomas Jefferson and the New Nation*. New York: Oxford Univ. Press, 1970.

Phillimore, Augustus. *Life of Admiral of the Fleet Sir William Parker*. London: Harrison, 1880.

Pittis, Donald, and Susan Henders, comps. *Macao: Mysterious Decay and Romance*. 1940. Hong Kong: Oxford Univ. Press, 1997.

Platt, D. C. M. *Finance, Trade and Politics in British Foreign Policy 1815–1914*. Oxford, U.K.: Clarendon, 1968.

Poolman, Kenneth. *The* Speedwell *Voyage: A Tale of Piracy and Mutiny in the Eighteenth Century*. Annapolis, Md.: Naval Institute Press, 1999.

Potter, E. B., ed. *Sea Power: A Naval History*. 2nd ed. Annapolis, Md.: Naval Institute Press, 1981.

Prescott, Victor, and Clive Schofield. *The Maritime Political Boundaries of the World*. 2nd ed. Leiden, Neth.: Nijhoff, 2005.

Rahman, Chris. *The Global Maritime Partnership: Implications for the Royal Australian Navy*. Papers in Australian Maritime Affairs 24. Canberra: Sea Power Centre–Australia, 2008.

Ritchie, Robert C. *Captain Kidd and the War against the Pirates*. Cambridge, Mass.: Harvard Univ. Press, 1986.

Robinson, W. Courtland. *Terms of Refuge: The Indochinese Exodus and the International Response*. London: Zed Books, 1998.

Rodd, Francis Rennell. *General William Eaton: The Failure of an Idea*. New York: Minton, Balch, 1932.

Rogers, P. G. *A History of Anglo-Moroccan Relations to 1900* (printed in London, unpublished).

Ross, Robert S. *The Indochina Tangle*. New York: Columbia Univ. Press, 1988.

Rowan, Roy. *The Four Days of Mayaguez*. New York: W. W. Norton, 1975.

Rutter, Owen. *The Pirate Wind: Tales of Sea-Robbers of Malaya*. New York: Oxford Univ. Press, 1987.

Sherry, Frank. *Raiders and Rebels: The Golden Age of Piracy*. New York: Hearst Marine Books, 1986.

———. *Pacific Passions: The European Struggle for Power in the Great Ocean in the Age of Exploration*. New York: William Morrow, 1994.

Solomon, Richard H., and Masataka Kosaka, eds. *The Soviet Far East Military Buildup*. Dover, Mass.: Auburn House, 1986.

Sondhaus, L. *Preparing for Weltpolitik: German Sea Power before the Tirpitz Era*. Annapolis, Md.: Naval Institute Press, 1997.

Spence, Jonathan D. *God's Chinese Son: The Taiping Heavenly Kingdom of Hong Xuquan*. New York: W. W. Norton, 1996.

Starkey, David J. *British Privateering Enterprise in the Eighteenth Century*. Exeter, U.K.: Univ. of Exeter Press, 1990.

Starkey, David J., E. S. van Eyck van Heslinga, and J. A. de Moor. *Pirates and Privateers: New Perspectives on the War on Trade in the Eighteenth and Nineteenth Centuries*. Exeter, U.K.: Univ. of Exeter Press, 1997.

Swanson, Claude A., ed. *Naval Documents Related to the United States Wars with the Barbary Powers*. Washington, D.C.: U.S. Government Printing Office, 1939.

*The Taiping Revolution*. Peking: Foreign Languages, 1976.

Tarling, Nicholas. *Piracy and Politics in the Malay World: A Study of British Imperialism in Nineteenth-Century South-East Asia*. Melbourne, Australia: F. W. Cheshire, 1963.

Teng, Ssu-yü. *New Light on the History of the Taiping Rebellion*. New York: Russell and Russell, 1966.

Thakur, Ramesh, and Carlyle Thayer. *Soviet Relations with India and Vietnam*. New York: St. Martin's, 1992.

Thomson, Janice E. *Mercenaries, Pirates and Sovereigns*. Princeton, N.J.: Princeton Univ. Press, 1994.

Timlin, Thomas. *The Use of SOLAS Ship Security Alert Systems*. Working Paper 154. Singapore: S. Rajaratnam School of International Studies, 2008.

Tracy, Nicholas. *Attack on Maritime Trade*. Toronto: Univ. of Toronto Press, 1991.

Trocki, Carl A. *Prince of Pirates: The Temenggongs and the Development of Johor and Singapore, 1784–1885.* Singapore: Singapore Univ. Press, 1979.

Tsamenyi, M., and Chris Rahman, eds. *Protecting Australia's Maritime Borders: The MV Tampa and Beyond.* Wollongong Papers on Maritime Policy 13. Wollongong, Australia: Wollongong Univ., 2003.

United Nations. *Review of Maritime Transport 2008.* New York: Conference on Trade and Development, 2008.

U.S. Congress. House. Committee on the Judiciary. *Orderly Departure Program and U.S. Policy Regarding Vietnamese Boat People: Hearing before the Subcommittee on Immigration, Refugees, and International Law.* 101st Cong., 1st sess. (Washington, D.C.: U.S. Government Printing Office, 28 June 1989).

U.S. Energy Dept. *Piracy: The Threat to Tanker Traffic.* Washington, D.C.: Government Printing Office, September 1992.

Vermeer, E. B., ed. *Development and Decline of Fukien Province in the Seventeenth and Eighteenth Centuries.* Leiden, Neth.: E. J. Brill, 1990.

Vermonte, Philips Jusario, ed. *Small Is (Not) Beautiful: The Problem of Small Arms in Southeast Asia.* Jakarta: Centre for Strategic and International Studies, 2004.

Villar, Roger. *Piracy Today: Robbery and Violence at Sea since 1980.* London: Conway Maritime, 1985.

Vo, Nghia M. *The Vietnamese Boat People, 1954 and 1975–1992.* London: McFarland, 2006.

Wannan, Bill. *Legendary Australians: A Colonial Cavalcade of Adventurers, Eccentrics, Rogues, Ruffians, Heroines, Heroes, Hoaxers,* *Showmen, Pirates and Pioneers.* Adelaide, Australia: Rigby, 1974.

Williams, J. B. *British Commercial Policy and Trade Expansion 1750–1850.* Oxford, U.K.: Clarendon, 1972.

Wong, J. Y. *Yeh Ming-ch'en, Viceroy of Liang Kuang, 1852–8.* London: Cambridge Univ. Press, 1976.

Woolery, William Kirk. *The Relation of Thomas Jefferson to American Foreign Policy.* Baltimore, Md.: Johns Hopkins Univ. Press, 1927.

Xiu Guojian. *Yuedong mingdao Zhang Baozai.* Hong Kong: Xiandai jiaoyu yanjiu she chuban, 1992.

Ye Linfeng. *Zhang Baozai de chuanshuo he zhenxiang.* Hong Kong: Shanghai shuju, 1970.

Yoshihara, Toshi, and James R. Holmes, eds. *Asia Looks Seaward: Power and Maritime Strategy.* Westport, Conn.: Praeger Security International, 2008.

Young, Adam J. *Contemporary Maritime Piracy in Southeast Asia: History, Causes and Remedies.* Singapore: Institute of Southeast Asian Studies, 2007.

Young, Marilyn B. *The Vietnam Wars, 1945–1990.* New York: HarperCollins, 1991.

Yu Zufan. *Zhongguo Jiandui Shi Lu* [The Real Record of the Chinese Fleet]. Shenyang: Chunfeng wenyi chubanshe, 1997.

Zonis, Marvin, Dan Lefkovitz, and Sam Wilkin. *The Kimchi Matters: Global Business and Local Politics in a Crisis-Driven World.* Chicago: Agate, 2003.

## About the Contributors

Robert J. Antony: PhD in Chinese history, University of Hawai'i (1988); associate professor of Asian and maritime history, University of Macau. Author of *Like Froth Floating on the Sea: The World of Pirates and Seafarers in Late Imperial South China* (University of California, Berkeley, Institute for East Asian Studies, China Monograph Series, 2003) and *Pirates in the Age of Sail* (W. W. Norton, 2007). He is currently working on a book on the origins of modern piracy on the South China coast from 1837 to 1937 and on a documentary history of the pirate Zhang Baozai in the Canton Delta.

Sam Bateman: Senior fellow, Maritime Security Program, S. Rajaratnam School of International Studies, Nanyang Technological University, Singapore. Author or editor of numerous publications, including Rothwell and Bateman, eds., *Navigational Rights and Freedoms and the New Law of the Sea* (2000); Bateman and Bergin, *Future Unknown: The Terrorist Threat to Australian Maritime Security* (2005); Bateman, Ho, and Raymond, *Safety and Security in the Malacca and Singapore Straits: An Agenda for Action* (2006); and Herbert-Burns, Bateman, and Lehr, eds., *Lloyd's MIU Handbook of Maritime Security* (2008).

Penny Campbell: Commander, Royal Australian Navy, and currently Command Legal Officer to Border Protection Command, Australia. Author of "Indonesian Archipelagic Sealanes" in *Australian Maritime Issues 2005,* edited by Gregory P. Gilbert and Robert J. Davitt; and "Hot Pursuit and Australian Fisheries Law" in *Australian Maritime Issues 2006,* edited by Andrew Forbes and Michelle Lovi.

Bruce A. Elleman: Research professor, Maritime History Department, U.S. Naval War College, with an MA (1984) and PhD (1993) from the History Department, Columbia University; MS (1985) in international history, London School of Economics; and MA in national security and strategic studies, with distinction (2004), U.S. Naval War College. Recent books include *Modern Chinese Warfare: 1795–1989* (New York: Routledge, 2001); *Naval Mutinies of the Twentieth Century: An International Perspective,* edited, with Christopher Bell (London: Frank Cass, 2003); *Naval Blockades and Seapower: Strategies and Counter-strategies, 1805–2005,* edited, with S. C. M. Paine (London: Routledge, 2006); *Waves of Hope: The U.S. Navy's Response to the Tsunami in Northern Indonesia,* Newport Paper 28 (Newport, R.I.: Naval War College Press, 2007); and *Naval Coalition Warfare: From the Napoleonic War to Operation Iraqi Freedom,* edited, with Sarah Paine (London: Routledge, 2008).

Andrew Forbes: Deputy Director (Research), Sea Power Center–Australia, Canberra. Master's degrees in defense studies (1989), maritime policy (1998), and public administration (2001). Visiting senior fellow at the Australian National Center for Ocean Resources and Security at the University of Wollongong and research fellow at the Center for Foreign Policy Studies at Dalhousie University, Halifax, Canada. Author of *Protecting the National Interest: Naval Constabulary Operations in Australia's Exclusive Economic Zone* (2002) and editor of *The Strategic Importance of Seaborne Trade and Shipping* (2003); *Australian Maritime Issues 2006* (2007), *Australian Maritime Issues 2007* (2008); *Sea Power: Challenges Old and New* (Sydney: Halstead, 2007); *Asian Energy Security: Cooperation in the Malacca Strait* (Canberra: Sea Power Centre–Australia, 2008); and *Australia and Its Maritime Interests: At Home and in the Region* (Canberra: Sea Power Centre–Australia, 2008).

Charles W. Koburger, Jr.: Captain, U.S. Coast Guard Reserve (Ret.), master's degrees in history (Niagara) and political science (Oregon) and graduate of the Armed Forces Staff College. Research fellow at London Polytechnic (navigation systems) and a former captain of infantry. Author since retirement of over fifty articles for professional journals and sixteen books on maritime affairs, including *Sea Power in the Falklands* (Praeger, 1983) and *The Cyrano Fleet: France and Its Navy, 1940–42* (Praeger, 1989), which was translated into French.

Andrew Lambert: Laughton Professor of Naval History, Department of War Studies, King's College London, with an MA in war studies (1979) and PhD (1982) from King's College London. Recent books include *The Crimean War: British Grand Strategy against Russia 1853–1856* (Manchester, 1990); *The Last Sailing Battlefleet: Maintaining Naval Mastery 1815–1850* (London, 1991); *The Foundations of Naval History: Sir John Laughton, the Royal Navy and the Historical Profession* (London, 1998); *War at Sea in the Age of Sail* (London, 2000); *Nelson: Britannia's God of War* (London, 2004); *Admirals: The Men Who Made Britain Great* (London, 2008); and *Franklin: Tragic Hero of Polar Navigation* (London, 2009).

Samuel Pyeatt Menefee: Senior associate, Center for National Security Law; Maury Fellow, Center for Oceans Law and Policy; and adjunct professor, World Maritime University. Author of *Contemporary Piracy and International Law* (Institute of Marine Law, University of Cape Town, 1995) and *Trends in Maritime Violence* (Jane's Information Group, 1996). IMB Fellow of the International Chamber of Commerce–International Maritime Bureau (London), fellow of the Regional Piracy Center (Kuala Lumpur, Malaysia), and formerly chair of the Maritime Law Association's Working Party on Piracy and rapporteur of the Comité Maritime International's Joint International Working Group on Uniformity of the Law of Piracy and Maritime Violence.

Arild Nodland: Former United Nations project manager and security adviser for the European Union with ten years of work experience in global conflict areas. Officer with the Norwegian military in numerous NATO and UN peacekeeping missions. Master's degrees (1993 and 2006) from the Graduate School of International Studies at the University of Birmingham, one specializing in defense and security and one specializing in political risk analysis and religions' role in global politics. Founder and chief executive of Bergen Risk Solutions, a risk-management consultancy, which publishes the monthly *Niger Delta Security Report* and quarterly *Nigeria Maritime Security Review.* Author of several articles on the Gulf of Guinea security situation for *Scandinavian Oil and Gas Magazine* and presenter on shipping and geopolitical risk at Oslo Maritime Security Seminar (October 2007) and Oslo Shipping Forum (June 2008).

Catherine Zara Raymond: Associate at the Corbett Center for Maritime Policy Studies, based at the Defence Studies Department, Joint Services Command and Staff College, Shrivenham. PhD student at King's College London, writing her thesis on Islamic radicalization in the United Kingdom. Previously worked as an analyst for the security consultancy Control Risks in Singapore and as an associate research fellow at the Institute of Defence and Strategic Studies, also in Singapore. Coeditor and contributing author of the volume *Best of Times, Worst of Times: Maritime Security in the Asia-Pacific* (World Scientific, 2005) and a policy paper, *Safety and Security in the Malacca and Singapore Straits* (IDSS, 2006). Articles published in the *Harvard Asia Quarterly, Maritime Studies Journal,* Jamestown Foundation's *Terrorism Monitor, Journal of the Australian Naval Institute, Straits Times,* and a number of other publications. Latest papers were published in the *Journal of Terrorism and Political Violence* and in an edited volume, *Maritime Security in Southeast Asia* (Routledge).

David Rosenberg: Professor of political science, Middlebury College, Vermont, and visiting fellow in the Department of Political and Social Change in the Research School of Pacific and Asian Studies at the Australian National University, Canberra. Regional editor for the *South China Sea in the WWW Virtual Library of Asian Studies,* www .southchinasea.org/. Recent publications include "Dire Straits: Competing Security Priorities in the South China Sea," *Japan Focus* (March 2005); "Managing the Resources of the China Seas: China's Bilateral Fisheries Agreements with Japan, South Korea, and Vietnam," *Japan Focus* (August 2005); "ASEAN-China Relations: Realities and Prospects," review, *China Journal* (July 2006); "Maritime Security in the South China Sea: Coordinating Coastal and User State Priorities," coauthored with Christopher Chung, Center for Defence and Strategic Studies, Research School of Pacific and Asian Studies, Australian National University, *Ocean Development and International Law* 39, no. 1 (January–February, 2008); and "Fisheries Management in the South China Sea," Sam

Bateman and Ralf Emmers, eds., *Security and International Politics in the South China Sea* (Routledge, 2008).

Robert F. Turner: Cofounder and associate director of the Center for National Security Law at the University of Virginia School of Law, where he teaches seminars in advanced national security law. Former Charles H. Stockton Professor of International Law at the Naval War College and distinguished lecturer at the U.S. Military Academy at West Point. Author or editor of more than fifteen volumes, including the law school casebook *National Security Law* (Durham, N.C.: Carolina Academic, 2005); *The Real Lessons of the Vietnam War: Reflections Twenty-five Years after the Fall of Saigon,* edited, with John Norton Moore (Carolina Academic, 2002); *To Oppose Any Foe: The Legacy of U.S. Intervention in Vietnam,* edited, with Ross A. Fisher and John Norton Moore (Carolina Academic, 2006); and *The Jefferson-Hemings Controversy: Report of a Commission of Scholars* (Carolina Academic, forthcoming).

Gary E. Weir: Chief Historian, National Geospatial-Intelligence Agency, Bethesda, Maryland. Specialist in undersea warfare, intelligence tradecraft and collection, and related technologies. Author of *Forged in War: The Naval-Industrial Complex and American Submarine Construction, 1940–1961* (Washington, D.C.: Brassey's, 1998); *An Ocean in Common: American Naval Officers, Scientists, and the Ocean Environment* (Texas A&M University Press, 2001); and *Rising Tide: The Untold Story of the Russian Submarines That Fought the Cold War,* with Walter Boyne (Basic Books and Perseus, 2003). Founder and editor of the *International Journal of Naval History.*

# Index

11 September 2001  14, 79, 84, 92, 110, 113, 202

## A

Abd al Qadir  176

Abd el Malek  187

Abhyankar, Captain Jayant  90, 232

Abu Sayyaf Group (ASG)  72, 84, 145

Abuja  195, 200

Aceh  74–75, 114–15, 141–42

*Acorn*  55

*Actaeon*  55

Adalbert, Admiral Prince  186

Adams, John  160, 162–63, 165, 170n54

Aden  51, 209

Aden, Gulf of  156, 207–209, 216, 218, 233, 240

Adeniyi, Rear Admiral Peter Shola  200

Admiralty  *See* Royal Navy

Admiralty courts  v–vi, 3–6

Aegean Sea  177

Afghanistan  101, 151n4

Africa  vi, 13, 15–16, 42, 80–81, 85, 155–221 *passim,* 224, 230, 239
*See also* East Africa; North Africa; West Africa

Africa Command (AFRICOM)  *See* United States Africa Command (AFRICOM)

African Partnership Station  203

Afweyne, Mohamed Abdi  211–12

Agricultural and Allied Workers Union of Nigeria (AAWUN)  196

agriculture  *See* farmers

Ajibade, Captain Mufutau  201

Alauddin Bahini Gang  129

Alboran Island  174

Alger, Horatio  48

Algeria  15, 156, 173–74, 176, 180, 185, 188

Algiers  158, 161, 166, 168–70

*Aliya*  126

al-Qa'ida  110, 145, 214

*Amazon*  124

Amazon River  29

Amile, Akinshola  195

Amoy  37, 47

amphetamine-type stimulants (ATSs)  *See* methamphetamines

'Amr ibn al-'As  1

Anambas Islands  66

Andaman Sea  109, 141

Anding Gate  58

Anglo-Dutch Wars  4

Anglo-Moroccan Treaty (1856)  185, 187

Anqing  60

Antigua  vi

Anti-piracy Coast Guard Program  87

*Anzac*  68

A'Pak  43

Arabian Gulf  156
*See also* Persian Gulf

Arabian Sea  85, 156, 214

*Ardeal* 129

Argentina 9

*Argus* 166

*Ariel* 129

*Arktis Crystal* 122

*Arleigh Burke* 213–14

*Arrow* 51, 54

Arrow War 13, 42–43, 51–63, 240
*See also* Opium War, Second

ASEAN Chiefs of National Police meetings
148

Asia 19, 50n17, 52, 80–81, 84–85, 87, 113, 207,
215, 219, 221n36, 234
*See also* Central Asia; East Asia; South Asia;
Southeast Asia

Asia Pacific and Africa Inter-Regional
Cooperation 85

Asia-Pacific 73, 79, 140, 219, 224

Association of Southeast Asian Nations
(ASEAN) 87, 102–103, 116, 148–49, 230

Atlantic Ocean 6, 156, 177–80, 182, 204, 240

Auckland, First Lord of the Admiralty 177–79

Australia vi–vii, 10, 51, 67–70, 73, 85, 88, 97,
99, 103, 105, 208, 217–18, 226, 235, 239

Austria 62

Austria-Hungary 62

Automatic Identification System (AIS) 87–88,
111, 117, 230, 236, 239

Azanen Bay 174, 185

**B**

Badawi, Abdullah Ahmad 113

Bahrain 215–16

Bai Ling 41

*Bainbridge* 239, 242n33

Baki Billah Bahini Gang 132

Baltic Sea 184

Bangkok 66, 72, 74

Bangladesh vi, 15, 88, 96, 116, 119, 121–36,
139, 141, 144, 225, 230

Barbary Coast v, 157–71

Barbary pirates v, 157–71, 208, 224

Baring, Sir Francis 179–80, 186

Barisal Division 121, 125–29, 132

Barre, General Muhammad Siad 209, 211

Bashshu Bahini Gang 128

Basra 214

Batam Island 74, 87, 226

Bayelsa 194, 196, 198, 201, 205n3, 206n19

Beijing 37, 49, 53–58, 60–62, 100–101, 106

Beijing Convention 58

Belgium 62

Bellamy, Samuel "Black Sam" v

Bengal, Bay of 96, 126–28, 130–32, 233

Benin 192

Benin River 196

*Benvalia* 122

Bergen Risk Solutions 196, 205n1

*Betsy* 158

Bhola 126, 129, 131

Biafra 195

Bias Bay 44–47, 50n25

*Bittern* 55

Black Flag 98

black market 53, 70, 84, 102, 112

Black Sea 230

blimps 25

*Blue Sea* 124

"boat people" 14, 97–108, 225–26

Boggs, Eli 42

Bomba 166

Bonaparte, Napoleon 8

*Bonhomme Richard* 162

Bonny River 196

Border Protection Command (Australia)  235

Borneo  2, 65, 67–68, 76, 145

Botoya Point  185

Bowring, Sir John  54

Britain  *See* Great Britain

Bruce, James (Lord Elgin)  54

Brunei  66

Bu Gafar  174–75, 183, 187

Bugis pirates  2

*Bunga Mawar*  123

Burma  96, 143
*See also* Myanmar

Busan  80

Bush, George W.  202–203

**C**

Caesar, Julius  v

Cai Qian  37, 39

Cai Qian Ma  39, 48

Cala Tramontana  76, 185

Calabar  200

Calcutta  55

*Caldera*  42

California  42, 88

Cambodia  14, 34, 66, 70, 96–97, 100, 140, 143

Cameroon  156, 192

Canada  97, 105, 235

cannabis  140

Canton  38, 40–41, 43–44, 47–48, 52–55

Cao Bang  101

Cape Lopez  192

Cape of Good Hope  51, 156, 240

Cape Palmas  192

Cape Tres Forcas  174–76, 181, 185–86

Caribbean Sea  v–vi, 7, 208

Carter, Jimmy  100–101

Cathcart, James Leander  159, 162, 164–65

Caucasus  151n4

Celebes Sea  68, 96, 118, 146–48

Central Asia  151n4

Central Command (CENTCOM)  *See* United States Central Command (CENTCOM)

Ceuta  174

Ceylon  *See* Sri Lanka

Chaozhou  38, 47

*Chaumont*  73

*Cherry 201*  75

*Chettinad Glory*  123

Cheung Chau Islands  47

*Cheung Son*  35–36, 47, 73

Chief of Naval Operations  216, 234

Chile  9, 42

*Chilean Express*  124

China  2, 12–13, 16, 34–63, 66, 71, 73, 80, 85, 88, 96–108, 116, 139–40, 143, 192, 203, 205, 218–19, 223–26, 230, 239, 241

Chittagong  15, 96, 121–36, 225

Chittagong Port Authority (CPA)  124

choke points  81–82, 216

Cholon  103

Christians  52, 69, 166, 187

Chu-apoo  42

cigarette smuggling  84, 137, 139, 142

civil war  16, 27, 45–46, 51–63, 195, 199

Clinton, Hillary  32n34

coalitions  *See* naval coalitions

cocaine  140

"Cod Wars"  9–10

Cold War  73, 209, 223

Coloane Island  47

Combined Task Force (CTF) 150  207–208, 212–14

Combined Task Force (CTF) 151  218, 239

commerce 2, 3, 8, 10, 14, 24, 29, 37, 56, 65, 157–58, 160, 162, 164, 174, 208, 220n16, 226, 234

Communism 45–46, 49, 102

Congress (U.S.) 113, 161–63, 168, 169n3, 170n39, 170n42, 203

*Constellation* 166

*Constitution* 167

consulate (U.S.) 159

Container Security Initiative (CSI) 87

Continental Congress 8, 158, 161

continental shelf 9–10

Convention for the Suppression of Unlawful Acts against the Safety of Maritime Navigation (SUA) 89

convoy system 7, 43, 51, 54, 233, 239–40

Cooke, George 43

*Cooperative Strategy for 21st Century Seapower, A* 236

Copenhagen School of Strategic Studies 153n29

*Corsicana* 71

Cotabato 140

Council for Mutual Economic Assistance (Comecon) 99

Council for Security Cooperation in the Asia Pacific (CSCAP) 149, 152–53

Council of Islamic Courts (CIC) 214

*Crane* 68–69

Crimean War 185

Cruiser's Act 6

Cuba 100

*Cuthbert Young* 173

Cyprus 129

**D**

Dagu Repulse 56–57

*Dai Hong Dan* 213

*Daihung* 123

Dale, Captain Richard 162–64

Dampier, William 7

*Danzig* 186

Darwin 99

Davis, Sir John Francis 52

*Dawson* legal case 22

*De Xin Hai* 239

Decatur, Lieutenant Stephen 166, 168

Declaration of Paris 8, 51, 54

decolonization 14, 66, 69

Defoe, Daniel v

Deng Xiaoping 100–101

Denmark 62, 105

Derne 166, 170n54

*Dewi Madrim* 75

dhows 70, 76, 209–10, 213

diesel smuggling 139, 142, 151n2

Dokubo-Asari, Alhaji Mugahid 198–99, 206n20

*Dona Ramona* 145

Dongresilli, Bernard 3

*Dragon* 186

Drake, Sir Francis v

droit 5, 6

drug running 46, 70, 74, 83–84, 86, 139–41, 146, 193, 223, 236–37

Drummond Hay, John 176–80, 182–83, 185, 187

Dubai 72

Dundas, Vice Admiral Sir James 179–82

Dutch *See* Netherlands, The

*Dynamic* 129

**E**

East Africa 209

East Asia 61, 224

East Indies 65–66

East Timor 217

Eaton, General William  15, 157–71

economic sanctions  157

ecstasy  140

Egypt  1, 156, 165, 202

El Aolde  210

El Mann  210

Elgin, Lord  *See* Bruce, James (Lord Elgin)

Elizabeth I, Queen  3

Ellen, Eric  11

England  *See* Great Britain

*Enterprise*  162

environment  11, 15, 25, 85, 88–89, 117, 146, 236

ephedrine  140

Equatorial Guinea  192

*Erria Inge*  73

Escravos  196

Essaouira  *See* Mogador

Ethiopia  156, 209, 214

Europe  v, 2, 7–8, 14–15, 40, 42, 44, 65, 80, 109, 151n4, 157–58, 160–61, 168, 174, 187, 202, 223–24, 239
*See also* Western Europe

European Command (EUCOM)  *See* United States European Command (EUCOM)

European Economic Community  229

European Union  80

"Ever Victorious Army"  61

exclusive economic zone (EEZ)  10, 28, 85, 89–90, 92, 146–47, 225, 229, 237, 241n2

Exercise MARITIME SAFARI–LAGOS 2008  202

extraterritoriality  98

*Exxon Valdez*  193

"Eyes in the Sky" (EiS) patrols  87, 115–16, 148, 230

**F**

*Faina*  238–39

Falkland Islands  51

*Fantome*  175

Far East  67

farmers  193, 227

Faruk Bahini Gang  127–28

*Feisty Gas*  212

firearms  11, 35, 40–42, 45, 53, 60, 67–70, 74, 99, 112, 115, 125–27, 140–41, 145, 147, 150, 161, 174–75, 197, 201, 210, 214, 231–32, 236–38, 240

fisheries  v, 2, 8–11, 15–16, 32, 35–37, 39–43, 46–47, 61, 66–68, 70, 72, 76, 79, 81–83, 85–86, 99, 102–105, 107, 112, 125–37, 139, 141–47, 150, 152n14, 174, 193–96, 207–21, 224–27

Fishtown  194

Five Power Defence Arrangements  237

floating production storage and offloading vessels (FPSOs)  197, 205n1, 206n19

floating storage and offloading vessels (FSOs)  197, 205n1

*Flora*  173, 186

*Forbes*  v

Forcados Export Terminal  198

France  5, 8, 15–16, 20, 51, 55, 58, 62, 65, 97–98, 105, 159, 173–75, 184–85, 188, 208, 214, 219n2

Free Aceh Movement  72, 75, 115, 140

free trade  82

French Indochina  *See* Vietnam

*Fu Tai*  74

Fujian Province  36–37, 39–41

Funing  38

*Furious*  55

**G**

Gabon  156, 192

Ganges River  121

Gardiner, General Sir Robert  181, 185

*Gaz Lion*  123

Gbomo, Jomo  199

General Santos  140

Geneva Conventions on the Law of the Sea  9, 25, 27, 228

Gerakan Aceh Merdeka (GAM)  *See* Free Aceh Movement

Germany  88, 105, 122, 184, 186, 190, 202

Ghana  156, 193

Giap, No Nguyen  102

Gibraltar  15, 162, 173–83, 185, 208

Gibraltar, Strait of  174–75, 187, 225

Giffard, Captain Henry  186

*Gladiator*  181

*Glasgow*  217, 220n31

Glasspoole, Richard  40–41

Global Maritime Partnership  237, 239

Global War on Terror (GWOT)  89, 202, 208

globalization  81, 137–38

Golden Age of Piracy  7

*Golden Nori*  214

Gordon, Charles  63n25

Gortney, Vice Admiral William  218

Grand Canal  53

Grant, General Hope  57

Great Britain  v, 3–10, 13, 15–17, 22–23, 42–45, 51–63, 65–67, 69–70, 88, 98, 107, 122, 157–58, 160, 163–64, 173–90, 208–209, 211, 214–15, 217, 238

Great Exhibition (1851)  184–85

Great Yarmouth  5

Greater Sunda Islands  140

Greece  1, 165

Grotius, Hugo  1–2, 20, 23, 31n9

Guangdong Confederation  39–41, 49n13

Guangdong Province  38–41, 52

Guangxi Province  52

Guangzhou  *See* Canton

Guelaya Peninsula  174

*guerre de course*  4

Guinea, Gulf of  16, 191–93, 204, 251

Guizhou Province  38

Gulf of Guinea Guard Force  16, 192

Gurkha  213

**H**

Habir Gedir subclan  211

Hadi, Ibnu  85

*Hai Sin*  73

Hainan Island  12, 41–42, 90

Haiphong  100

Hakka  52, 62n4

Han dynasty  37

Hangzhou  53, 60

Hankou  53, 55

Hanoi  98–99, 102

Haque, Nurul  125

Harardhere  16, 212–13, 219

Harris, Steven  220n32

Hart, Robert  60

Harvard Draft Convention on Piracy  19, 23–27

Hawiye clan  211

Hayes, Bully  43

Hedges, Sir Charles  vi

Henry V, King  3

Henry VIII, King  5

heroin  140, 151n4

high seas  1, 9, 11, 15, 21–23, 25–28, 31, 67–69, 77, 105, 108, 147, 168, 217, 220, 224–25, 228, 240

Ho Chi Minh  102

Ho Chi Minh City  *See* Saigon

"Hoa" Chinese  97–108

Holland  62
*See also* Netherlands, The

Honam Point  55

Hong Kong 12, 22, 42, 44, 46–48, 50, 53–54, 61, 72, 103

Hong Xiuquan 52, 61

Hope, Admiral James 57, 60

Horn of Africa (HOA) 16, 207–21, 239

*Hornet* 55, 166–67

Hossain, Shahadat 124

House of Commons 179

Huai Army 60–61

Huang Ting 38

hub ports 71, 80, 84

Hubei Province 38

Hull, Lieutenant Isaac 165

Human Rights Watch 204

*Hupeh* 46

Hutan Melintang 141

*Hymen* 173, 187

**I**

Iban pirates 2

Ibebuka, Ekene 200, 205

*Ibn Qutaibah* 129

"ice" *See* methamphetamines

Iceland 9–10

Ijaws 199, 205

Ilocos Sur 74

*Inabukwa* 73

India vi, 55, 72, 85, 88, 96, 116, 121, 123, 130–31, 139–41, 209, 213, 223, 230, 233, 238

Indian Ocean vi, 73, 85, 114, 156, 207–208, 210, 233, 237

Indian Ocean Naval Symposium 237

Indonesia vi, 11–13, 35–36, 47, 66–75, 80–82, 85–90, 102, 109–20, 122, 133, 137, 139–43, 145–48, 151n2, 152n14, 152n16, 152n21, 226, 229–30

Industrial Revolution 8, 234

*Inflexible* 55

Information Sharing Center (ISC) 89, 109

International Chamber of Commerce (ICC) 10, 207–208, 214, 220n16

International Convention for the Safety of Life at Sea (SOLAS) 114, 229

international law 2, 8, 19–32, 105, 108, 147, 215, 225, 227, 239

International Law Commission (UN) 25, 27, 31

International Maritime Bureau (IMB) 10–12, 15, 19, 29, 79, 83, 86–87, 90, 109–10, 112, 114, 121, 142–43, 152n14, 191, 205, 207–208, 210, 212–14, 220, 230–32, 239–40, 250

International Maritime Organization (IMO) 10–11, 19, 25, 29, 87–88, 90, 92, 110, 117, 142–43, 148, 201, 216, 220n16, 221n36, 228–30, 236–37

International Seapower Symposium XVII 216

International Ship and Port Facility Security (ISPS) Code 119n8, 143, 191, 229, 231, 241

International Transport Workers Federation 90

Inventus UAV 216

Iran 151, 156, 215–16

Iranun pirates 2, 17n4

Iraq 84, 86, 156, 163, 202, 208, 214–16

*Iron Prince* 44

Israel 74

Italy 62, 105, 184, 209

Itu Aba Island 66

Ivory Coast 192

**J**

Jakarta 72, 88, 117, 141, 148, 151

Jamaah Islamiah 73, 145

*James E. Williams* 213

*Janus* 185–86

Japan 34, 38, 46, 66, 70–72, 80–81, 85, 87–89, 98, 105, 113, 116, 141, 213–14, 229–30, 239

Java 96, 138, 141

Jay, John 159, 161

Jefferson, Thomas 8, 15, 157–71

*Jeune Dieppois*  173, 187

Jiaqing emperor  41

Johnson, Captain Charles  v, vii

Joint Revolutionary Council  197

Joint War Committee (JWC)  86–87

Jones, John Paul  162

*Joven Emilia*  185

"junk piracy"  52

junks  37, 39, 41–46, 52, 54, 61, 70, 76

**K**

*Kalifornia*  152n16

Kalimantan  118, 140

Kampong  81–82, 142

Kangxi emperor  38

Kaohsiung  80

Karachi  51

Karamanli, Hamet  158, 164–66, 168

Karamanli, Yusuf  15, 158, 163–64, 166–68

Karimata Islands  66

Karnaphuli River  121–22

*Karya Sentosa*  122

*Kawsar*  125

Kelley Barracks  202

Kenya  156, 219, 229

Khulna Division  121, 129–31, 135

Kidd, William  43

Kismaayo  210

*Koei*  71

Koh Tang  70

Koizumi, Prime Minister Junichiro  89

Korea  34, 116, 141, 213
*See also* North Korea; South Korea

*Kota Tegap*  125

Kowloon  45, 50

Kuala Lumpur  87–88, 110, 117, 148, 151, 213, 230

Kutubdia Island  123

Kuwait  215–16

**L**

*Lady's Captivity among Chinese Pirates, A*  42

Laem Chabang  80

*Laemthong Glory*  122

Lagos  196–97, 200, 202–204

Lai Choi San  46, 48

Lang Son  101

Lantau Island  47

Lao Cai  101

Laos  14, 96–97, 140

Laraiche  180

Lawrence, Thomas Edward (a.k.a. "Lawrence of Arabia")  163

Lay, Horatio Nelson  58–60

Lay-Osborn Fleet  58–61, 63n25

*Le Ponant*  214–15

League of Nations  21–22

Lear, Colonel Tobias  166–67, 170n54

Lebanon  86, 182

Leiden (Leydon)  3

Leizhou Peninsula  41

letters of marque and reprisal  2–6

Li Hongzhang  60

Liberia  71, 191–92, 202

*Liberty Spirit*  122

Libya  156

Liem Sioe Liong  36

Lilius, Aleko  46

Lin Shuangwen Rebellion  38

Lingga Islands  66

*Lively*  173

Lloyd's Market Association  86

Logan, James  7

Lombok Strait  71

London 158, 173, 184, 188n10

Long Range Identification and Tracking (LRIT) 236

*Lotus* legal case 21

Loviot, Fanny 42

**M**

Macassar 2

Macau 9, 12–13, 40–44, 46–47

Madeira 179, 181

Madison, James 161–62, 164–65, 167

*Maersk Alabama* 239

Maheshkhali Island 125

Maine 168

Makassar Strait 72

Malacca Strait vi, 12–14, 19, 30, 31n32, 47, 66, 71–73, 75, 81–88, 96, 107, 109–20, 139–44, 146–48, 152n14, 224–26, 229–31, 233, 235–36, 240

Malay pirates 98

Malayan Emergency 69

Malaysia vi, 12, 35, 66, 68–69, 72–73, 80, 85, 87–89, 96–97, 102–103, 109–20, 137–43, 147–48, 151n2, 207, 216, 219, 229–30, 239, 241n10

Malaysia-Singapore-Indonesia (MALSINDO) patrols 87, 91, 114–15, 148, 230, 240

Malmesbury, Foreign Secretary Lord 186

Malta 176

Malvinas *See* Falkland Islands

*Mammoth Monarch* 71

Manado 140

Manchuria 53

Manchus 37–38, 48, 51–63

"Mandate of Heaven" 52

Manila 66, 70–71, 80, 84, 151, 152n16

Manila-men 42, 50

*Marblue* 130

*Mare Liberum* 1–2, 20

"Marine Electronic Highway" 91–92

marine environment 15, 89, 117, 146, 150, 228

maritime domain awareness (MDA) 234–37

Martin, Ricky 49

Massachusetts 168

Masum Bahini Gang 132

Mauritius 51

*Mayaguez* 70

*Mayer Doa* 127

McCleverty, Commander James 176–77

Mediterranean 15, 156, 162–63, 168, 170, 173–75, 177–80, 182, 184, 208, 224, 230

Meghna River 121, 125, 127–29

Melilla 174, 178, 182, 187

Merca 210

methamphetamines 140

Mia, Kalu 125

Miao Uprising 38

Middle East 81, 85, 151n4

Mindanao 118–19, 139–40

Ming dynasty 36–38, 48

Mirs Bay 47

Mitee, Ledum 205

*Mobile Bay* 217, 220n32

Mogadishu 208, 210–11, 213–14

Mogador 177–79

money laundering 46, 90, 140

Mongla 132

Mongolia 53

Monroe, James 161

Montauban, General Cousin de 57

Montemayor, Isabelo 67

*Moon Bird* 122

Moro Liberation Front 73

Moroccan Jews 185

Morocco 15, 156, 158, 173–90, 233

Moros 67

Morris, Captain Richard  163

Moscow  100–101

Motaleb Bahini Gang  131–32

Mount Thistle  52

Movement for the Emancipation of the Niger Delta (MEND)  197–99, 206nn19–20

Movement for the Survival of the Ogoni People (MOSOP)  193, 205

Mugdug  211, 220n13

Mullen, Admiral Michael  16, 216, 219, 234, 237, 242n21

multinationals  58, 194, 201

Muslims  16, 69, 73, 203, 205

mutiny  11, 24, 26, 165

Myanmar  12, 88, 121, 139–40, 143
See also Burma

**N**

*Nagasaki Spirit*  73

*Namoa*  44

Nan'ao Island  48

Nanjing  53, 61

Nanking Decade  37

Napier, Sir Charles  177–85

Naples  177

*National Geographic*  109

National University of Singapore  82

Nationalist Party  45

Natuna Islands  66

naval coalitions  217

Navigation Acts (1651)  6

Nelson, Horatio  8, 166, 217

Netherlands, The  1–5, 7, 17, 20, 62, 65–66, 88, 105, 208
See also Holland

New People's Army  140

New Zealand  218

Ngubane, Brigadier General Lawrence  201

Nha Be  72

Nichols, D. W.  67

Nicolson, Commander Frederick  175

Niger Delta  193–95, 197–201, 204

Niger Delta Joint Task Force  200–201

Niger Delta People's Volunteer Force (NDPVF)  197–98, 216n20

Niger Delta Summit  199

Niger Delta Vigilante  197

Nigeria  16, 156, 191–206, 224, 233

Nigerian National Assembly  198

Nigerian Navy  200–201

Nigerian Trawler Owners Association  196

*Nimrod*  55

Ningbo  43, 47, 60

North Africa  159, 170n46, 223

North America  vi, 7, 80, 223

North Atlantic Treaty Organization (NATO)  217–18, 230, 237–38, 251

North Korea  213

North Sulawesi  140

North Sumatra Fishery Office  86

North Vietnam  99

Norway  88, 105, 191, 205n1

*Nuria 767*  67, 70

Nyon Arrangement (1937)  26–27

**O**

Obama, Barack  32n34

O'Bannon, First Lieutenant P. N.  164

Obasanjo, Olusegun  199

Odili, Peter  204

Ogbainbiri  194

Ogoni  204–205

Okah, Henry  198

Okpo, Admiral Ekpenyong  201

Oman  215–16

Oman, Gulf of  156

Omehia, Celestine  201

"Open Door" commercial treaty  187

Operation GOLDEN TIGER  131

Operation STABILISE  217

opium smuggling  43, 47, 52–53, 72, 151n4, 223

Opium War, First (1839–42)  37, 41–42, 98, 223

Opium War, Second (1856–60)  51
*See also* Arrow War

Organisation for Economic Co-operation and
Development (OECD)  82

Osborn, Sherard  59–60

*Ots Uranus*  129

**P**

Pacific Ocean  vi, 85, 230

Pakistan  101, 121, 208

Palau Bidong  104

Palmerston, Foreign Secretary Lord  54, 57,
177–79, 181–86

Pan Pacific Hotel  71

Panama  73, 90, 122, 129–30, 191

Paracel Islands  66, 99

Paris  159, 173, 180

Paris Declaration  8, 51, 54

Paris Memorandum of Understanding on Port
State Control  229

Parker, Admiral Sir William  175, 177, 179–82,
184, 186

Parkes, Harry  54

Patenga Point  124

*Pax Britannica*  vi, 65

Pearl River  45, 48

Penang  51, 139

people smuggling  70, 84–85, 119, 138–39, 142,
146, 237

*People v. Lol-Lo and Saraw* legal case  22

People's Liberation Army (PLA)  101

People's Republic of China (PRC)  *See* China

Permanent Court of International Justice  20,
31

Persian Gulf  71–72, 85
*See also* Arabian Gulf

Peru  9

*Petro Concord*  74

*Petro Ranger*  110

Philadelphia  161

*Philadelphia*  166

Philippines  vi, 12, 22, 31n14, 34, 65–69, 73–
74, 80, 86–88, 90, 96, 102, 118, 139–41, 143,
145–51, 226

Phillip Channel  71–73

Phillips, Richard  239

Phnom Penh  100

Pickering, Timothy  163

piracy and

    aircraft  24–26

    bribery  41

    coastal states  10, 22, 28, 31, 81–82, 84–92,
146, 228–29, 232, 234, 236–37, 240

    cruise ships  22, 85, 145, 212

    extortion  2, 38, 41, 43, 46–47, 84, 131, 141

    flag states  20, 51, 54, 70–71, 73–75, 81–82,
90, 146, 157, 223, 228–29, 232, 235–36,
240–41

    globalization  81, 137–38

    hijacking  35, 44–47, 70–71, 73–75, 82, 84,
90, 111, 128, 130, 132–33, 142, 197, 213,
225, 234, 236, 238–39

    "hot pursuit"  65, 76, 89, 91

    insurance  11, 13, 29–30, 75–76, 82–83, 86–
87, 90, 143, 188n10, 230

    international shipping  vi, 2, 4–5, 8, 10, 13–
14, 16, 19, 25, 28–30, 41, 45, 53, 62, 71–73,
80–83, 85–88, 90–92, 97, 105, 109–10, 117,
133, 138, 143, 145, 148, 184, 191, 193, 195–
96, 200, 213, 224–37, 239–41

piracy and *(continued)*

kidnap for ransom  12, 15, 41, 43, 46–47, 70, 75, 82, 111–12, 116, 130–33, 148, 150, 191, 195–200, 207

law enforcement  28, 30, 70, 72, 76, 81–83, 86, 88, 91, 116, 122, 124–29, 131–32, 141, 146–51, 196, 200, 204, 225, 227, 231–34, 238, 240

liquefied petroleum gas (LPG) carriers 123, 145

littoral states  31n32, 82, 88, 92, 114, 117, 119

maritime crime  9, 11, 13, 15–16, 19–32, 79, 84, 123, 128, 133, 137–53, 196, 208–209, 214–16, 219, 221n36, 224–28, 240–41

multilateral naval response  16, 110, 114, 116–17, 146, 148–49, 216–17, 224, 227, 230, 237–38, 241

murder  7, 24, 35–37, 39–40, 42–43, 46–48, 70, 75, 84, 86, 98, 103, 105–106, 111, 127–29, 131–32, 152n16, 158, 166, 175, 180, 183, 185–86, 196, 232, 239

occasional pirates  14, 39, 43, 97

opportunistic pirates  36–37, 39, 42–43, 45, 81, 90, 93, 104–107, 137, 145, 174, 223–28

phantom ships  74, 90, 111, 142, 223

port states  146, 228–29, 236, 241

professional pirates  13, 14, 36, 39, 43, 45–47, 97, 104–107, 125

prostitution  46–47, 84, 104

ransom  v, 40–42, 44–47, 70, 74–75, 82, 111–12, 128, 130–33, 157–58, 160, 174, 185, 187, 195–96, 199, 211, 214, 218, 225, 239–40

rape  14, 24, 47, 70, 97, 99, 103–104, 115

sanctioned piracy  4, 36, 39, 42–43, 51, 53, 69, 97–98, 102

shipmasters  12, 41, 143, 164, 230–33

shipowners  7, 56, 70, 74–75, 82–83, 87, 90–91, 127, 143, 146, 188n10, 196, 213, 224, 228, 230–33, 239–41

syndicates  13, 36–38, 42, 45–47, 49n10, 71–72, 74, 141, 224

terrorists  11, 15, 24, 41, 73, 75, 79, 82–86, 88–89, 110, 113, 138–41, 144–46, 148–49, 152n16, 157, 168, 202, 208, 214, 218, 234, 236–37

three-mile territorial limit  8–9, 22, 115, 224

twelve-mile territorial limit  9, 28, 115, 213, 225

Piracy Reporting Center (PRC)  12, 87, 110, 216, 230

*PK 504*  99

*Plumper*  181

poaching  85–86, 131

pollution  15, 32, 79, 85–86, 88, 117, 150, 191, 193, 199–200, 228

*Polyphemus*  175–77, 181–82

Port Harcourt  194, 196–97, 200

Port Klang  80, 111, 144

*Porter*  213–14

Portugal  3, 41, 43, 62, 65, 226

Poulo Condore Islands  66

poverty  v, 15, 48, 81–84, 121, 149, 151, 174, 194, 204, 211, 216, 223, 227

Powell, Lieutenant Richard  185–86

*Powerful*  181

*prahus*  70, 76

Pratas Islands  66

Preble, Commodore Edward  166

President's Emergency Plan for AIDS Relief (PEPFAR)  203

*Prince Regent*  180

privateers  v, 1–17 *passim*, 24, 36, 42, 51, 54, 69, 102, 185, 208, 223, 226, 237

Privy Council  22, 24

Protection of Vital Sealanes initiative  117

Prussia  62, 173

pseudoephedrine  140

Pulau Bidong  104

Pulau Perak  112

Puntland Autonomous Region  211, 219n2

Pusur River  130

**Q**

Qatar  215–16

Qianlong emperor  36

Qing dynasty  36–38, 41, 47, 52, 55, 57, 61–62

**R**

Radjasa, Hatta  118

*Radwan*  124

Raju Bahini Gang  132

Rapid Action Battalion (RAB)  132

Reagan, Ronald  31n33

Red Banner fleet  40

Red Sea  209

Redman legal claim  177, 180–82, 189n16

Regional Commission for Fisheries (RECOFI)  215–16

Regional Cooperation Agreement on Combating Piracy and Armed Robbery against Ships in Asia (ReCAAP)  19, 89, 109, 112, 116, 119, 230, 240, 241n10

Regional Maritime Security Initiative  113

*Renmin Ribao*  100

Revolution of 1911 (China)  37, 45, 47–48

*Reynard*  181

Riau Islands  2, 66, 138, 142

Riff musket  175–77, 185

Riff pirates  15–16, 173–90

Ripert, Jean-Maurice  215

Robert, Bartholomew  7

*Rodney*  179–80

Romans  1

Royal Australian Navy (RAN)  13, 67–68, 217

Royal Malaysian Marine Police  72, 219

Royal Malaysian Navy  219

Royal Navy  v–vi, 7, 42, 44, 51–52, 54, 58, 65, 68, 164, 177, 184, 186, 208–209, 233

Russell, Foreign Secretary Lord John  185

Russia  51, 55, 58, 62, 74, 129, 151n4, 184–85, 238–39
See also Soviet Union

*Ruth*  173–77

**S**

Sabah  70, 118, 139

Sabinagi  74

*Safina Al Bisarat*  213

Saigon  66, 110

Samal pirates  67

Sandakan  140

*Sans Pareil*  54

Santa Cruz de Tenerife  179

São Tomé and Príncipe  192

Saro-Wiwa, Ken  193, 195, 205

Sattahip  70

Saudi Arabia  129, 156, 215–16

Schleswig-Holstein conflict (1848–50)  184

Scotland  4, 164

sea lines of communication (SLOCs)  225

*Seabourne Spirit*  212–13

sea-lanes  15, 66, 85, 91–92, 117, 121, 238

Second Barbary (Algerine) War  168

Secure-Ship  87, 91, 216, 231

Security Council (UN)  30

Security Council resolutions (UN)  26, 30, 208, 239

Seymour, Admiral Michael  54

"shabu" *See* methamphetamines

Shanghai  42, 45, 47, 53, 60–61, 73, 80

Shanwei  35, 49

Shap-ng-tsai  42

Shell Oil Company  198, 206n19

Shenzhen  80

ShipLoc  87, 91, 216, 232, 240

Si-Amil Island  68

Sichuan Province  38

Sicily  177, 208

*Sidon*  180–81

Silva-Sam, Governor Timipre  201

*Sinar Merak*  152n14

Singapore  vi, 12, 31n32, 35, 42, 51, 65–67, 71–75, 80, 82–84, 87–89, 98–99, 102, 109–20 *passim,* 148, 151, 152n14, 226, 229–30

Singapore Strait  31n32, 83, 87–88, 143–44, 146, 148, 226

Sinkiang  *See* Xinjiang

Sino-American relations  100

Sino-British relations  51, 54, 66, 240
*See also* Arrow War; Opium War, First; Opium War, Second

Sino-Japanese War (1937–45)  46

Sino-Soviet border  101

Sino-Soviet war (1969)  108n19

Sino-Vietnamese border  39, 101

Sino-Vietnamese War (1979)  98–100, 102

*Sirius Star*  218, 239

Sitakunda  124

Slave Trade Act (1825)  23

Slovenia  123

Society of God-Worshipers  52

Socotra Archipelago  214

Soebijanto, Admiral Slamet  113–14

Somalia  16, 30, 86, 133, 156, 207–21, 224, 236, 238–41

Somaliland  209, 211

"sonic boom" gun  231, 239

South Asia  14, 224

South China Sea  10, 12, 14, 36–37, 47, 65–77, 79–93, 105, 143, 147, 224

South Korea  34, 80, 88, 96, 124, 230, 251

South Pacific Forum Fisheries Agency  215

South Vietnam  9

Southeast Asia  11–12, 14–15, 17, 38, 40, 42, 49, 71, 73, 75–77, 82, 85, 87, 90, 93, 99, 105, 108, 110, 116, 119–20, 138–39, 141–42, 144–46, 149–50, 151n4, 152n16, 152n20, 223, 226, 230–31

Soviet Union  vi, 73, 100–101, 107, 209

Soviet-Vietnamese relations  100

Spain  2, 7, 15, 22, 31n14, 62, 65, 67, 69, 156, 167, 173–75, 183, 185, 187–88, 214–15, 226

*Spark*  44

Special Operations Forces (SOF)  105, 113

*Speedwell*  7

Spithead  178, 180, 184

Spratly Islands  66, 77, 89, 106

Sri Lanka  116, 141

*St. Bridges Bay*  69

*St. Vincent*  181

Stapleton, Commodore James  217–18

*Star Bird*  122

Sterrett, Lieutenant Andrew  162, 164, 179n39

Stromboli  181

Stuttgart  202

submarine cables  28

submarines  27, 70

Sudan  156, 238

Suez Canal  209

sui generis  20, 23, 28

Sukarno, President  69

Sulawesi Island  118, 141
*See also* North Sulawesi

Sulu region  67–69, 138–39, 146, 150, 224

Sulu Sea  2, 96, 139, 146–47

Sumatra  71, 73, 86, 114–15, 138–39

Summer Palace (Beijing)  58

Sunda Strait  71

Sundarbans mangrove forest  121, 130–32

*Superferry 14*  84, 145, 152n16

Surabaya 141

Suzhou 61

Switzerland 105

Sydney 51

Syria 156, 183

**T**

Taipa Island 47

Taiping Island *See* Itu Aba Island

Taiping Rebellion 13, 36–37, 41, 51–63, 224

Taiwan 34, 38–39, 48, 66, 96, 140, 151n2, 235

Taiwan Strait 35

Tamelan Islands 66

Tamil Tigers (LTTE) 141, 152

Tan, Tony 113

Tanjung Pelepas 80

Tanjungpriok 80

*tauke* 142

Tausug pirates 69

Tawau 68

Tawi Islands 66

Taylor, Rear Admiral James E. 105

Tâyson pirates 39, 98

*Te Kaha* 217, 220n31

Teach, Edward "Blackbeard" v, 7

technology vii, 13, 16, 25, 32, 59, 79, 86–87, 93, 214, 217–18, 228

Tetuan 178

Tew, Thomas v–vi

Thailand 12, 66, 70, 87, 96–97, 99, 102–104, 107, 139–41, 143, 148, 150

Thailand, Gulf of 152n20, 224

Thakurani River 130

thirteen colonies vi, 6–7, 158, 223

*Three Sisters* 15, 173–90

Tiananmen Square massacre 106

Tianjin 55–58, 62

*Tirta Niaga IV* 74

*Tobruk* 68

Togo 192

Tokyo 92

*Torgelow* 212

Transitional Federal Government of Somalia 238

Trans-Ramos crude-oil pipeline 198

Treaty of Friendship and Cooperation 100

Treaty of Paris (1783) 158

Treaty of Tianjin 44, 55–58, 60

treaty ports 42, 55

Triad Uprising 38

Trilateral Coordinated Patrol *See* Malaysia-Singapore-Indonesia (MALSINDO) patrols

Tripoli 15, 158–59, 162–67, 170, 208

Truman, Harry S. 9

tsunami 75, 77, 114, 118

Tunis 159, 163–65

Turkey 20, 156, 177, 184

Turner, John 41

**U**

Uduaghan, Emmanuel 201

Uganda 156

Ukraine 238

Ulrich, Admiral Harry 230

Union of Soviet Socialist Republics (USSR) *See* Russia; Soviet Union

United Arab Emirates (UAE) 215–16

United Kingdom *See* Great Britain

United Nations (UN) 9–10, 16, 92, 208–209, 214–15, 217, 227–28

United Nations Convention on the Law of the Sea 1982 (UNCLOS) 1, 10, 23, 27–30, 31n9, 31n33, 85, 88, 207, 225, 228–29, 238

United Nations Development Program 92

United Nations Operation in Somalia (UNOSOM I and II) 209

United Nations Security Council  *See* Security Council (UN)

United Nations Security Council resolutions *See* Security Council resolutions (UN)

United Nations World Food Program  208

United States (U.S.)  vi–vii, 8–10, 14–16, 21n33, 28, 31n14, 55, 58, 70, 74–75, 77, 84, 87–90, 92, 99–101, 105, 108n41, 113–14, 141, 150, 157–71, 192, 195, 201, 203–208, 213–14, 216–20, 221n36, 223, 229–30, 233–36, 238–39, 241n2

United States Africa Command (AFRICOM) 16, 192, 202–204

United States Central Command (CENTCOM)  202

United States Coast Guard  90, 114

United States Department of Defense  vii

United States EP-3 incident  90, 241n2

United States European Command (EUCOM) 202

United States National Intelligence Council 195

United States National Strategy for Maritime Security  235–36

United States Naval Historical Center  217

United States Naval War College  vi, 216

United States Navy  vii, 10, 75, 84, 105, 161–63, 208, 213–14, 216, 221n36, 230, 234, 239

United States Pacific Command (PACOM) 202

**V**

*Vanguard*  180–81

Versailles, court of  161

Versailles Peace Treaty (1919)  228

Vietnam  vi, 2, 12, 14, 17n4, 34, 39–40, 66, 85, 96–108, 129, 143, 223, 225–26
*See also* North Vietnam; South Vietnam

Vietnam War  14, 98–99, 223

*Violet*  173, 185–86

**W**

Wad Garet  183

Wai  70

Wang Huizhi  38

War of 1812  8

War of the Spanish Succession (1702–13)  7, 226

Ward, Frederick Townsend  60–61

Warri  200–201

Warri Naval Base  201

Washington, D.C.  100, 159, 163–64, 166, 203

Washington, George  159–61, 165

weapons  *See* firearms

Wei Suoni  36

Weng Siliang  35

West Africa  vi, 202

West Indies  vi

Western Europe  2, 8

Western Pacific Naval Symposium  237

White Lotus Rebellion  38

Wilson, General Sir Robert  176, 180, 183

Winstanley, Commander Keith  233

*Winston S. Churchill*  213

World Bank  92

world trade  19, 80–81, 228

World War I  45, 150, 209, 223, 227–28

World War II  14, 45, 65–67, 69, 150, 223, 227

World Wildlife Fund  193

Wu Ping  48

Wuchang  53

Wushi Er  41

**X**

Xinjiang  101

**Y**

yachts  10, 107, 144, 214

Yang Jingtao  49

Yangzi River  53, 55–56, 58, 61

*Yankee*  8

Yar'Adua, Umaru Musa  192, 199, 201–203, 206n20

Ye Mingchen  54–55

Yellow Sea  34, 96

*Young II*  122

**Z**

Zaffarine Islands  183

Zambia  156

Zamboanga  140, 145

zeppelins  25

Zhang Bao  37, 40–41, 48

Zhang Mingzhen  38

Zhejiang Province  37, 39, 98

Zheng Chenggong (Koxinga)  37–38, 48

Zheng Yi  36–37, 39–40

Zheng Yi Sao  41, 48

Zheng Zhilong  37

Zhengzhou  38

Zhou Yu  38

Zhu Fen  39

zinc anodes  15, 122–23, 125, 129–30, 133

CPSIA information can be obtained
at www.ICGtesting.com
Printed in the USA
LVHW111931221121
704136LV00006B/418